Lee and Jackson's
Bloody Twelfth

Lee and Jackson's Bloody Twelfth

The Letters of Irby Goodwin Scott,
First Lieutenant, Company G,
Putnam Light Infantry,
Twelfth Georgia Volunteer Infantry

Edited by Johnnie Perry Pearson

Voices of the Civil War
Peter S. Carmichael, Series Editor

The University of Tennessee Press / Knoxville

The Voices of the Civil War series makes available a variety of primary source materials that illuminate issues on the battlefield, the home front, and the western front, as well as other aspects of this historic era. The series contextualizes the personal accounts within the framework of the latest scholarship and expands established knowledge by offering new perspectives, new materials, and new voices.

Library of Congress Cataloging-in-Publication Data

Scott, Irby Goodwin, 1840-1925.
Lee and Jackson's bloody twelfth: the letters of Irby Goodwin Scott, first lieutenant, Company G, Putnam Light Infantry, Twelfth Georgia Volunteer Infantry / edited by Johnnie Perry Pearson. — 1st ed.
    p. cm. — (Voices of the Civil War)
Includes bibliographical references and index.

ISBN-13: 978-1-57233-935-4
ISBN-10: 1-57233-935-7

  1. Scott, Irby Goodwin, 1840–1925—Correspondence.
  2. Confederate States of America. Army. Georgia Infantry Regiment, 12th. Company G.
  3. Confederate States of America. Army. Georgia Infantry Regiment, 12th.
  4. United States—History—Civil War, 1861–1865—Personal narratives, Confederate.
  5. Georgia—History—Civil War, 1861–1865—Personal narratives.
  6. United States—History—Civil War, 1861–1865—Regimental histories.
  7. Georgia—History—Civil War, 1861–1865—Regimental histories.
  8. Virginia—History—Civil War, 1861–1865—Campaigns.
  9. Soldiers—Georgia—Putnam County—Correspondence.
10. Putnam County (Ga.)—Biography.
  I. Pearson, Johnnie Perry.
  II. Title.

E559.512th S38 2010
973.7'82—dc22   2010015359

To Porter P. Pearson, my father,
born and raised in Putnam County, Georgia.
His family stories about the Civil War
in Putnam County ignited my interest in the war.

Contents

Illustrations

Figures

Maps

Foreword

The "fog of war" did not disappear with the final shots of battle. Confusion, uncertainty, and fear were the particles of a misty veil that never lifted, entrapping Civil War soldiers even when they returned to camp, where the crossfire of constant rumor and the enforcement of Spartan discipline was an inescapable fact of life. As much as the men wanted and needed a reprieve from the horrors of fighting, orders immediately crashed down on them from above, often feeling arbitrary and random, reminding them of their lack of free will and warning of the predictable restrictions and punishments that would follow the slightest infraction. How a man adjusted to the stern realities of military discipline, to an existence defined by unrelenting hardship, and to a war that indiscriminately consumed life largely determined whether he would become a reliable soldier or a man who disappeared from the rolls because of sickness, fatigue, or a broken spirit. Irby Goodwin Scott of the Twelfth Georgia Infantry did not fall by the wayside, miraculously completing the journey from naïve recruit to hardened veteran while seeing action in virtually every major battle of Robert E. Lee's Army of Northern Virginia.

Scott's remarkable letters attest to the ways the war profoundly changed him, turning him into a person he seemingly did not know, but one he had to become in order to live with the sorrow and sacrifice that infused his world. Near Spotsylvania Court House on May 10, 1864, Scott's regiment was routed, and in the confusion he became separated from his brother Nicholas Ewing, affectionately called "Bud." After his unit counterattacked and drove the Federals from the field, Irby searched vainly in the darkness for his brother, going to sleep that night a survivor of another battle but filled with the gnawing anxiety of a man headed into combat, worried over the whereabouts of his brother, whose corpse happened to be a hundred yards away from where the Twelfth Georgia camped.

The next morning Bud's body was discovered, and Irby, after inspecting the head wound, could not imagine that his brother uttered a word or even moved after the bullet passed just above his left eye and exiting from the back of his head. Knowing that his brother had fought gallantly was of some comfort, but Irby was disgusted to see that his brother's pants pockets were turned out, emptied of personal effects and mementos. Before Irby's unit was ordered away, he found a blanket and two brand-new tent shelters for a makeshift coffin, leaving the burial of Bud to the hands of strangers. Irby returned to the gravesite to grieve for a loved one who was too "young and full of promise" to die. "I have felt sad ever since his death," he confided to his parents. "I have not shed a tear. I cannot cry. I wish I could it would to some extent relieve my feelings [for] it seems that all the finer sensibilities of my nature are gone."

The devastating loss of a brother forced Irby to look inward and see, maybe for the first time, that a part of himself had died in military service, never to be resurrected as long as he was subjected to the savagery of war. Through it all, Irby was determined to find higher meaning and purpose in fighting for the Confederacy, even when his most treasured Christian beliefs, the stuff that gave his life humanity and decency, were trampled upon in the army. He asked his parents after Bud's death to remember that "it may be that he was taken from us for some good and we must try and resign ourselves to Gods will." His use of "may" suggests a degree of doubt as to whether a higher power actually guided the war, an understandable reaction when considering all that Irby had endured and witnessed.

Existential questions, though deeply felt, could not be pondered for any sustained amount of time, as Irby's letters make clear. Always on the move, always fighting, and always trying to stay alive inflicted a dizzying array of duties on Irby, filling nearly his every waking hour. Trying to live off army rations, pay, and clothing was impossible. Even though he received a steady stream of clothes and fresh food from home, price gouging from sutlers and local farmers nearly impoverished him. After Gettysburg, Irby gave the folks back home a glimpse of the economic reality of life in Lee's army. "Things not bought from the government cost us much higher Irish potatoes from $2.00 to $3.00 per bushel, snap beans $1.00 per gallon, water mellons (common size) from $4.00 to $6.00 & so on," he wrote. "The commissary bill for our mess for the month of August was $101.16 this includes only what we bought from the government." Irby, unlike most of his comrades, was fortunate to come from a family of moderate wealth, having enough resources to loan him slaves to cook, clean, and wait on him and his messmates. Even though his most basic material needs were often satisfied because of his privileged position, Irby knew he had to become a different man in order to persevere and return to his Georgia home and family that he loved so dearly. Just a year into service, after passing unharmed through an arduous campaign in western Virginia, Irby dismissed his family's suggestion that he buy a substitute and leave the army. "I have," he asserted, "become so hardened as to stand anything." How Irby stood up to the physical and emotional duress of war is poignantly conveyed in his correspondence, revealing how all ordinary soldiers, Union or Confederate, invested great meaning into the daily trials of living in the ranks. For the essence of soldiery sacrifice in Irby's mind was contained in the seemingly mundane experiences of survival.

Peter S. Carmichael
August 2009
West Virginia University

Acknowledgments

I became aware of the Irby Goodwin Scott letters while reading Robert G. Tanner's excellent work, *Stonewall in the Valley*. During transcription of the letters, I enlisted my wife as the first of many who would help make this project a reality. Mary Anna transcribed letters, newspaper articles, and Compiled Service Records, tramped over battlefields, worked as a research assistant at a number of repositories, never objected to my research trips, and, most of all, supported and encouraged me throughout this entire project. For her support and encouragement I am forever grateful.

At the first University of Virginia Civil War Institute at Bridgewater College in June 1999, I met Keith Bohannon, who reviewed the transcribed Scott letters and encouraged me to bring them to public light. Through the years, he has given advice and encouragement. As one of the University of Tennessee readers, he provided additional advice and encouragement at a crucial stage in the publishing process. I developed a friendship with Robert K. Krick at the University of Virginia Institute. Over the years, he has allowed me access to his extensive research library. Bob's advice and encouragement, to a novice, helped me through this project. Also through the UVA Institute I met Robert E. L. Krick, who provided encouragement throughout the project and suggested expanding the final chapter of this work. Peter Carmichael, another UVA Institute faculty member, has been a continuous source of encouragement. All of the staff and faculty of the UVA Civil War Institute programs have become good friends and have been an ongoing source of information and support. To all of them, I am grateful.

Early in my research I contacted T. G. Scott, a descendent of Irby G. Scott, to determine if additional Scott letters survived. Unfortunately, he possessed no additional ones, and did not know of the existence of the letters at Duke University. He has been a gracious host over the years as I have invaded his home a number of times. Early in the process, he shared with me the two photographs of Irby G. Scott, and his encouragement has meant a great deal to me.

I am indebted to two additional Scott descendants, who have preserved a small number of the Irby G. Scott letters. Patsy Scott Prickett took the time from her busy schedule to share a number of valuable letters. Tom Atkins not only shared a Scott letter, but was the person who placed me in contact with Mrs. Prickett. To these Scott descendants I am ever so grateful for their generosity and time. This book is better because of their willingness to share their ancestor's letters.

My friend and former minister the Right Reverend Lane Sapp has read every word of the manuscript more that once and has liberally applied editorial comments throughout. He and I have trekked most of the fields on which the Twelfth Georgia camped and fought. I thank Lane for his friendship and for all the time and effort he has give me and this project over the years. The project and I are better because of his friendship, help, and encouragement.

Without the assistance of John Weaver, none of the illustrations in this work would have been possible. His ability to turn my photographs and other illustrations into usable images is a marvel. I am deeply indebted to James P. Marshall, Jr., president of Eatonton, Putnam County Historical Society for his friendship and help, not only with this project but with other research I have conducted in Putnam County. The company roster is far better because of his assistance.

I want to thank Julie Krick for the excellent maps in this book. Julie responded to the challenge of producing the maps on a short timeline. She took my vague ideas and an overwhelming collection of marked-up maps to produce useful and attractive finished maps.

To Elizabeth Dunn at the Rare Book, Manuscript, and Special Collections Library, Duke University, I extend my thanks for granting permission to publish the Irby G. Scott letters from the Irby H. Scott Collection. Mrs. Dunn has been helpful over the years when I have had questions.

I offer my thanks and gratitude to other historians, friends, and associates who have helped and offered encouragement. Two special people are my cousins, Rhoda Bowen of Conyers, Georgia, and Fay Morrison of Eatonton, who have helped on research trips and been a source of encouragement. Special thanks go to Brent Smith for his dedication to preserving the physical history of the Civil War, and to Greg Biggs for his knowledge of Civil War flags and generous assistance. Others include Mike Andres, Mrs. Cathy Arnold, Mac Atkinson, Bill Avery, Phyllis Baxter, Tim Bjelke, Russell Brown, Chris Calkins, Mrs. Amanda Cook, John Coski, Harriet J. Davis, Mrs. Martha Dozier, Steven W. Engerrand, Rick J. Espelage of Rock-Eagle 4-H Center, Ashley and Mike Hattaway, Scot Henson, James J. Krakker, Ph.D., W. Hunter Lesser, Tom and Bev Lowry, Mrs. Jodi Middleton, Eric Mink, Mrs. Jesse Powell, Charlotte Ray, Dalton Rayer, Cheryl Reed of Rock-Eagle 4-H Center, David Rich, Christopher Stokes, Reverend Adam

Spaugh, Mrs. Miriam Syler, Richard Vernon, Leon Wier, Marshall Williams, and Eddie Woodard. I offer special thanks to proof readers Betty Cole and Suzanne Thompson.

Many archives, museums, National Military Parks, and libraries assisted me. I am especially grateful to the staffs of Alumni Affairs, Georgia Medical College, Augusta, Georgia; Alabama Department of Archives and History; Antietam National Battlefield; Archaeology and Anthropology Department, National Museum of Natural History, Smithsonian Institution; W. C. Bradley Library, Columbus, Georgia; Historic Beverly, West Virginia; Calhoun County, Georgia, Historical Society; Cobb Memorial Archives, Valley, Alabama; Rare Book, Manuscript, and Special Collections Library, Duke University, Durham, North Carolina; Special Collections, Emory University, Atlanta, Georgia; Fredericksburg and Spotsylvania National Military Park; Georgia Department of Archives and History; Madison, Georgia, Records Archives; Monongahela National Forest, West Virginia; National Park Service Southeast Archeological Center, Tallahassee, Florida; Museum of the Confederacy; National Archives, Washington, D.C.; Petersburg National Battlefield Park; Richmond National Battlefield Park; Darlene Mott at the Sam Houston Regional Library and Research Center, Liberty, Texas; Rock Eagle 4-H Center, Eatonton, Georgia; Special Collections Library, Alderman Library, University of Virginia; and Mrs. Stephanie Macchia at the Washington Memorial Library, Washington, Georgia. While conducting research at many of these institutions, the staffs directed me to additional sources, and for their guidance and direction I am very grateful.

Last I want to thank my associates at the University of Tennessee Press. Without their help and support this book would not have become a reality. Scot Danforth and Thomas Wells, acquisitions editors, provided the necessary help and encouragement from the beginning to ensure the success of this book. I am indebted to series editor Peter Carmichael for his guidance over the years, and the two readers whose advice and suggestions were most welcome. This book is better because of their efforts. My thanks to freelancer Walt Evens, who expertly copyedited the manuscript. Any remaining errors are my own. Thanks also to Managing Editor Stan Ivester, who assured me that no problem I might think was major could not be overcome. This was most true when additional letters were discovered after the copy editing stage. My thanks to everyone in the Design/Production Department and to Cheryl Carson and Tom Post.

Introduction

When Georgia seceded from the Union on January 19, 1861, it literally became a state without a nation. Citizens throughout Georgia celebrated secession with picnics, barbeques, and general euphoria. In early February 1861, the Confederate States of America (CSA) became a reality at Montgomery, Alabama. Confederate authorities outlined from the beginning their intent to field an army and naval force to defend the borders and protect the interests of the newly created nation. Initially Governor Joseph E. Brown of Georgia tendered state militia units to the Confederacy. As the call to arms spread, volunteer companies mustered throughout the state.

About April 26, 1861, Richard T. Davis, a member of the Georgia Secession Convention and a successful attorney in Eatonton, Georgia, began raising a volunteer company. Calling themselves the "Putnam Light Infantry," these volunteers became Company G of the Twelfth Georgia Volunteer Infantry Regiment. Going into camp near Eatonton on June 1, the Putnam Light Infantry received additional drill instruction, and the company organized with the necessary officers and noncommissioned enlisted men. Events on two fronts in Virginia soon required the Putnam Light Infantry at the seat of war.

In April 1861, filled with the southern patriotic spirit that raced through Putnam County, Georgia, twenty-one-year-old Irby Goodwin Scott enlisted as a private in the company being formed by Captain Richard T. Davis. His official enlistment date was June 15, at Eatonton. Irby served as a private through the sojourn in the mountains of northwestern Virginia and with Jackson's "Foot Cavalry" during the now famous 1862 Shenandoah Valley campaign. Leaving the valley of Virginia with Jackson's army, he next saw service during the Peninsula campaign. In early August 1862 he was elected junior second lieutenant. At the beginning of the Battle of Second Manassas, Scott's brief experience in the officer ranks ended when he was wounded on August 27. He would return to the army in March 1863 in time to participate in the Gettysburg campaign. He was promoted to first lieutenant in late April 1864, just as the 1864 Overland campaign began. In early April 1865, Irby was in command of Company G during the surrender of the Army of Northern Virginia at Appomattox.

Men from Putnam County accounted for all but two of the initial recruits of the Putnam Light Infantry. Baldwin and Morgan Counties furnished one man each to round out the company when it left Eatonton. In the 1860 Putnam census, the majority of the company's older men listed their occupation as farmer. Other occupations included four clerks, two doctors, two overseers, students, attorney, dentist, money lender, bookkeeper, wheelwright, minister, carpenter, and a livery owner. Only ten of the original recruits owned slaves, and of this number not one would have been considered a planter. Sons of planters, like Irby, did compose a large number of the original volunteers. The youngest member of the company was fifteen, and the oldest was fifty-seven.

Captain Richard Davis wrote Governor Brown on May 1, 1861, "We have about seventy five men drilling regularly under competent instructors. . . ." Davis added that in "ten days or two weeks the company would be organized and uniformed." He desired to know if the state would furnish equipment to volunteer companies upon their organization, or only upon being mustered into service. Anticipating that equipment would only be supplied at the time of muster, Davis asked the state to furnish tents, cartridge boxes, and knapsacks for his company. Whether or not Governor Brown responded with all the needed equipment is not known.

On Friday, June 14, Reverend John H. Corley, a Baptist minister serving the Eatonton Church, delivered a farewell sermon from the text "contend with him in battle." At the conclusion of the sermon, Miss Fannie Jane Reid, eighteen-year-old daughter of Judge David Henry Reid and Sara Elizabeth Adams Reid, presented the company with a flag made by the women of the Military Aid Association of Putnam. Irby Hudson received the flag on behalf of the company "with an address which won golden opinions from all who heard it." The banner was of the first national design with a blue field containing seven stars representing the seven seceding states in June 1861. In the blue field below the stars was embroidered, "Putnam Light Infantry." The obverse side featured in the blue field below the stars the Latin phrase, *Venimus ut Vincamus,* which translates "We came that we might Conquer." "If the boys don't fight under that beautiful banner, and beautiful address we shall have to give them up as hopeless cases," exclaimed the author of a newspaper article appearing in the *Southern Federal Union* on June 25, 1861.

Irby G. Scott and the men of the Putnam Light Infantry left Eatonton on Tuesday evening, June 18, 1861, on a spur line of the Central Georgia Railroad with ninety-one officers and men and six servants. They departed for the seat of war without rifles or sufficient cooking utensils.

Before Irby left Eatonton, Thomas G. Lawson, a prominent attorney, addressed the company and the assembled throng. Captain Davis responded, giving personal thanks on behalf of the company for the kindness of the

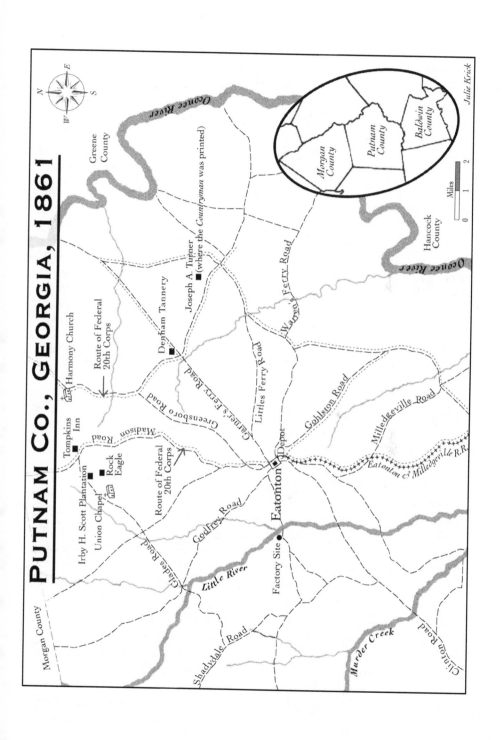

PUTNAM CO., GEORGIA, 1861

Julie Krick

county's women in preparing the men for the field. "Their departure was not so sudden and hurried . . . and we had more time to bid them the fond *adieu*, and our brave women had more time to prepare for them the needed comforts of camp life," reported the *Southern Federal Union* on June 25. No doubt countless tears fell on behalf of Irby, shed by his father, mother, relatives, and friends who gathered at the depot to wish him Godspeed for a safe and victorious return to the family fireside.

Shortly after Irby arrived in Richmond, he and his company mustered into Confederate service. Dispatched to northwestern Virginia soon after being mustered, the regiment was to reinforce the Confederate forces under General Robert S. Garnett, located at Laurel Hill. They arrived too late to be of any support to Garnett.

Approximately seven miles northwest of the Eatonton Court House square on the Athens-to-Milledgeville Road (also known as the Madison Road or Post Road) stood the plantation of Irby G. Scott's father, Irby Hudson Scott. On December 11, 1838, Irby Hudson Scott married Mary Ellen Tompkins in Putnam County. To their union ten children were born, six boys and four girls. Their first-born son, Irby Goodwin Scott, arrived March 2, 1840. Their second child, Nicholas Ewing (Bud) Scott, was born five years later on April 28, 1845. Nicholas (Bud) entered the army in the same company as his brother in June 1863. Bud survived the rigors of combat until his death on May 10, 1864, during the counterattack to recapture the works at Doles' Salient at Spotsylvania Court House, Virginia.

Education appears to have been important to the Scott family. For a time Irby H. Scott served as treasurer of the Board of Trustees of a school near his plantation, most likely located at Union Chapel Methodist Church. In 1855, Irby H. Scott felt led by his religious faith to donate to the trustees of the Methodist Episcopal Church South of Putnam three and three quarter acres of his land for Union Chapel Methodist Church. His gift may have been influenced by his mother-in-law, Sarah Tompkins, a longtime member of Union Chapel Methodist Church. In several letters home Irby G. Scott asked his family to give his respects to Mr. Shell and family. Asa A. Shell, a teacher in Putnam, conducted a school near the plantation of Irby H. Scott, at Union Chapel Methodist Church. In 1850, Irby G. Scott was shown attending school, most likely with Mr. Shell. By 1860, Irby appears to have completed his formal education; however, his brother Nicholas and two of his sisters were students, probably with Mr. Shell.[1]

Near the former plantation site of Irby H. Scott stands the Tompkins Inn. Tompkins family lore says that Giles Tompkins, a planter in Putnam living near the Athens-to-Milledgeville Road, wanted to obtain news from the legislators traveling back and forth from the capital. He would invite many of them into his home. To promote domestic tranquility, Tompkins purchased the northern half of Land Lot 132 for $2,000 from George L. Bird on November 19, 1812. Bird had paid $850 for the property in 1808, thus indicating improved property when Tompkins purchased it in 1812. Tompkins made additional improvements to the property, including building Tompkins Inn as a place he could meet and entertain the many travelers. Tompkins Inn became a focal point for news from the capital. Oral history indicates that political events, horse racing, horse trading, and fox hunting thrived on the property, bringing additional activity to the inn from surrounding counties.

Irby Goodwin Scott could have walked to Tompkins Inn from his father's home. His mother and grandmother descended from the Tompkins family, and this allowed him entry into the adult world of the inn. His visits to the inn during the tense years before the Civil War would have brought him in contact with legislators and business travelers. His interaction with educated travelers and his own education exposed him to the larger arena of Georgia during the period preceding the Civil War. His letters to his father and family from 1861 to 1865 reveal a literate adult with an ability to express his feelings, concerns, and thoughts during the horrors of war.

Irby and Nicholas resided in the home of their father and mother on the property their father bought in 1847. Nothing remains today except the foundations of the main house and detached kitchen. Their home, located on high ground, would have been the typical "Piedmont Plain" two-story, usually consisting of two rooms over two rooms, two shed rooms, chimneys on each end, a roof covered with shakes, and siding made from locally sawn timber. A detached kitchen with a central chimney stood to the left rear, with a covered porch connecting it to the house. There is some evidence these early "Piedmont Plain" homes were imported from Augusta and constructed on site. White quartz rock lined the well in front. Split-rail fences surrounding the house kept wandering livestock from disrupting the home environment. A low rock wall a short distance in front of the house welcomed visitors to the Scott home. From the porch on the front of the home, family lore says, the Rock Eagle could be seen. This is not likely, as the Rock Eagle is several hundred feet from the homesite.[2]

By 1861, the Scott plantation contained 1,008 acres, with only five hundred acres improved, the remainder unimproved. The 1861 Putnam County tax digest listed landholdings at a value of $10,040, and slave property valued at $16,500. The value of all property, which consisted of land, slaves, money, and solvent debt of all kinds, plus household and kitchen furniture over $300 and all other property, amounted to $29,563.

In 1860, Irby H. Scott seems to have avoided the temptation to devote his livelihood and land entirely to cotton production. He had forty-one bales of cleaned cotton on his plantation at the time of the 1860 agricultural census, produced on twenty acres of cultivated land. His remaining cultivated land produced wheat, rye, and corn. A large garden for plantation use would have been part of the cultivated land. On his unimproved property he raised cattle and large flocks of sheep and swine. His production animals consisted of eight mules and two yoke of oxen. Milk cows and horses rounded out his livestock holdings.

As a planter, Irby H. Scott owned twenty-six slaves on his plantation. His chattel property cooked the meals, provided household services, tended the livestock, and cultivated and tended the fields, orchard, and household garden. Scott fed, clothed, housed, and provided them with medical care. In 1860 fifteen males, ages two to sixty-six, and eleven females from infant to age sixty-six, resided on his plantation. His slave property was small compared to neighbors with similar landholdings.[3]

Irby G. Scott's letters reveal how some Confederate officers and enlisted men received great benefit from the slaves that accompanied them to the army. Not only did these slaves assist personally in camp, they also brought the companionship of home. Two slaves from the Scott plantation, Franklin and Tom, called body servants by Southern soldiers, exercised a surprising degree of autonomy in the ranks. Typical services included cooking and cleaning utensils, washing cloths, cleaning quarters, and other household chores. Franklin was encouraged to earn money on the side, and they were allowed to forage outside the boundaries of camp. Most Confederate soldiers, however, never enjoyed the services of a body servant.

When Irby left Eatonton for the seat of war, no plantation slave accompanied him. His letters home in 1861 and 1862 indicate that a messmate's body servant provided camp services. In April 1863, nine months after his election as a junior officer, Irby suggested that Franklin, a slave on the Scott plantation, come up to the army and "bring with him several good razors, shaving brush . . . if he wants to make a few dimes." The slave accompanied Irby's brother Nicholas to the army. Franklin must have taken with him shaving supplies, for in no time he had earned $80, providing shaves, a portion of which he sent home to his wife and children. Tom, another Scott slave, came to the army after Franklin returned to the Scott plantation.

Irby's early letters provide a glance of the assistance the body servants provided the men of the company. The slaves were of great service to the company's many sick men during the fall and winter of the war's first year. Irby's letters are particularly revealing of the relationship between Irby and his body servants Franklin and Tom. Franklin clearly held the confidence of Irby and the Scott family, being allowed to earn income and then forage vegetables while the company was on detached service, in the winter of 1863. Tom apparently spent most of his time with the wagon train and may have been of little service to Irby. Anyone with an interest in the work of body servants for Confederate soldiers will find value in the Scott letters.

In August 1865, sixteen of the former Scott plantation slaves bound themselves by a signed contract to Irby H. Scott "until the 25th day of December next," to work the plantation for one-sixth of the entire crop. Irby H. Scott agreed "to furnish said freed men and women and their children now members of his family with food, and clothing and to ——— them in every way humanely." This signed contract suggests that a number of the emancipated adult slaves remained for at least a season on the Scott plantation.[4]

When he penned his first letter home, Irby Goodwin Scott did not intend for his letters to be a tribute to himself or the men of Company G, or the Twelfth Georgia. His letters offer vivid testimony to the confusion, hardships, sickness, and difficulties Irby endured during the Civil War. A Japanese proverb says, "To endure what is unendurable is true endurance." The Irby G. Scott letters clearly show that Irby was made of hardy material. Irby's letters named and provided details on nearly all men of the company. Separated from family and friends, Irby portrayed a group of men with the capacity and willingness to sacrifice all and to endure this tumultuous period in American history.

Irby Scott provided fresh accounts of service in the mountains of northwestern Virginia. His letter of September 21, 1861, provides details on the aborted attack on the Federal camp on Cheat Summit. Two days after the Federal attack on Camp Bartow, October 3, 1861, Irby gives an account of his regiment's activities. His letters during the 1862 Valley campaign are short on battle details. They do, however, provide excellent descriptions of the marches, camp life, hardships, and confusion faced by Irby and the men of the company and regiment. By the end of the Peninsula campaign, worn out from the incessant marching and fighting, Irby stated he had seen "a plenty killed & wounded . . . but I never saw anything to equal the last battles." He expressed a desire to see the folks at home, where he could rest and recuperate. Through the remainder of 1862 and 1863, his letters focus on describing marches, camp life, and the condition of the company men. His June 8, 1864, letter provides an account of the May 10 battle at Spotsylvania Court House, and the breakthrough of the Doles' Salient, where his brother Bud was mortally wounded.

The single most important occurrence from a military point of view for Irby was possibly Edward Johnson's appointment as colonel of the Twelfth Georgia. An old army officer, Johnson brought the military discipline and training the regiment needed in the early months of its existence. Johnson, a no-nonsense, rigid disciplinarian, demanded absolute obedience. He led from the front and was everywhere on the field of battle. In no small way, his example and discipline transformed Irby and his fellow volunteer soldiers into one of the hardest fighting regiments in Confederate service.

Irby wrote his early letters as a private. After a little more than a year of service, Irby wrote home as a junior company-grade officer. At the time of his last letter home he was in command of the company as first lieutenant. Irby rose in rank during the war, with the associated leadership responsibilities. Elements of friendship and camaraderie strongly bound Irby and the men of Company G to one another, more so than reason or ideology.

Irby and the men of Company G were like most southern soldiers who volunteered in the early months of the war. They were sons of slaveholding planters and yeomen farmers. As volunteers, the soldiers lacked the military skills of drill, manual of arms, patrolling, and picket duty. They also were ignorant of household skills when they formed the "Putnam Light Infantry." On June 25, 1861, Irby informed his father that when cooking, "It goes right hard not knowing how and not being use to it." Then, on June 29, he told his father, "If I had some one to show me a few things I could do very well." In no time Irby mastered the military skills and "do very well" cooking and performing household duties. Colonel Johnson ensured the men mastered the military skills, and necessity required the mastery of cooking and household chores.

Irby wrote most all of the war letters home to his father. There is no indication why he addressed his letters to his father and not his mother. It is reasonable to assume that his mother, the daughter of a planter, had received the benefit of education and could read and write. It is more likely Irby addressed his letters to his father because the elder Scott was a former Georgia militiaman called up during the Second Seminole War in 1836. (Irby's great-grandfather served as a soldier in the Revolutionary War.) Thus, Irby may have felt a closer association to his father because of past family military experience. He perhaps felt he could be more open and honest with his father in his observations of military life. There is also the possibility that Irby addressed his letters to his father knowing his father, as head of the household, would have more interaction with other men of the community. The elder Scott would share the contents of the letters with other families.

Irby wrote home frequently. Unfortunately, a few gaps exist in his letters. From the middle of August 1862 until early March 1863, no letters came forth because of regimental activities at the beginning of the Second Manassas campaign and because Irby was wounded and on furlough. He fell wounded August 27, 1862, in the opening stages to the Battle of Second Manassas. A second gap is the winter of 1863-1864. In his letter dated January 6, 1864, while camped near Piedmont, Virginia, Irby says he "should have written before now but did not have a chance to send my letters." Scott's brother Nicholas did pen four brief letters during this period, but he is not the chronicler like his older brother. During this gap in the letters the regiment was on detached service in the mountains of Virginia, being recalled to the army for the Mine Run campaign. Once the conflict on Mine Run had been resolved, the regiment returned to the mountains to round up army deserters and absentees. While on detached service there would not have been the logistical support the army usually supplied.

From early 1864 to the first part of June, letters home were infrequent, especially when active campaigning began during the 1864 Overland campaign. One of the last surviving letters is dated June 8, when Irby detailed the death of Bud, his brother. His last letter home is from February 25, 1865. Here Irby exclaimed, "I never was so near worn out in my life. I scarcely have any energy left." In late June 1864, Irby and the Twelfth Georgia and the Second Corps had marched to Lynchburg, Virginia, under the command of General Jubal Early, to oppose the advance of Federal forces into the Shenandoah Valley. Once the danger at Lynchburg had passed, the regiment and the Second Corps marched down the valley (northward) in what is known as the 1864 Valley campaign. Hard marching occupied Irby. After the aborted attack on Washington City, Irby and the men continued marching and in active combat, allowing little time for letter writing.

The entrance of Federal troops into Atlanta on September 2, 1864, disrupted mail service to Putnam County, as did Sherman's March to the Sea. Both wings of the Federal army passed through Putnam County on November 20–21, with the 20th Army Corps advancing on the Madison Road from Madison to Eatonton. Irby's family lived adjacent to the Madison Road in the direct path of the Union bummers and foragers who plundered all the homes in their reach. It may be that some of the letters at his parents' home were destroyed during Sherman's march through Putnam County in November 1864. General Sherman's departure from Savannah, Georgia, and entrance into South Carolina again disrupted mail. There is also the possibility that over several generations, the Scott family lost a number of the letters. Though a small number have been preserved by the family and for the first time are presented here.

Irby was not the strong individualist who would balk at the discipline and authority demanded of a soldier. His letters are devoid of the petty complaints and personal affronts typical from a southern soldier. This is especially seen when many in the company became dissatisfied that Colonel Zaphaniah Turner Conner might not be appointed colonel of the regiment. Irby wrote that he would be satisfied that President Davis would ensure the "best officers that can be had" would command. His only disappointment with any of the officers or men was with Captain Davis. This does not appear to be with military matters, but rather how Davis handled affairs with several of the men. In another letter he states in general his disappointment with some of the officers, not with military matters, but with what appears to be partiality shown some of the men.

As was typical of soldiers from North and South, Irby tells his family how receiving "a letter from home from those we love . . . buoys us up and stirs our sleeping patriotism." Throughout his military service, Irby continued to look for letters from family and friends to reaffirm the link between home and the front. Correspondence from home constituted an important ingredient in Irby's morale during the war.

Considered notoriously poor, the Confederate postal service delivered mail and packages from home irregularly throughout the war. Most often, mail from the men of the Putnam Light Infantry reached recipients via soldiers returning home because of illnesses or furloughs. Likewise, soldiers returning to the regiment after a trip home would bring back to camp mail and packages. Early in the war, family and friends visiting the soldiers in camp became another source. In return, these visitors carried mail back home. Early in the war, mail delivery by the Confederate postal service to the Twelfth Georgia was complicated, as two regiments had been numbered Twelfth Georgia. In August 1861 one of these regiments, commanded by Colonel Thomas W. Thomas, became the Fifteenth Georgia Infantry Regiment.

When campaigning and the routines of camp life began in earnest, life became much different than the grand adventure Irby and most of the men expected. He informed his father that some in the company wished they had stayed home. Irby was not immune to thoughts of home, writing his father on July 21, 1861: "I had rather see you all than anything else on earth. I never knew how dear home and friends were untill I left them." In his letter of November 6, 1861, Irby tells his father after receiving a letter from home, "It is one of the greatest blessings that we enjoy away from the comforts of home, the society of old and cherished friends, in the mountain wilds of an almost wilderness country surrounded by dangers on every hand and exposed to the relentless vengeance of a hireling foe."

Irby's letters are written by a man mature beyond his years. During periods of both inactivity and active campaigning, rumors ran rampant throughout the company and the regiment. Irby put no faith in the many rumors that abounded on military and other subjects. In his November 6, 1861, letter Irby states: "I have long since learned that we need not listen to reports or rumors to get any information that can be relied on, but must wait untill we receive positive orders from our officers." Not giving credence to rumors served Irby well during his service and helped him avoid becoming frustrated or disheartened.

Irby wrote his parents that he appreciated their desire to "fix him up" and make him comfortable in camp. He knew, though he had no prior military experience, that whatever arrived from home or what he might purchase would have to be left or carried on his back. In early July 1861, on the march from Staunton into the mountains of Virginia, the Staunton–Parkersburg

Turnpike became littered with cast-off items, as many of the men soon found their endurance did not exceed their desire to be comfortable.

When his family suggested a substitute, Irby told them, "Do not trouble yourself to much." Irby's frugal maturity comes out when he states, "Besides it would cost a good deal besides in the way of money." Prior to telling his parents not to trouble themselves, in his July 7, 1862, letter he informs them that he "would give almost anything for the quite retreats of home." He goes on to write, "if others can stand it, why can I not do it?" In his July 10, 1862 he clarifies his position on a substitute.

Pay was another morale builder for Irby and the men. Irby, in his second letter home, informs his father, "I wish to be as econoimical [economical] as I can and not spend my money foolishly." By November 1861, Irby had $95 on hand. In his September 10, 1863, letter, he informs his father, "while I am in the war I am going for comfort if it takes all I make." His statement "if it takes all I make" is in stark contrast with his second letter home. Though Irby intended to be comfortable, his letters throughout the war tend to reflect his ability to conserve financial resources, even when promoted to the officer ranks and paying for much of his subsistence. Irby routinely sent part of his savings home to help the family with living expenses and taxes.

Irby's letters reflect that duty to the army and to the men of the company became increasingly important, and the men became his extended family. This is most evident in his letter of June 8, 1864, when he tells his family "we have no officers left in my opinion capable of commanding. . . . I have nothing now to bind me to the Regt or Co. more than to be with those I am acquainted." His sense of community with the men of the company and regiment became the bond that carried him through the remainder of the Civil War. In his June 8 letter, Irby expresses the strongest feelings of any of his writings home. He now commanded a contingent of his brigade's sharp-shooters, a position of much responsibility. His brother had been mortally wounded, and Colonel Edward S. Willis, who Irby considered the best friend of the regiment, had suffered the same fate. For Irby, the war had become more intense, more personal, and he had no control of events. His bond of brotherhood with the men of the company now became his foundation.

Irby only gives the reader of his letters small snippets of the reasons he entered military service in June 1861. We can suppose, from his letters, his motives included duty to his country, a desire for liberty, self-government, and defeating the Yankees. His October 15, 1861 letter allows us an early glimpse of his motives and his August 27, 1863, letter gives an additional glimpse of why he and the men fought: "The soldiers are in fine spirits and willing to fight to the bitter end, if need also to sacrifice all they have not only their property but their lives." After the death of his brother Bud, Irby gives us another glimpse of why he fought when he tells his family Bud "died fighting gallantly for his Country and his rights." In the letter dated June 8, 1864, Irby states his hope for being "permitted to live and return home once more as a freeman to enjoy the blessings of peace & liberty for which I have toiled so hard."

Irby G. Scott wrote with a legible hand, which made editing the original letters, located in the Irby H. Scott Papers of the Special Collections Library, Perkins Library, Duke University, a pleasure. A small number of letters are held in private hands of two Scott descendants who have been gracious enough to share them with me. All of his letters are written without paragraphs, from the left margin to the right margin, using the entire sheet of paper. To keep the letters true to the original form, no paragraphs have been created. Irby used periods liberally, and in the editing process the editor has made necessary corrections. Spelling has been left alone in the letters. Those few missives penned by his brother display a noted contrast in form and language usage. This may owe to Bud Scott's youth and his not taking advantage of his school instruction. The editor has used brackets [ ] to clarify some spellings. Where a word could not be read in the original, a blank space is inserted. Annotation is included to identify the first occurrence of soldiers' and other individuals' names. Events or places are also annotated in the letters. Because the Scott letters are as much about the men of the company as they are about Irby G. Scott, a roster of Company G, "Putnam Light Infantry," Twelfth Georgia Volunteer Infantry Regiment, is included.

Duke University acquired an initial component of the Irby H. Scott Papers as early as 1942. Acquisition records at Duke show three additions to this collection, one in 1957 and two in 1958. None of the letters have been published as a whole. However, some of the letters have been quoted in published books, such as Peter Cozzens's *Stonewall Jackson's Valley Campaign: Shenandoah 1862*; an essay by Keith Bohannon in Gary W. Gallaher's *The Shenandoah Valley Campaign of 1862*; Robert K. Krick's *Conquering the Valley: Stonewall Jackson at Port Republic* and *Stonewall Jackson at Cedar Mountain*; W. Hunter Lesser's *Rebels at the Gate: Lee and McClellan on the front Line of a Nation Divided*; and Robert G. Tanner's *Stonewall in the Valley: Thomas J. "Stonewall" Jackson's Shenandoah Valley Campaign Spring 1862*. With the exception of the work by Lesser, none of the letters have been used as a resource for the period when Irby and the men of the Twelfth Georgia saw service in the northwestern Virginia mountains from the summer of 1861 through the winter of 1861–62. During their time in the mountains of Virginia, Irby G. Scott and his fellow soldiers came together as a true band of brothers. Likewise, none of the Scott letters have been used in other works as a resource for the remainder of the war.

Chapter 1

Seat of War

"The boys are all well and in good spirits."

Colonel Zephaniah Turner Conner, an antebellum Georgia militia officer, had the responsibility of moving to Richmond several companies that became the Twelfth Georgia Volunteer Infantry Regiment. The men and officers assumed that Conner would command the regiment. Instead President Jefferson Davis appointed Edward Johnson, a forty-five-year-old regular army officer and West Point graduate, who had seen service in the Seminole and Mexican Wars, as colonel on June 26, 1861. Conner became the regiment's lieutenant colonel.

At Camp Reservoir the ten companies that composed the Twelfth Georgia came together for training and organization. Camp rumors ran rampant in the regiment that the men would be sent to Manassas Junction, Virginia. They ended up in the mountains of northwestern Virginia.

While in the Richmond camps, illnesses appeared in the form of diarrhea and the common cold. Camp diseases took the lives of more than a few men during their relocation to the mountains of Virginia. To protect the men from more serious diseases, Confederate authorities vaccinated them against smallpox. Four days after arriving in camp at Richmond, Irby Scott and the men in his company who had not been inoculated were vaccinated.

Camp Fairfield, Richmond Va.[1]
June 21st 1861.
Dear Father,[2]

I take this opportunity to write you a few lines. After leaving on Tuesday we arrived here this morning and have struck our tents about three miles from the city. I do not know which way from it—whether North, South, East or West. I think we will be tolerably comfortable in a few days. We are

going to get cooking utensils this evening and other necessary things. There are a great many soldiers here drilling. I saw three camping grounds as we marched out here. We had no accident on the way here. The boys are all well and in very good spirits. I have not heard whether there is much sickness or not among the troops. This is a very pretty country although a little hilly. I have heard there was a man to be shot here today for drawing a pistol on his officer. There has been fighting at Harpers Ferry and some other points. It is said our troops came off victorious by taking 3000 prisoners at Harpers Ferry.[3] There are a great many soldiers all along the route we came drilling &c. as captain Davis is going down to the city.[4] I must close and write to-morrow or next day and give you a full account of things. Nick is well, also Wat.[5] Give my love to the whole family, Grandma and all inquiring friends.[6] I have written in a great hurry nothing more at present. Remaining your affectionate son,
I. G. Scott

(Camp Fairfield)
Richmond Va. June 25th 1861
Dear Father & Family
    I wrote to you last Sunday morning but I never felt less like writing in my life but knowing you were anious [anxious] to hear I thought I would write any how. There was so much confusion every way. I felt bewildered and almost foolish, added to the loss of sleep, travel &c, I thought I never could get use to it but I have got straight and am a great deal better satisfied than I was first. It seems I have been here a month and still when I count it up it has been only five days since I arrived at this place. We cannot hear much news here, more rumors than any thing else. We can buy a Richmond paper every day from the news boys.[7] Among the rumors which I heard to day was that there was an insurrection in Augusta Ga which resulted in five hundred killed on both sides together which rumor I do not believe to be true as it came by no newspaper or telegrath [telegraph] as I can find out.[8] There is considerable dissatisfaction on the part of the companies composing our regiment as to the course Colonel Conner has pursued, in bringing us here we supposing that he was to command our regiment but since his arrival here which was night before last we have found out that he was never commissioned by president Davis, and some of the companies say if he does not command the regiment that they will go back home, but if they do it will cost them some three or four thousand dollars.[9] The captains of the regiment have consulted and I think came to an understanding in the matter. We had a company meeting this morning and decided to leave the matter in the hands of Capt Davis to do as he thought best. President Davis says he will give us the best officers that can be had. Since I have been writing

Capt Davis came from the city a letter from you. I was glad to hear that all was well. I did not expect a letter so soon, but can say I never recd [received] a letter with more pleasure in my life. Capt Davis says we will be mustered into service this evening at five Oclock. That will be rather a solum time with me as I cannot tell how long I shall have to stay or what my fate will be yet, I trust that I shall again be with you soon. There has been some talk that we will move our camp to the west side of James River if the place will suit. There is also talk that we will be stationed here at this place but know nothing certain yet about it. Charles Badger who cut his throat last Friday night is getting well pretty fast he is able to walk about camp and seems to be in his right mind.[10] No doubt it was from the effects of liquor which he drank in Eatonton while encamped there. The company are all well with the exception of colds & diarhea [diarrhea]. There has not been much diarhea [diarrhea] in our company. I have a cold but not sick from it at all. I have been vaccinated and it is taking very well.[11] The boys generally are lively and in high spirits Nick and Wat are well. Rest assured if I should get sick I will let you know and take the best care of myself that I can. Tell Bud I think that he had better remain at home that there is enough men here for the present the whole country is alive with them.[12] We are tolerably comfortable now. We have set up trees before our tents got the most of our cooking utensils and plenty to eat so far. I give you our bill of fair in my last letter we have put Feiler at the head of our mess and raised a fund to be kept by him to buy any thing the mess may need.[13] I have cooked some Bread, meat, Coffee, rice &c. It goes right hard not knowing how and not being used to it, but my mess and the boys generally pitch right into it like they were not affraid. Tell Abner that I am sorry he is sick and cannot come on to us as he expected but hope he will soon be with us and to be certain to bring Jim with him as he will be a great help to him.[14] If I should need any thing which I cannot get here I will write to you and I will try to write as often as I can and conceal nothing from you. I have not been to the city but once since I have been here though I could have gone often if I had wanted to, but it is some three or four miles from the main part of the city which is a right smart walk. We can ride there and back for half a dollar but I wish to be as econoimical [economical] as I can and not spend my money foolishly. I do not exactly like the arrangements as to our regiment but I feel were we to go back it would disgrace us. June 27th 1861 To day finds us up on a new camping ground I think rather westward from the city.[15] We had to march to the capital to be mustered in yesterday. I did not go with the company to the capital, but had to remain with four others to guard the baggage, we moved to this place (I do not know what is the name of the place) because there is a nice piney grove plenty of water &c. Our whole regiment is encamped here there is between 900 or 1000 men in it. We do not know who our officers are yet the President appoints them. Our regiment is complimented as being the finest regiment from Ga. There is not a great deal of sickness in the camp. Some diarehea [diarrhea] colds & though none of them that I know of dangerous. I am very well excepting a slight cold which is the case generally in our company. The reason I did not finish and send this letter off sooner was that we have been very busy since yesterday morning taking down tents packing up baggage moving &c. and having to fix every thing again. I must stop and write again soon. You spoke of sending me some things by Abner or the Express company. I thank you for thinking of me and wishing to fix me up and make me comfortable but you cannot know as I do what will be best for us. I do not want you to send me a pillow, (Rolster Linen Cravat) as pants as they will be in my way more than do me good. The middle of the day is warm but the nights are cool so do not send them, if you wish to send anything let it be something worsted or garn—. I do not care about summer cloths. If Abner does not leave before you get this send me some Butter also tell Mr. Morton to send Wat some.[16] If Abner has gone he is alone untill Caps Davis comes home and I write again. I am very well satisfied do not Backen your letter to —— regiment. Nothing more now. Give my love to all the family and inquiring friends. Yours affectionately.

I. G. Scott

P.S. Nick & Wat are well

Richmond Va. June 29th, 1861

Dear Father,

I know you all want to hear often and I shall try to write as often as possible. Yet sometimes it may be several days between letters, if anything should occur or we have to leave for some other point I will let you know immediately. The President has not appointed our Officers yet. The whole regiment are encamped together near the reservoir in a pine grove and as comfortable as we could expect. There was a fine rain here last night. I want to hear whether you have had rain, what is the prospect for a corn crop &c, the crops here around Richmond are very fair, though a great deal better than in Georgia. Alexander Reid received a letter from home which stated you had written me a letter of importance and wished to know whether I had received it or not?[17] I have not received but one letter since I left home from you which was dated the 20th, in which you advised me how to act in case I took the measels [measles], mumps and to write to you in case I needed your assistance in anything.[18] I am glad to say I am actually in need of nothing at present. There is some things which would be a convenience and help to me, but still we must be contented as far as possible and learn to conform to things which are unavoidable. If I were to buy things I should have to leave them whenever we received orders to march to some other place. There is

one thing which troubles me might that is cooking & washing. If I had some one to show me a few things I could do very well. I have been looking for Abner for a day or two past. I wish he would come along. I want to see some one from home. Capt Davis thinks of going home as soon as the regiment is fully organised [organized]. O'Neal who refused to be mustered in service as Badger will soon leave for home.[19] There is some of the company sick with diarhea [diarrhea] but none unable to be about. I have not had it and hope by being prudent to miss having it, my health is very good with the exception of cold, which is a general thing among the troops. I saw Major Perryman yesterday he belongs to a company from Texas, Matt Talbots regiment has gone to Winchester near Harpers Ferry.[20] I went over to his camp several times to see him. Jeff Davis rode out near our camp. I did not get a good look at him but one thing I can say if I had not known who he was I should never have taken him for the President of the confederate states. I cannot describe him, Jake Feiler sends his respects to you all, a good many of the boys who were so anxious to come here say if they were back in Georgia they would never come again unless compelled to do so. Nick says tell his father and mother he is well and doing very well Wat is also well. There is my news here as to what is going on at any of the places north of this at least nothing reliable. I want to see you all bad enough. Kiss all the little ones for me. Give my love especially to Grandma also to all of my friends. My love to you and all the family. I ever remain your most affectionate Son.
Irby G. Scott

Richmond, Va, July 5th, 1861
Dear father,

Contrary to my expectations when I wrote you the other day I am still here we expect to have left yesterday, but did not. Again to day every thing was made ready to leave at three Oclock this evening, yet we are still here. Now the cry is we leave here in the morning at 7 Oclock. I am pretty certain we will go at that time. We have to leave a great many of our things here at this place. Richmond Reid has the appointment of Commissary for the regiment.[21] He had our things placed in a house where they will be safe, I think, and he says that he will have them sent to us if we need them. Abner Zachry and Mr Marshall arrived here to day about twelve oclock we gave a hearty welcome and a cheer we were all glad to see them.[22] They are both well. I received yours and Mr Shells letters and was glad to hear you were all well, but should liked to have heard that you had rain enough.[23] I received by Abner a good many things that are very nice, indeed rarities with us here in camp, they came in a bad time just as we are about to leave. I had to leave the cloths you sent me and Nick because we could not carry them in our knapsacks. The eatables we will carry with us as we have to carry along two days rations. I got my hams that we did not cook in a box that we will carry with us. I also got my butter in which will be of great benefit to us. I thank you for your kindness in fixing up all these things for me, but I had rather you had not sent me the cloths. I put them in Mr Eakins trunk and they were also deposited in Richmond. I let Abner take my carpet bag for his boy to carry his cloths in. I heard a man tonight while I was writing that we would not go to laurel hill [Laurel Hill] but to a place call Martinsburg where they have been having some brushes.[24] I do not know whether it is true or not. I should like to go to some place where we could travel all the way by railroad. There is some dissatisaction [dissatisfaction] in our regiment about our having a Virginia[n] instead of a Georgia[n] colonel. I cannot tell when I can write again, but promise to do so at the first opportunuty [opportunity]. Our company is all up except John Denham who was sent to the hospital this evening.[25] We will have to leave him behind. Wat and Nick are well I believe I gaining in spirits, and very well, tell Bud to stay at home. I must close as it is getting late. The other boys have gone to bed. Tell grandma I was sorry to learn she had been so sick, but I hope when this comes to hand she will be much better. Give her my love and say to her I have not forgotten her. I often set and think of every thing about home how every thing is arranged &c, tell Mr Shell I was pleased to receive a letter from him. I will try and answer it some time. Dear father and family do not be uneasy on my account for I think I am among friends who will care for me should anything happen that I should need attention. Give my love to all my friends. My best love to the whole family, white and black. Nothing more to night. I therefore bid you an affectionate farewell.

Yours devotedly untill death,

    Irby G. Scott

Chapter 2

Mountains of Northwestern Virginia

"I had rather see you all than anything else on earth."

When the Twelfth Georgia arrived at Staunton, Virginia, quartermaster arrangements had not been made for transporting camp equipment or knapsacks. Because there was no place to store excessive baggage, except in open country, each soldier had to decide what to carry or discard. The Putnam Light Infantry hired a wagon to carry their knapsacks and camp equipment. After the first day's march the Staunton–Parkersburg Turnpike was littered with items once deemed necessary for a soldier's comfort. This early experience of traveling light set an example for future marches, which earned the Twelfth Georgia the title "Jackson's Foot Cavalry."

From Staunton the regiment marched through the mountains of northwestern Virginia on the Staunton–Parkersburg Turnpike. The turnpike, cut into the sides of mountains, followed the natural contours of the landscape, with a minimum of grades. Built on the popular macadam model, the road was fifteen to twenty feet wide, allowing two wagons room to pass each other. Nearly a decade of neglected road maintenance, floods, and mountain weather had rendered portions of the road impassable, muddy, and sorely in need of repair.

After marching nearly seventy-two miles from Staunton, the soldiers arrived at the summit of Allegheny Mountain on July 13. Colonel Edward Johnson received a dispatch from Colonel William C. Scott of the Forty-fourth Virginia Infantry that he was in full retreat, with a long wagon train marching toward the Greenbrier River at the base of Allegheny Mountain. When Colonel Johnson and the Twelfth Georgia arrived at the Greenbrier River, they heard a report detailing the death of General Robert Selden Garnett, and the shambles of his command, the flight of the Forty-forth Virginia from Beverly, Virginia, and the commissary and quartermaster stores warehoused at Beverly. To his credit, Colonel Scott had managed to safely carry off a large quantity of these stores.

Fearing a Federal pursuit of unknown force, Colonels Johnson and Scott decided to withdraw to Monterey, Virginia. Traveling all night under the command of Colonel Johnson, the regiments returned to the summit of Allegheny Mountain at dawn on Sunday. After a three-hour rest period on the summit, the command took up the line of march to Monterey, a distance of eighteen miles. They arrived just before dark on July 14.

After three days' rest at Monterey the Twelfth Georgia, with their artillery, received orders to return west on the turnpike to the summit of Allegheny Mountain. Arriving on the summit at 11 o'clock on Friday, July 19, Lieutenant Colonel Conner of the Twelfth communicated to General Henry R. Jackson his opinion that their current position risked being flanked from both the front, sides, and rear. He also indicated that securing necessary water would be difficult.

Believing there was a strong position in advance of Allegheny Mountain, a reconnaissance under the command of Colonel Johnson went forward on July 28 intending to advance the regiment to a stronger position near the enemy fortified on Cheat Summit. A second reconnaissance, numbering two hundred of the Twelfth Georgia under the command of Lieutenant Colonel Conner, scouted the vicinity of the turnpike and the Greenbrier River on August 11. This second reconnaissance in force was in preparation for the movement of the regiment to a new camp located at the junction of the turnpike and the Greenbrier River.

The foul, wet weather of the mountains exacerbated illnesses among the soldiers, such as the common cold. Diarrhea and dysentery, which first appeared while the company camped in Richmond, continued to plague the company. These afflictions often weakened men to the point of not being fit for duty for weeks at a time. Measles and mumps spread through the regiment while camped on the summit of Allegheny Mountain, and at one point Irby Scott believed one-half of the regiment was not well because of various illnesses, most notably measles.

Rumors, disease, the foul mountain weather on a summit at 4,400 feet, and a diet much different from home intensified longing for the comforts of the family fireside. These homesick feelings first appear in the letters from Scott on the summit of Allegheny Mountain. Campaigning and the routines of camp life were much different from what most of the men of the Putnam Light Infantry expected. Many anticipated a grand adventure and a short war.

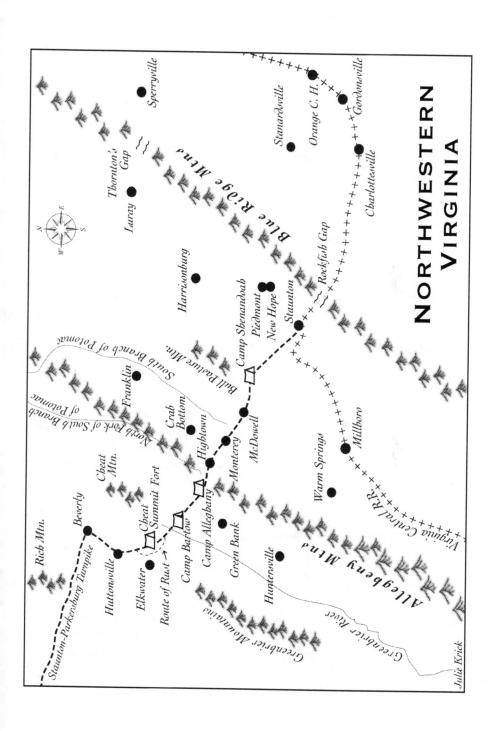

NORTHWESTERN VIRGINIA

Sperryville

Thornton's Gap

Luray

Blue Ridge Mtn.

Stanardsville

Orange C. H.

Gordonsville

Charlottesville

Rockfish Gap

Harrisonburg

Camp Shenandoah

Piedmont

New Hope

Staunton

South Branch of Potomac

Bull Pasture Mtn.

Franklin

Crab Bottom

Hightown

North Fork of South Branch of Potomac

McDowell

Monterey

Warm Springs

Millboro

Virginia Central R.R.

Cheat Mtn.

Beverly

Rich Mtn.

Staunton-Parkersburg Turnpike

Huttonsville

Cheat Summit Fort

Elkwater

Route of Rust →

Camp Bartow

Camp Allegany

Green Bank

Huntersville

Allegany Mtn.

Greenbrier Mountains

Greenbrier River

Julie Krick

Montery [Monterey], Highland Co. Va. July 15, 1861

Dear Father,

As it has been some time since I wrote you, and as this is the first opportunity I have had to write I will embrace this to let you know our where abouts &c. We left Richmond last Sunday was a week ago for Laurel Hill, we had to march from our camp in Richmond to the depot about three miles and ca[r]ry all our plunder on our backs, the day was exceedingly warm as it was about ten or eleven Oclock in the day. A great many were exhausted and had to stop and get under the shade trees along the streets. I reckon you have heard about John Bidelle [Bedell] fainting from being overheat[ed].[1] He was very sick for awhile but when we left he was getting better, we have not heard a word from him since we left Richmond. We also left Cincinnatus Griggs there he was sick and I reckon he has gone home before this.[2] We also left John Denham there sick with the Pnunmonia [pneumonia]. We went through by Railroad to Staunton about one hundred miles got there just about day the next morning. We then remained there until next morning which was Tuesday. We than started on our march of about one hundred and twenty miles all the way through the mountains. We hired a wagon in Staunton to carry the knapsacks for our company. We got on very smoothly for seventy miles when we had to retreat back to this place the cause of our retreat was owing altogether to Colonel Scott's forty fourth regiment which we met at green brier creek [Greenbrier River].[3] Retreating in confusion, we reached that [this] place just before dark after having traveled eighteen miles that day. We stoped [stopped] and took a snack to eat and then turned about and commenced our retreat, we were told that the enemy were marching on us fifteen thousand strong and was not more than fifteen miles off. We marched all ~~night~~ Friday night and yesterday, in all about 30 miles, there was a sad occurrence that took place on Friday night, as we were marching along in good order, Col Scott's Va. Regiment had some prisoners which tried to make their escape. They were fired upon by the guard, which produced the greatest excitement among the whole regiment, who thinking they were attacked fired at random and killed eight of their own men and wounded several more. There was one of the same regiment shot himself accidentally yesterday morning he died from the wound, also another shot his hand nearly off today. I had rather they were not so close to us. We have not had the first accident since we left Georgia. I cant tell what we will do now, we met here at this place a regiment from North Carolina. We have here about three thousand men and are expecting Gen. Garnett with about 5 thousand more.[4] I do think there is any danger of an attack here. We have had a rough time marching through the mountains. The roads are fine nearly all turnpike we stood it fine, traveling about 15 miles a day. Our company are generally well. I have been a little sick with cold settled on my

———— but have got about straight again. Wat, Nick, Abner and the rest of my mess are all well, they ~~are~~ all send their respects to your all, some of the boys got letters here today. You had better direct your letters to Richmond they will send them on to us. Write to me soon. I am very anxious to hear from you all. Give my love to grandma and say to her that I hope her health has improved. I want to see you all as bad as I ever did in my life and hope that I may soon be able ~~soon~~ to be with you all. I must close and send my letter to the office. I will write again soon if I have the chance. I am looking for a letter from home. Abner received one from home this morning stating you were all well, which was welcome news to us, you must remember me to all my friends especially to Mr Mortons family. Mr Shell's and others around. This is a wild romantic country thinly settled. You must not expect anything extra of me in my letters I cant give you a description of this mountainous part of the world. There is nothing but mountains some of them covered with a flowering ivy which is beautiful. It is nearly cold enough here for frost every night. I would prefer to be stationed at some place to moving about but we will have to take it as it comes whether is suites us or not. My Love to the whole family do not be uneasy if I should fail to write when you are expecting a letter. Kiss all the children for me, nothing more at present. I remain your most devoted son untill death.

Irby G. Scott

Highland Co. Va. July 21st 1861[5]

Dear Father & Family,

I wrote you last from Monterey I am at this time about fifteen miles from there on the top of the Aleghany [Alleghany] mountains. Our regiment was ordered here by Gen. Henry R. Jackson we are in nine miles of Green Brier [Greenbrier] creek the place that we retreated from last night was a week ago.[6] It is said that the enemy are on the top of Cheat mountain about 15 miles distance from here.[7] We have a beautiful camping ground. We do not know what we were sent here for, some say to keep the enemy in check I cannot see how one regiment can do it by themselves. Col Conner says it cannot be fortified. There was considerable murmuring among men and officers. It seems that we are to do nothing but to trot over the mountains backwards and forwards from one place to another. We are here among the mountains where we can buy no vegetables or get any thing to eat except what is given us. Without we are reinforced I think we will have to fall back again. T. A. Walker, Bill & Oliver arrived here last Friday evening.[8] I received two letters and some money by Mr. Oliver, he says he brought ten dollars for me and twenty five for Alexander Reid he paid the money over to Liut. Marshall as Alexander had gone to Staunton with some prisoners and was not here.[9] I let Marshall keep the money untill Alexander comes back and opens his letter and I know how much Mr. Reid sent Alexander. I do not understand how the mistake could have been made you stated twenty dollars. I am afraid he spent it on his way here. I will know soon and write you again upon the subject. The Government has not paid us yet and I dont know when they will, if they ever do. I was not in need of money at this time as I have twenty eight dollars now on hand and nothing to buy I thank you for it and I will try and take care of it untill it will do me some good. I was glad to get yours and mothers letters I began to think I was not going to get any more. I was sorry in deed that you had been so dry and had such bad prospects ahead I am in hopes it will be better than you think and that the latter rains will make cotton and help the corn. It will be hard to have to buy both meat and bread especially such times as these, but let us hope for the better. I learn here from the boys that the crops in some parts of Putnam are fine. We get plenty to eat, Bacon, Flour, Beef, Rice, Coffee, Sugar & so on. You wished to know how my clothing held out. It holds out first rate so far. I will have plenty untill fall unless some accident should happen and I should loose it. I do not know what I will need. I will let you know as soon as I can what I need, how to have it made and so on.[10] I will need as warm cloths as I can get for is cool here now at night. I am in hopes if we have to stay here untill winter that they will move us lower down to take up winter quarters. As to Tom I do not need him now Abners boy Jim is plenty, he is very handy, cooks well washes and does all we want done.[11] If at any time I should need Tom I will let you know. We have had the good luck to have our knapsacks carried in a wagon so far. If we have to carry them on our backs over these mountains we will have to throw away some of our things. I should like to be stationed at some place to stay, this one difficulty in our way about cloths we move so much that unless our knapsacks are hauled we cannot carry them. I reckon you have heard of the death of Gen. Garnett who was Commander of all the forces around here he has been Susspecioned [suspicioned] since his death of being in a plot with the enemy. I do not know much about it. Some two or three hundred prisoners pass here yesterday on parole of honor that were taken at Laurell Hill who were under his command and they were Virginians. The first Georgia regiment had a battle at Laurell Hill and are scattered they will rendevous [rendezvous] at Staunton.[12] I have seen some of them they say there was not many killed on our side there was eight of the enemys scouts killed by our scouts at Green Brier [Greenbrier] creek day before yesterday. We have a great many rumors here which I pay no attention to as they are false, it is the hardest matter in the world to get the truth of anything. While we were in Montery [Monterey] the officers raised a false alarm to try the men there was a great deal of excitement all over the camp the men responded promptly to the call and seemed ready to do their part. I was excited but not much frightened. There is some sickness in the regiment mostly diarhea [diarrhea] we left some of our boys at Montery [Monterey] and they have since gone to Staunton. I do not think there was much the matter with the most of them. We received a letter from John Biddelle [Bedell] yesterday stating that his health was improved, but his physicians advised him not to enter the service again as he would be subject to another attack. I think he will return home as soon as he can get a discharge. I believe there is less sickness in our company than most any in the regiment. I have been fortunate so far. I have had a bad cold and the diarhea [diarrhea] but am nearly well of both. I have not laid up for either there has been mumps and measles [measles] both in our camp and some now. I have escaped both up to this time although I have been exposed to them. If I should take them I will remember your advise and do the best I can to take care of myself for I want to get back to Georgia to see you all again. I had rather see you all than anything else on earth. I never knew how dear home and friends were untill I left them. I am getting on as well as I can expect under the circumstances. I hope the war will close so we may get home by Christmas. To day is Sunday and seems sometime like Sunday ought to be. Mr Marshall preached for us.[13] It has so happened that we have been on the march every sabbath since we left Richmond except to day it dont feel right to me though we are sometimes compelled to do it. I was glad to learn through your letter that Grandmas health had improved. I hope it will continue to improve tell her I think of her very often and feel when I think there is a probability of our never seeing each other again. I never did want to see you and the family as bad in my life. It seems an age almost since I left. You may rest assured that you are upper most in my thoughts. I have to banish the thought of home and friends as much as possible from my mind to keep my spirits from being cast down though it is a hard task. Tell Bud that I do not want him to come for he will find it different from what he expects there is many things he has never thought of and many quite different from his idea of it there are some in our company who were badly mistaken and wish now they had staid [stayed] at home, but it is to late for them now to get out it. I have no doubt he could stand our marches as well as some of us, but it worsts the best of them. I think of the peaches and watermelons often there is none here so I have made up my mind to do without them. Capt Davis thinks we will be home by fall. I cannot see upon what his notions are based. Give my love especially to Grandma. Mr Morton & family. Mr Shell & family, Mr Criddelle & wife and the rest of my friends.[14] Direct your letters to Richmond and I will get them. Write me soon as I want to hear often from home. Tell Bud and Charlie and Tom Morton to write to me.[15] Wat, Nick, Abner and all of my mess are well. I have written a long letter. I do not think there is much danger of an attack on us here. My love to all the negroes, except all of my love for you have it all unto death. Yours truly and affectionately.

Irby Goodwin Scott

Pocahantas Co. Top of Aleghany [Alleghany] Mountain July 29th 1861

Dear Father

I reckon you begin to want to hear from me as it has been several days since I wrote you. I am well and doing well. There is a great deal of coughs and colds in the regiment some mumps, measles, &c. I do not think there is more than half of our regiment that are well. The weather is very change-able it rains about every other day. It may be perfectly clear and in fifteen minutes it will be raining and then clear off in the same length of time.[16] There is no news here of importance no end to rumors which have ceased to have any effect upon me. I know you have heard of the Battle at Manasa [Manassas] in which our troops achieved a glorious victory.[17] It is not worth while for me to say what I have heard about the battle for you know more about it than I do. We get very few news papers here and it is hard to hear or get one to read. You said you would send me one if I wanted it. I want one but do not send it for I would not get them and then we will be mov-ing about from one place to another. Our mails come very irregular so do not send it for it would be but throwing money away. The battle at Manasa [Manassas] has raised the spirits of the boys tolerably high and there seems to be more confidence among the mess. The reverses our troops met at Rich Mountain and Beverly seemed to dispirit them. I understand that we will have an army or force of about fifteen or twenty thousand men in this part of the state. We hear that Gen. McClenland [McClellan] has been ordered to Washington to the assistance of Gen. Scott with part of his forces.[18] I learn that we have now about four thousand men in this vicinity and more on the way. It is said here that Gen. Beareguard [Beauregard] has posesion [pos-session] of Alexandria and Arlington heights they say it will be an easy mat-ter for him to burn or take Washington City.[19] While the battle of Manasa [Manassas] was going on the firing of the cannon was heard near this place a distance of over a hundred miles. Col Johnson with two companies went out yesterday on a reconnoitering expedition.[20] They camped last night at Green brier [Greenbrier] creek about ten miles from here in the direction of Cheat mountain where there are some of the enemy encamped. Their tents may be seen from this place with a spy glass. I do not know what will be our future movements. I would not be surprised if we did not move on in a day or two some eight or ten miles but this is just my own conjecture and it may not be so for privates know very little of what is going to take place untill the time comes for things to [take] place. Our company is getting on very well there is not much sickness among them some of them who were sick when we left Monteries [Monterey] went back to Staunton to recruit up. Several of them have returned and we are expecting the others soon. Nick Whaley has been complaining but is better and I think will soon be all right. The rest of my mess are well and send their respects to you all. I will give you a programe of each days business. The first thing in the morning is reville at five oclock when we all get up and the roll is called all who are not present except duty are marked, next comes police call when all the rubbish and filth is cleaned away from the tents this begins 5 1/2 Oclock and the recall 6 1/2, sergeons [surgeons] call at 7 1/2 when all the sick who are able are marched to the surgeons quarters to be examined at 7 Breakfast call, 8.45 guard call, 9 guard mounting 9 1/2 to 11 drill, Dinner 1 pm, 3 1/2 to 5 Drill again, sun down retreat and roll call, 8 roll call again, 8 1/2 all go to bed and lights extinguished &c, this is the daily routine of each day. I have to stand guard about once a week there are so many sick, we put on a 9 A.M. and have to be on duty 24 hours, we stand 2 hours and are off 4. I do not find it as hard as I expected. Our meat is mostly beef we get Bacon about every three days, we have had good luck so far in getting plenty of butter we do not get any meal except what we buy and little at that as it is very scarce up here. There is not much corn raised the productions are mostly grass hay some wheat and oats. They make their money principly [principally] upon stock. The people are mostly Dutch. There are large quantities of maple sugar made up here in the mountains. We are now encamped in a large maple grove. The land around here is rich but it is to cold and the seasons to short to be worth much. I was very much surprised to find so much wood land in Virginia. Georgia looks almost three times as old it does here. I do not think I have seen a red hill since I have been here the land is broken and hilly but does not seem to wash like ours. I saw some of the finest fields of wheat I ever saw between Richmond and Staunton. I expected to see a great deal of tobacco growing but have seen but little. We have not been in the tobacco region. I wrote you about the money you sent by Oliver. Alexander Reid came back from Staunton and we straightened it all up. Mr Reid wrote him that you and him concluded not to send so much for fear I might not get it. I am glad you did not send me any more for I have plenty at present. I received the ten dollars. I am going to get an overcoat from the Government which will come out of the pay I would receive for my services. It costs eight dollars. I do not know what to write about the cloths you spoke in your letter. In the first place I hope we will not be here in the winter, in the next if we were stationed I could take them and keep them but as it is if we move much I will have to throw away some I have now for we will have to carry them in our knapsacks on our backs. I will need some shoes or boots in the fall and winter if you come you could bring them. I have a pair of boots at home which

I think are very good as far as I can recollect. I dont know what to say about the matter. I am completely puzzled as to what is best. I dont know what the others are going do about theirs, are you all fixing up cloths for us or not. I will wait a while and see what we are going to do and try and let you know in time. I should like for you to let me know when you expect to come on so that I may let you know in time what to do in the matter. I have plenty until winter. I am afraid I will take the mumps or measles though I have been exposed long enough to take them, this is a bad place to have them. If I take them I shall try to get in a house here untill I am well. I hope I shall not take them. I have written a longer letter than I anticipated at first but if you are like I am you like long ones best. Write me soon I want to hear from home, give my love to all my friends especially Mr Morton & family, Mr Criddelle & wife Mr Shell & family and all inquiring friends. My love to Grandma, tell her I would like to write some to her but my letter is written as much to her as any of the family. My best love to all of the family, remember me to the negroes.
Yours most affectionately
    Irby G. Scott

Chapter 3

Camp on the Greenbrier River

"I rather suspect that there will be a battle here. . . ."

On a rainy August 13, 1861, to get closer to the enemy fortified on Cheat Summit, the Twelfth Georgia marched down Allegheny Mountain to a new campground at the junction of the Staunton–Parkersburg Turnpike and the East Fork of the Greenbrier River within ten miles of the enemy. On this march the men toted knapsacks, blankets, muskets, and accoutrements because they were without wagon transportation. Leaving their sick at Camp Allegheny, the remainder of the regiment marched the ten miles in three hours.

As the month of August progressed, more Confederate regiments were assigned to the First Brigade, commanded by General Henry R. Jackson, and posted at Camp Bartow with the Twelfth Georgia. Reliable intelligence was a vital ingredient missing in the planning of any campaign by Confederate forces in the area. On the other hand, loyal Union citizens in the area quickly reported every move of the Confederates. With additional manpower now at hand, larger and more aggressive scouting parties were sent from Camp Bartow and Camp Allegheny into the surrounding countryside toward the enemy. These scouting parties were often gone for days, their objective being to observe the movements of Federal forces and, if possible, capture Federal soldiers, from whom intelligence could be gathered and passed to headquarters.

After a successful reconnaissance of Cheat Summit, General William Loring, on September 8, issued orders for Colonel Albert Rust and his Third Arkansas Regiment to turn the enemy's position on Cheat Summit at daylight on September 12. General H. R. Jackson, with the remainder of his force, would proceed on the turnpike to the eastern base of Cheat Mountain. Colonel Edward Johnson and his command would occupy the enemy on the eastern base and cooperate with the attacking force of

Colonel Rust. Once the pass on Cheat Mountain was carried, General Jackson with his entire force would move toward Huttonsville. Colonel Rust never attacked as planned. His command captured a Union soldier who gave a false report of the total number of Union troops stationed at Cheat Summit Fort and the surrounding area. This soldier also informed Rust that his movement had been discovered, which was another ruse. Hearing no gunfire, Colonel Edward Johnson did not push forward on the eastern base of Cheat Mountain with his command.

Regular camp routine, drilling, guard duty, camp labor, and caring for the sick continued day in and day out on the Greenbrier River. Any new activity provided a welcome diversion. Irby Scott's father arrived at Camp Bartow to visit his son and their friends from Putnam County. Visits to camp from family members or friends were always welcome, as visitors usually brought clothing, food items, letters, and news from home. This was an especially welcome visit for the younger Scott because he was ill with measles and his father helped nurse him during his brief visit.

Constant rain, mud, exposure to cold temperatures, and the damp mountain environment took a toll on the clothing the men had brought with them. Letters written home during the time at Camp Bartow repeatedly asked loved ones to prepare winter clothing and heavy blankets. Ladies Aid Societies established at the beginning of the war for the purpose of supplying clothing for the troops and bandages for the wounded now began knitting gloves, wool socks, and winter undergarments for the men stationed in the mountains.

Camp Bartow Pochahontas Co. Va. Aug 29th 1861[1]

Dear Father

Knowing that you will expect a letter at the time I promised you to write and also that you will be disappointed if you do not receive one I now return that promise hoping that you have reached home safe and well before this comes to hand. Also that you may find all well there and everything right. I have no news of importance to write. There has been no change in our program that I have heard of every thing remains the same as it was when you left. Some of our company as usual are complaining but none but what are able to be about except Capt Davis James Reid and Solomon Batchelor.[2] Capt Davis and James Reid are both improving and I think will soon be well. Batchelor is quite sick. My mess are on the improve. I am feeling very well for the last few days and shall take my place in the ranks in a few days. I am stouter now than I have been since I had the measles and I dont think I can stand it much longer to lay up here and do nothing and see the rest of the boys doing their duty when I feel as well as I now do. Nick seems to be doing very well and I think he will soon be well Feiler has got

about straight. James Eakin is very unwell and has been since you left.[3] The rest are well as usual. I think we all will soon be well for we have some good old ham to eat mixed with a little brandy it is a great luxury here. Also some of the best pickles perhaps we are living higher. Tom Carter let us have half a ham which made about one whole one.[4] We are very saving with it not with standing it tastes so well. I have nothing to write about as nothing has transpired since you left except a two days raid. The clouds have broken off and the sun is shining bright the first time since day before yesterday. I forgot to write about our mess having a nice plate of peaches given us by Alexander Reid they were of this years crop put up in a can. There is a rumor here that Gen. Beauregard had crossed the Potomac into Maryland but there is not much confidence placed in it.[5] I was very sorry to see you leave last Tuesday and would have insisted on your staying longer but I knew it would be best for you to go as matters at home required your attention and you could do no good by staying. I confess that when you left I could with difficulty restrain the tears from my eyes when we shook hands. I could not trust myself to speak my heart but the sad word farewell it was hard to part but it had to be so but I hope to join you at home soon. I shall try to come home christmas if we should have to stay here during the winter. Give my very best love to Grandma and my thanks for the blankets which I would like to bring home with me if I am so fortunate as to get back remember me to all friends. The mess sends their respects to you and family. Abner Wat & Nick send their love to their families. Wat says he will write about Sunday. Give my very best love to all the family also remember me to the negroes. You must excuse bad writing and mistakes as I have a sorry pen and have written in a hurry to send my letter this evening. Nothing more at present. I remain your most affectionate son.
Irby G. Scott
P.S. Direct you letter to Travelers repose [Traveller's Repose]. Pochahantas [Pocahontas] County Virginia.
   I.G.S.

Camp Bartow, Sept 5, 1861
Pochahantas [Pocahontas] County, Virginia
Dear Father & Family,
   I wrote you last Thursday and as I have a chance to send a letter by Leut Marshall who leaves here this evening for home I thought I would not let this opportunity slip and not write you. He comes home on business for the regiment such as cloths, shoes, hats &c. I expect he will remain about a month or more. As it will be no little trouble for him to get all the cloths &c for every company from the different counties being scattered as they are. There has nothing of interest transpired since you left everything remains

the same. The health of our regt. is still very bad. There has been several deaths since you left, two last night. Our company is improving in health. All up and able to be about except three or four, Sol.[Solomon] Batchelor has been quite sick with the fever but is better and on the improve.[6] James Eakin has been sick ever since you were here, and at this time is quite sick. I am afraid ~~with~~ he also has the fever. I hear that Green Alford has succeeded in procuring a discharge and he will come home with Marshall.[7] I am well and fattening some. I have been on guard once, and had nice weather it being dry clear and warm. I have felt well and strong for a week or more and do not think there is much danger now. Nick has not taken his place in ranks yet. He is not improving fast and I am afraid it will be some time before he will fully regain his strength yet he is up and about every where around the camp. Yet it seems he is very weak he keeps in good sprits and does not seem to mind it much. ———— is not very well to day though I do not think it is anything more than cold. The rest of the mess are all well, Abner is on guard and he has bad time of it. It has taken a notion to rain and it rains, we had the best spell of weather for the last four or five days that we have had since we have been in the mountains, but last night and to day there has been a continual rain and there seems no prospect for the Sun to shine to day. It is said that we will receive our pay in a few days. Capt. Davis has made out his pay roll. I do not know how much we will get or whether it will be paid in money or Government bonds. If I get it I think I shall send it home by Mr Boswell if he comes on.[8] As to overcoats and other clothing that the government will supply, we have heard nothing from them though Capt. Davis says they will be certain to come. You all can do as you think best about them whether you will send them from home or let the boys get them here. I think they will be certain to get them for there was a man sent on to get them and bring them here. I am now looking every day for a letter from you. I want to know whether you got home safe or not. I am very anxious to hear. I received a letter a day or two since from mother and Emma stating that all were well also enclosed I found a letter to you from Nick Featherston wanting to know where I was.[9] I think I will write him in a few days he said his college chum was in our regt. I found him and showed him the letter. He did not know that Nick was in the battle of Manassa [Manassas] and said he would write to him. I was sorry to hear that the crops were so much injured by the rains. Emma stated in her letter that she had written to me, but I have never received it. Abner received two letters last night saying that all were well at home except Grandma who had been quite unwell for several days but was better. Nick also got one from home. Wat and Abner have both written home. Wat also received one from Mr. Morton who said that he had not received but two letters from him since he left Richmond, but I know that he has written at least eight or ten. I do not see why some of our letters should go right and others do not. War matters remain about the same so far as I know. I believe the men here are anxious for the fight to take place. They are tired of lying here in suspense, and all we want is the word to march, whenever we receive that, someby [somebody] will be hurt. I have dreamed of home for the last two nigh[ts] though not at all home sick. In the first I thought I was at home in mothers room with all the rest of the family sitting around the fire talking, every face seemed familiar as when I left. Grandma was also there sitting in her chair and looked quite natural. I dreamed that there was another person there a certain young lady, (but I will not name her) when I waked to find it all a dream it made me feel very bad for a while. In the second I dreamed that we had taken a stand at John Waltons and were expecting an attack every minute from the Indians, but I waked at this part and found myself wraped [wrapped] up snug and warm in No. 9 the reason I dreamed the last. I supose [suppose] was from hearing of the yankees taking those forts in North Carolina.[10] I want to see you all the worst sort, but would not go home now if I had a furlough for I would not go over the parting scene for nothing , but if I should live and can, I intend to come to see you in the winter. If Mr Boswell does not come on you can send our things by Marshall, but I would prefer for you to send them by Mr Boswell. P.S. (Give my love to Mr Criddelle and wife) Marshall will have so many to trouble him that they might not come as safe. I have written about all I can think of at present. Jim Pike has been sawing on an old fiddle all the morning playing nothing in particular but keeping up a noise he plays. Tell Turner that Jim says howdy and that he wishes he was here to knock the bones while he plays the fiddle, that he is enjoying himself finely and is in good health.[11] Also to tell his wife when he sees her that he will not write often as there is no use in it. Give my love to Grandma and say to her that I think of her often and nothing would give me more pleasure then to see her. Remember me especially to Mr Morton & Family, Mr Shell & Family, Mr. Boswell and Family, Mr Whaley & family and all inquiring friends, also to all the negroes.[12] The boys all send their love to their families and friends. Also their respect to you all. I am looking anxiously for a letter from you thinking you would be certain to write as soon as you arrived at home. Write me often and about every thing. I will send back Nicks letter that you may see it and get his address. My best love to you and all the family. Yours as ever.

Irby G. Scott

Camp Bartow. Sept 11th, 1861

Dear Father,

I have looked anxiously for a letter for several days, but have not received a line from you. I do not doubt but that you wrote to me as soon as you arrived at home and that the letter has been delayed somewhere on the route, Abner received one from Mrs Boswell yesterday evening saying that you had got home safe and that all were well which I was glad to hear, but I cannot write the same good news to you in respect to our health which is any thing but good.[13] When you were here there were a good many sick and since that time there has been a good many deaths and there are now many who are unable to do duty the fever seems to be the worst disease amongst us at this time. I am very fearful that it will increase. I wrote Mr Morton day before yesterday that Wat was sick with slow fever. I cannot say that he is any better now. I think that he will have a hard spill and probably a long one, he has been rather delirious for several days. We are doing all we can to make him as comfortable as possible, but cannot do much in that way. We have procured plank and made a good floor in our tent which is much better than lying on the ground. It is a hard matter to get anything for the sick to eat, but what the government give us. There are several others in our company that are quite sick with fever James Eakin has had a hard spell since you were here he was sick when you left and is not able to sit up much now. I think that he will get a discharge and come home as soon as he is able. Green Alford has got a discharge and is now ready to start for home but Capt Davis wants him to wait untill Eakin is well enough to go with him. The old man Hollis has been quite sick and I do not know that he is any better.[14] Homer Paschal, T. A. Walker and Rickerson are all quite sick with fever.[15] There are others of the company complaining but none of them confined to their beds. My own health is very good at this time. The mess excepting Wat and Eakin are well and send their respects to you and family. I think from the prospect this morning that we shall have a rainy day. The first Ga regiment arrived here on last Monday they look very well and can turn out a great many men than we can.[16] We were glad to see them for we know that they would do to depend upon in any place. On last Tuesday three battalions of five hundred men each left to join Gen. Lee and we received orders this morning to put a white stripe upon our hat and to draw the loads from our guns and clean them. This is all I know and will have to guess at the rest. I rather suspect that there will be a battle here in a few days from the signs, though as I said before it is all guess work with me. You can show this letter to Mr Morton. I have written just how Wat was the best I know. I have kept nothing back but have written plainly. Some tried to persueede [persuade] me not to write that he was so sick that it would only make them uneasy at home and do no good. I cannot but know that Mr Morton wishes me to write the truth so I have written, and never expect to write any other way. Nick is doing well and has nearly recovered his strength he has not taken his place in ranks yet. Give my best love to Grandma and tell her that I think of her often and that it would give me great pleasure to see her which I hope will soon be.

Give my love to all my friends. My very best love to Mother and all the children except a large share for yourself.[17] Yours as ever.
Irby G. Scott

Camp Bartow Pochahantas [Pocahontas] Co. Virginia
Sept. 21st 1861
Dear Father
I received your letter of the 11th Sept last night. It gave me great pleasure I assure you for I have been looking for one from you and it seemed to me it would never come to hand. I must now make some excuses for not writing myself. I wrote to Mr. Morton last Monday was a week ago that Wat was very sick with the [typhoid] fever.[18] Two days after I wrote again to you stating as best I could Wats condition. In that letter I stated that we were ordered to cook two days rations and to be ready to march at a moments warning. So that night about one Oclock we left our camp our destination being Cheat mountain. We were kept out of camp for five days and nights up there. So I had no opportunity to write while we were from camp. When we got back on Monday evening about sun down I found that James Eakin was dead, and that the surgeon had removed Wat to the hospital the day before being very tired and worn out from the fatigues of the last five days and nights I did not go to see him until next morning. I found him very low, he did not know me. I tried to rouse him and to talk to him but could not make him understand anything I said to him, he was so crazy as any one you ever saw, he raved and talked a great deal but you could not understand or make any sense of what he said. I remained all day with him at night was relieved by Jacob Feiler who remained all night. The next day Mr. Marshall staid and attended to him until evening when myself and Thomas Spivey relieved him and set up with him untill about two oclock when he died and with the help of one or two others of our company we shrouded and laid him rest.[19] I knew as soon as I got back to camp and saw him that there was no chance for him to live his sufferings were great and as long as he had strength but for an hour before he died he lay perfectly quiet and died very easy. We shrouded him in his uniform. Frank Suther made him a very nice plain coffin as good as could be had here.[20] He died the 19th inst at 15 minutes past 2 Oclock and was buried day before yesterday evening. I cut his name on a plank which was placed at the foot of his grave the initials of his name is also marked on a rock at the head of his grave. I wished very much to talk to him before he died to know if he wanted any message sent home to his family, but he was so deranged in his mind that I never had an opportunity. Capt Davis wanted me to write to Mr. Morton of his death, but I did not know how to do it. So he (Capt Davis) wrote to Mr. Morton the day he died. I intended to write you the same day but having slept none the night before I thought I would sleep

in the morning and write my letter in the evening. So I laid down and slept untill dinner the order came for us to tear down our tents and move. So I had to go to work and could not write that day. Yesterday I was very busy all day fixing up our tent cutting ditches, brushing up &c. Our present locality is upon the top of a high hill just over back of where Col Scott was encamped when you were here or rather if you recollect as you come this way about two or three hundred yards this side of the house where the stage stops on the right side of the road not more than seventy yards from the road. This place is not a pretty place to camp but I think it will be much healthier than the old one was. We had to dig and drag the dirt down the hill about like the turnpike road to get places for some of our tents, but I believe all are very comfortably fixed. I had like to have forgotten to state that Mr. and Mrs. Jenkins of Eatonton was here they came last Wednesday was a week ago from some springs the name of which I have forgotten and found Robert Jenkins quite sick with the fever he was taken about the same time Wat was and has been very sick but is improved now and with proper treatment will get well.[21] I do not know how long they will stay. They have tried to get a furlough for Bob but, I believe they were only allowed the privilege of taking him to Staunton. I dont know yet whether they will carry him there or not. There is still a great deal of sickness among the soldiers and we have some in our company who have been very sick but the most of them are improving none I believe dangerous. As for myself I believe I have much enjoyed better health since I have been in Virginia. Abner had a slight attack of fever but he is now nearly recovered entirely from it. Nick is still on the sick list and his health is not good he is up and about the camp all time but seems to be weak and unable to gather his strength he looks a little thin. I think if he had Brandy to drink it would help him and also if he had something besides beef and biscuit without any shrotning [shortening] to tempt him that would soon be well. The rest of the mess are well, we only number five now and Jim (Pike) making six in all. I deeply regret the deaths of Morton and Eakin and sincerely symphasize with the relatives of the deceased, but God has so ordered it and we must submit. If I had not been away from camps I should have written every other day to you or Mr. Morton how Wat was getting on and should have given him all the attention I possibly could, but I was compelled to leave but I think while I was away he was well attended to. We are rather at a loss to know what to do with his cloths, as we have as many of our own as we can manage. He has some little things which I intend to bring or send home to his family. I thought that I would give his cloths to Capt Davis and let him give them to any of the company who might need such things. His money is in the hands of Capt Davis. Jim Pike (Abners boy) had a hard time waiting on Wat and James Eakins while we were gone. There was only two well men left to take care of the sick. He set up with them four nights without any one to relieve him and they say he attended to them well. I will now try and give you a little of our trip to Cheat mountain. We left Camp about one oclock on Wednesday night in the rain with oil cloths and blankets strapped on our backs and two days rations in our haversacks there was about two thousand men in all. The 1st Ga regt. was in the lead. It took a long time to cross the creek which was bridged with wagons clear across. Our regt went next to the 1st Ga then the artillery consisting of four cannon and equipment, following that was Col. Scott 44th Va regt. Besides some militia cavalry &c. It was about twelve miles from our camp to where the Yankees are encamped upon Cheat mountain. Such a march I have never had since I have been in Virginia. It was raining when we started and had rained all the day before, the night was dark as pitch and the holes all full of water which you could not avoid stepping in. The mud about shoe deep all the way. The road just about like it had been greased (you would have thought so to if you could have seen and heard the boys falling every few steps) we could not turn right or left for branches but wade right through as if it was perfectly dry. So as we went through rain mud and water part of the time in double quick untill about sun up the next morning when we found ourselves in about two miles of the Yankee camp when we stopped [to] eat breakfast and rest awhile. We again took up the line of march and had not proceeded far when a Yankee picket fired at Col Johnson who was at the head of the column from the bushes, but missed his aim. Old Blucher as we call him here kept perfectly cool and laughingly remarked that the picket was a darn poor shot.[22] We sent out men to flank the mountain but the picket escaped after being at once. This delayed a little time when we marched on but our ears were again startled with the roar of musketry in front (the road being a circuitous winding around the mountain side we could only hear without seeing) in a few minutes we heard a tremendous shouting as we supposed our troops pursuing the yankee pickets, but when found out who it was that we were shooting every face seemed cast down and all the life and ammunition the men had just before exhibited was completely gone we were firing into our own advance guard consisting of one hundred men under Luit. Dawson which was sent out at 8 oclock the night before through the mountains cut off and surprised the yankee pickets.[23] They went around the first pickets and fired some about three quarters of a mile of the enemys camp killing 7 that we found and wounding a good many more that ran off through the bushes as we got 16 guns the same number of cartridge boxes a good many blankets, hats &c. The guard after firing into the pickets were making their way [into] the bushes along the road side expecting to meet more pickets running toward the yankees camp when they saw the first companies of the 1st Ga regt coming around a bend in the road and fired upon them they the 1st Ga supposing them to be yankees without waiting for a command fired in upon them but as soon as it was found out that both parties were Georgians the firing ceased immediately. There was three killed and about the same number wounded. This detained us for some time when we marched on towards the enemys Camp distance about two miles. We proceeded untill we reached the top of the mountain in full view of the enemys camp we there halted and seeing the yankees formed in line inside of their works the cannon were brought to front and the men arranged in order of battle, but the yankees declined to meet us so we remained untill evening and started back to our camp when we got in about four miles we met a dispatch and had to go back half a mile to a cabin where there was an opening and camp for the night. We built fires eat our supper and then all laid down and slept upon the ground. Early next morning we started again towards the yankee camp everyone being certain that we would have a fight that day. Gen Jackson came around that morning talking to his men in such a manner that we were double sure of a fight. We went up and occupied the same ground that we did the day before, but could not get the yankees out of their strong hold. We remained untill evening and returned to our camping ground of the night before. Here we met wagons with provisions and cooking utensils, we again slept upon the ground around our fires the next day which was the third day we did not move but remained where we were that day and the next also which was Sunday doing nothing but cooking and eating. They said we were waiting for orders from Lee. I was on picket guard from Saturday evening untill Sunday evening in one of the worst mountain thickets you ever saw. You could not see a man more than fifty yards. On Monday we again moved up the mountain in sight of yankees this day we tried to draw the yankees out into an ambuscade but could not succeed. We remained untill evening and returned to camp where we arrived just at night about as tired a set of men as you ever saw. On Sunday night it rained and we had to take it sitting around our log heap fires and when it quit raining we laid down and slept on the wet ground all night. On Monday we intend to remove our camp in sight of the yankees and went to work cleaning away the bushes, logs, and to dig ditches when we had worked about an hour we received an order not to try to hold the place where we [were] fixing for our camp on the top of Cheat about a mile and a half from the enemys camp but to fall back to our old camp at Greenbrier on our way back we met our tents and came back here. I think that we will fortify here and not try to attack them on Cheat mountain. They are to well fortified for us to do anything with them. Col Rust, was also out with about the same number of men that we had and was to attack them in the rear and us in front, but he did not attack them.[24] Two regiments was ordered to Petersburg from here but they have been ordered back here one of them has returned and the other is at Allegheny. But I have written as much as I can get in an envelope and will save some for next time. I was glad to hear that you got home safe and that all was well. If you send us butter put it in several small cans so that we will not have to open all at once. I think it will keep better. Remember me especially to Grandma. Give her my best love and affection and that if I can come home this winter for you dont know how bad I want to see you all. Give my love to all my friends. Say to Mr. Morton that I deeply simpathise with him for he has lost a son, I a mess mate and friend. Remember me to the negroes. My best love to mother and all the children and except a large share for yourself. I have fattened up considerably on biscuit without any grease in them and beef that eats like it is old enough to be of age.

Yours untill death

Irby G. Scott

P.S. I shall look anxiously for the good thing you inumerated [enumerated] in your letter it made my mouth water to read that part of your letter.

IGS

Chapter 4

Cannon Fire on the Greenbrier

" . . . I passed through unscathed."

Throughout the South there was bewilderment as to why the victorious army at the Battle of Manassas was not being put to better use. On October 3, 1861, Confederate President Jefferson Davis and Generals Joseph E. Johnston, Pierre G. T. Beauregard, and Gustavus W. Smith met at Centerville, Virginia, to discuss strategy. The generals advised concentration in Virginia, for the defense of Virginia, and considered western Virginia a priority. While President Davis and his generals discussed strategy, the men of the Twelfth Georgia fended off an attack on Camp Bartow by superior Federal forces.

Brigadier General Joseph R. Reynolds, in command of the Federal forces in the Cheat Mountain area, encouraged by the aborted Confederate attempt in September to gain Cheat Summit, planned to attack Camp Bartow. Though his own force had been reduced by the withdrawal of regiments to the eastern theater, he felt he had a sufficient force at hand to dislodge the Confederate defenders at Camp Bartow and clear the Staunton–Parkersburg Turnpike to the east. He planned a "reconnaissance in force" against the Confederates at the Greenbrier River crossing of the turnpike.

Confederate troops under command of General Henry R. Jackson were entrenched at Camp Bartow. On October 2, General Jackson informed authorities in Richmond that his force had been reduced by sickness and by regiments detached for other service, and that he could only field about 1,800 effective troops. About nine miles to the southeast, on the Staunton–Parkersburg Turnpike, at the top of Allegheny Mountain, Colonel John Baldwin and the Fifty-second Virginia guarded the rear of Camp Bartow.

About seven o'clock on the morning of October 3, the head of the advancing Federal column made contact with the forward Confederate picket line three miles in advance of Camp Bartow. Retiring to the main guard, now reinforced to one hundred, a mile in advance of Camp Bartow, Confederate pickets delayed the Federal advance for at least an hour. After the Confederate guard retired to Camp Bartow, Colonel Nathan Kimball's Fourteenth Indiana was directed to the Confederate front and right to clear a position for Loomis's Battery. Loomis's Federal Battery was brought into action six to seven hundred yards in advance of Camp Bartow. Soon after Loomis's Battery began firing, additional Federal guns came into play on Camp Bartow.

The men in the Twelfth Georgia initially ignored musket fire heard in direction of the advanced guard. The Virginians that were in the Laurel Hill and Rich Mountain fight were convinced it was an attack and at once formed and took position in the entrenchments. The men of the Twelfth and the First Georgia continued with "their regular morning duties." It was not long before the men of the Twelfth received orders to be ready to move at a moment's notice. The regiment formed and marched toward the river.

Aroused by a courier on the morning of October 3, Colonel Edward Johnson heard of the pending danger to Camp Bartow. A second courier soon arrived, confirming that the faint sound of musketry was a Federal advance in force. Johnson apprised General Jackson of the possibility of a pending assault. Johnson and one company of the Thirty-first Virginia rushed to the front to investigate.

When Johnson reached the main guard he found the advanced pickets scrambling back. Johnson at once took control of the main guard and the fleeing advance pickets, deploying them on either side of the turnpike. He ordered the men to load and fire as rapidly as possible. Confronted by a hundred muskets, the Indiana regiments staggered and moved off the turnpike. A stubborn Confederate resistance bought enough time for Jackson to deploy the regiments into the entrenchments at Camp Bartow.

Federal infantrymen pressed forward on Johnson's flanks, forcing him and the grand guard to give ground stubbornly. After about an hour, Johnson and the guard retired to the entrenchments of Camp Bartow. Johnson commanded his section of the entrenchments with the same cool haste displayed on the other side of the river.

With the time bought by Johnson, General Jackson formed the defenders of Camp Bartow along a mile-long front. In the early morning three companies of the Twelfth Georgia were dispatched to the extreme Confederate right, to protect the main body from an enemy flank movement. Soon the entire regiment received orders to cross the Greenbrier River at the double quick. Before fully deploying into line of battle, the regiment received orders to "right about," crossing the river again and deploying in a branch, the remains of a mill race. Remaining in the water of a mill race throughout the battle, the regiment repelled a Federal advance on the right flank. Irby Scott states the regiment drove the enemy back "with out firing a gun." Observing Federal forces deploying in the woods, on the Confederate right flank at the base of Burner Mountain, Confederate artillery fire repulsed the Federal advance. After four and a half hours Federal General Reynolds broke off the engagement and took up the march for Cheat Summit Fort, which he reached at about sundown.

Following the Cheat Mountain campaign, many men in the Twelfth Georgia were sick and unfit for duty. They had been exposed for four days to cold rain and cold night air, with only a blanket each for protection. Arrangements were made to move many of the sick to Crabb Bottom, Staunton, and Harrisonburg, Virginia. By early October, the Twelfth Georgia moved its camp up the mountain to what they hoped would be a healthier location.

The weather at the end of September and the beginning of October was still rainy, but also cool and windy, exacerbating living conditions at Camp Bartow. Heavy frosts and fog in the mornings greeted the men in early October. Later in October, temperatures during the day had dropped and nights were quite cold, with days of snow and sleet.

November began with blowing wind and rain continuing into the next day. High winds flattened tents and tore canvas. A correspondent to the Richmond Daily Dispatch reported, "The mud is ankle deep, both inside and outside of the tents." Weather conditions at Camp Bartow grew progressively worse during the month, with a foot of snow falling on the morning of November 16. The next day, a snowball battle took place between the First and Twelfth Georgia. One chronicler declared the Twelfth Georgia victorious, while another stated the affair ended in a "dawn [drawn] battle."

Camp Bartow Sept 30th 1861

Dear Father,

You can see above that we have not changed our camp and I am afraid from what is going on here that we many have to stay here this winter, we are fortifying on a large scale by digging entrenchments, throwing up breastworks and cleaning up the woods all around. The trees are cut upon each other forming a kind of jungle which makes it almost impossible for a man to get through it. Since we have commenced fortifying every well man is on some kind of duty nearly all the time which makes it pretty hard.[1] The weather has for a few days past has been quite cool, cold enough for ice a quarter of an inch thick and every where white with frost. Abner had a bad time of it standing guard (Grand Guard) he had to go over the creek.[2] It

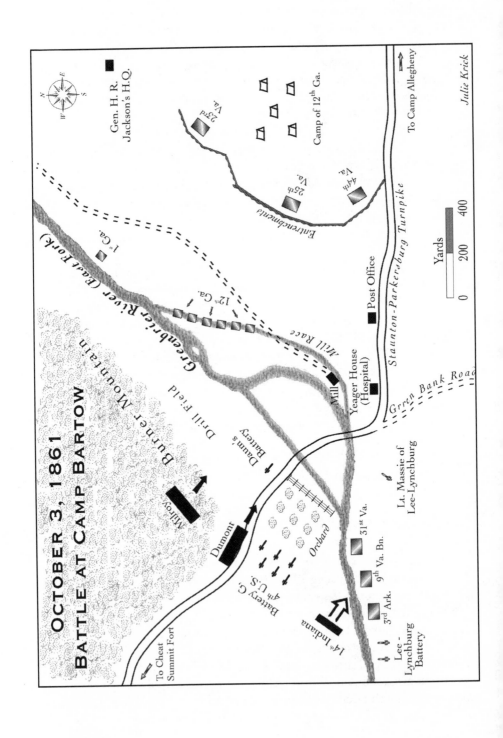

OCTOBER 3, 1861
BATTLE AT CAMP BARTOW

Gen. H. R. Jackson's H.Q.

Camp of 12th Ga.

23rd Va.

Entrenchments

25th Va.

4th Va.

To Camp Allegheny

Julie Krick

Buner Mountain

Greenbrier River (Bad Fork)

1st Ga.

12th Ga.

Drill Field

Mill Race

Post Office

Staunton-Parkersburg Turnpike

Yards

0   200   400

Mill

Yeager House
(Hospital)

Green Bank Road

To Cheat
Summit Fort

Milroy

Dumont

Daum's
Battery

Orchard

Battery G.
4th U.S.

Lt. Massie of
Lee-Lynchburg

31st Va.

9th Va. Bn.

3rd Ark.

14th Indiana

Lee-
Lynchburg
Battery

was raining in the morning when he left and continued to rain all day and all night. The wind commenced blowing and it began to turn cool and kept getting cooler till there was plenty of ice. The creek was higher than it has been before since we came here. The guard over the creek could not be relieved at the proper time and they had to stay two days on account of higher water. Another one of our company died yesterday morning and was buried yesterday evening. William Hitchcock who has been in bad health ever since we left Richmond his disease was typhoid fever.[3] All of the sick that were able to stand the travel left yesterday for Harrisonburg. Some where near Staunton which is said to be a nice place.[4] There was fourteen of our company that went, leaving three unable to go (viz) old man Hollis who is improving slowly. Henry Rickerson who is very bad and Bob Jenkins who has also been very low and in all probability would have died had it no been for the timely arrival of his parents, he is getting better, we have also sent of[f] all our extra baggage, which went from here to Montery [Monterey]. Mr and Mrs Jenkins will leave for home this evening and will be the bearer of this. I regret very much to see them leave for they have been very kind to the sick since they have been amongst us, for which I know they will receive the thanks of every man in the company. I have been very well for some time but for a day or two have been suffering a little from a bad cold. I also have a little soarness just below my ears, which I am rather afraid will turn out to be mumps. Because I write this I do not wish you all to be uneasy for I am not certain that it is mumps. My self I received a letter about two days since from Mr Morton but if he got Capt Davis letter and you got mine you will see that Wat was dead over a week before it got here. I would like to know whether he intends removing him or not. Nick is improving a good deal and if he keeps on I think he will soon be well. The rest of the mess are well. We received an official dispatch stating that Gen. Price of Missouri had almost demolished Fremont's command by killing three thousand.[5] Taking the same number of prisoners sixteen thousand Stand of arms and sixteen pieces of artillery. It is generally believed to be true. As to our future movements I have not the least idea, but you can here [hear] almost anything you would like yet nobody knows anything definite if we have to stay here during the winter there will be great distaffaction [dissatisfaction] among the soldiers. I have written about all the news of importance and will write again in a few days. My mess only numbers six now including Jim. We are rather on the lookout for Steve Marshall. Give my love to Grandma and say that I have not forgotten her, and often think what a pleasure it would be to sit in her room by the fire and relate to her as she used to me. My adventures among the wild mountains of western, va. My love to all friends to mother, Bud and all the children. [*cross drawn on left side of letter*] and except [accept] a large share for yourself.   Irby G. Scott [*Irby signs name in tall bold script not seen in any of his other letters*]

Camp Bartow Va. Oct. 5th 1861
Dear Father

I know you will hear through the newspapers of the battle on the 3rd. Knowing that you will be uneasy untill you get a letter, I embrace this opportunity of writing you a few lines to say I passed through unscathed. I did not fire a single gun during the fight it was because I did not have a chance. Thursday morning the yankees took a notion to come down and whip us. They drove in the guard and advanced to within a mile of our camp when they commenced throwing their shell and ball into our camp. They came thick and fast in every direction. Our cannon soon responded and there was a regular fire kept up for four hours. Fortunately our sick had been removed a few days before except a few who were quickly taken out of the tents in wagons and sent to Allegheny. Nearly every tent has a hole in it and one burnt clear up. You could hear shell and ball whistling in every direction. Some of the shell that we picked up after the fight weighed ten and twelve pounds. Some would burst it seemed a hundred feet in the air over the camp. They made two attempts to flank us. In the first attempt Col. Rusts Arkansas regiment poured a deadly fire of musketry upon them and they retreated in the next it came to ours and the 1st Ga time to drive them back which was done with out firing a gun. In the morning our regiment was formed over the field where we drilled when you were here where we remained untill they attempted to flank the mountain on that side when we double quicked across the open field to the creek and got down as flat as we could in a little branch some of the boys up to their knees in the water and some lying flat down in it, here we remained to await them.[6] Every now and then a ball would whistle close over our heads. One little fellow was shot through the arm missing the bone. There was a small canon reserved in case they tried to flank us. This turned loose upon them a galling fire causing them to scatter through the mountain and to scamper back as fast as possible. So we did not get a chance at them at all, by this time I suppose they had got enough and took with a leaving back up the road towards Cheat some say in double quick I could not see them. It was a big battle for it was fought most altogether with cannon. Our loss is said to be 2 killed and 7 wounded.[7] That of the enemy we dont know as they carried them away as fast as they were killed in wagons. Col. Ramsey who was cut off in the morning and was upon the mountain where he could see, says they were hauling off their dead & wounded all the time of the fight he also thinks their force was five thousand men.[8] There certainly was a good many killed. There was several horses crippled and killed. Col. Johnson had his horse shot under him. He commanded the whole battle in every respect and he was every where in the thickest parts of the fight as cool as if nothing was the matter. He is certainly a brave man, as brave as ever lived. We received a dispatch here which has been confirmed that Gen. Lee had routed Rosecrans and was in his rear pursuing him.[9] It seems things are working fast in these parts now. Some suppose that these yankees who attacked us wished to get out from Cheat as times above them are getting rather warm. We are still cutting down the woods around our camp and throwing up fortifications. Among the trophies obtained was a large nice company flag which the enemy left part of the staff being shot off.[10] As it went through the camp it called for the many a lusty cheer. There was a good many ball of descriptions picked up all over the camp and some in the woods. Some of the boys had several chickens in a coop. A cannon ball killed one of them and turned the rest out. I was perfectly cool all the [time] and did not feel afraid every[one] seemed to ready and there was very little excitement among the men. The Virginians occupied the entrench- ments around the camp and the Georgians and Arkansasians were pitted against each other to prevent them flanking us. So I suppose I shall call it a great victory. I must close as I am tired. Give my love to Grandma mother and all the rest of the family also all inquiring friends. We may be attacked again before long but as to this I know nothing. I think we can whip them every time they come with 3 to 1. I must close by remaining your Affectionate son

    Irby G. Scott

Camp Bartow Pochahantas [Pocahontas] Co. Va
October 13th 1861

Dear Father & Family

    It has not been many days since I wrote to you but having nothing else to do I concluded I would write you a short letter knowing also you are al- ways anxious to hear. I have been sick with the mumps and had to expose myself the day of the fight so much. I got my feet and legs perfectly wet and they had to remain so the most of the day. I think I took a little cold from it and it made me worse than I had been. I was right sick for several days but I now am about straight again. Every thing has been very quite here since the battle, but we are still going ahead throwing up fortifications and arranging our defences.[11] You would not know the place now if you were here every- thing is altered so much. Four recruits arrived here last Thursday, Robins, Batchelor, Lawrence and Adams.[12] They left Steve Marshall in Richmond sick.[13] Mr. William Terrell arrived here last night by the stage.[14] He had been down to see the Brown Rifles and came from there on here.[15] The boys on the coast have had a little skirmish with the yankees.[16] We keep sending the sick and all who are unable to do duty back to Staunton. Nick and Mark Cochran left today.[17] Nick disliked very much to go, but had to obey the order. I understand that the boys at Harrisonburg will also be moved to Staunton so Nick will be with his friends and I think he may be benefited by the change. His health is somewhat improved. I do not know what to think, whether we will winter here or go back to Staunton. I reckon we will soon know. I think it will be almost impossible for us to stay here. It is quite cool now which troubles us a great deal. Standing picket guard not being allowed to have fire at night. I understand that old man Hollis is dead. I have heard none of the particulars of his death. The day of the battle he with the rest of the sick were removed up to Aleghany [Allegheny] where the old man died. We thought that he was improving some while he was here. I would not be surprised if the excitement and then being hauled in a wagon over these rough roads was not the cause of his death. Mr. Jenkins and his wife went from here to Richmond where they obtained a furlough for Bob. Mr. J. sent it back in a letter to Capt. Davis thinking that he would not come back, but hearing of the fight he immediately started back leaving his wife in Richmond. He staid here several days waiting for the furlough to come so he took Bob and set out for Staunton intending to leave him there and go on to Richmond and get another which he would send back to Staunton or telegraph for Bob to come on. He tried every way that he could to get one here but could not succeed. Old Green was very contrary about it and made Mr. Jenkins very mad several times.[18] The health of our company except those sent off is very good. We hear through the papers that Joe Brown was elected Governor by a large majority.[19] I received several letters by the recruits from you and one from Mr. Shell. You sent almost to many good things. I dont know how we will manage it all. There is only four of us now. Nick is gone. I will be sorry if Nick does not get a chance at some of the good things for he has talked so little about them. I want to see you all very bad and think of your very often but I cant tell when I shall have that pleasure. I am affraid that I shall not be able to get a furlough as it is so hard to get one now for a man that is sick. If a man is diseased so that they know he will never be fit for duty they will not give him a furlough. Give my love especially to Grandma and tell her that I have not forgotten her but think of her very often and nothing would give me more pleasure than to see her and that I hope soon to have that pleasure. If we take up winter quarters here I dont know how it will be about getting the mail from Staunton here. The roads will be blockaded with snow. Give my respects to Mr. Shell and tell him I was glad to hear from him and I hope he will write again soon. Is he going to teach for you all another year? I received a letter from Nick Featherston last week which I have answered. He is near Fairfax Station. He did not write any news of importance. He said that his health was much improved. I reckon we will keep up a regular correspondence from this time on. He has got to be Captain of his company his captain dying soon after the battle of Manassa [Manassas]. We received four more cannon the other day. Two twelve pounder and two six pounders rifle cannon. We have now twelve in all and the way they are placed it will be almost impossible for an enemy ever to reach our camp. Since we have thrown up fortifications and fixed this is a strong position and we can whip the enemy three to one. I believe the mess are all well. They send their respects to you and family. I dont think Mr. Terrell will stay more than a day or two. I dont think he looks well. Give my love to all inquiring friends, tell Emma and Sue that I received their letters.[20] Tell them to write again. I received a letter from Lou Jones wanting to know all the perticulars of Wats death.[21] You will please show her the letter I wrote you about it. Except my best love and wishes and may we meet soon is my ernest desire.

Irby G. Scott.

Remember me to the negros.

Camp Bartow Pochahontas [Pocahontas] Co. Va
Oct 15th 1861

Dear Father

I wrote you day before yesterday, but as Mr Terrell leaves to day I thought that you would be disappointed if you did not get a letter through him. I am about well though I have not gone on duty, but shall in a few days if I continue to feel well. I was enjoying fine health untill I took the mumps and when I get over them I hope I shall enjoy the same blessing again. I hope these lines may find you all well and doing well. The company are generally well with the exception of a few cases of mumps. I have not heard from any of the sick that are gone to Harrisonburg since they left. I hear a report here that they will all be removed to Staunton in a few days, every thing is very quite here nothing of interest turned up since the battle. We are still cutting down the woods around the camp and erecting batteries some of them masqued. Leut Marshall nor any of our things have arrived yet. They may be stoped in Staunton, but as to this I am not advised. You wrote me that any extra clothing I had I could sent back by Mr Terrell. There was a order that our regiment should box up all the extra clothing we had and let them be sent back as far as Montery [Monterey]. So we packed up our trunk full and sent it to Montery. I had several things to send back home but as they are in Montery I cannot get them and shall have to wait another opportunity. Mr Morton wished me to send back Wats cloths but they too are in Montery and I cannot get them. As to his money that will be sent by Mr Terrell. It is in the hands of Capt Davis he had only twlve [twelve] dollars and about sixty cents on hand when he died. He loaned his Cousin John Zachry ten dollars.[22] I saw Zackry yesterday but he did not have the money nor could he borrow it he said he intended to write to Mr Morton soon and that he would make arrangements with his father to pay it. Bob Jenkins owes him two dollars and a half which Mr Morton can get as Bob will be at home soon. Also John Biddelle [Bedell] owes him five dollars that he can collect from Bedelle, if any one else owes him anything I do not know it. I sent some little things by Mr Jenkins a small ——— a tooth brush and his letters. His pocket knife was lost and I never could find it. I am very sorry that I cannot send his things, if I should have an opportunity I will send them. I wrote rather discouraging in my last letter about getting a furlough there will be a great many who will want to go home, but reckon I will stand as good chance as any of the privates. At any rate I intend to try what I can do. I want to see you all very bad and shall be sadly disappointed [if] I do not have that pleasure this winter. Nothing could give me more pleasure than to sit around a good warm fire and converse with you all. I may see you and I may not but it is my greatest desire. Give my love especially to grandma and tell her that I know her time is short on earth, but it is my earnest prayer that I may see her once more and talk over my hardships in the mountains. I would be delighted to sit down and give her a full history of my travels since I entered the service. As to the war closing this winter I have lost all hope and how long it may be protracted we cannot tell any how we are in for the war and will remain untill it closes whether it be long or short. But I will content myself the best I can. I have become so that I am satisfied with almost anything in reason, but am perfectly disgusted with some of our officers, the way in which they act about some things. If you will go to see Mrs Jenkins she will tell you about some things.[23] It is said the putnam light infantry means the marque [marquee]. That is when things are sent to the company the marque gets the benefit of them such as wine, brandy &c. If at any time you send any thing send it in my name and I will derive the benefits of it. I do not wish to complain of our officers but cannot help it when things are so plain. I do not wish anything said about it as it might get back and I might suffer for it as they have me in their power, but I guess when the war closes and if we all should live to get home they will hear something of it. I will also say there is partiality shown some of the messes. The weather here at night is quite cool, ~~at night~~ there are white frosts every morning but the middle of the day is quite pleasant. The leaves upon the trees here are turning yellow and beginning to fall every thing looks like fall. I supose [suppose] we will winter about Staunton but as to this we know nothing definite. I wish I had some thing to send you all by Mr. Terrell but this is a poor place to procure anything fitten to send. I have two laurel rings which I will send to Emma and Mollie and if I can I will send ——— one to keep in remembrance of me.[24] They are made of laurel root and are not very nice as they are the first I have tried to make. I will also send Bud a plain one which I have been wearing. Tell Bud to write to me. I will send them by Mr Terrell. I will write again soon and shall expect a letter from home before long. It seems they come very slow yet I know you write. Give my love to mother and say to her that I hope soon to see her, for her not to grieve about me for if I am killed. I die fighting for her freedom and rights and that I think our family should be represented. How could I stand back and no one in the field to fight for my family, shall others do it all and we lay on our oars and when our independence is gained receive as much benefits as any one and do nothing towards it. It is a very unpleasant business to me. I had much rather enjoy the sweets of home but my country calls upon me and I am obeying the call. Give my love to Mr Shell and family, Mr. Morton & family, Mr Whaley and family, Mr Boswell & family, Mr Creddelle and wife and all inquiring friends. Give my love to all the children and kiss them for me. Give my love to all the negroes. I must close by wishing you and affectionate

Farewell for the present. Irby G. Scott

P.S. The mess are all well and send their respects.

Camp Bartow Pochahontas [Pocahontas] Co. Va
Oct 21st 1861

Dear Father

As Mr Robins and Lawrence leave for home this evening. I write you a few lines by Mr Robins. Mr Robins is sick with cold and has been ever since he has been here. Him and Lawrence are dissatisfied with things here and rather home sick to so they have concluded to go back home. I am doing very well at present with the exception of a cold and cough. My cough has been pretty bad but it is getting a great deal better now. Our company are generally well with some exceptions. Thomas Spivey and John Dannelly [Danielly] have both been quite sick, but are improving.[25] We have moved our camp again on the Turnpike towards Montery [Monterey] about a mile and a half from where we were. We cleared up a new place in the woods, which we like very well. We have rather been on the lookout for another attack on us here and have had several alarms by the yankees firing on our picket guard. Small parties attempting to slip down and cut off our outside pickets but they could not succed [succeed], the only injury done was the wounding of one man through the ankle. For several days every thing has been very quite and I rather think the dread of another attack has passed off. We are still busy as bees fortifying and making this a strong position. It is currently reported here that we will leave here in a short time. Some say two weeks. We get it from pretty good authority. I do not know where we will go. I heard today that we would go as far as Richmond.[26] We have not heard a word from Leut Marshall since the recruits came, nor a word from our things. My notion about it is that they were ordered to be stoped in Staunton and they do not wish us to know it because if we did we would know that we were going back. I am afraid that a good many of our things will spoil before we get them. I have not heard a word from Nick since he left. He promised me that he would be sure to write as soon as he got to Staunton. I also made him promise to write home every week. I do not know what is the reason he has not written. I am afraid he is sick though he was pretty well when he left. Mr Batchelor the recruit that came on has taken his brothers place who will return home. He has been in bad health for some time. I wrote you that I would send some rings by Mr Terrell, but I forgot to give them to him. So I will send them by Mr Robins. There is nothing more of interest to write. The mess are all well and send their respects to you and family. I have not received a letter from you since the recruits came and I am beginning to become anxious for one. Jim Pike has the mumps. He is doing well. Several of the boys also have them at this time. Give my very best love to Grandma also to all friends. Remember me to the negroes. I have written in great haste as I did not know they were going to start this evening untill it was late. Except [Accept] my best love for yourself, mother and all the children. I remain as every your most affectionate son untill death.

I. G. Scott

P.S. I wrote to uncle Ben Wright the other day.[27]

Camp Bartow Pochahantas [Pocahontas] Co. Va
Oct. 29th 1861

Dear Father

I received your letter of the 15th Oct a few days since and it gave me great pleasure to hear from home that all were in the enjoyment of good health but, was sorry to hear that Grandma was still in very febble health. I hope when this reaches you that her health may have improved. You stated that mother was also not well. I hope she has also entirely recovered by this time. I am well and enjoying good health at this time. The health of our company and also of the regiment have improved a good deal. We can muster at this time about five hundred men fit for duty. The sick have all been sent off to Harrisonburg and Staunton. Spivey and John Danielly left here for Staunton a few days ago. The weather is quite cool here. We had the whitest frost day before yesterday morning I ever saw. It looked like a snow all over the mountains, every bush was perfectly white. It is getting very disagreeable standing picket guard these cold nights without fire. Everything is very quite here now and has been for several days. We had a false alarm several nights ago. The outside pickets fired their guns and retreated back to the main body of the guard reporting that a large body of men had crossed the bridge and was flanking down the river. It was about eleven oclock. Two companies from our regiment were out and the same number from each regiment here to reinforce the guard and give them battle but they could not find a single trace of the enemy. It is suposed the guard became frightened at some noise. The yankees have not molested our guard for some time. The last time they came down they drove back the first guard and set fire to a house which burnt up. The guard all got together and drove them back across the river.[28] All the injury they have ever done us in that way was the burning of the house and wounding one man through the ankle. It is nearly the first of November and we are still here but I think we will leave soon from the indications and from what I can hear. We know nothing definite as yet where we will take up winter quarters. There are plenty of rumors stating the place but I put no confidence in any of them. They are puting up a good many houses at Aleghany [Allegheny]. Col. Baldwin has a regiment there.[29] We are about done fortifying this place and it is very well done. I forgot to say that there was a slight fall of snow here several days ago. We are about to get our pay at last. The quarter master is here and has paid off some of the companies. We are only paid for two months and a half which will amount to about twenty seven dollars. Mine will be about twenty five as I drew a pair of shoes from the government. I shall not send home untill I see what the chances are for my getting a furlough to come home. I have on hand about 40 dollars. Everything is very high here and what you buy you have to pay for it. We have received none of our things yet. We got a letter from Leut. Marshall yesterday stating he had gone back to hunt up some of the things that were left behind. We heard through Capt. Brown that a good many of the things were at Staunton as he was just from there.[30] I expect that a great many of our eatables are spoilt. If we are to leave here soon I do not care now, whether they bring them here at all or not for they would be a great deal of trouble in moving. I have not heard a word from Nick since he left for Staunton although he promised to write to me as soon as he got there. If I had the paper and envelopes I would write and find out about him how he is doing &c. I will be very sorry if Nick should not have a chance with us at the good things from home as he looked anxiously for them to come before he left. If there was any way to send him some of them I would do it but if we do not go to Staunton or he does not come back it will be a bad chance. There is plenty of wagons but I would not trust them. We are making out fine on biscuit, beef and coffee, in fact we have got so we can eat almost anything. We have also learned to cook our provisions up in different ways so as not to tire of the same thing every time we go to eat. We get a chance every once and awhile at some butter and sometimes a cabbage. We get a little bacon every seven days which we take good care of to put in bread and so on. Our commissary stores are getting pretty low. There is only enough for about a week more, but in that time they can bring in enough to last a month. Mother wrote to know whether I had enough bed clothes. I have enough for the present. If we move I have as many as I can carry. I can draw blankets here from the government but, they are not very good and cost five dollars and a half a pair. I shall wait till we get in winter quarters before I get anything of the kind. I will let you know if I need anything of the kind. The mess are not well. Jacob Feiler had a chill night before last but, he is now about. Haskins has a very bad cold.[31] The rest are well. They all send their best respects to you and family. You said in your last letter than you had not received a letter from me since the 21st Sept. I try to write one letter home every week. I rekon you have received several since you wrote. I received the letters you sent by Marshall and only one since which is about three weeks between your letters. If you cannot write make Bud write or Emma and Mollie. It seems out of all of you I might get a letter once a week or once in two weeks at fartherst. I am complaining a little just as you would do were you in my place, a thousand miles from home. I have written about all I can think of for this time. Give my best love to Grandma, mother, and all the family, white and black. I want to see you more than ever. My love also to all inquiring friends, except my warmest love for all of you and believe me when I say that my thoughts are often upon home and the dear ones there. I will close by remaining your affectionate son untill death.

I. G. Scott

P.S.: Tell Emma and Sue Morton they write very slow. Also try and get Bud to write.

I.G.S.

Nov 6th 1861

Camp Bartow Pochahantas [Pocahontas] Co. Va.

Dear ones at Home,

    I received your letter last night about nine oclock and nothing could have given me more pleasure but to have seen you all. It is one of the greatest blessings that we enjoy away from the comforts of home, the society of old and cherished friends, in the mountain wilds of an almost wilderness country surrounded by dangers on every hand and exposed to the relentless vengeance of a hireling foe. It is but natural that the spirits of a man at times should be gloomy and cast down, but to receive a letter from home from those we love it buoys us up and stirs our sleeping patriotism. It makes us firm in our purpose to conquer or perish on a bed of honor, but enough on this point. Already I am afraid you think I am low spirited and longing for home and its sweets but I can assure you that I am cheerful as a man could possibly be under the circumstances. I enjoy good health get plenty to eat, have good warm cloths to wear. It is true we see some pretty hard times but nothing short of this a soldier need not expect to see in this cold mountainous region. You can see from the place I write that we are still at our same old stand, but I feel confident that we will not remain where we are much longer, but as to [where] we are to take up winter quarters I am entirely ignorant. I heard this morning that we are going to leave for Georgia soon, but this report like the thousand and one others I hear I pay no attention to. I have long since learned that we need not listen to reports or rumors to get any information that can be relied on, but must wait untill we receive positive orders from our officers. I hope and trust that we may be ordered to Georgia, but my faith is weak about getting to Georgia this winter. I think we may be sent back as far as Staunton or probably Richmond. Some think we will go to Kentucky, but I do not believe we will go there this is the only thing that troubles me much. I do [not] wish to stay here any longer than we can possibly get away for it is getting disagreeably cold. While I write it is raining and if it gets much colder I think it will sleet. On last Sunday it commenced snowing and continued untill Monday. The mountains around were perfectly white and remained so for two days. It did not snow as much about our camp because we were rather under the mountain. We have to stand picket guard and at the outside posts are not allowed to have fire but all the other posts they can have fire. I was out the other night and it sleeted and rained all night. The wind blew tremendous hard and take it upon the whole it was the most disagreeable night I have ever spent in my life. We have become inured to hardships untill we look for nothing else taking things as easy as possible doing the best we can. Men in army when they get home will know how to appreciate them. Lieut. Marshall got here last week (Friday I think) Abners box came on Saturday, but mine did not get here untill yesterday and I only got one. The other one is behind somewhere there is not many of the things come yet. Lieut. Marshall has gone back to Montery [Monterey] to see about them we are expecting every day. The box of mine that came contained our uniform a bag meal, some cakes, dryed fruit, figs and peaches, our shirts, hams &c all in nice order nothing at all injured. We also received three cans of butter and lard 2 for me and Nick and one for Abner they were not boxed up also some potatoes which were all spoilt. The one that packed Abners box deserves great credit and knew what they were about. There was nothing broke except a small jar of honey. I have tried on my coat and it fits fine my pants I have not tried yet but know they are all right. Nick has not returned yet. Lieut Marshall saw him in Staunton and said that he was improving very fast. They offered him a discharge but he would not accept of it. He ought to have accepted it and went home through the winter and then if he wished he could return to army. His cloths and such things as will keep. I will box up with the rest of boys cloths who are off sick and they will be in care of Capt Davis. Such things as will not keep I shall use up. I do not know whether Capt Davis intends sending them off now or keep them untill we go back. It is a bad chance to send them from here. He will get them I think in a short time. Mark Cochran has a discharge and is going home. We have received pay for our services at last.[32] I drew for my part 48 dollars and 86 cents for two months and a half. We got 21 dollars for our first uniform and 11 dollars a month for our services. I have now on hand 95 dollars. I received from the government a —- dollar confederate bond which I should like to send to you to help pay taxes and so on if had the chance. I would then have plenty left for my use enough to bring me home if I should get a chance to come. If I come it will only cost me half price. I would be afraid to send it by letter from here. I want you to accept my part of mine and Buds cotton and use it any way you think proper. You must except my warmest thanks for all you have sent me. I never will forget it while I keep my sense nor cease to be grateful that I have a father and mother to provide for me. If I should be spared I will try and repay you in part for I never can in full. Tell Major I have plenty of balls to shoot yankees with if they would [give] me the chance, that I am going to send him something for getting me chestnuts and crab apples.[33] Jacob Feiler says tell Mary Jane Moore he will not forget her for sending him those nice socks and gloves.[34] The yankees have got off raid of our pickets. They shoot at them about three quarters of mile. Our pickets killed five of them last week in the night and it was dark as pitch. The yankees were trying to cut them off none of our men were hurt at all. My best love to grandma and all friends. The mess are well and send their respects to you and family. Remember me to the negroes. I write this letter to all of you, except my warmest and best Love now and always.

I. G. Scott

P S I forgot to give the rings for the Little girls to Mr. Terrell, but sent them by Thomas Robins when he left.[35] See him and get them. I was sorry to hear Mr. Shell was going to leave you all another year but was glad he is not going far. I have plenty of cloths and bed cloths for the present. I am looking for the other box every day. There no news of interest here. You sent me a package of papers to read we have papers to read every day nearly both Augusta and Richmond papers but I will look them over. I have written in a hurry as it is very cold and my hands are numb.

Yours affectionately.

I. G. Scott

P S Nov 7th, As I wrote my letter yesterday morning and did not send it off I concluded to add this postscript to let you know my other box came to hand yesterday evening all safe except one bottle of lemon syrup for Nick 1 bottle of something else and my jar of higdom salid [salad].[36] These were all broken and the contents lost. Nicks jug of honey was also cracked but no honey lost. I also got my bed tick, Pillow some medicine my leggins and some other things which I have not time to mention. My things are all straight I reckon I will let you know in my next letter which [will] be in a few days. My self and the mess are all well.

Yours as ever

    I. G. Scott

Camp Bartow Pochahontas [Pocahontas] Co. Va
November 12th, 1861

Dear Father

    Having to go on picket or grand guard tomorrow it would be two days before I could have an opportunity of writing. I am well with the exception of a cold. A man here need not look for anything else exposed to all kinds of weather. It makes no difference what comes when it comes round your time for duty there is no getting around or putting off untill another time, but these things must be so and of strickness in these respect. I do not complain. There is no news of interest here everything is dull enough about camps. The yankees continue to trouble our pickets, though they take care not to come to near since we killed and took prisoner five of them one dark night not long since. They will come in about a half a mile of our first picket stand fire and then run. Of all the tramps and scouts that I have had since we came into this mountainous country none ever exceeded one on yesterday morning. Each regiment and battalion take their turn to reinforce the pickets when they are attacked ~~and~~ when it is necessary. Yesterday was our time and just after light there the picket guns echoed through and around the mountains, in a few minutes the order came for our regt to march to their relief. About sun up we left the most of us without breakfast and went it double quick about a mile to Col. Johnsons quarters where we received our orders and again took up our march to the last picket post. Just after we left camp it commenced raining and continued so untill we got back to camps again. We marched to the last post at the river and found three yankees only had made their appearance.[37] We remained a short time and was returning to camp when the firing of guns was heard and we came to a halt. Righted about and marched back again to the last post at the river. The yankees had fired but kept themselves under cover where they could not be seen. So we remained a while to see if they would show themselves, but not a hair of them could be seen and we returned to camp as tired and hungry a set of men as you ever saw.

N. B. we marched yesterday about 12 or 15 miles and got back by 1 Oclock in the evening.

We were wet and muddy as pigs when we came back we were halted at Col. Johnsons quarters and all treated to a good dram of whiskey. The Colonel is very much taken with our new suits and wants a pair of pants like them if

he can get a pair that will suit Capt Deshler Col Johnsons aid and I hope will be our future Col. at some if Johnson be promoted (which is very probable) took old man Hollis's suit.[38] We are faring sumptuously on the good things you sent us. I received every thing you mentioned in your list. There was as many boxes sent to our company as there was to the rest of the regt. The society sent us enough cloths for twice.[39] We have boxed up what we did need and it will be sent back either to Montery [Monterey] or Staunton. A report reached here yesterday that we would leave here in a few days and go to Raleigh N. Carolina. There seems to be some confidence placed in it coming through very good authority.[40] I guess we will know in a few days whether it be so or not. I see from the papers that the federals have taken posession [possession] of some forts on the coast of South Carolina. Also of a fight in Missouri in which we were victorious. Hannah wished me to name her boy before I knew what you all called him.[41] I and some of the mess had come to conclusion to name him Bartow. So the name suits all around. So let it be Bartow. Tell Hannah to take good care of him and be sure and raise him. I received your and mothers letter dated Oct 30th yesterday evening and was glad to hear that you were all well, but was sorry to hear that grandma was still in very [bad] health. I hope ere this reaches you that her health will be some what improved. In case we should be ordered away from here in a few days, I think we will be troubled about getting our things carried as the means of transportation will be limited. But we have always succeeded in some way so far and if there is any chance will succeed again. I hardly know what to write as there [is] nothing of much interest going on. You stated that you had heard nothing of Nick since he left us. I got a letter from him when Leut. Marshall came on. He said he had written home twice. His health was improving but all this I wrote in my letter before this. Mother wished me to send Sue Morton a ring I had thought of this and have one which I will put in this letter for her. It is made of cow hoof. Major wanted one if I can get one before I seal my letter. I will send it to him. I have written all of any interest to you all and will close my wearisome epistle. Give my love and affection to grandma and ask her to accept my thanks for the nice Bottle of wine she sent me. Remember me to all friends, also to the negroes. Accept my best love and affection for yourself and all the rest of the family. I remain yours truly.
Irby G. Scott
P.S. Chap Hudson has been and is now quite sick with fever.[42] The rest of the company are all able to be up and about.

Chapter 5

Camp Allegheny

" . . . no idea that we could ever stand the winter."

On October 18, 1861, Confederate troops at Camp Bartow and on the top of Allegheny Mountain received orders, to begin constructing huts, storehouses, and a hospital to serve as winter quarters. Captain William H. Tebbs of the Third Arkansas oversaw the construction of sufficient facilities to accommodate two thousand troops. His working parties came from the commands located at Camp Bartow and the top of Allegheny Mountain. Lieutenant Colonel Seth Maxwell Barton of the Third Arkansas was responsible for general supervision of the work. Colonel Barton had authority to "demand and obtain the requisite tools and implements." The brigade quartermaster provided transportation to move the command and to execute the work.

Though they began in ample time, the construction crews did not complete sufficient cabins to house all the men who would be stationed atop the mountain. The Twelfth Georgia reached the top of the mountain last, on the evening of November 22. When they arrived, they found all of the available cabins taken. Because most of their tents had been destroyed at Camp Bartow, many of the men slept on the frozen ground. On the morning of November 23 they awoke to several inches of snow. Colonel Johnson wasted no time in putting everyone to work on shelters. Those already in cabins toiled on the defenses of Camp Allegheny.

General Loring continued to block the turnpike through the winter. Irby Scott's letters of November 26 and December 9 are filled with the frustrations and confusion facing the men as generals and government authorities considered the various options for a winter campaign in northwest Virginia. Added to the confusion at higher levels was the "indignation among officers" of the Twelfth Georgia, hoping to get the regiment away from the winter weather in the mountains of northwestern Virginia.

Included in the surviving Scott letters is one dated December 15 in which he told the family of the December 13 Federal attack on Camp Allegheny. Federal troops commanded by Brigadier General Robert H. Milroy advanced from Cheat Summit Fort on December 12. Ambushed at former Camp Bartow, the Federal column of almost 1,900 men rested at Camp Bartow, where General Milroy divided his command, one part to attack the Confederate left flank, by way of the Green Bank Road, and the other by the right flank, by the Staunton–Parkersburg Turnpike. A simultaneous attack by both wings was expected at 4:30 on the morning of December 13. Poor coordination between Milroy's divided command allowed the 1,200 Confederate defenders, commanded by Colonel Edward Johnson, to repulse the separate Federal attacks. Confederate casualties amounted to 146 men, while Federal casualties numbered 137. At the end of the fight, the Federals returned to Cheat Summit Fort.

Scott, in his letter of March 27, tells his father they had received orders to "pack up all of our extra baggage and ship it to Staunton." He did not know that General Lee and General Edward Johnson had been in regular contact with each other since March 15. On March 21, Lee instructed Johnson to "send a competent officer to examine the Shenandoah Mountain . . . in case you deem it advisable, or be forced to take a position secure from being turned." Shortly, events in the valley required Scott and the men to deploy to Shenandoah Mountain.

Scott ends his March 27 letter with a postscript to his younger brother Bud, with a "little advise" as a veteran. He knew of his brother's desire to join the army, and as an experienced soldier tells his brother he is too young and could be of great help to their father. Irby Scott had the best interests and welfare of his brother in mind when he crafted his postscript.

November 26th 1861
Camp Aleghany [Alleghany] Pochahantas [Pocahontas] Co. Va[1]
Dear Father,

Doubtless you are getting uneasy at my long silence. I should have written before this but have had not the first opportunity for several days and had I the opportunity I could not have sent my letter off. We have had no mail now for a week untill today, nor should I be at all surprised if we get it once a month after awhile. We have taken up winter quarters at last on the Aleghany [Alleghany] near where we were camped before. We had no expectation of ever stoping here. We received orders from Richmond to go to Staunton and expected to leave on the 22nd of this month but did not have wagons enough and had to stay untill the next evening. The day we left orders came from Gen. Loring to stop here.[2] We were sadly disappointed after making all of our arrangements to go to Staunton. We made a great sacrifice in burning many valuable things thinking that we could replace them when we arrived at Staunton and another reason was we could not get wagons to carry all. So we disposed of butter, lard and many other things which [we] would not have given up so willingly had we known that this place was our destination being unwilling for the yankees to have what we left. We burned them up. We left Greenbrier late in the evening and after a muddy march we reached here about sun down only three or four of our tents got here and in them we all had to be packed for the night. In the night it commenced snowing and it has been snowing nearly ever since untill today. The day after we got here we had an alarm. The yankees came in about two miles of our camp and took one of the 1st Ga regiment prisoners. He was sick and left at a house on the road. We did not have a picket guard out that day but since that time we have had them out regular every day and night. On the second day they crowded us into two houses thirty to each one. Today they gave us another house and we now have twenty to each house. I think we will build more as soon as possible. Our houses are not very good being built of logs with part stick and dirt chimneys. We have commenced to throw up some fortifications and are doing other things which should have been done before this time. There are only three regiments here. The 1st Ga and one of the Virginia regts have been ordered to Manassas. There is great indignation among officers and men about our having to stay here and Virginians going off. Our Captains are going to make a trial to get us away from here, but I am affaid it is to late now. They have a petition which they will send on to the war department. If this fails they say they intend to make an application to congress for our relief. The two Virginia regiments at this place, one of them is from Staunton and the other from above here, both of them you may say were raised right here in the mountains and it does not seem hard to keep us here when there were plenty other Virginians here that could have staid and who have not suffered near as much as we have. But considering every thing the boys keep in fine spirits. It seems nothing can daunt them for they will be lively it makes no difference what turns up. The company is generally well. Rich Reid is sick with the jaundes [jaundice] Joe Porter is also sick.[3] Chap Hudson is improving Green Spivey arrived here yesterday evening.[4] He came on to Staunton to see his brother and to try and carry him home. He will leave in the morning and will be the bearer of this letter to you. I have almost dispared of seeing you all this winter if we should have to stay here but if there is any chance I will try and come. I am well with the exception of a cold. The mess are all well and send their respects to you and family. I have not heard from Nick Whaley since Leut

Marshall came on. I have written to him but have not received an answer. I shall have to make my letter short as my candle is nearly out. Give my very best love to Grandma and say to her I would like very much to see her but I am affraid that I shall not be able to do so this winter. I want to see her and all of you worse than I ever did and nothing on earth could give me more pleasure than to pay you all a visit. I have made up my mind to take things easy and to get along as well as I can for being discontented does one a great deal of harm. I wrote you about sending some of my money home. You wrote me not to send it but I know money is scarce and you will be hard run to get enough to pay your debts this winter so I have concluded as I have ninety five dollars to send you by Mr. Spivey fifty dollars in confederate money, which I wish you to accept and use. Also whatever my cotton brings you will please accept. You can get the money from Spivey as I not enclose it in my letter. Tell Bud to take and wear any of my cloths that he wants and not to let them lay and get old. I will have plenty of money in case I should come home and to spare. Give my love to all friends and also to the negroes. I will write soon if I can send it off. I do not know how it will be about the mails. My love especially to mother and all the children except for the whole family my best love and affection for you all untill death.

Irby Goodwin Scott

Camp Aleghany [Alleghany] Pochahantas Co. Va
December 9th, 1861

Dear Father,

Doubtless you are getting anxious to get a letter, and to hear the news from this part of Virginia, but as to news there is any quantity. Such as it is, mostly rumor. One day we are going to Georgia the next we will have to winter here. Capt. Blanford has returned from Richmond with good news.[5] He says the war department had issued an order for our removal before he got to Richmond. They are carrying back the provisions from here and I learn also from Monterey. Some think this portion of the State will be evacuated entirely and we will all fall back and protect the railroad. But this is merely conjecture. It is said that the 12th Ga will go as far as Staunton. We have no idea where we will be sent from there. We have done a great deal of work at this place and it is very well fortified. I received your letter in reference to Wat Mortons removal home. Capt Davis also received the one Mr. Morton wrote to him. I read Mr. Mortons letter and would have been glad to have complied with his request. Capt Davis wrote back to Mr. Morton without ever trying in any way to see what could be done he promised me that he would see Col Johnson about it but he has never done it and as soon as I knew he had written to Mr. Morton that he did not intend to do it. It was

to much trouble for him and he was affraid Col Johnson might bluff him. He attended to this about like he attends to many other things. There is no chance to do anything through him. I think Mr. Morton will have to try some other plan than through Capt Davis. I know it would be a great deal of trouble especially at this season of the year but if Capt D. [Davis] would have procured me a furlough I would have attended to the whole of it willingly, which I know I could have done as well as any one. I should like very much to see you all, but I have to depend on the Capt. of our company to procure me a furlough I am affraid I shall not have that pleasure this winter, but this is enough about such things unless there were better. Col Conner with thirty men came into camp yesterday from Harrisonburg among them were six of our company. They are looking well. We are all getting along very well at this time. The weather has been very cold, but at this time is quite pleasant. By tomorrow it may be snowing. I think from appearances that we will leave here in a few days. The company are generally well. I am getting along finely and with the exception of a cold I am enjoying good health. My mess are all well and send their respects to you and family. I have heard nothing from Nick Whaley lately. If we leave for Staunton in a few days I shall not write again untill we get there. Give my love especially to Grandma and tell her I think of her very often. My love also to all my friends. Remember me to the negroes. You must write me soon as I am anxious to hear from home. Tell Bud I will write to him some of these days when I have a good chance. We are crowded so much it is almost impossible to write. Give my love to whole family and accept a share for yourself.
Yours as ever
    Irby G. Scott

Camp Aleghany [Alleghany] Pochahontas [Pocahontas] Co. Va
December 15th, 1861

Dear Father

When I wrote you last I expected to write from Staunton, but I am still here and cant tell when we will get away. We have had orders to go to Staunton for more than a week and have been making preparations for leaving. You will learn the news about the battle that was fought here on Friday last. I would have written you sooner but have not had an opportunity untill now. On Friday morning about two oclock we were all aroused from our slumber by the alarm drum, and the call of our officers to fall into line, that the yankees were approaching. We all got ready as soon as possible and three companies of our regiment (ours among the number) were marched down the Green Brier road to ambush.[6] The rest with the exception of Jackson's regt. (which was posted to the back of our camp upon the hill) were sent to the ditches. About sun up they had flanked around and came down on Jackson's regt. when the fight commenced.[7] As soon as we heard this we rushed up the hill to their assistance. Two more companies were sent from the ditches, with these we fought them two hours. We drove them back three times before we could satisfy them that they could not overrun us. Their object in this movement was to rush right into the camp and take it by storm. A few of them reached the tents at one time but were quickly driven back and did not return. The fighting was severe on both sides. Both parties using muskets, the balls seemed as if raining while this was going on another party attacked our men in the ditches did but little harm. The enemy did not have any artillery, and we could not use ours to any advantage, but had to depend entirely upon our muskets, the fight lasted in all about six hours. We only took two prisoners and they took one or two or ours. We suffered pretty severely. I have not learned the exact number in killed and wounded but will try to do so before closing. My own company suffered severely. William Davis was killed dead upon the field.[8] Algernon Little received a severe flesh wound in the thigh, Woodson Haskins a flesh wound in the hip, Alex. Middleton a flesh wound in the groin, W. T. Arnold a flesh wound in the thigh, Tuck Thomas a slight wound on the back of the head, Ed. Davis in the arm flesh wound, A. M. Marshall was also slightly wounded in the arm, Muckelory [McLeroy] shot through the leg.[9] In all one killed and eight wounded. None of the wounds are considered very dangerous. Littles & Haskins are the worst of any. The boys are doing very well and receive a good deal of attention. I suppose they will be sent off as soon as they can travel. I was in all of the fight and did not receive a scratch. It looked like it would be almost impossible for a man to escape, but thank God I am still living. I expect we will have to remain here several weeks before we can leave on account of the wounded. The yankees had in all about three thousand men. They were about equally divided and attacked us on two sides at the same time. Their loss was severe but I do not know how many they carried off a great many of their dead and nearly all of the wounded. I cannot ascertain our loss. I supose [suppose] not over thirty killed and sixty wounded. It looks as if they intended to take our camp anyhow, but they were sadly mistaken in this. I must close and will write you again soon. Give my best love and affection to Grandma, mother, Bud, and all the children. Also to the negroes and all my friends. I sent you some money by Spivey let me know when you get it. I see they have passed a dog law in Georgia taxing all the dogs a man has except one. I think you had better go to killing mine. If I was there I would kill them before I would pay tax on them. Write soon the weather is now warmer than it has been and the snow has all melted off. I received a letter from Nick Featherston a day or two since he had been sick, but had got well again. Except my best love and esteem for yourself and the whole family. I remain yours truly untill death.

Irby G. Scott

Camp Aleghany [Alleghany] Pochahontas [Pocahontas] Co. Va
December 25th, 1861

Dear Father,

It is with sorrow that I attempt to communicate to you the death of Nicholas Whaley who died this morning about one Oclock after a few days sever illness. This attack was severe and sudden. The disease was Pneumonia. He was well only two days after he got into camp. I deeply symphasise with the relatives of the deceased more especially as I feel that if it had not been for me he would never have come, but he died in the defence of his country and if he had been permitted good health he would have made and excellent soldier. We attended to him the best we could under the circumstances, but he grew worse and worse suffering a great deal until death came to his re-lief. He will be buried this evening. Leut Reid received a letter from Ed Davis who is in Staunton announcing the death of James Reid.[10] The wounded boys are doing well with the exception of Algenon Little whose recovery is almost dispaired of. He is very low and I should not be surprised at his death at any thime. A good many of our company are complaining, but none seriously.

To day is Christmas and it is one of the dullest times I have ever seen. Everything goes on just the same I can hardly realize that Christmas is here. Evey thing looks rather despondingly. Times are pretty hard but we look for and expect nothing else. I wrote you a letter about two days ago we are still fortifying this place, which is now in a very good state of defence. There is no news of importance nothing more than mere camp rumors. Capt Davis wrote Mr Whaley a letter this morning apprizing him of Nicks death as the Capt. had written to Mr Whaley I concluded that I would write to you think-ing you would get the letter sooner than Mr Whaley.[11] You must read this for Mr Whaley as I wrote it for his satisfaction. Going out on picket Guard these cold nights is very disagreeable indeed these cold nights. I understand that there will be houses built for them. You wished me to send you a lock of my hair, which I will enclose in my letter. I also will send some of Nicks to Mr & Mrs Whaley. Every one has given up the idea of getting out of the moun-tains this winter. I heard that the people of Putnam had sent a petition on to the war department for our relief, which think will do no good whatever. I send some little things by Mrs Jenkins to Mr Morton which I never have known that he received. I must close and write again soon. Give my love to Grandma and tell her that I often think of her, but have almost dispaired of seeing her this winter. My love to the whole family. I want to see you all very

much but if I cannot have that pleasure I will try and bear my disappoint-
ment the best I can. Remember me to all friends also to the negroes. I will
close by wishing you all a happy Christmas. Your most affectionate son.
Irby G. Scott
P.S. The cloths we sent to Monterey have just been brought back.
   IGS

Camp Aleghany [Alleghany] Jan. 9th, 1862
Dear Father,
   It is with much pleasure that I attempt to write you a few lines this morning. I have made several attempts to write but owing to one thing or another
I have postponed it untill the present. I received your letter of the 22nd of
December, and it gave me the greatest pleasure to hear from home, and that
you had received my letter of the 15th Dec. We learn from a letter received
here a few days since that Capt Davis in his letter only mentioned the town
boys who were in the fight and did not mention one of the country boys. I
do not know the reason he did this, but I know that the country boys fought
just as brave as the others. It has caused some feeling in the company. As for
myself I do not care anything about it. I think he should not have mentioned
any if he did not mention all. In my last letter I wrote you about Nicks death
also of Algernon Littles. I wrote my letter in the morning and did know of
the arrangement to send them home untill evening. Milton Little started the
next morning with them to Staunton and I thought it would be useless for
me to write as they would get there as soon as the letter.[12] Mr William Little
met them in Staunton and was to convey them home.[13] I wish you to pay
over to Mr Whaley five dollars for me Nick had only five which I concluded
not to trouble about sending home and let you pay Mr Whaley. He had never
drawn any for his services. I let Jacob Filer have his new shoes as he needed
them. Let me know what they cost and he will pay for them. I also let him
have his comfort and some of his little things. The rest of his cloths are nearly
all worn out. I did not expect that his remains would be sent home, but was
glad for it to be done as I knew his parents would be better satisfied. He had
very little to say while he was sick. Part of the time he could only whisper.
I deeply sympathize with his parents in their loss. From the way you write
you think that we have not yet taken up winter quarters. We are in winter
quarters now, but do not know how long we will remain here. Our supply
of provisions is small not more than enough to last a week or two and I understand they have stopped the wagons from hauling. They will either have
to bring provisions or we will have to leave. I cant tell what we will do or
where we will go. There is no chance for furloughs now. Gen. Jackson would
not allow Milton Little to go any farther than Staunton with his brothers re-

mains. You can see from this that the chance is a bad one. You stated in your letter that mother had made all her arrangements to come and nurse me in case I had been wounded. I had rather had her than any one else, but would rather have suffered for want of attention than for her to have come here and been exposed in this cold mountains climate. The wounded are well attended to and receive plenty of attention. Alexander Middleton is doing well and will soon be up. Woodson Haskins is pretty low.[14] His wound was a severe one, and I am affaid if he ever gets well that he will be a cripple for life. It seems from the way you write that you think I had to loose the most of my things when we left Greenbrier. I did not loose any of my clothing. I lost or rather had to sell some of my butter &c. I have plenty of cloths for the present. I find it best for a soldier not to have much clothing for he will be certain to loose some every time he moves and besides they are a great deal of trouble to him. You wanted to know what I had to eat. I get plenty of Flour, Beef sometimes Bacon, Rice or peas, sugar, coffee &c. I cannot grumble at my fare, we buy Butter, occasionally a shoat and many other things to tedious to mention. My mess are as follows. Abner Zachry Filer, Tom Pearson, Milton Little, Robert Little, Henry Marshall, Henry Etheridge, Haskins and three others who are at Staunton.[15] I have a very good mess and we get along finely. We have two cloth tents put up so as to form but one where the negroes stay and do all the cooking. We also have a table in the tent and a first rate chimney. So you see we are doing very well. I do not want you to send me anything to eat or any cloths untill I know whether we are settled here or not. I reckon I will know in a few weeks. I was proud of the locks of hair sent to me. I wanted to see the little fellows bad enough before, but I want to see them worse now. I shall try to keep it as long as I can. Tell major I have not forgotten his ring. The reason I have not sent it I wanted to get a nice one for him. I will send it before long. I had heard of the marriages you wrote about before I received your letter. If you have a good chance you may send me a good hat if there is not a good opportunity you need not trouble yourself as my old one will do for a while yet. I learn that several of our Putnam friends will be here soon. The weather has been very cold and the ground covered four or five inches in snow. I must tell you of a scout we had about a week ago. A party of yankees came down to Greenbrier one evening and set fire to several little houses and had tremendous smoke which we could plainly see from our camp. We rather expected an attack the next morning, but were disappointed. So the next day after dinner our Regt and the 52nd Va Regt were ordered to go down there and give them fight. The distance there and back was about eighteen miles. We did not find any yankees and started back a little before sun down when it commenced raining and sleeting. The roads before this was hard frozen the ice on the ground was an inch thick and slick as glass. Night came on as dark as pitch and such walking I have never seen. It was one continual slip down all along the road. One place we had to get on our hands and knees to crawl up. Sometimes four or five would fall and be piled up together. Our cloths on the outside was a solid sheet of ice. We finally reached camp about eight Oclock and all gave it up to be the worst scout they had ever had. I must close this wearisome epistle. Give my very best love to Grandma and say to her I was very sorry to hear her health was so feeble, but hope by the time this reaches you she may have improved. Remember me to all friends also to the negroes. My love to mother, Bud and all the children and expect a large share for yourself. I remain as ever your most affectionate and devoted son untill death.

Irby G. Scott

P.S. I get letters very seldom, but lay it to the carelessness of the postmaster for I know you write.

IGS

Camp Alleghany, Jan. 19th, 1862

Dear Father.

Doubtless you are getting anxious to hear from me as it has been several days since I wrote you last. There is no news of any importance with us. Everything is perfectly quiet. I received a letter from you a day or two since which gave me great pleasure to hear from those who are near and dear. You wished me to write fully all the particulars of Nick Whaleys death. In my letters I wrote you all about it. He had very little to say while sick and bore his suffering very patiently. He did not say whether he was willing to die or not. He made no request only that he told me he would be certain to die and that he wanted me to see him buried. I asked him where he wanted to be buried. The answer was any-where here upon the mountain. I was asleep when he died. Jacob Filer was sitting up with him and did not wake me until after he was dead. He died much sooner than any of us expected. I believe this is all but what I have written before. I have his pocket knife and one or two other little things which I will send by the first one passing. You are very anxious for me to get a furlough and come home but I assure you that nothing would give me more pleasure than see you all. It seems that we are not to have any furloughs. I have not tried to get one for I knew it was of no use. If there should be a chance I will be certain to try and get one. You sent me a slip of newspaper containing an act passed by congress relating to furloughs. That will do us no good unless the officers in command are willing to give them to us. Gen Johnson is opposed to giving furloughs.[16] One of the Leut. in our regiment procured a furlough from the war department and Gen Johnson would not allow him to leave so he left anyhow and Johnson sent after him to bring him back. You can see from this that it is no easy matter to get furloughs. I understand that a good many of the Brown Rifles have been home. The weather has been extremely cold but at this time it is quite warm and raining. We are all getting on very well. The company, those who are here, are generally well. The company received a few days since a casque [cask] of hams which had been laying over in Stanton for two months. My mess got eight or nine. We are living pretty well. We buy butter but have to pay fifty cents a pound. Everything else is high in proportion. I sold my pistol the other day for forty dollars. The reason I sold it was that I never have found any use for it. It was a great deal of trouble to keep in order and I was affraid [afraid] it might be stolen as there has been two stolen from our company in a short time. I was sorry to have to part with it but I thought it best to let it go. Selling my pistol and drawing twenty dollars from the government, I have now about one hundred and eight dollars on hand.[17] Give my love especially to Grandma and say to her that I hope to see her once more. Your petition and hers to Capt Davis will do no good. Remember me to all my friends and to the negros. My love to mother, Bud and all the children. If I get a chance I will send you some more money. Yours affectionately.

Irby G. Scott

Camp Alleghany Pochahontas [Pocahontas] Co. Va
Jany. 25th 1862
Dear Father,

We were very surprised much at the appearance of Mr. Suther in our camp on last Thursday evening but it was a very agreeable surprise for we are always glad to see any one from home.[18] I have nothing new to write but cannot afford to let this opportunity slip without writing you a few lines. I received a letter from you by him and was very glad to hear that you were all well and enjoying good health but was sorry indeed to hear that Grandma was so feeble. I hope ere this comes to hand she may have improved in health. I should like above all things to come and see you but do not know when I shall have that pleasure. They say they intend to give furloughs but men of families will get them first. The weather is very cold. Yesterday we had a severe snow storm and today the ground is covered some four or five inches. It is the largest we have had this winter. The cold does not hurt so much now. We have become inured to it. There is another rumor in our camp that we will leave here soon. This like all others I cannot believe until we make the start. I think I shall send you some money by Suther. I have one hundred dollars and fifty is as much as I need. If I can get some money changed I shall sent it. I will write more about it before I close my letter. I intend to send my buoy [bowie] knife home by Mr. Suther. I have not received the things you sent me yet but they are on the way and I shall get them soon. We were expecting them yesterday. The snow may stop a few days. I did not particularly need them. I need a hat which cannot get here which I wish you to send me the first chance. I was glad to hear of the boots you are having made for me. My shoes are wearing out very fast having to walk so much on the frozen ground. My over coat looks fine. The last suit of clothes you sent us are not much account. Are beginning to wear out. If you have the chance send me a good pair of pants. This is all I need and do not need anything else. I get plenty to eat and am getting on very well every way. The health of the company is very good, better than it has been. I believe I have written about all I can think of now. I see from your letter that you think we have fallen back to Monterey but we are still at Camp Alleghany. We should have fallen back had there been a large force at Huntersville but they only burnt up the town and returned back to Cheat.[19] Remember me to all friends and the negros. My love to mother, Bud and all the children. Except a share for yourself. Yours most affectionately

Irby G. Scott

P.S. I send you fifty dollars by Mr. Suther.

P.S. I received all the things you sent me and was very proud of them. Your as ever

IGS

Camp Alleghany
February 2nd, 1862
Dear Father,

As today is Sunday and I have nothing else to do I will write you a few lines. I am well and enjoying very good health at this time. The cold weather does not hurt me at all although it snows every three or four days and sleets and rains. I do not see that it affects me any more than it does in Georgia. I have learned this much that man can become accustomed to many things which at first would seem almost impossible for him to endure. The health of the company is very good much better than it has been for some time. The boys are in good spirits and seem to enjoy them selves as well as they can under the circumstances. I learned yesterday that Alex. Middleton was dead as soon as his wound would permit he was sent to Staunton and there died. I did not learn the disease. It could not have been caused from his wound for that was nearly well and at first was not a dangerous one. I have nothing new to write you but thinking you would like to hear from me I concluded to write. I expect that Capt Davis and some of the boys will be home soon on furlough. Their furlough which were sent to Loring & Jackson for approval have been returned and they now await the return of Gen. Johnson from Monterey before they know whether they will get to come home or

not. You will be some what surprised when you learn that we had a severe fight here a few days ago. There was about one thousand engaged on each side. You will be equally surprised when I tell you that nobody was hurt. It was a snow ball fight and the whole brigade was engaged in it. I received a letter from you dated the 20th of last month. I received all that you sent me by Mr Suther. I was very proud of my vest, which Mrs Boswell presented me with. I think it is very nice and I know from experience that it is warm. Tell Mrs Boswell that she will please accept my thanks for it. It is very much admired by all who see it. I want to know if it is home made goods. I wrote to you not to send me anything untill I wrote for it. At that time the camp was full of rumors that we would not remain here long and I did not wish to have to loose again as I did when we left Greenbrier, but I think we will not leave here this winter and you can send me anything in the eating line you wish to. Do not take this as a hint that I am in need of anything to eat for I get plenty. My mess eat up six dozen eggs this morning for breakfast. Do not send me more cloths untill I write for them except what I wrote you for. A hat, pair of pants and those boots you had made for me. I do not know yet whether I shall apply for a furlough or not. I am affraid that I would be refused as my excuse for absents from camp would not be sufficient. I entirely forgot to send Nicks things home by Mr Suther, but will do it the first chance. Give my very best love to Grandma, mother and all the children. Remember me to all friends and also to all the negroes. Accept my warmest love for yourself and the whole family. Your devoted son untill death.
Irby G. Scott
P.S. The mess sends their best respects to you and family.

Camp Alleghany, February 16th, 1862
Dear Father,

I take this opportunity to acknowledge the receipt of yours, mothers & Emmas letters by Bob Jenkins & the boys from Putnam. It was a source of great pleasure to me to receive letters from those I love. Nothing could possibly give me more pleasure than to see you. The boys arrived in camp on Friday last. We were all glad to see them and hear from home. I was very proud of the things you sent me, and you will accept thanks for them. My boots are fine to wade through the snow with and fit firstrate. My hat was rather large and the crown to high, but it will do very well. Everything in the trunk came safe except a bottle of honey which was broken and all spilt. It did not get on any of the cloths nor injury anything. We are living well at this time and was also living fine before we received those things from home. We live much better now than we have since we have been in the service. The health of the company is also better than it ever has been. Abner has been sick for a day or two, but has got about well again. There is nothing

new in this part of the country. Everything very quiet and all getting along well. The weather continues cold and it snows every day or two, but we do not mind it at all. The boys are snow balling or playing in it all the time. I made a trip to Green bank [Green Bank] last Tuesday as a guard with some wagons which were sent for lumber. It is about ten miles, we went down there and back the same day. Green bank [Green Bank] is a little village with two churches a store &c.[20] It snowed on us all day and me and Abner broke down coming back. It was a severe walk. My own health is very good as good as it ever was in my life. From the papers we learn that we gained a victory in Kentucky but lost one at Roanoke N. C. we also learned of the death of Gen Lee.[21] I received a letter from cousin Lizzie Reid by Mr Suther which I have answered.[22] She said Sally Collie did not like my not sending her a ring.[23] I send her a nice laurel ring with a book cut on it. I also send major one with a heart on it. I will put them in my letter and hope they may come safe to hand. I think I shall apply for a furlough in a few days whether I get one or not. Chap Hudson has come back to camp and looks quite well. I sent you fifty dollars by Sandy Suther when you get it you will please let me know. Tell Mr Whaley that I have plenty of money and did not keep the five dollars because I needed it, but that was the least trouble for me to keep it and let you pay him. As he has made me a present of it I will accept it and in return he will accept my thanks. My best love to Grandma, mother, Bud and all the family. Remember me to all friends and also to the negroes. Nothing more but my best wishes for your welfare through life.
Affectionately yours.
I. G. Scott
P.S. Tell Bud to stay at home and to never come here to join the army.

Camp Alleghany March 10, 1862
Dear Father,

As Leut. Reid & Jesse Bachelor are going to leave tomorrow for Putnam I will avail myself of this opportunity to write you a few lines.[24] I am well and getting on finely. Milton Little arrived in camp camp yesterday. Capt Davis and the others are expected here tomorrow or next day. There is nothing very new up here. It is reported that the yankess are advancing upon Winchester with a large force. Our regt and one of the Virginia regt. are ordered tomorrow to blockade the roads towards Green Brier & Green Bank.[25] I do not know what this means. There are many conjectures all through the camp as to what it is done for. Some think that we will fall back but this is all rumor and there is no dependence to be placed in it. I do not think there is any danger of an attack here. We are well fortified and it will take a many a very large force to drive us from our entrenchments. The health of the

company is very good. All well except Mr. Marshall who is recovering. I applied for a furlough but have heard nothing from it yet. I do not expect to get one now for I do not think there will any more be given. Jim Pike is coming home with Leut. Reid. I send some little things to Mr. Whaley & Morton by him. I must close and write more another time. I am looking for a letter by Capt Davis. Give my love to Grandma & all friends. Remember me to the negroes. I should have written more but did not know they would [leave] so soon. My best love to mother, Bud and all the children and accept a large share for yourself. Yours until death
Irby G. Scott

Camp Alleghany, Va
March 16th, 1862
Dear Father,

It has been a week to day Since I wrote last which letter I sent by Liut. Reid. Capt. Davis & Leut. Ethridge arrived in camp on last Tuesday evening. I expected to get a letter by them but was disappointed. They brought some five letters with them and left the rest in Richmond in a box, which has not yet come to hand. I waited Several days to get your letter before I wrote but there is no telling when it will get here now. I thought that Capt. D. would certainly have brought the letters through with him. I am well and in good health. The health of the company is generally good with the exception of a few cases of diarrhea. There is no news of any importance with us. Every thing is very quiet. Of course there is always rumors in camp, but they so seldom prove true, that they are not much noticed. There is a rumor now on hand that the Yankees are advancing on Winchester in two columns of twenty thousand each, and that our forces are falling back from Manasas [Manassas] & from Winchester which if true we will be compelled to fall back also.[26] We have learned here of Prices Great victory in Arkansas.[27] We have been blockading some roads to prevent them from bringing canon [cannon] to our rear, and we will blockade the Green bank road also. We have been strengthening our fortifications also, and should the Yankees attack us they will meet with a warm reception. Gen. Johnson says his little squad (as he calls his brigade) can whip fifteen thousand. Capt D. told me that you were all well, which I was glad to hear. He said you and mother spent a day with him while he was at home. He says he thinks mother has more fire and zeal for our cause than anyone he saw at home. He says you set [sat] and let mother & Cousin Sarah Reid do all the talking.[28] I should have liked to have been there concealed to hear their many questions. I want to come home very much but do not expect to come in some time yet, for I do no think any more furloughs will be granted to any of the soldiers in this division of the army. Spring is also fast approaching, and with it also the advance of the enemy will be expected. The most of our company have improved considerably (I mean physically). I can say I have improved —— little myself. I weigh over one hundred and sixty pounds. When I left home I did not weigh more than one hundred and 40 pounds at the outside. I can now stand my hand with any of the boys at almost anything. We all have plenty to eat and to wear, and are generally in fine spirits. I received a nice pair of pants, gloves & also a ball of thread by Milton Little which I was very glad to get. Tell mother that the next money I get I shall send to her. I do not know when we will draw, but according to the way we have been drawing it is time now that we had our money. We will draw about fifty dollars. I have now almost forty on hand, and should I draw soon I expect to sent it all home. I am willing to remain in the mountains now. I have a good mess and plenty of friends. The company is somewhat split up into two parties and I feared for a while that there would be a terrible collision yet things have subsided and I hope well remain so. There has always been some feeling between the town & country boys with some few exceptions, but enough of this.[29] I should have said nothing about it, but know you will never say anything to anyone about it. From what I hear from Isham some one has been trying to injure me at home, but let them go ahead.[30] All will come right some of these days. My mess all wish to be remembered to you and family. Let no one you cannot trust see this letter. I have nothing else to write. The weather still continues bad though not quite so cold as it has been. Give my love to all friends and relations. My very best love to Grandma, mother, Bud and all the children and accept a large share for yourself, your son truly until death,

Irby G. Scott

P.S. You must excuse bad writing for I have a bad pen and Isham is shaking the table washing the dishes.

Camp Alleghany, March 27th 1862

Dear Father,

I received a letter from you a few days since (Dated 13th March) which make but two since Robert Jenkins left them. The one you sent by Capt Davis I have never received. It looks hard that I cannot get letters from home any oftener than I do considering how many of you might write. Bud, Emma & Mollie could write me a letter once & while, and if you all knew how anxious I was to hear from you all you would certainly write to me oftener. I try to average one letter a week. There is very little or no news with us. Rumor says that we are to fall back from here in a short time. We received an order the other day to pack up all our extra baggage and ship it to Staunton by the first train of wagons returning to that place. This smells of something & then considering how much advanced we are to any other portion of our army and besides having such a small force and no chance to get reinforcements in case we should need them I should not be surprised that we will fall back as far as Staunton in a short time from now. They are also making tent pins which indicates that tents are to be used shortly and if we are to remain here we would have no need for them. I do not have exactly the same feelings upon this subject that I did when we first came here from Greenbrier. I then had no idea that we could ever stand the winter as well as we have and besides we had no fortifications at all. We are now about as well fortified and fixed up as we can be, and now to leave here and march to Staunton carrying our knapsacks upon our backs will be no light task taking the condition of the roads into consideration. Winter has not broke here in the mountains yet the ground has as much snow on it as it has had at any one time during the winter. We have no tents which are any account and to leave our houses where we have good bunks and straw to lay on. To lay upon the cold ground will certainly make many of us sick. If we go to Staunton we will have plenty of work to do fortifying again. I rather dread to move. Some think we will probably go to Winchester to reinforce Jackson.[31] I do not think so myself for were we to go there this road would then be entirely open and the enemy could either go to Staunton or get in our rear. Besides the whole country below this would be exposed to their ravages. I am almost certain that we will go somewhere. I shall send off all my cloths which I cannot carry in my knapsack. The company are generally well. Abner has taken a severe cold and is quite unwell. I think he will soon get over it. I have a pretty bad cold myself but feel very well. Can eat as hearty as ever, and weigh more than I ever did in my life. Several of our boys have come back from the hospitals among them J. D. Johnson, Notley Maddox, & Elijah Vining, Frank Jenkins &c they all look pretty well.[32] Dr Etheridge has not been appointed Surgon as yet he is now acting in the surgons place.[33] We have no Colonel that we know of. We hear that Maj Smead will be appointed Col, Capt Hawkins, Lieut Col & Capt McMillan Maj.[34] There is great opposition to Smead. I do not suppose there is a single man in the regt. who had not rather have almost any one else. It seems they intend to throw Col Conner out of office who is now at home on furlough. Furloughs is now done with, they grant no more. I feel disappointed in not getting to come home, but will live in the hopes of seeing you all at some future day. I dream occasionally of going home but wake up and do not find my self there. We have drawn pay for two months some of the company drew for four. I do not understand why we were not paid for four months as well as some of the others. It is said that we will draw next time for 4 months and our cloths. I understand that the Society in Eatonton expects us to pay each ten dollars for the last suit of cloths sent us. If they furnished them I am perfectly willing to pay the ten

dollars when we receive pay for them. I know it takes no little to cloth all the soldiers from Putnam.[35] I have nothing else to write. Give my love to all friends and relatives and my very best love to Grandma, mother and all the children, accept a large share for yourself. I remain yours most devotedly.
Irby G. Scott
P.S. I wish to add a few words to Bud, he wrote in a letter which I never answered only through your letter. Dear Brother, I know you will not object to a little advise from me who wishes your welfare as much as his own. I should not doubt that you are anxious to join in the struggle for our independence. I have some experience in this matter having now been in the service for over nine months. If I were in your place I would not engage in it at the present for various reasons. 1st you are entirely to young, your constitution may be injured by hard service and exposure, your habits are not formed, and there is not a worse place in the world than in the army for boys to be led astray. Besides there are innumerable hardships and privations to be gone through with of which you have never thought about. Lastly there is no need of your services at the present time and being under age no one can ever ——— you for not going. Besides you can be of great help to your father in many ways. My advise to you is not to go unless necessity compels you. If it were necessary for you to go I would never advise you to stay at home and see your country overrun, but it is not now necessary and I advise you to remain at home for you will never find war as you expect it. You would be exposed to all the diseases of the camp which there is no means of escaping and worse to be dreaded than the enemys balls. I know you must be anxious to go, for you could not stay at home and be otherwise. I desire your welfare as much as my own and therefore advise you again not to leave your home yet for the field of battle. Write to me. Accept the love of an affectionate Brother.
I. G. Scott

Chapter 6

1862 Valley Campaign

"I have become so hardened as to stand anything."

On March 23, 1862, events in the Shenandoah Valley took an unforeseen turn, when a Federal division repulsed the small Army of the Valley, under "Stonewall" Jackson, at the battle of First Kernstown. After several hours of intense fighting, Jackson's Army of the Valley retreated up the valley. Though a Federal victory, the Battle of First Kernstown initiated the ultimate defeat of Federal offensive operations in 1862 in the Valley of Virginia.

General Edward Johnson, as directed by General Lee, examined Shenandoah Mountain and found it a strong position. On the morning of April 2 Irby Scott and the men departed Camp Allegheny for Shenandoah Mountain, which they reached on April 5. On April 6, General Order Number 10 was issued, stating the encampment would be known as "Camp Shenandoah," located about twenty-four miles west of Staunton, Virginia.

After the battle of First Kernstown, a revised Union plan called for Federal General Banks to push up the Shenandoah Valley and dislodge "Stonewall" Jackson at Rude's Hill. Federal troops would then advance on Harrisonburg, threatening Staunton from the north. Federal General John C. Fremont would push toward Staunton from the west on the Staunton–Parkersburg Turnpike. On April 17, Banks's force routed Jackson from Rude's Hill, forcing the Valley Army to retreat to Swift Run Gap east of Harrisonburg, allowing Banks to occupy Harrisonburg.

On Saturday evening, April 19, Irby Scott and the men departed Camp Shenandoah in the rain. As the regiment advanced, the men stopped at Buffalo Gap to wait for the additional regiments, wagon train, and artillery to close up. On Easter Sunday morning, April 20, Scott and the men arrived at West View, Virginia. General Johnson then rode to meet "Stonewall" Jackson near Swift Run Gap for a lengthy conference on the evening of April 20. From April 20 to May 6, 1862, Scott and the men encamped along the Staunton–Parkersburg Turnpike at West View.

On the evening of May 7, Johnson's men spent a quiet night in their former camps, near Shenandoah Mountain. Again, with Johnson's brigade in the lead, the men resumed their march on May 8. Halting near the top of Bull Pasture Mountain, Johnson conducted a reconnaissance from Setlington's Hill, located on the south side of the turnpike. Observing Johnson's reconnaissance party, a Federal skirmish line was sent up Setlington's Hill to drive off the Confederates. Hoping to secure the hill, Johnson at once called forward all of his regiments, placing the Twelfth Georgia on the crest of the hill, forming the center of his line. A spirited fight of four hours' duration ensued as Federal troops tried in vain to dislodge Confederate troops from Setlington's Hill. After the battle, Federal troops destroyed stores in the village of McDowell, retreating toward Franklin, Virginia. Shortly after the McDowell fight the Twelfth Georgia transferred to a brigade commanded by General Arnold Elzey, to which they were assigned through the 1862 Valley Campaign.

In his letter of May 12, Irby Scott told how devastating the Battle of McDowell was on his company. All of the commissioned officers were either killed or wounded. The noncommissioned officers of the company now had to take charge. Without tents or knapsacks, Scott and the men were traveling light. This was the norm for the duration of the Valley Campaign.

It was not until May 26 that Scott penned his next letter home. In this letter, though sparse on details, he gives the reader a description of the marching the men had endured since the Battle of McDowell, including fights at Front Royal on May 23, at Strasburg on May 24, and finally at Winchester on May 25. Though held in reserve on May 25, Scott and the men pursued the retreating Federal army through the town of Winchester.

On May 27, "Stonewall" Jackson detached the Twelfth Georgia to Front Royal to guard Federal prisoners and help remove the sizable quantity of quartermaster and commissary stores captured on May 23. Some in the regiment felt they had been detached to recover from their trials or that General Jackson favored them. It is more likely that the regiment, now numbering fewer than four hundred men, was sent to Front Royal with the belief that Colonel Conner could manage this important assignment.

The day after the regiment arrived in Front Royal on May 29, a Union prisoner who had been captured the night before claimed Federal General James Shields was en route to Front Royal with a Federal division of fourteen thousand men. Conner at once asked for orders from his commander, General Arnold Elzey. If he ever received a reply, it is not

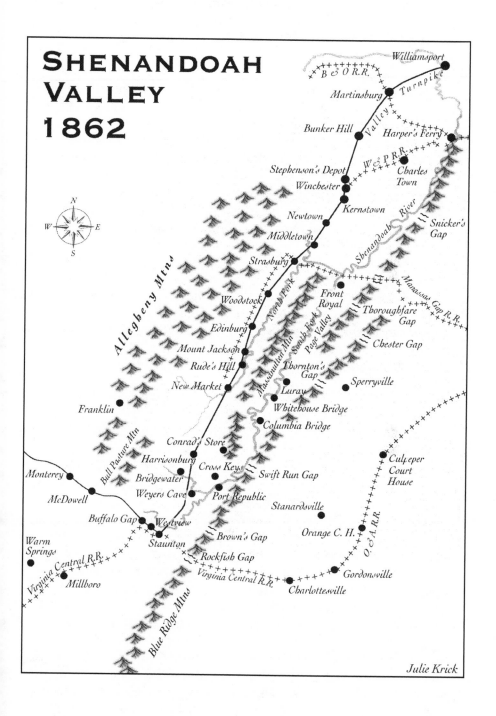

SHENANDOAH VALLEY 1862

Williamsport

B & O R.R.

Martinsburg

Valley Turnpike

Bunker Hill

Harper's Ferry

Stephenson's Depot

W & P R.R.

Charles Town

Winchester

Kernstown

Snicker's Gap

Newtown

Shenandoah River

Middletown

Strasburg

North Fork

Front Royal

Manassas Gap R.R.

Thoroughfare Gap

Woodstock

South Fork

Page Valley

Chester Gap

Edinburg

Massanutten Mtn

Mount Jackson

Thornton's Gap

Rude's Hill

Luray

Sperryville

New Market

Whitehouse Bridge

Franklin

Columbia Bridge

Allegheny Mtns

Conrad's Store

Harrisonburg

Cross Keys

Culpeper Court House

Monterey

Bull Pasture Mtn

Bridgewater

Swift Run Gap

McDowell

Weyers Cave

Port Republic

Stanardsville

Buffalo Gap

Westview

Orange C. H.

O. & A. R.R.

Warm Springs

Staunton

Brown's Gap

Virginia Central R.R.

Rockfish Gap

Gordonsville

Millboro

Virginia Central R.R.

Charlottesville

Blue Ridge Mtns

N
W   E
S

Julie Krick

known. Clearly, Conner was concerned that a large Federal force was headed in his direction from the east. To Conner's credit, he moved a large wagon train and his regiment toward Winchester before Federal cavalry entered Front Royal on May 30.

These Union horsemen, a New Hampshire cavalry battalion numbering one hundred men, of the First Rhode Island Cavalry, drove the retreating Confederates across the last bridge out of Front Royal, slashing and shooting as they advanced. What had begun as an orderly retreat ended, as Scott states, with the Georgians running for their lives. Major Willis A. Hawkins, in command after Colonel Conner fled to Winchester, proposed surrender at an officers' council. None of the men surrendered until they were overtaken by the Federal cavalry, who demanded their submission. When Colonel Conner arrived in Winchester, in advance of the regiment, Jackson had him arrested and eventually cashiered from the army for his conduct at Front Royal.

Since May 6, when the Twelfth Georgia left Valley Mills, Irby Scott and his comrades rested no more than two days during the Valley Campaign. By June 12 only twenty-six men remained in the company, with no commissioned officers or noncommissioned enlisted men. Scott did not know at the time he wrote on June 12 that his first twelve months of service were only the beginning of the war horrors he would witness. This letter clearly shows that he was worn down and slightly discouraged, and needed time to rest.

Camp Johnson, Augusta Co. Va.[1]
April 6th, 1862

Dear Father

I reckon you will be a little surprised when you get this letter and see that I am not at Alleghany. In my last letter to you I anticipated a movement of our brigade in a short time. We left Alleghany on last Wednesday morning and camped that night at Montery [Monterey]. Resumed the march next morning and camped at McDowell where we remained one day & two nights. On yesterday we came to this place which is about forty miles from Alleghany Mountain. Our brigade is now somewhat scattered. There is two regiments on the top of Shenandoah Mountain [one] I believe at the foot on this side, at Reynolds hotel, where there is a toll gate and two or three here.[2] We are encamped in a nice valley in the woods. It is only about 24 miles from Staunton. Our company have only a few tents. We drew three new ones yesterday and with the old ones make out very well. I supose we will draw more tents in a few days. Our company stood the march well and are generally in good health. I am well and hearty. I have not received a letter from home since the 13th March. We did not get any mail for a week before we left Alleghany. We found some yesterday at Reynolds but not a single letter for me. I understand there is some at ——— not far from here which has not yet been brought in. If I do not get a letter in that I will not know what to think. We rather looked for the yanks to attack or try to pursue us the morning we left but we heard or saw nothing of them. I understand they were making preparations to come around by Huntersville and cut us off but we were too fast for them. If they should take a notion to come down here they will meet with a warm reception. For Shenandoah Mountain is naturally a strong position. We can place cannon on the top and rake them for miles but, I do not think they will molest us here. It is the opinion of some that we will not remain here long. As to this I know nothing. I call this place Camp Johnson as I know of no other name. I expect that is what it will be named. You can direct your letters as heretofore and I will get them. I cannot write you a long letter today. One reason is that I have not yet got entirely over the effects of the march and do not feel like writing at all. I am very anxious to hear from home and hope I may get a letter this evening. Write soon. Give my love to all friends. Remember me especially to Grandma, mother, Bud & all the children. Also to the negroes. You will accept a large share of love yourself. I remain your devoted son untill death.

Irby G. Scott

PS: The name of our camp is Shenandoah. Direct your letters to one as Camp Shenandoah Augusta Co. Va.

April 11th 1862

Dear Mother:

As I did not have an opportunity to send ——— off my letter after writing it, I concluded to add a postscript in it to you. I wrote this letter the day after we reached this place and intended mailing it the next morning but very unexpectedly about ten oclock that night orders came to our regiment to cook up two days rations and be ready to march by light next morning. The 12th Ga went on a scout back as far as McDowell that day and intended to march that night to Montery [Monterey] and attack a squad of yankees there but, when we arrived at McDowell we learned that they had been reinforced by two regiments finding them too strong for us, we remained in McDowell all night and returned to camp next day. It snowed very hard on us all the way there and continued to snow and rain all night. It was a very large snow. The trees were almost broken down with ice. I had to go two miles farther and stand picket but, spent the night very comfortable around a large fire in an old blacksmith shop by the roadside. The rest of the boys scattered about some sleeping in hay in stable lofts, &c. We had quite a rough trip of it but all got back safe. We had only one days rest after our march from Alleghany before we took this. You may say we marched seventy miles in all but, the boys did not seem to mind it much. Since we returned from this scout the weather has been extremely cold and disagreeable untill part of yesterday & today which prevented me from writing untill the present. Myself & mess have also been very busy at work putting us up a cabin which is now nearly completed. We are doing this of our own accord. We went to a sawmill and bought as much plank as we wanted, and are progressing finally with our work. I received your and fathers letters, of the 25th and which was a great treat to me not having received one so long before. You wished to know whether I needed any clothes or not and to let you know. It is now to late for you to get this letter before Jim Pike leaves.[3] I am not much in need of anything. I will need about three shirts for summer (I mean cotton shirts). I have plenty of socks (woolen) but they will not be good for summer. So you can send me 3 pr of thick cotton socks. I have plenty of drawers. I should like to have a good pr of shoes for summer wear, not too heavy and would prefer them made in Madison if convenient.[4] I want them with broad bottoms and heels. I also want two rows of large headed tacks in the heels to prevent the rocks from wearing them off too soon. I have worn my boots ever since I got them besides marching in them and they are now pretty good. It does not take long to wear out shoes in this country. As to your sending wine, I do not know whether it would be allowed or not. I do not care particularly about it no how. I cannot think of anything else now. In my next if I should think of more I will write. You can send these by the first opportunity. I am very well. The company is generally well. Nothing more at present. I wrote to Cousin Lizzie Reid not long before we left Alleghany but have not received an answer. Find out whether she received it or not and let me know in your next. I was glad you was proud of your ring but was sorry it was broken. I think you can very easily mend it with Spaldings Glue.[5] Did you get the one I sent Sallie Colly. Tell Tolbert I was very sorry indeed to hear of his bad health but hope he may soon recover.[6] Give my very best love to Grandma and tell her that I very often think of her and hope we may meet again. I want to see you all very bad but do not know when I shall get a chance to come home. My love to all friends & the negroes and especially to father, Bud and the children. Accept a large share for yourself. I remain your affectionate son untill death.

Irby G. Scott

[*April 11 letter is included with April 6 letter.*]

Camp Shenandoah Augusta Co., Va.
April 18th, 1862
Dear Father

In my last letter I promised to write again soon knowing your anxiety at all times to hear. I merely write to let you know that I am well for there is nothing new or even worth writing about in the mountains, but still if there is no news in a letter that I get from home, it does me as much good to hear all are well and going on right as if it were full. We are all getting on finely & the company are generally well with a few exceptions. We are now pretty well fixed up to live. Moving and settling down again is quite a troublesome piece of business. We had an alarm yesterday morning about ten oclock and all the regts. on this side of the mountain were marched up to the top of Shenandoah where our batteries and fortifications are erected. It proved to be only a scouting party of the enemy trying to reconoiter our position. After a little skirmish with a few of our cavalry & picket guard they left. We then returned to camp about four miles distance. One company from our regt. and two or three from others were sent up the road last night but for what purpose I have not learned. Shenandoah Mountain is naturally a very strong position being very steep on all sides. We will soon have it well fortified and then we defy the yankees to come and take it. If Stonewall Jackson will maintain his ground and not fall back any farther we will hold this mountain untill the cows come home. I think Gen. Johnson is offering them every inducement to get them to attack us but I hardly think he will succeed unless they have at least three to our one. We have had beautiful weather for a day or two. Yesterday was exceedingly warm, there is not much sign of spring here yet the woods look like the dead of winter. The buds are beginning to swell a little. We are beginning to look for Leut. Reid and his recruits. From the time we heard they were to leave home it is now about time they were here. I suppose you have heard that Conner was our Colonel, Smead Leut. Col, Capt Hawkins (as was) major.[7] I understand Col Conner will be here in a few days. You wished to know if Dr Etheridge was our surgeon. He is not surgeon as yet but, is filling at this time the surgeons place.[8] Dr. Green has been granted a hearing and will return to answer to the charges prefered against him.[9] There is no chance for him to ever be surgeon of this regt again. If he comes back there are more charges that will be brought to bear of a more —- than any that has already been brought up. Dr. Etheridge will take his place as soon as he is disposed of. Gen. Johnson has issued an order that no more transportation will be furnished to carry clothes or edibles more than is allowed in the army regulations. Everything we get from home hereafter we will have to hire transportation, and if we have more clothing on hand than we can carry on our backs it is that much lost. I have found from experience that two good suits of clothing is as much as a soldier can well take care of. All that is necessary is a change. I have a good many things in Staunton which I have never had any use for. I intent if I should get the chance to send these home. I was glad to hear that Leut. Reid was bringing us tents. We will not be so badly crowded and they are much better than the government tents. I noticed in the Countryman the sale of Old man Cockran's negroes.[10] I was surprised to see them sell so high.[11] What has become of Davie.[12] It seems that our government intends to strain every nerve to hold the enemy in check by passing the conscription Bill.[13] I think it a good law. We learned with feelings of much regret of the fall of Fort Pulaski and also have great apprehensions that Savannah may also fall into the enemy's hands but, we much look more on the bright side of things in order to keep our spirits up and also remember the old maxim that all things works together for good.[14] I want to see you all worse than ever since spring has set in. Spring here is quite different from what it is in Georgia. I think of home and the loved ones there almost a hundred times a day. Do not think I am low spirited or grieving for such is not the case. I have learned to take all things easy however hard they may be but, rest assured that as soon as an opportunity shall present itself of a chance to come home I shall avail myself of it. You have rather urged upon me in several of your letters to try and get an office. I have no particular desire for one at this time. There is no vacancy except a corporal place which I care nothing for. As soon as Dr. E. [Etheridge] becomes surgeon there will be a vacancy in the company for a Leut place which office I do not feel capable of filling as it ought to be. Nor do I know whether I could get it or not. If I should try, an officer has as much duty to do as a private. They have the advantage in only a few respects. I will bide my time.[15] Perhaps things will work right some of these days. I spoke of sending mother some money but not drawing as much as I expected and having to spend some fixing up our quarters here, also for some provisions which we bought, I have concluded not to send any at present. I have nearly sixty dollars on hand. It will soon be time for us to draw again. I send little Fannie a ring in this letter.[16] I must close as it will soon be time to drill. We have to drill four hours every day now. I have written in a great hurry to get through but hope you can read it. Give my very best love to Grandma, mother, Bud and all the children. Remember me to all friends also to the negroes. Accept a large share for yourself. Yours affectionately.

    I.G. Scott

P.S. Kiss babies for me.

Augusta Co. Va. Six miles from Staunton at Valley Mills or West View[17]
April 24, 1862

Dear Father

    It is about time I was letting you know something of my whereabouts &c. I wrote you last from Shenandoah Mountain, which place we left on Saturday the 19th of this month. Orders came to us about ten oclock in the morning to get ready but we did not leave until nearly night. It rained all day and the greater portion of the night making the roads quite muddy. Sometimes half leg deep reaching Buffalo Gap about midnight.[18] We built up fires and remained until morning. The reason for our stopping there was that we were the advance regiment and the wagons & artillery were behind some distance on account of the conditions of the roads. They caught up next morning and we came on here a distance of six miles from Staunton. We moved again yesterday morning about a mile further towards Staunton to get a better camping ground. It has been raining nearly all the time since we left Shenandoah and today it has been snowing but, it melts nearly as fast as it falls. We are all comfortable and generally well. The cause of our falling back here was to prevent the enemy from getting in our rear and cutting us off as well as our supplies. Stonewall Jackson was compelled to give back and is now somewhere between Harrisonburg & Staunton. If he could have held his ground we could ours but when he fell back we were also compelled to do the same. I learn this morning that Jackson has been reinforced. If this be true and the reinforcements sufficient I expect we will remain here some time but, as to this there is no knowing anything about it. We managed to get all our things hauled except cooking utensils & knapsacks. The latter we brought upon our backs & the former were broken to pieces. We could have put them in the wagon with our other things but did not wish to load them heavy and the quarter master promised that we should put them in another wagon but, we did not get that wagon & the other gone so we broke them to pieces. Since we have been here we have gotten up a few and make out to cook &c. Jim Pike reached camp just as we were packing up to leave Shenandoah. I received a letter from you & mother by him and was glad to hear you were all well but, was sorry to hear Grandma had lost her sight of one eye and likely to loose the other. Give her my best love and tell her I desire to see her once more but, am affraid that I never shall for there is no chance for me to get home at the present. I want to see you all the worst sort but, shall have to wait patiently until I can get the chance to come home. I have asked Jim many questions concerning you all, and from his statements you must have asked a good many yourself. Leut Reid and his recruits have not reached us yet. They came on us as far as Charlottesville and there I understand went back to Richmond. I supose he will be here in a few days.[19] William Pearman met us here.[20] This is a nice section of country. The fields are perfectly green. Quite a contrast between here and Alleghany [Allegheny] Mountain. Now while I write it is snowing & sleeting and from apperances it is likely to continue the rest of the day. I do not know how I will get this letter off but shall try and get some one to take it to Staunton. The people there were panic stricken & have left by the wholsale. I must close as Abner wishes to write some in my letter. I have given you all the news of any importance. My love to Grandma, Mother, Bud & all the children. Also to all friends. Remember me to the negroes, accept my best love & affection for yourself, truly your affectionate Son.

Irby G. Scott.

PS: If any thing turns up I will write immediately. We are now in no danger of being cut-off but may have to move farther back.

March 26, 1862

[It appears Scott was unable to mail his April 24 letter. Therefore the date is more likely April 26.]

Contrary to my expectations I did not get my letter off. The evening I wrote orders came for two companies of our Regt & also two from a Va Regt to go out on a Scout the next morning at six oclock. We accordingly left at the appointed hour and went back as far as Buffalo Gap where we remained all night and returned to camp this morning. We were more of an advanced picket guard than a scouting party. The day and night passed off quite pleasantly. We saw nothing of the yankees. I do not suppose there is any camped nearer than Shenandoah. A scouting party wounded one of our cavalry a few days ago. Our movements depend entirely upon Gen. Jackson. There is nothing new in camps. All generally well. Abner has concluded not [to] add a postscript but write a separate letter. My best love to all the family and yourself. Yours affectionately.

Irby G. Scott

Kiss the little buddies & sissees for me and the larger ones if they will let you.

Camp Valley Mills, West View Augusta Co, Va
May 4th 1862

Dear Father

I embrace this opportunity of writing you a few lines. We have just finished a pretty good half day work. Soon after breakfast we rubbed & cleaned up our guns. We then had a dress parade after which there was a brigade inspection. Gen Johnson and staff rode round and inspected the whole command. He complimented our regiment by saying that it was the best looking on the ground. Our company was complimented. This is the first time we have ever had a brigade inspection. This evening we have another dress parade. We have beautiful weather and vegetation is springing every where. The fields are a solid green mostly covered with grass and clover. This is the finest section of country I have ever seen. It is full of the finest horses & stock generally you ever saw. We get plenty of nice bacon to eat. Today we drew some beef which is the finest we have had since we left Shenandoah which makes it quite acceptable. There is no news of any importance. Every thing is now quite. As usual there is many rumors in camp. I will give none of them as we can place no confidence in them. Jackson has been reinforced but I do not know exactly where [he] is, there is no keeping up with him.[21] There is no telling how long we may remain here. We have rather been looking out for Gen Jackson to make an attack on the yankees. We heard here the other day that he sent to Staunton for twenty battle flags.[22] One for each regt. I supose. It is thought here that he has the rise of twenty thousand men. I should not be surprised if our forces and Jacksons were not consolidated before a great while. We are now not very far apart. The health of the brigade is very good. I expect better than it has been since it entered the service. There is no sickness in our company. Some of the boys have had colds which is nothing uncommon. I have seen some nice looking girls since I have been here. Every time one passes along you can see the boys crawl out of the tents and take a look. Gen Johnson rode through our camp the other day with one in a buggy. The boys as he passed all gave a loud cheer. He took it all in good humor, but I think he was annoyed a little. I expect you think we are very foolish, but when you remember that we have not seen a woman worth looking at for ten months I think we are perfectly excusable. We have heavy guard duty to perform there are so many roads to look after. I never want to seen the mountains again as a soldier. The things you sent by Leut Reid have not reached us yet. I do not know where they are. Our tents were also left at Gordonsville and I doubt whether we will ever see them. You can send anything you wish to me. I do not know whether it will be carried on the railroad ——— or not. Gen Johnsons order I think only meant that wagons would not be furnished for transportation of eatables from home. You can send clothing for the government has as much as it can do to supply those in the army who cannot get the things from home. Our surplus baggage which was sent from Alleghany to Staunton has been removed to Lynchburg and I fear we will loose it. We hear the whistle of the car every day and by going out a little way from camp we can see them as they pass.[23] They continue to run a short distance above here. I have written all of any interest and will close my wearisome and badly written epistle. Give my very best love to Grandma and tell her that I often think of her in her afflictions and would give everything I posess to see her and all the rest of the family. I have ceased to be home sick long since and take things quite easy hoping and believing there is a better time not far distant where all who survive will be allowed to return to their homes. I often think of the day (should we be victorious) when we shall arrive once more in Eatonton. I imagine some will be joyful others sad, but enough of this. My love to all friends and the negroes. My love to mother, Bud, and all the children. Accept a share for yourself.

Your affectionate Son

Irby G. Scott

P.S. I understand that some of the boys in our company has written Sue Morton a letter. Just for mischief I want to find out who he is. Tell Emma to find out from Sue and let me know. Also tell Bud I am anxiously looking for that promised letter from him.

Camp Near Franklin Pendleton Co. Va.
May 12th, 1862
Dear Father

It is with feelings of great gratitude to God that I am still alive and can write you that I passed through the battle at McDowell on the 8th without injury. I was in the thickest of the fight from the beginning to the end and, although my companions fell all around me there was only one ball that touched my clothes. It was a hard fight of four hours duration part of it in the night. It was day before the dead and wounded could all be taken from the field. I shall not write many of the particulars of the fight. You will have learned who were killed and wounded long before this reaches you. I will mention those killed on the field. Edd Ried, Edd Davis and Frank Williams.[24] There was twenty seven killed and wounded from our company. From the regt. one hundred and eighty five. I have learned since I left that Rich Reid started for home the day after the fight with his Brother & Edd Davis. You can see him and learn all you wish to know. We left McDowel the morning after the fight in pursuite of the enemy and have had small skirmishes along the route. Our force is fifteen or sixteen thousand strong. That of the enemy suposed to be eleven thousand. When we got to Monterey we turned to the right in the direction of Winchester and are now about twenty miles from Monterey. It seems the enemy is about to make a stand or pretend they are. There has been some skirmishing and a little cannading [cannonading] but no injury done. What we will do I cannot tell. We are now camped. We have no tents or knapsacks. Fortunately the weather is good. There is only thirty men with us in the company. We have no commisioned officers. Leut. Bell [Beall] of the Jones Vol. has command of it he is a nice clever man.[25] The boys are standing the march very well. If we can whip the enemy I expect we will either go to Winchester or take down the valley and come in the rear of Banks army.[26] Ab Zachry was left sick at West View and was not in the battle. I must close as Billy Paschal wants to write in the same letter with me.[27] We had to borrow this sheet of paper. We will direct this letter to Mr. Paschal who will forward it on to you.[28] My best love to you, Grandma, Mother, Bud & all the children. Also to all friends. I cannot tell you where to direct your letters. Your affectionate son.
Irby. G. Scott.

Starsburg
Camp Near Winchester
May 26th 1862[29]

Dear ones at home,

I know you are very uneasy not having heard from me in some time I should have written you before this but have not had the first opportunity and orders may come for us to march before I can finish this. We left west view on the 6th of March and have been steadily on the march ever since. We drove the yankees on the Alleghany line as far as Franklin in Pendelton Co. We then turned back as far as Shenandoah and cut across into the valley passing through Harrisonburg, New Market.[30] At the last named place we left the main turnpike and passed through Luray in Page county. From there to Fort Royal in Warren county where we rousted the enemy and took nearly a regt prisoners besides commissaries and many other things.[31] The next day we attacked the main body of Banks army at Strasburg routing them also.[32] The next day which was yesterday we attacked them at the place and pursued them some four or five miles when we stoped but the cavalry kept after them.[33] Our brigade was held back as a reserve and have not fired a gun but were in the chase after them. Yesterday we were in sight of them about 4 miles our men and them running as fast as they could. We ran them through town, the Ladies cheered and thanked us as we passed. They tried to burn their stores but the fire was put out and nearly everything saved. They must have lost everything they had for I never saw the like of plunder in my life. I do not know their force. Our force consisted of Jacksons, Ewells & Johnsons armies.[34] I supose about 30 thousand men. There was not many killed on either side that I can hear of. We have between two & three thousand prisoners. I cannot tell whether we will go any farther or not. I expect we will move somewhere today. I am well and are doing well except sore feet. We have marched 250 miles you may say without rest. The company are generally well. Lut. Reid received a letter from Henry Reid stating that Capt. Davis was dead and that the other boys were doing very well.[35] We were sorry to hear of Capt. Davis death. I received your letter by Mr. Reid and also one written just before informing me of Grandmas death.[36] It made me feel quite sad but when I thought of her age and affliction I knew she was better off. Our loss was her eternal gain. I should have been glad could I have seen her once more, I was not surprised to hear of her death for I had been expecting it some time. A better woman never lived. I got my shoes & socks but did [not] get a chance to see Mr. Reid. We are having pretty tight times but are making out very well. I cannot tell what I would give to come home & see you all but do not make any calculations when I shall have that pleasure. I want to hear from home very bad. I cannot tell you where to direct your letters. You can direct as you think best. You will see our movements in the papers and can tell best. If I should get wounded I should like for you or some friend to come and take care of me. I will close. My love to all friends. My very best love and affection to mother, Bud, & all the children. Accept a large share for yourself. Your affectionate son untill death, Irby G. Scott

Camp Near Port Republic
Augusta County Va June 12th 1862
Loved ones at home,

I know you wonder and are uneasy at my long silence but you must not blame me. Circumstances have been such that I could not write or even mail a letter. I wrote you when we were in Winchester and sent my letter to Staunton to be mailed. I am affraid you never received it. I have a chance this evening or tomorrow to send another. I eagerly embrace the opportunity. Since I last wrote there has been several changes in our company. Eleven of our boys are prisoners, they were taken at Front Royal on the 3rd of this month.[37] After running the enemy from Winchester the 12th Ga regt was sent back to Front Royal to guard some prisoners and property. Jackson with the other forces proceeded on to Harpers Ferry when Shields Division tried to cut him off.[38] We had to run some distance to save ourselves and retreat to Winchester. A good many of the boys tired down and scattered through the woods where they were picked up by the enemys cavalry. Some few escaping. The cavalry charged into our rear shooting and cutting but only wounded 4 men, Ben Adams & Dave Ried in our company.[39] Neither one hurt very bad. I reckon you have heard all about it before now. Abner Z was among the number taken and also Jim Pike. We have seen hard times and are still seeing them. We left Valley Mills with about seventy men besides the recruits that have since came in and we now have only 26 men with us. The regt. had about six hundred, three hundred and seventeen have been killed, wounded & taken prisoners. We report only about one hundred and seventy five for duty. Our company has no commissioned officer or noncommissioned either. Sid Ried is in Staunton sick. Leut. Taylor is in command of the company.[40] We fought three Sundies [Sundays] in succession besides skirmishes nearly every day since we drove the enemy from Front Royal. After running Banks into Maryland Freemont [Fremont] & Shields armies both came upon us, and we were compelled to retreat which we did untill Saturday when we made a stand on the Shenandoah river. Shields in front of us one side of the river & Freemont [Fremont] in our rear.[41] Early Sunday morning Shields attempted to burn the bridge to cut off our retreat; but we drove him back and held posession of the bridge. Freemont [Fremont] also attacked our rear when we had a severe fight. I suppose of six hours duration when the enemy fell back and we lay all night near the battlefield. Our Regt did not engage the enemy with muskets, but were placed in rear of the artillery to support it. We lay in an open field just behind the canon. During the whole fight solid shot, grape and bombs seemed like they were raining down upon us. During the whole action one shell struck and bursted in our ranks killing & wounding 9 men. G. G. Mahone in our company was mortally wounded having since died.[42] Both his legs were broken and mangled

just about his knees. Milton Little was severely wounded on the right shoulder and has been sent to the hospital at Charlottesville. The flesh was nearly all torn from his shoulder. On Monday morning our whole force crossed the river, burned the bridge and pitched into Shields routing and running him ten or fifteen miles. Freemonts [Fremont's] force came to the river but could do nothing but look on being unable to cross the river. Our loss as well as the enemys was large but I do not know how many on either side. We have just got here and camped and I cannot tell how long we will remain here. We have not been stationary two days since we left Valley Mills the 6th of May. Marching part of the time night and day. I am in hopes we will be allowed to rest at least for a few days. I am well and have not been sick at all. Since we have been on the march my feet have been very sore but have become hard. I can stand almost anything. Lay down at night on the ground without a tent, with my clothes perfectly wet in a single blanket and sleep as sound as if on a feather bed. I shall write you every chance I get & if you do not get letters from me it will not be my fault. I dreamed last night of seeing you & mother. Oh how I would like the reality. I still live in hopes of seeing you all once more though times are dark with us now. Do not think I am low spirited from the way I write. I have become so hardened as to stand anything. I have not received a letter from you in some time and am getting very anxious to hear from home. I must stop writing for this time. I will write again the first opportunity there is to get off a letter. A few more days and I will have been in service 12 months having been in five hard battles, but thank God only one ball has come near enough to touch my clothes. Homer Paschal says tell his father to send him a hat & a pair of shoes by the first one coming on to the company. I expect he could send them by Dr. Ethridge or Bob Jenkins. I have never got my box you sent me it is in Staunton. Do not try to send me anything to eat for I will never get it. My very best love and affection to yourself, Mother & all the children. Also remember me to all friends & the negroes. Direct your letters to Staunton. Your affectionate son untill death,
Irby G. Scott

Chapter 7

Seven Days to Cedar Mountain

"I thought I had seen a plenty killed & wounded men. . . ."

Irby Scott and the men camped from June 12 to 16, 1862, near Port Republic to rest and collect abandoned Federal equipment left on the field. On the evening of June 17 the Valley Army broke camp and began moving toward Waynesboro, Virginia. In Scott's letter of June 19, he provides clear statements of the effects on the company after more than four hundred miles of marching and fighting in at least five battles. His company had been reduced to thirteen men, and for the past two weeks had no company officers.

Unfortunately no letters exist between June 19 and July 7. This is owed in part to Scott marching and fighting in the Seven Days Battles. Throughout June, Scott and the men battled the huge Federal army of General George B. McClellan, pushing the Federal army south of the Chickahominy River to Harrison's Landing on the James River. In his first letter home after the Seven Days Battles, on July 7, Scott writes about the "hard fighting" and that he had "seen a plenty killed & wounded men." He was worn out in body and mind from all of the marching and fighting.

Richmond had been delivered from the invading Federal army. McClellan was at Harrison's Landing preparing to return with his army to the Washington area. Federal forces that had earlier threatened the Shenandoah Valley now occupied northern Virginia. A new Federal army under Major General John Pope marched toward the vital rail junction of the Virginia Central Railroad and the Orange & Alexandria Railroad at Gordonsville. From Gordonsville, railroads radiated to Richmond, Staunton, and Manassas. Control of this rail junction would sever Richmond from northern Virginia.

Early in August, General Jackson welcomed the arrival of Ambrose P. Hill's division. Now, with a sizable force at hand, Jackson assaulted the lead elements of Pope's army assembling at Culpeper Court House. On *the morning of August 9 Jackson's army was northwest of Mitchell's Station on the Orange & Alexandria Railroad at Slaughter's Mountain, also know as Cedar Mountain, a rise north of Rapidan Station.*

During the Battle of Cedar Mountain, August 9, General Jubal Early praised the Twelfth Georgia and called it "his fighting regt." Irby Scott, in his August 15 letter, expresses pride in his regiment's actions. Unfortunately part of the August 15 letter Scott wrote home is missing. Camped five miles from Orange Courthouse on August 18, he wrote his last letter during the campaign. Nine days later, Scott received a wound in the opening fighting of the Battle of Second Manassas.

Camped Near Charlottesville. June 19th, 1862

Dear Father,

I wrote you last from Port Republic at which place we remained until Tuesday last when we began a wearisome march over the Blue Ridge and found ourselves this evening at this place. I guess you will wonder where we are going to. I am not able to enlighten you in the least. Some say we are going to Richmond. Others that we will cross the Blue Ridge again to get in the rear of Banks & Shields in the valley by coming in at Front Royal or somewhere near Winchester but no one knows except Jackson. We have only had five days rest after marching about four hundred miles. On stretch we have only a piece of a Regt—only about 140 men in ranks. There has been 325 men killed, wounded & taken prisoners since the 6th May. The rest are scattered about at the hospitals and some broke down on the road. Today there was 13 men in ranks in our company. Some of the boys came in from Staunton this evening. Liut. Reid among the rest. We have had no officers with us for two weeks. There was a great many reinforcements sent on to Staunton but the cars have been passing all day full inside & out. They are going on towards Richmond.[1] Important movements of some kind are on foot and you will know what it means in a few days. Jacksons army is called the foot Cavalry. Our field officers are still under arrest. Capt. Philips put us here this evening and will remain so tonight. He comes after remains of Mahone of our company who was killed near Port Republic.[2] Milton Little's wound is very bad. It is a doubtful case whether he will ever get well or not. He is here in Charlottesville. We are expecting some of his relations to come to see him in a few days. I got a chance to send to Staunton a few days ago after my box, which had been broken open. I got the card, butter & syrup which had not been touched. It came in good time for we are living none of the best since we left Valley Mills the 6th May. We get flour & beef or Bacon and thats all untill today. They gave us rye & sugar. I do not want you to try to send me any more for I cant get them. They are also liable to be stolen. I can make out with what the government gives us, there is not much chance

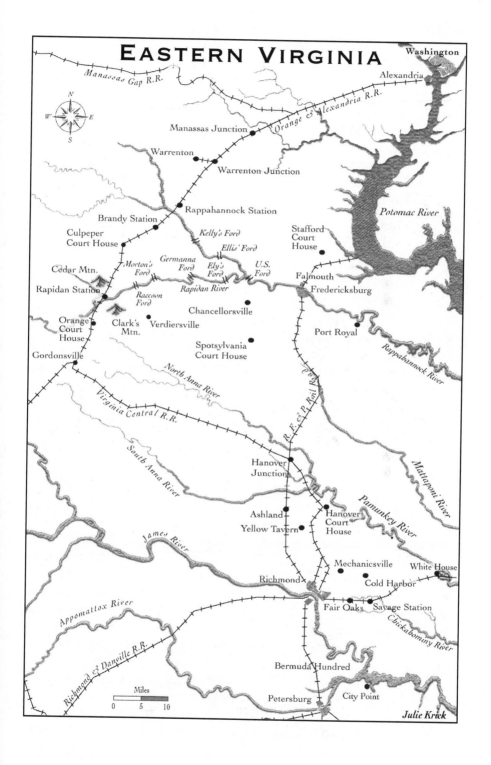

to get any clothing from home. I lost my knapsack that was left in Stanton with all my clothes except what I had on. I got some more from the boys and with what Henry Thomas bought I have plenty.[3] Chap Hudson is the only one of our boys that escaped from the yankees at Front Royal.[4] He traveled 13 days through the mountains being a prisoner twice. I am well and have been so all the time. I hope I will remain so. I want to get a letter from home. I have not received one since Henry Reid came on. They move us about so much that no one knows where to send our letters. Mr. A. M. Marshall is going on to Richmond tomorrow I will send this by him.[5] Remember me to all friends and the negroes. My love to yourself, Mother & all the children. Yours truly untill death,

Irby G. Scott

Kiss the little children for me.

July 7th, 1862

Dear Ones at Home,

(Kiss the little children for me).

    With great pleasure that I attempt to write you a few lines to let you know that I am still safe & well but how long I may remain so is hard to tell for there is danger on every side. We are now 25 miles from Richmond near Charles City within a short distance of the enemy. We have been here three days and the enemy fortifying all the time. Our pickets & theirs are in a very short distance of each other. I cannot tell what will be done. We have had some very hard fighting & will have more to do in all probability in a few days. I thought I had seen a plenty killed & wounded men before but I never saw anything to equal the last fights, suffice it to say that we have whiped in every engagement. The Yanks are now under protection of their gunboats. We are having hard times indeed but I hope they will soon improve and get better. I received the letters by Bob Jenkins which is the first for a month or more. You may know they were read with unspeakable pleasure by me. There was three of our company wounded slight in the fight Tuesday night, Jake Filer, Bob Young, H. Alford.[6] I expect they have all gone home before this. We have heard nothing more of the Front Royal boys. I expect they are all in some northern fort. We have twenty men along with the company. My general health is pretty fair but I am worn out with so much marching and also worn out in mind. There is so much loss of sleep and excitement every way. I never craved rest more in my life. I would give almost anything for the quite retreats of home but if others can stand it, why can I not do it? You want to send me a substitute which I am affraid you could not find easly. Besides it would cost a good deal besides in the way of money. You would have to get a man that was perfectly sound every way & a native from America. I would gladly be relieved for I feel that I need rest and there is no chance to get it any other way. If you can get one without to much trouble & without having to pay too much I will try and get off. Do not trouble yourself to much to get one if you find one let me know before you send him on. You can sell my horse if you wish or think best. I never wanted to see you all as bad in my life as I do now. I believe I would give the whole confederate states if I owned them to be with you all again. I think if nothing happens, I will see what can be done for an office. Perhaps I might stand a better chance in many things. Tell Alfred he must look to you for protection while I am here.[7] If I ever get a chance to come home I can then make some arrangements for him. I can do nothing now. If I should die or be killed I want you to let him choose his master. I know you will take good care of him.[8] Dr. Ethridge is here and surgeon of the Regt. Also Rich Reid. I must close for this time. My love to all friends & the negroes. I was sorry to hear that the children had the hooping cough, but hope they are all well by this time. Accept now the love of a devoted son & brother who will love you untill death. You had better direct your letters to Richmond. Affectionately adieu

    I. G. Scott.

PS: I saw Tom Morton the other day. He was well. Charlie was at Richmond sick but not sick much I reckon.

Camped Near Richmond
July 10th, 1862
Dear Father

    I wrote you a few days since which letter I hope you have received ere this but knowing your anxiety to hear from me, I concluded as I had time this evening to write & send my letter to Richmond in the morning. Since I wrote last we were twenty five miles from this place, within a mile & a half of the enemy who had taken a position in the fork of the Chickahominy Creek & James river under cover of their gun boats.[9] We remained there several days but did not have any fight with them. Our pickets and theirs were posted in two hundred yards of each other. They passed occasional shots. My Regt. was out the first & second days. In fact we drove their pickets in and posted ours in a quarter or half mile of their camp. We could hear them laugh & talk. In fact they even cursed us, called us rebels &c. We have fallen back (I mean Jacksons forces). I do not know where Johnsons forces are camped. There is so many Soldiers here that you can Scarcely find a division. If you inquire for a regt. you cannot find one man in a thousand that knows anything about it. I cannot tell what our future movements will be. We have a good camp & I hope will be allowed to remain here a short time to rest & recruit up. Our company is generally well. There is now about thirty men in ranks. We are improving some and if we could but stay here a short time we could have a very respectable company. My own health is very good with the exception of

a slight cough caused from cold but of which I am nearly well. You said in your letter that you heard I was troubled with a sore throat & cough. I had several times last fall & winter a cough but I do not remember having a sore throat more than once or twice since I left home. You cannot imagine how glad & how much surprised I was the other day when I received news that several of the boys who were supposed to be prisoners had escaped and would be in camp that day. I will mention their names. A. R. Zachry, William Winchel, Frank Jenkins, Frank Maddox, W. Pearman, James Davis, Thomas Carter.[10] They scattered through the country between Winchester & Front Royal, put on citizen clothes and worked until they could get a chance to slip through the Yankee lines. They fared well being in a Section of country where the citizens are all loyal. We gave them several hearty cheers as they came up. When I first heard the report of their coming I could scarcely believe it until I saw them. In my letters I have said very little about the battles which have been fought—not being able to give you anything like a description of them. They were so extensive and there were so many engaged, suffice it to say that we payed dear for the victories gained. Our losses in killed & wounded was great—as well that of the enemy. For particulars I refer you to the papers. I do (not) see how I have escaped so well but thanks to a kind providence I have not received the slightest hurt. I heard today that John Pearson of the 44th Ga was dead & that Dr. Monteith was dying last night.[11] That regt suffered terribly. I have seen the company once since the fight. Chap Hudson has obtained a furlough and gone home. He was struck by a piece of shell, but not hurt much. The skin was not broken. I saw William Hudson the other night. He belongs to the 9th regt.[12] He was looking very well. Mat. Talbert was not with his company being in Richmond sick. I wrote to you something about a substitute and I have wished ever since that I had written you not to try to get one for it will be a troublesome piece of business and then I should not like to remain at home and all the other boys in the war. If I could get a furlough I would be satisfied. I do not wish you to put yourself to any trouble. If you meet up with a good chance see what can be done but be sure to let me know before you make any final arrangements in the matter. If you or Bud wish to keep my horse for your own use you can do so. If not I expect you had better sell him as he is getting old and you can get a good price for him. This I leave entirely with you to Judge. I am getting very anxious for a letter from home. I want hear how the children are getting on with the hooping [whooping] cough. I was sorry to hear of Bartows death.[13] Tell Major & Bobbie I would give a thousand dollars to see them, in fact I am bad off to see you all.[14] I must close as Leut Reid is going to town. I expect we will get the clothes that we left here last summer. My love to all friends & the negros. My best love to yourself, Mother, Bud, & all the children. Your affectionate son until death.
Irby G. Scott

Camped Near Gordonsville July 19th 1862

Dear Father,

I wrote you last from Richmond which place we left last Monday on the cars for this place, we made but a short stop at the capitol, much shorter than I anticipated. The weather has been extremely wet since our arrival here. In fact we have had rough times for the last few days camped in the woods without tents or shelters and it pouring rain almost incessantly, but the sun had at last come out and we are getting strait again. Our tents which were behind in the baggage wagons came in last night. So after the rain is all over and we do not particulary need them, we have them to keep out of the weather. If we had had them there when it was raining they would not have done us much good for day before yesterday evening it was reported in camps that the enemy were in five miles of us advancing. The regt was immediately ordered out, raining as it was, remaining all night on picket and the next morning were taken up behind cavalry men proceeding on some ten or twelve miles farther to try to capture some cavalry which were on this side of the river it being very full from the rains, but they did not succed the enemy swam the river. They came back last night on the cars which we run as far as Orange Court House. They were without something to eat for a day and a half. I[t] was between midnight and day when they got back tired, hungry and muddy from head to foot. It was certainly a hard trip. I was not with the company. Some of the boys had just come in from the hospital when a guard was called for. They were detailed and having no guns I let one of them take mine. So having no gun I was excused. I generally like to be with the company, but I did not care much if I was out on (the) scout. I employed myself while it was not raining to much cooking up provisions for the boys, knowing how hungry they would be. I had fried chicken, Irish potatoes, peas, meal & buiscuit all served up. (I mean for my mess for we bought the chickens & vegatables.) Which we consider great eating here in the army & which was ate as if it might be good. I understand those Yankee cavalry who caused the alarm the other evening intended coming to Gordonsville not knowing I supose that we were here.[15] The enemy are in camp some fifteen miles distance. I cannot tell where we will make a strick, this may be a feint and then make the attact [attack] somewhere else. We may remain here a few days or we may be ordered away at any time. Every thing is kept very secret now in the army. (I mean its movements.) When we are ordered to march we never know where we are going. The company are generally well, Wm Waller & Athon are sick here in the hospital though not very sick I believe.[16] We have now nearly forty men in the company & about three hundred & twenty five in the regt. I am very well myself & so is all boys from our part of the county. James A. Beall who was wounded at McDowell has just arrived in camp from Lynchburg.[17] He still limps badly.

He says the reason he came back so soon that they did not give him scarcely anything to eat. He has tried to get a furlough, but could not succeed. He is not fit for duty and if we have to march he cannot keep up with us. I expect he will be left here at the hospital. I reckon Jake Filer & Henry Alford also Chap Hudson have reached home ere this.[18] How I wish I could have the pleasure of coming home to see you all, but I do not wish to be wounded to get the chance & that is the only way that furloughs can be obtained now. While we were camped at Richmond I went into the city once where I met a good many old acquanintances from Putnam. Among them A. F. Bird, James Zachry, Wm Gatewood & others.[19] Mr Batchelor was also at our camp he came on to see about his sons who are in Richmond sick.[20] James Zachry brought his brother a substitute, for whom he payed [paid] a thousand dollars. Freeman Perryman was going home with them, he had been & was still sick he looked very bad.[21] James Beall says that Woodson Haskins was a perfect skeleton not being able to help himself at all, why does not some of his friends come and take him home? It makes me feel bad whenever I think of it for him to lay there and suffer probably die without a friend near him. Something ought to done for him. If it should fall to my lot to get wounded I want you or some friend to come after me immediately. For the wounded suffer at these Hospitals. If I should be killed you will probably never know where I am buried or how. These are sad thoughts and I must not dwell on them any longer. Though the goodness & mercy of God I have been spared thus far & I hope & pray that I may live to see this war over, peace once more restored, the country in a prosperous condition and myself with those I love better than anything else on earth. I am awfully tired of this war, but there is no retreat now for us if we give up our lives will be no satisfaction to us & we will be disgraced forever. I have not received a letter from you in a long time and am very anxious for one. Our boys keep coming in. Hudson Adams & McGetrick have just arrived.[22] I think Hudson will he discharged, he ought to be. I must close as commissary Adams is going to town and will mail my letter. My love to all friends & the negroes, accept my love for your self mother & all the children. Yours as ever
I. G. Scott

Camp at Gordonsville, Va
July 20th 1862
To loved ones at home, Father,
Mother, Brothers & Sisters

I wrote you yesterday by mail but as McGettrick and others leave in the morning for home. I should not feel that I was doing right to not write you by them. How I should like to accompany them. To visit those I love. To look once more where I have passed the happiest of my life. To meet friends and engage as in days gone by in conversation around the family board. To enjoy eating some of the nice melons & peaches of which I know there are an abundance. Man has no idea how many ties there is to bond him to his home untill he leaves it to shift for himself in the world. As for myself I consider that I have no home as long as I am a soldier. I am at home any & everywhere I find myself in the confederacy. It may suit some men to live roving life but as for myself, I do not like it at all. Especially the kind of life we have had in the army for the last few months past. But man can stand almost anything for a time. Yet after awhile he can feel the effects very sensibly. If I had been told when I first entered the service that I could have gone through as much as I have, I never could have believed it, and now I can stand it better than at first for the reason that I know how to take the advantages on a march or anywhere else I may be placed, and besides I have become accustomed to this mode of life. I reckon you have tired of this kind of stuff long since and would prefer some of news from this section of the country. News with us is as scarce as hens teeth. We hardly know anything that does not come under our own observation. We seldom get a chance to read the papers. As for rumors and reports we have any amount of them for what they are worth. For instance it was reported that our Regt would be sent to Macon Ga. to guard prisoners and the Regt there would take our place here. I do not supose such a thing was ever thought of by our commanding officers. I have come to the conclusion that it [is] useless to think of being shown any favors for it seems that those who have done the most all the while are expected to take the lead and keep it. Every thing has been quite for the past few days. This evening it is reported that the enemy are at Beaver Dam a small station on the rail road between here and Richmond some forty miles distance from this place. I do not know weather to place any confidance in the report or not. We hear so many of the same kind which are untrue. William Wilson and Donnelson Pritchard of our company have been discharged and will leave tomorrow.[23] Hudson Adams too I expect. I do [not] know whether he has his discharge yet or not. Milton Little will also be discharged. He has lost the use of his arm. The boys are all well. Abner is complaining a little. I think [it] is only cold he has taken. He and I are all now that is left of mess No. 9 who have escaped thus far. I look upon him almost as a brother & missed him no little while he was cut off among the yankies. The mails must be very badly managed for we never get any letters now. I have not received but three or four letters since the first of May, but still I know that you write to me. To me the cause of my getting no letters must be owing to the derangement in the mails or post-masters. I heard when we were at Richmond that there was ten days mail lying in the office there for the army which had not been opened. Your last letter was by Bob Jenkins. I have heard from home pretty regularly through people coming from there. I cannot tell you

where to direct your letters we never stay in one place exceeding a week at a time. Direct them where you think best. While I was in Richmond I got the cloths you sent by Leut Reid also a pair of pants I left there last summer.[24] I am now pretty well supplied except shoes which I will draw from the government whenever I want them. I need a hat which is not to be had here and if you were to send me one from home I probably would never see it. I may meet up with a chance to get one here in my travels. My health is very good with the exception of a cold. Abner says tell his aunt Emerline that he wrote to her yesterday and will write again in a few days.[25] I sometimes imagine how large the children have grown and what changes in their looks &c. I want to see Major & Bobie worse than any of them. Tell mother if I never get home I want Bud to have my breast pin and Major the collar button. She must buy Bobie something. I have written about all I can think of at this time. If we remain here I will write again in a few days. I hope you get my letters. Remember to give my love to all inquiring friends also remember me to the negroes. Accept my best love and affection for yourself, mother Bud and all the children. I remain your most affectionate son untill death.
Irby Goodwin Scott

Camp 6 miles from Gordonsville
July 25th, 1862
Dear Father,

As an opportunity presents itself for me to send you a letter by hand I avail myself of it to let you know that I am well and doing well as I can expect. I send this by John Denham who has been at the Hospital at Lynchburg since the fight at McDowell at which fight he was wounded in the leg. Failing to obtain a furlough, he came back to the regt where he obtained one & will leave for home in the morning. The health of the company is generally good. I wrote you last from Gordonsville by McGettrick. We are now six or seven miles from Gordonsville in the direction of Federicsburg [Fredericksburg]. We have a beautiful camping ground. Plenty of good water & wood. Also plenty to eat. We have been rather reorganizing our army which is badly torn to pieces. We drill three times a day. Today we had a brigade inspection and besides drew four months pay & commutation for clothing making in all sixty nine dollars. I have now on hand ninety one dollars in my pocket and some owing to me, enough to make a hundred. I would like to send some of it home but I do not know when I will draw again or what use I may have for it and the chances for sending it now does not exactly suit me. There is no news of any importance in this part of the country. The yankees are on the other side of the Rapidan River some twenty miles from this place. I heard it rumored that they are fortifying which will do them no good if Stonewall takes it into his head to flank them. I do not know whether to

think we will remain here some time or move in a few days. I supose [suppose] our movements will depend upon those of the enemy. The yankees did us some damage in the Central Railroad by burning up a depot, seven hundred barrels of flour and a train of cars.[26] I have heard nothing of them since. I supose [suppose] it was a party of cavalry who did it. This is a fine section of country and the crops as far as I have seen are fine. Our camp is near the old residence of James Madison (once President of the United States). I have visited his grave. He has a large fine monument erected over his remains. It is a nice place and shows till now how much pains he took in arranging everything around.[27] Abner received a letter from Mrs. Boswell dated the 15th. I was glad to hear from home. I know you were all well or Mrs Boswell would have said something about it. I reckon your corn crops are fine for I understand that the seasons have been good up to the 15th of this month. We have one consolation if there is no prospect of peace. There is a prospect of something to eat. Several more of our Regt who were cut off at Front Royal came in yesterday. From them we learn the death of Thomas Gorley.[28] They dug his grave but thought it not prudent to remain at the burying. They say he was buried very nicely and there were a good many of the citizens in attendance. We can hear nothing of Henry Thomas. I have nothing more to write at the present. I cannot see why I cannot get a letter from home. I have not received one by mail since the 1st of May. My love to all friends and the negroes. Accept now my best love and affection for yourself and the whole family.
Your affectionate son
   Irby G. Scott

Camp 7 miles Gordonsville Va.
July 28th 1862
Dear Mother,
   I wrote home a few days ago by John Denham but ~~not~~ having written so seldom of late I never know how to stop now. I have an opportunity. The morning Denham left us we had received orders to be ready to march and accordingly packed up every thing ready to move. We were marched to Gordonsville and remained untill evening when we returned to our former camp. The cause of our removal was that the enemy was advancing upon Orange Court House (which is in Orange County) but finding out that it was false we returned to camp. We are resting up and reorganizing our army. We are drilling three times a day. Our Regt is daily increasing in numbers. A good many are coming in from the hospitals and also some of the wounded from home. Henry Marshall, Andrew Gorley & Isham arrived in camp yesterday evening.[29] We were very glad to see them back to hear from home and receive letters from those we love. I received two from you and I assure

you nothing could possibly have given me more pleasure unless I could see you. I was glad to hear the children were getting better of their cough, but was sorry to hear of the loss of the two little negro children, and Tolberts continued bad health, but I hope the next time I hear from him he will be better. You wrote concerning my clothing. I have plenty for the present. My coat is nearly worn out, but I thought I would try and make it do untill fall. I have plenty drawers & shirts also socks to last me untill fall. I received by Henry Marshall my hat, which was very acceptable. I had the day before cut out the crown of my old one and sewn it back in. Also patched it up in many places. The one you sent is a great deal better than any that can be bought here. I tried in Richmond but could not find anything but straw hats which I would not buy. It is a very difficult matter to get anything from home I do not want to send me anything unless you can send them by some one coming on to the company, do not try to send me cakes or anything to eat for it is that much lost. I get plenty to eat. You said you would send me some flour by Jake. I do not want it. You can send me a coat by Jake Filer when he comes on. If you get this letter in time to make it like the last one a frock coat. I will need some socks, pants, drawers & an over coat this winter, but do not try to send them untill I need them for I might loose them. There will be some chance in the fall. I have plenty of blankets for the present. It would be difficult to get them from home. I supose there will be some arrangements made to supply us this winter. We have plenty scattered about if we could ever them. I will also need a pair of over shirts. I live in the hopes of coming home myself in time to get what I need for the winter but I cannot tell when I can come home it depends entirely upon circumstances. I want to come home more now than I have since I have been in the service. You can also send me a pair of shoes by Jake if he is willing to bring them. Jake will know what he can bring and give information about anything you want to know. You can send anything you wish that Jake will agree to bring. You say it looks like the world is for itself. If you can find a friend in these times of trouble who will stick to you he is a friend indeed. It is very easy to find what a person is. Do not mind it because those people were not willing to bring me anything. It is very troublesome I know to have much baggage. Perhaps the time may come when I can tell them of it. If you or any of the family come on and they want you to bring something to Abner be sure to bring it for I consider him as one of my best friends and I do not think he takes after his relations in that respect. Jake Filer is also one of my best friends. I believe him to be a clever and honest a man as ever lived. If he is a foreigner and it has been thrown up to him by some in the company.[30] I think I have a good many friends in our company and I do not know of any that are enemies. I had thought of trying for a Leut place as there will be two to elect. It seems father is anxious for me to have an office. I do not know whether I can get it or not. I have ~~not~~ made known my intentions to very few in the matter as yet. I will close. Tell Bud, Mollie & Emma that they must write to me or I will begin to think they do not care any thing for me.[31] My love to all friends and the negroes. Accept the love of an affectionate son, for yourself and the whole family. Yours most affectionate son

I. G. Scott.

P.S. Abner is not well he had a chill to day and has some fever.

P.S. I received ———— a bottle of brandy cherries and handkerchief

P.S. 29th July 1862

Dear mother since I wrote my letter we have been marching and instead of sending it to the office I am here in Gordonsville and will mail it myself. I do not know where we are going. May be to Richmond or the valley. No body knows. I am well Abner is not well I am afraid he is taking the fever. I have not time to write now. So I bid you affectionately adieu for the present.

Your loving Son

I. G. Scott

Camp 7 miles Gordonsville Va.

August 5th 1862

Dear Father,

It is with pleasure that I attempt to write you a few line this morning. I wrote to mother last week to which letter I added a postscript that we were on the march and did not have any idea where we were going. Contrary to the expectations of all we went about five miles below Gordonsville and camped, where we remained untill Sunday last. When we were ordered back again to our old camp above Godronsville. The day we were ordered here there was considerable fight between our cavalry & the emeny's at Orange Court House.[32] I suppose that we are kept here to suport the cavalry in case they should need it. Our orders are to hold ourseleves in readiness at anytime. We have a pretty large force. Gen Hills division has been sent from Richmond. I heard that Longstreet was also coming up, but as to this I do not know. It is also said that the enemy has a large force. There may be a big battle fought here soon or there may not be we cannot tell anything about it. I have been quite unwell for several days. I took medicine yesterday and feel better to day. I have had a little fever. I hope to be entirley well in a few days. The company is generally well a few complaining but none sick much. There is no news of any importance with us. If you see Jake Filer before he leaves home say to him that J. D. Johnson & Abner Zachry wishes him to bring them a hat. They say if any one can find them Jake can. Some of the boys are getting bad off for hats. I think a great deal of my hat that you sent me. The sizes of Johnsons & Zachrys hats are 71/4 & 7. Abner received a letter yesterday from Mrs Boswell. She stated that you were all well except

Tolbert. Poor old fellow he sees a hard time I reckon. I feel sorry for him. If we stay where we are for a few days I should not be surprised if the elections for officers in the company did not come off. I think Abner will run for Leut. The other candidates will be R. Jenkins, J. D. Johnson and I think probably Jesse Batchelors name will also be proposed to the company. Chap Hudson has been looking forward to an office but there is no chance for him. I have said but very little to anyone about trying myself. I have been told that my chance was very good. Abner will be pretty certain to be elected. He says that I can also be elected and is very anxious for me to run. I have not time to write more now as the mail will go off in a few minutes. My best love and affection to the whole family also to all friends and the negroes. Abner says tell Mrs Boswell to sned him two cotton shirts and two pair of drawers some cotton socks, a coat, a hankerchief &c. You may send me a pair of pants. If you cannot send my things by Jake you can send them by Leut Marshall.
Yours Most Affectionate Son.
I. G. Scott

Camped 7 miles from Gordonsville Va
Aug 13th 1862
Dear Father
It is with pleasure that I attempt to write you this morning after having been through another fight. I supose Jackson wished to attack the enemy. So we left our camp on last Friday evening our brigade in advance. The attack was made about 3 Oclock in the evening of Saturday. Our brigade engaged the enemy for some time when reinforcements came up and the battle raged from that time till after dark. Our loss was small that of the enemy pretty large. I do not know the numbers killed and wounded on our side. In our regt. there was about 7 killed and 30 wounded. Among the killed was one of our company, Reubin Welch.[33] He was killed by a piece of shell or grape shot from the enemy cannon. Harvey Lynch was shot through the leg with a musket ball, bone not touched.[34] William Winchel was struck in the head by a spent ball, but the skin was just broken.[35] Several of the other boys were struck by pieces of shell, which only made slight bruises upon them. Welch was killed instantly the ball passing entirely through his breast. We drove the enemy back and slept upon the field that night. The next as was expected the fight was not renewed and we fell back a short distance on Monday there was sent in a flag of truce from the enemy to bury their dead which was agreed to. On Monday night we left marching all night and part of yesterday when we reached this our old camp. I cannot tell why we fell back, but I supose they were either to strong in position or numbers for us or the object may be to draw them out and fight them on our own ground. Our regt opened the fight and received great praise from Gen. Early on the field for

their gallant conduct during the fight.[36] I was struck by a spent ball on the hip but it did not hurt me any.[37] My health is not very good at this time. I have rather been complaining for ——— than a week. Yesterday I was taken with the camp colic and the sun being so very warm I was quite sick all day.[38] I threw up a good deal of bile and to day feel a great deal better, but still am not well. I think probably in a few days I will be all right. The company are generally well. The election came off in our company as was anticipated and Abner Zackry was chosen 2nd Leut. and myself 3rd there was several who were candidates, but Bob Jenkins was the only opponent that was in the way. There was three ballots before it could be decided between I and Bob. Bob before the election was certain he would be elected and after it was over seemed to feel great disappointment. I received your letter of the 31st of July yesterday evening which I was glad to get. I was sorry to hear of the drought and the failure in the crops, but hope you will make enough to do you. I and Abner now need a negro to cook for us. Abner received a letter that they would send Charles by the first one coming. If he was not coming I would want you to send me one, but one will be enough for us both, and I hope he will soon be here as we need him. Send me the cloths I wrote for by the first opportunity. We are looking for some of the boys on from home and are also looking for the boys who were taken prisoners at Front Royal as they have been exchanged and are in Richmond

[Letter stops here]

[The letter dated August 15, 1862, is written on stationery, with an image of a hand holding a staff with the first national Confederate flag flowing from the staff, and the word BARTOW near the bottom of the staff.]

Camped 7 miles from Gordonsville Va
August 15th 1862

To Loved ones at home

I wrote you a few days since and in that letter stated that I was not well knowing that you will be uneasy until you hear again. I cannot keep from writing you a few lines to inform you that I am improving. I think you need to have no fear of my having anything like fever. I was affraid my self at first that I would have a hard spell, all I need now is a little time to gather my strength and all will be right. In my last letter I wrote you something about the fight, but I was feeling so renewed at [the] time. I expect you can gather very little information from what I wrote. I see the Virginia papers claim that the attack and also the praise is due to the Virginians this is a mistake for the 12th Ga made the attack and was the first regt on the field. Gen. Early rode up to our regt just as the fight closed, and said the 12th Ga was his fighting regt he has seven or eight regts in his brigade. It is said that some if not all his

Va regts gave back. Some of them almost running from the field. I like a good name, but I think we have most too much of it for our own good. It causes us to be placed in many places of danger that otherwise we would not. It is reported here that McClellans army is leaving Richmond and coming around up this way, and that our forces are also coming up here. It is also reported that the enemy are bringing a large force through N. W. Virginia. I know nothing as to the truth of these reports. Every thing has been quiet since the fight a very good indication that something important is on foot. We are anxiously looking for some of the boys who were prisoners and have been lately exchanged. Some few have come in to the regt. It is time Chap Hudson, Filer and some of the others on furlough were reporting back as their time is about out. I want them to come along as I expect letters by them, and am exceedingly anxious to hear from home. I feel great solicitude on your account the times are so hard and every thing so high. I do not see how you all are to get along then sell your cotton at such a low price. I wish I could send you some money, but at this time I have none to spare. I have to buy all rations and pay the cash for them everything is high here as well as it is in Georgia. Bacon is worth from 35 to 50 cents a pound, flour $5 per hundred &c. this is what we have to pay the government. I have about $80 on hand, which is plenty for the present when I draw it again I [intend] to send you all I can spare for I know you must need money. Has Mr Whaley ever drawn Nicks pay from the government or not he can drawer it very easily he has administration on Nicks estate. All he has to do is send on to some one here a power of attorney and it can be collected. If I were in his place I would get it. I have forgotten how much is due Nick, but I think it is a good large sum. I dreamed of coming home the other night and when I got there I thought mother told me she wanted me to go right back and whip out the yanks, close the war & c. I did not think you were all very glad to see me, but if I could get the chance to come home I would very soon see whether my dream would prove true or not. I sometimes try to imagine how every thing looks and what changes have taken place since I left I do not expect I would hardly know the little children. Let one get a little sick and he can think more of home than any other time. I wish I could come home and stay a short time. Nothing on earth could possibly give more pleasure, but it seems I never was born to be lucky like some there is some who have been home twice but I will wait patiently, my time I hope will come some of these days. You wish me to send you my ambrotype which I will do if I can ever get the chance to have one taken. The weather has been extremely warm for some time past but for the last day or two it has been showery and pleasant. There is the first corn crops in this section I ever saw grow the upland looks like the very best bottom. I wish yours was so. I could feel a great deal better satisfied when you write let me know about every thing for you know not how much anxiety I feel for your welfare we hear that William Paschall is dead. The company is generally well and the whole army in very good health so far as I can learn. I wrote you in my last in reference to a negro we need one here I intended to write to you for one, but Abner is looking for his uncle Joes Charles by the first one coming on and he will be enough for us both.[39] I would have preferred one of my own but as Charles is coming he will do as well. There is some danger of loosing a negro here. Since writing the above orders have come round to cook up rations and be ready to [*This page ends here, and it appears a page is missing. The top of the next page begins with*] tell Tolbert I am sorry to hear of his protracted sickness and hope he will again get well. I should like to see him very much. I want to see you all very bad but cant tell when I shall have that pleasure. I see from the papers that the officers who were taken the other day have been sent to Richmond and put in irons I do [not] exactly like this for the yankees may get me prisoner some time and they will be certain to do us the same way, but I shall try to keep out of their way if possible. Abner received a letter from home saying they heard he was very sick this he wishes me to contradict by saying that it is not so. He is perfectly well. I leave you to do as you think best about selling my horse if you think best sell him. I must close as the mail will leave in a few minutes. My love to all friends and the negroes. I will write again in a few days. My best love for yourself, mother, Bud, and all the children. Your affectionate Son untill death.

Irby G. Scott

PS direct your letters to Gordonsville

Aug 18th 1862

Dear Father

Since writing my letter we have moved I supose some ten miles in the direction of Fredericksburg. The enemy advanced nearly to the river opposite Orange Court House. I supose the object in moving us down here was to get in their rear or make a flank movement upon them but I understand that they were all falling back yesterday to their former position. I should not be surprised if we have a big fight here in a short time. Gen Lee is here and there is a large force around here.[40] We may advance upon them or we may not. I can't tell anything about it. There is no news of any importance with us. I send this letter by the ambulance to Orange Court House I do not know whether there is any office there or not, but I thought I would try it. I am very well and hope this may find you all enjoying the same blessing. The company is generally well and in very good spirits a good many of the exchanged prisoners are coming in, but it seems the exchange is not exactly completed and they cannot take up their arms yet; none have come to our company as yet. My best love to the whole family. Your affectionate son.

Irby G. Scott

Chapter 8

Fredericksburg Front

"If they intend to fight . . . , I should like for them to do it here."

No letters survive that Irby Scott wrote home giving details of his wound-ing on August 27, 1862. The Twelfth Georgia was marching toward Manassas Junction before sunrise on the morning of August 27 to as-sist two regiments of Confederate General Isaac R. Trimble's brigade. Also on that morning, Federal General George W. Taylor and his New Jersey brigade, with two Ohio regiments, advanced toward Manassas Junction. It was during a skirmish with these Federal troops that Scott received wounds to a shoulder and thigh when a shell exploded nearby, killing and wounding several men. Scott sent word to his family after being wounded and removed to a private home in Middleburg, Virginia. Scott's father arrived in Middleburg on September 28, and on October 4, at Gordonsville, Irby received his wounded furlough, and he and his fa-ther journeyed home.

During his furlough, Irby Scott likely purchased a sword manufac-tured by W. J. McElroy of Macon, Georgia. This sword, which still sur-vives, is etched with cotton and tobacco leaves and a large "C.S.," with the name of the manufacturer included as part of the decoration. A distin-guishing feature of the swords manufactured by McElroy is the "stopped" blade, something not usually found in southern swords. Scott's name is not etched on his sword, as is often found on swords made by McElroy. In all likelihood, Scott also received new clothes, shoes, and other necessary items before his return to the army.

As the year 1863 opened, the Army of the Potomac and the Army of Northern Virginia faced each other on the banks of the Rappahannock River. General Burnside's huge Federal army was licking its wounds after the disastrous December 13 attack at Fredericksburg. Another Federal advance, on January 22, ended almost as soon as it began, in the mud, on the north bank of the Rappahannock, and has become known as the "Mud

March." Once again Lincoln replaced an army commander when General Joseph Hooker became the commander of the Army of the Potomac.

On the Confederate side of the Rappahannock River the army was in need of reorganization, owing in part to attrition. On January 19, 1863, Trimble's brigade was broken up, with the regiments assigned to other brigades. The Twelfth and the Twenty-first Georgia Regiments became part of a new brigade, which included the Fourth and the Forty-fourth Georgia, commanded by Brigadier General George Pierce Doles, former colonel of the Fourth Georgia.

Shortly after the Twelfth Georgia joined Doles's brigade, Lieutenant Colonel Edward Willis of the Twelfth was promoted to colonel, January 22, 1863, and placed in command of his regiment. Willis had been absent from the Twelfth Georgia for most of 1862 as a member of General Stonewall Jackson's staff. At only twenty-two years of age, Willis led the Twelfth Georgia until shortly before his death in 1864.

Though young, Colonel Willis had attended the United States Military Academy and saw the need to train the regimental officers. Shortly after taking command of the regiment, he began classes for officers. Irby Scott remained absent when the first classes began. Because Scott had been a lieutenant for only two weeks before being wounded, officer training benefited him before the coming campaign.

In a letter to his father dated April 21, Scott says that Colonel Willis authorized Lieutenant Marshall to muster Bud Scott into service with Company G, Twelfth Georgia. Irby also told his father how Bud should travel to the army. Franklin, a slave on the Scott plantation, accompanied Bud to the army. Franklin apparently had the family's trust and also permission to earn income outside the plantation. In no time, Irby sent home some of the money Franklin earned using the shaving supplies he brought with him. His May 8 letter survives, providing details on the Chancellorsville campaign.

Petersburg March 8th, 1863, Va

Dear Father & Mother

I arrived here this morning at seven Oclock and will have to remain here until four this evening. I am well, and doing well at the Bollingbrook Hotel.[1] The night after we left you in Madison we remained in Augusta at the Globe Hotel, took the train next morning and traveled straight ahead until last night at Weldon where we missed connection.[2] We have had no accident on our journey, and have procured seats [on] every train except this morning when we slept to late, and had to stand upon the platform, the cars have been crowded from Madison here.[3] We will have to remain in Richmond tonight and take the train for Fredericksburg in the morning and arrive at the Regt tomorrow evening if nothing prevents. I and Ab. have just been down and got our passports for Richmond, where will have to get another. We went to Concert Hall in Augusta and were well entertained until Eleven Oclock.[4] Had an idea provisions would be scarce but I have found plenty all along by paying one dollar & a half per meal. Feel no uneasiness on my account for I know to take care of myself. I thought I would be homesick but I am not a bit of it. My mind often turns back to home and the loved ones there. I feel that I shall return again to that lovely spot (Called home). My love to Mother, Bud and all the children, also my love to all inquiring friends & relations. Remember me especially to Mrs Henry Reids family nothing more at present but remain your affectionate son untill death.

I. Goodwin Scott

Luit Co "G" 12th Ga, Regt

Camped near Fredericksburg Va

March 13th 1863

Dear Father

I arrived here safely on last Monday the 9th Inst. I wrote you from Petersburg which I hope you have received in this. I am well as usual with the exception of a slight cold. I had no difficulty whatever on my journey except having to lay over in Weldon, Petersburg & Richmond missing the connection at each of those places always getting a seat except from Weldon to Petersburg. I got to camp on Monday evening & the next morning we were ordered out on picket about 4 miles from camp where we remained for two days as a reserve to reinforce the pickets if necessary. I was detailed as officer of the guard to listen out for alarms &c. It rained sleeted & snowed the whole of the first day and night and I was compelled to remain out in it all, but stood it finely. I was very much surprised to find the boys fixed up so well they all have small huts or houses and very comfortable at present they all look well and generally are enjoying fine health there are only two or three complaining but none of them sick much. I never saw them look better or in finer spirits. They drew for furloughs this morning. Wm Winchel & James A. Beall are the next to come home provided they will give any more furloughs I hope they will succeed, there is nothing new up here everything quite, the weather is not very cold, it snowed a little this morning and looks as if it may snow more. Our rations are not very large at present, we get the regular allowance of flour, and 1/4 of a pound of bacon per day, no beef though we make out first rate. We have a nice camp, plenty of wood & water and are 4 or 5 miles from the railroad, about 8 miles from Fredericksburg. Suffice it to say we are well situated. I saw Thomas Morton him and Charley are well. Tom looks very well. I went over yesterday and saw Whit Tompkins he is well and has not had the smallpox yet.[5] Having just got here I have not had time to look round much or get my ideas arranged. When I was on picket I could see Fredericksburg very plain & also the yankee pickets, the next time I think I shall carry along some tobacco and swap it off for coffee, though we have some on hand yet. We drill every day, but I don't think we will today as the time for drill has passed. I have nothing more to write at present but will try to keep you posted as to our movements. My best love to mother, Bud and all the family. Also to all inquiring relatives & friends except for yourself a large share. Your son affectionately.

I. Goodwin Scott

P.S. If I had only known it I could have brought a trunk or box without much trouble. If it will not be too much trouble I would like for you to send me a small box through the Ga Relief & hospital association.[6] I want nothing only substantial eatables. I dont think there will be any difficulty in its reaching me.

Direct your letters to me

Near ~~Fredericksburg Va~~

Doles brigade, Rodes division[7]

Jacksons Corps

Near Fredericksburg Va

IGS

Hed Qrs 12th Ga Regt. March 24th 1863

Camped Near Fredericksburg Va

Dear Father

I have written you twice since I left home. I have been in camps over two weeks and have not received a letter. I am looking every day for one. I am very anxious to hear from you all, and hope I will get a letter to day. All the boys are still in bed taking their morning naps. I had to be present at roll call, and report to the Adj. whether all the men were present. Ab. & Charles are busy preparing breakfast and I am in the corner writing. In my mess are Capt Reid, Ab. Zackry, Parson Marshall and J. Adams. We are fixed up very comfortable. Our house (or part house & tent) is built in this order. We began with logs and raised it about four feet high then upon the top of that is stretched our tent, with a splended fire place attached. Now for the inside, there is a bunk large enough [for] five to sleep on. It is built like a scaffold forks are driven into the ground, upon them are placed stout pieces for the bed to rest upon next comes a covering of small poles and they are covered with pine brush upon which is placed a mattress & other bedding. You cannot imagen how well it sleeps. Underneath of the bunk are our trunks, bails & plunder &c. In the opposite corner stands a barrell which makes us a place for water then comes our cooking utensils, crocking ware &c. we are having a good time generally. When I wrote last it was snowing it was about five inches deep but has all disappeared leaving plenty mud in its staid. There is nothing new going on since the fight near Culpeper Court house every thing has been very quiet and will be apt to remain so until the earth drys. The prospect this morning is that we shall have more rain. I drew my pay from the Qr. Master soon after I got here in all amounting to six hundred & forty seven dollars. I expected when I drew [it] to have sent it home by Capt Reid or William Winchell who applied for a furlough a few days after I got into camp, but they have not been heard from. I do not think they can come home at present. I cannot tell how I will send it. I will keep a lookout and send it by the first opportunity that presents itself. My health is good. I have a cold, but I expected nothing else when I came here. The health of the company never was better. I saw Whit Tompkins two days ago he was well but his negro was then sick but was getting better he had a slight attack of pneumonia. Js [James] Ethridge came back a few days ago also T. A. Walker of our company. It is talked and generally believed that Gen Ed. Johnson will take command of this division he has been recommended by Lee & Jackson I hope it may be true.[8] Rodes is not very popular.[9] Col Willis is going to form a class of the officers to study the tactics and recite lessons to him every day.[10] I shall have to study pretty hard but think I can go through. I wrote to Aunt Emily Wright a day or two ago.[11] We get papers and the mail every day. I must close for I have about written out. My warmest love to mother, Bud & all the children, kiss the little ones for me, remember me to all inquiring friends and acquaintances accept a share of love for yourself. I remain your devoted son untill death.

I. Goodwin Scott

To Irby H. Scott

Eatonton Ga

12th Ga. Regt.

Camped near Fredericksburg Va. Apr. 5th 1863

Dear father,

Your letter of the 22d came safely to hand a few days ago and afforded me no little pleasure. I was very anxious to hear from home and than to hear that all were well makes me fell easy and satisfied. I went on picket guard last Monday and remained untill Thursday evening when I returned to camp the next morning. I was officer of the camp guard for one day being in all on duty five days. During this time I received three letters one from cousin Mary Thomason, another from Alex Reid and yours.[12] After getting those letters I came to the conclusion that I was not entirely forgotton. This conclusion I had almost come to not having received a letter since I got back to camp nearly a month since. There is no news of any importance all quite along the Rhapahannoc [Rappahannock] which will apt to be the case untill the snow melts and the ground has time to dry. We had a perfect snow storm last night and part of today. It has snowed about eight inches deep. We had a small snow on last Monday night while I was on picket. I was in sight of the yanks all the time. Only the river between us which is some one hundred to one hundred and fifty yards wide. On one day they had up three balloons.[13] One of them was not more that a mile and half from us. I had a good view of it. I could see the basket, the rope to which it was attached, the telegraph wire and also the men on the ground to manage it. The land being level for some distance on the other side of the river. Some of the boys wanted to see the basket fall with the man in it. Others wanted the rope to break and the wind to blow it over. You can see them up almost any clear day. We can go a quarter of a mile from camp and see over into yankeedom. I mean on the other side of the river. On fast day myself and several officers of my Reg went over to see the battle field near Federicksburg. I went to the palace where our boys charged them in the railroad. You can see now hundreds of old shoes. Shoes that belonged to our men. They leaving them and swaping with the dead yankees, knapsacks, canteens &c which were destroyed. Some places close to the ditch where our men were are all plowed up by cannon balls, trees shattered all to pieces. Besides many marks of muskets and minis. On my way back I got a mess of oysters &c. Fast day was pretty generally observed by the soldiers. It seemed more like Sunday than any day I have ever spent in the war. It was of the prettiest day we had since I have been here. This is a beautiful country and has been in a high state of cultivation. But an army can ruin and tear to pieces any thing that comes in their way. Along the river there are a great many fine residences but a good many are becoming delapidated. The company are generally well with a few exceptions none sick much. In reference to Bud, I wrote him a letter stating my views upon the subject, but if he wishes to come to my company let him come and I will do the best for him I can. If Franklin is willing to come I think he will be better than Tom and be very handy.[14] There is no telling where is the best place for we cannot look into the future. I was glad to hear from my box although I get enough to eat but of such things I do not especially ——— Bacon &c. I shall keep a look out for it at the station. Abner also has one on the road. I have no opportunity to send money home yet, but think I shall send you about five Hundred dollars. Who are the candidates for Governor? I think the soliders ought to be allowed to vote. I heard there was a law allowing it. If such be the case I don't think Brown will stand much chance in the army. Politics are not talked much here. Tell mother those things she spoke of will ——— good I know. As to clothing I have plenty for the present. As much as I can take care of when we leave here on a march. You can have me a coat and pants ready and I will write you when I need them. Bud had better not bring much clothing with him if he comes for he will have to carry them on his back. If you see a good chance you may have me a suit made of Confederate gray cloth (uniform) if the war last cloths will be higher. Also keep a lookout for a hat for me. My old one does fine. I must close for I have written out. When Bud leaves home and Charley gets fat, I think you had better sell him unless you need him yourself.[15] My very best love to mother and all the family. Also to all inquiring friends. Also remember me to the negroes, accept a large share of love for yourself. Let me hear from you at least once a week. I have written oftener than that. Write me soon what Bud will do. Nothing more but remain your affectionate Son

I. Goodwin Scott
I. H. Scott
Putnam Co
    Ga

P.S. April 6th 63

I wrote my letter yesterday but not sending it off and receiving yours of Mch 31st to day I will brake my letter and add a post-script. I was glad to hear from home that all were well and doing well. In reference to Bud I hardly know what to say. The only way or at least the best way for him to do will be to go to Macon and be mustered in before he is eighteen. Then he can draw a bounty of fifty dollars. If he remains untill he is of age he will be conscripted and cannot draw a bounty. There is no telling when Marshall will come on as to a furlough. I don't think he can get one. You had better go with him to Macon and then try for the furlough. I shall need some summer cloths. I would like for you to try and have me a uniform Leit made of gray cloth. I do not want the finest. Send it by Bud if you can get it ready. Nothing more at present. Yours as ever.

    I. G. S

April 8th, 1863
12th Ga Regt. Fredericksburg, Va
Dear Father

As Sid Reids boy, Ab will leave here this morning I have concluded to write you a few lines to let you know that I am well and getting on fine. There is nothing new with us. We heard yesterday that the fight had commenced at Charleston.[16] I hope our troops will give them a good licking. All the boys are well. I wrote two days ago. In that letter I wrote you about every thing. If you get me a suit, do not get the finish goods or have it to light a color. I hardly recon Bud can get in our mess as it is already full. I can get him a good mess I think. Ab will leave this at Mr. Terrell as he will come by Buck Head.[17] I would like to send you some money by him but I am afraid it might be stolen on the way. I will see before he leaves what I will do. Write me soon. Nothing more at present but remain yours affectionately.

I Goodwin Scott

P.S. I have concluded not to send money by Abb[18]

Camped near Fredericksburg Va
April 14th, 1863
Dear Mother

I reckon you think that I do not intend to write to you when I write to any of the family I consider it the same as writing to all. So when I write it is as much to you as if I had written to no one else. This is a lazy day with us. The sun is shining bright and warm and we are excused from all duty untill four oclock this evening when there will be inspection and dress parade. The boys are out just in front of my tent enjoying a game of marbles. Some are brightening up their guns for the approaching inspection. Ab. Zachry is lying just outside of the tent suning himself. Sid Reid is lying upon the bed asleep. The 21st Ga Regt is passing, giving us as good music as can be got out of drums & fife.[19] They have been out drilling. There is not much news for several days past we could hear occasionly [occasionally] the distant boom of cannon. It was currently reported through camps yesterday that the yanks had with drawn their picket lines on the river opposite to where we have to picket but there are plenty of camps and men in sight a short distance on the other side. I cannot imagine what their object is unless they are moving up the river various were the rumors upon the reception of this news. Some said we would cook up rations to day to march, others believe we will soon be on our way towards Richmond & hundreds of conjectures of all manner of shapes, forms & sizes. Sum them up and they all amount to nothing at least for myself I will not be surprised to leave here at any time. It is almost universally thought that there will not be another fight at this place but there is no telling, or looking into the future. If they intend to fight any more, I should like for them to do it here. I am glad that we repulsed them at Charleston.[20] I never feared their whipping us there. Spring has set in and the roads are getting dry. So you may soon hear of some active movements up this way let the yanks come when ever they wish, but we are ready and can thrash them at any time, our army is stronger in better health and spirits than I have ever seen it. Several men have been sentenced to be shot for running out of the Fredericksburg fight. It will have a good effect for it is better to go into the battle and fight taking the chances than to run and be shot certain. The evil of straggling is almost entirely cured if a man straggles he is certain to be court-martialed and punished severely. I recd fathers letter of the 6th and was glad to hear from you all that all were well as for myself I never was in better health and am getting on as well as I could ex-

pect. My wounded leg has improved a great deal since I have been here. It is only at times I am troubled with it and then very little in a month more I dont think I will feel it at all. I was glad to hear that Charlie was sold and am fully satisfied with the price.[21] If it had not been for Bud and he had been in good order I should have tried to have sold him when I was home. Does Bud walk to school? It is well enough for him to walk and be running himself by the time he has to join the Army. How does Stonewall come on?[22] I should like to see him. Is Bob as rude as ever, and Major as good?[23] I reckon he has a good time riding to the office to look for letters. I was sorry to hear of Mr. Mortons continued bad health which I hope will improve as the spring advances. I saw Thomas & Charles two days ago they are in good health and are stout robust looking boys. I have inquired in the 4th Ga Regt and tried to find some of my down the country kin but none of them belong to it.[24] I should like to know what Regt they are in? Tell Bud and Emma, Mollie to write to me. I am anxious to know what he has decided to do. I have in my letters before this given him all the information I can. If I knew whether he had decided to come to my company I could see Col Willis and get him to let ———— Marshall muster him in. Mother I want a suit of cloths which I have written to you about before. I do not want them to fine you can get them either in Atlanta or Macon also the trimmings. I would like for the coat to be cut like Abners double breasted do not have the collar too wide or too long. I want them for summer and fall wear. I see from the signs my coat will soon wear out. Put a black stripe of velvet or something of the kind on the leg of my pants though I don't care much about it. Tell Alfred I arranged for him before I left home in case of my death if he wishes to know tell him if he wants money to draw on father.[25] My love to all the family and all friends & relations. Your devoted son untill death.
I. Goodwin Scott

12th Ga. Regt. April 21st, 1863
Camp Near Fredericksburg Va
Dear Father

Your letter of the 13th came to hand this morning which afforded me no little pleasure to hear that all were well, we have just returned this evening from a tour of picket duty of two days. I must stop writing for some of the officers have just come in to hold an election for Lieutenant in our company a place being vacant on account of Lieut Marshalls resignation. I did not have a chance to finish my letter yesterday evening so this morning I resume the pleasant task. I supose you would like to know the results of the election. Robert Jenkins & Robert Little were the candidates which resulted in Littles election. It seems hard for Bob J. to make a rise he is a gallant soldier and deserves promotion. It was an unexpected thing to the most of us never having dreams of Marshall resigning we had a good deal of fun all day yesterday in teasing the candidates. Calling upon them for speeches, treats, &c. But I guess you had rather hear something else of more importance. I have report all along the Rappahannock quiet. I was upon the river three days in full view of the yankee pickets. Perhaps it may be the calm which precedes the coming storm. It is the opinion of a good many that there is no immediate danger of a fight here. The enemy have sent off a good many of troops to reinforce Rasencsand [Rosecrans] in the west and then our fortifications will keep them in the other side of the river. They dare not cross in the face of them. We have had fine times eating fish lately mostly shad. There a great many caught of different kinds some of our company caught three hundred and eighty at our hole with a small sine. They happen to strike a school of herrings. We are getting on very well especially in the eating line. Mine & Abs boxes are in Richmond, but we cannot get them here yet. The government has the railroad pressed bringing up provisions, ammunition, and forage for horses. I think we will get them shortly. I sent you five hundred dollars by Charlie Wiley who is adjutant of the 44th Ga he started home last Sunday morning he will send it to you by express from Macon.[26] Wiley is a cousin of Sid Reid so you may keep a lookout for it. Col Willis received a letter from Lt. Marshall also a short post & script to me in relation to Bud. Col Willis will send Marshall papers this morning authorizing him to muster Bud in the service get him transportation &c. as to Buds remaining at home after he is mustered you can see Marshall and make arrangements with him to let him stay at home a few days he will have to come and just as well come on at once if he was to stay a month longer when he leaves it will be the same thing. I dont know how he will manage traveling without some one along who could assist him he never having traveled any himself when he gets to Richmond there will be a guard there who will take him to a house called the soldiers home, where he will be kept all night and then be put aboard the cars next morning. Ab. Reid will stay at home about twenty days if Bud could come on as he does he would know how to manage everyway to get along the baggage &c. I cannot get him in my mess yet for we have already too many, but I can make arrangements for him for the present, and then I will see what can be done. Tell him not to bring too many cloths for he will have to carry them on his back. Tell Franklin to get up several good razors, shaving brush &c. if he wants to make a few dimes he can get fifty cts a head for shaving.[27] It will cost Bud about twenty five dollars to bring him here he had best bring provisions enough to last him from home here there are plenty on the road, but not knowing the points he might be troubled. Sometimes where the cars are crowded (as they are sure to be) he had better take Franklin in the car with him, which is often done & his baggage &c. he must keep close watch on all the time he will have to get a passport

at Petersburg to go to Richmond and then one in Richmond to come here (the passport to include him and Franklin both) he will get off the cars at Guinea Station unless we shall move in which event I will try and keep you posted, he can inquire for this Division, brigade, regiment & so on, he will have to have a showing from Marshall who will procure him transportation in Macon. He had best come via of Wilmington if he has much baggage there is always plenty of omnibusses, wagons &c. at all the depots ready. If I were in his place I should not buy any tickets for Franklin but pay his way it will cost no more and save him unnecessary trouble if they are in different coaches he had best give Franklin a little money to pay the conductor, but he can manage this (but lookout not to let both pay) write me as soon as you can when he will leave home the arrangements and so on.[28] In respect to the suit of cloths if you have not received my letter I want a uniform Gray suit not too light colored or fine. Made like Abs. double breasted
[*The remainder of this letter is missing.*]

Camped near Fredericksburg Va, May 8th, 1863
Dear Father,
　　Knowing how uneasy you all are to hear from me I hasten to inform you that I am safe and well. You doubtless have ere this been informed through the papers of the recent fights that have taken place upon the Rhapahannock [Rappahannock] and of our splendid victories.[29] I cannot give you a detailed account of the fight but will endever [endeavor] to give you some idea of it. On the morning of the 29th April we were startled by the roar of cannon and musketry near Fredericksburg.[30] We were immediately under arms and proceeded to the scene of conflict. Owing to the dense fog the yankees had but very little trouble in throwing across their pontoons. This was below Fredericksburg some three miles and about opposite Hamilton's crossing. We were halted at the last named place and were formed in line of battle towards the approach of the enemy but no fighting took place except a little cannonading on both sides. We remained there until the 1st day of May when between midnight and day we were again put on the march up the river having found that the enemy were only making a faint. Proceeding up the river some eight or ten miles we were again thrown into line of battle not doubting but what we would have to work. Again nothing but a little skirmishing. Night came so we bivouacked or camped. Early the next morning we resumed the march making a flank movement and reached the enemys flank about five in the evening of Saturday. Rodes division now ordered to advance and the struggle commenced. We charged the enemy through one of the thickest swamps and woods I ever saw. At last reaching the open field we encountered a battery but still pressing on through musketry, shell and grape shot we soon captured every gun and then came the pursuit which

lasted until dark, we having driven the enemy some two miles getting into dense pine thickets when the brigade was ordered to halt. The old twelfth still kept on and did not stop until they found themselves alone and within two hundred yards of another battery which commenced throwing shell and grape into us. We succeeded in reaching a little hollow where we lay down and protected ourselves as best we could. At last everything becoming quiet, the question now to get back to our own lines, so we started expecting every minute to be fired into by our own men and we could also hear the yanks advancing in our rear. We at last reached our lines in safety in about ten minutes. Owing to the confusion and darkness our own men did fire into each other wounding Stonewall Jackson causing him to have one of his arms amputated and also slightly wounding A. P. Hill.[31] We were fortunate in getting out at the time as no doubt some of us should have been killed. The fight then ceased for the night and we lay down and slept on the battle ground by lines. The next morning (Sunday) our lines were formed and moved forward. We had three lines of battle, ours was the third. During the night the enemy had constructed formidable breast works of logs. From these they were charged and driven by the first line. The second line were ordered on to charge a battery. This they refused to do (South Carolinians at that). Gen. Stewart [Stuart], the cavalry man was then commanding Jacksons corps.[32] We told him we would go and leaping over the breast works and led by Stewart we charged them taking a few broken guns &c and a great many prisoners. Our brigade being about the center of the line, as soon as we charged and broke the center of the yankee line, there was a general stampede on both wings. We continued to advance until we came near another battery and owing to our force being small and no suport [support], believing we were compelled to fall back behind the breast works we had just left. On our way back it seemed that the air was full of shell and grape. Our canon then came up and took position near the yankee works and an artillery duel took place. Our batteries succeeded in silencing their batteries and driving them from the field. This ended the fight of Chancellorsville and our brigade was ordered back to the rear to rest and collect our scattered men. Cannot give you any idea of the scene I saw of mangled bodies, the dead and wounded were lying thick everywhere but from what I saw I think the enemys loss far exceeded ours, say at least four or five to one. I never saw as much plunder in any fight as the yanks threw away coats, blankets, oil cloths, caps, canteens, Havre Sacks &c of which our boys supplied themselves bountifully. A man could have got almost anything he wanted. In the evening we were again ordered to the front where we were again put in order of battle and remained until the next evening. We were then taken out of our entrenchments by the roadside and put upon the left in the woods. We were told that we would have an hour and a half to fortify so at it we went with a will constructing breast works of logs &c including ——— to throw up dirt but about the time we had got up the logs the enemy advanced their skirmishes and drove in ours. We were then certain of a fight but they only wished to see what we were doing. We went to work again and by digging and spading soon had a good breast work thrown up. I was surprised to see them done so soon for it would have taken the same men a week to have done it any other time. Here we remained until Wednesday morning. W. W. Pearman was killed here in a skirmish. They were ordered to advance upon the enemy to see what they were going for the night before we could hear them cutting and driving distinctly. They advanced within two hundred yards of the enemy and were returning when Pearman was shot through the head and died instantly. While we were here it rained a day and night part of the time in torrents but having supplied ourselves with small yankee tents, we managed to keep pretty dry. Our time here and that of the enemy was not more than one half a mile apart. On Wednesday morning our skirmishers were again ordered to advance it being found out that the enemy was crossing the river and pick up all the stragglers who were not a few. About two oclock that evening we were ordered back to our old camp near Guines Station [Guiney's Station].[33] It still continues to rain and our camp being some eighteen or twenty miles off we did not reach it untill ten or eleven oclock that night and some or rather the most of the men came in next day. It was quite dark, raining and the mud in places knee deep. I never have seen but one time before that could come up with it. After getting here we went into our cabin and made a fire, but it was day by the time we had accomplished it. Our camp had been broken up and the waggons ordered off. So yesterday we were busy in putting up tents and getting every thing to right. I never was more tired and sore in my life but feel very well other wise. Last night I got a good nights sleep and rest being the first for nine days and nights. The casualties of our company are not very great considering the fighting we had to do. I will give you a list before I get through writing. I escaped well? Being with the company all the time and did not receive a scratch. ~~when I reached here~~ I felt very thankful to God for preserving my life and by his allowing us to again turn back the invader. I cannot imagine what will be the next move, but think we will remain here some time yet, probably untill the enemy makes some movement, which I do not think they will do in some time. I heard we took eight thousand prisoners. Gen Early fought ——— line but I cannot give you any other particulars of his fight. You will learn in from the papers. The enemy cavalry made a raid nearly to Richmond but did not do much damage. I see from the papers that Gen Forrest took sixteen hundred cavalry prisoners near Rome, Ga. I must close for this time and write again in a few days. I have never got my box yet. Capt Green went to Richmond and he says they were not there.[34]

I hope they will turn up soon. I received your letter of the 27th Apr. George Cochran is dead, he was sent to some Hospital sick and died.[35] I learned this from the officer of his company. When will Bud come on? I am anxious to know what arrangements you and Marshall made about his remaining a short time at home. I like the sample you sent of my shirt. I am afraid it is most to fine for me to ruin here in the war. I was gald the money came to hand so soon, but I knew it would be all right for Wiley is a clever man.[36] Nothing more at present. My warmest love to mother Bud and all the children, also all the negroes and especially to all friends. Accept a large share of love for yourself. Your most affectionate Son.

Irby G. Scott

List of Kill & wounded[37]

Wm Pearman killed

James Bullard leg cut off

Robert Young shoulder slight

Frank Maddox foot slight

McLeroy bruised slight

F Suther slight

———— Slight

C Batchelor

S Batchelor finger off

James Davis arm slight

The killed and wounded in the Regt   80 in number

P.S. I thought I would give you the outlines of the battlefield but have missed it. I don't think you can understand from my drawing but if I can I will draw another of the part of the field I was on and enclose in this. Whit Tompkins, Thomas & Charlie Morton were not hurt. Whit is now a lieutenant in his company. IGS

[Included on this letter is a rough outline of the battlefield.]

12th Ga Regt May 12th 1863

Near Fredericksburg Virginia

Dear Mother

I know you are always anxious to hear from me and more especially at this time. I hope you have received my letter ere this and have been relieved from an awfull suspense by hearing of my safety and good health. Through the protection of divine providence I escaped without injury where it seemed the missiles of death none could escape. Our loss was severe but nothing to compare with that of the enemy. A great many who were upon the battle field say that proportion is five to one. I do not think it is quite so large. I have been a little sick for several days past but have about entirely recovered. It was nothing more than the effects of cold and exposure. Everything has been remarkably quiet since the fight. Nothing of interest has occurred. There was a report in camp a day or two ago that the enemy were crossing the river about forty miles below here but it has all died out. Yesterday we received orders to cook two days rations and there is now a rumor that we will move camps or are expecting orders to march, where I have no idea. I hope they will allow us to remain here a short time. If we move I think it will only be to move our camps to some unprotected place along the river for I hardly think Lee will attempt to cross and Hooker cannot in some time. You no doubt learned from the newspapers of the death of Gen. Jackson. It is a serious loss to our cause and has cast a gloom upon the army especially his old troops who have followed him through so many trying places. Longstreet with his corps have arrived.[38] If he had been here during the fight our victory would have been greater and more decisive. I see our loss estimated at about eight or nine thousand and that of the enemy twenty to twenty five thousand. The weather is very warm here at this time and I never saw vegetation spring faster. The woods are almost green. Two weeks ago there was not a leaf to be seen and now they are half grown. Wheat is looking well. I received fathers letter yesterday and truly glad to hear you were all well and doing so well. How my mouth watered for some of those strawberries, milk & butter. If I could come home now I expect that I would eat, drink and get fat. But it is of no use thinking of such a thing unless I should be so unfortunate as to get wounded, if the wound was slight and get a furlough I should consider myself fortunate but then I should not like to take the chances for it is as easy to get a severe one as a slight. Therefore I would prefer not to have one of any kind. Father wrote that Lt Marshall had resigned. This we know and the vacancy has already been filled. Robert Little was elected. He also stated that Lt Marshall had not heard from Col. Willis in relation to mustering Bud in. Col Willis sent them some time ago and they ought to have come to hand long since. I hope they will get there soon so you will not be troubled with the conscript officers. Bud could be mustered in at Macon or Augusta and get transportation. But keep him at home as long as you can. I have never heard a word from my box. We heard they were in Richmond and have tried to get them here but have failed. I have given up all idea of ever seeing them. Capt. Reid sent up an application for a few days leave of absence to go to Richmond but I dont think it will be granted. Ab Reid got back from home on last Sunday.[39] From what he told us, while we were marching and fighting there was a May ——— in Eatonton. Dancing and enjoying themselves but this I do not think this any time for such things as dancing &c. They certainly cannot have much sympathy for the poor soldiers who while they are at the height of enjoyment is then upon the battlefield sacrificing their lives for the liberty of these very people. No doubt these were young men there who should have been here assisting and bearing their portion of the burdens of this war. I do not like to hear of such things and yet I dont know that I ought to have written a word about it. I should not be surprised if some of them felt bad when they knew that while they were dancing probably some of their near relations and friends was then upon the battlefield dying, but enough of this. Mother if you get this letter before Bud leaves you may send me a few pr. of cotton socks that with my suit is all I will need for the present. Buds having to come to the army troubles me no little. I would be willing if it could be so to serve for myself and him too. If he was here and we were to go into a fight I would feel miserable for fear he would be killed or wounded. If he were wounded there would be no chance for me to remain and attend to him. He like all the rest will have to take the chances. Do not let him bring too many clothes for there are no wagons to carry such things now. They are taken upon the shoulder. I was glad to hear that Mr. Mortons health was improving and hope it may continue to improve until he is fully restored to health. Give my best respects to his family. Tom & Charles were well a day or two ago. I have about written all I can think of now. Tell Bobbie to eat some strawberries for me. What is the reason Emma & Mollie does not write to me. Sometimes I see nothing to prevent them. They are certainly not so busy working that they cannot take time to write once and awhile. Give my love to all inquiring friends & relations. Remember me to Alfred and all the negroes. Mother I think of you all very often and sometimes dream of being at home but do not infer from what I have written that I am desponding for such is not the case. I have a strong hope of surviving this war and of returning home again but these hopes may all be blasted. None but God knows. I received a letter from Cousin Mary Thomason a few days since. They are all well. She wrote me about Uncle Lees ——— family having the small pox. Accept now the love of your devoted son for yourself and all the rest of the family. Yours affectionately. I. Goodwin Scott.

P.S. Capt. Reids leave to go to Richmond has come back approved. He will look up our boxes.

12th Ga Regt. May 16, 1863

Dear Father

As I have an opportunity of sending you a letter by hand I will avail myself of the chance to inform you that I am not exactly well yet. Since our return to this camp from our recent exploits I have had the diarhea [diarrhea] and pretty bad too. My box and Abners came to hand last night all right. Dr. Etheridge says I must eat light but I could not make any promises on that score for to just peep into one of the boxes to make him feel like eating and I am going to eat (moderately though). I am not sick much now except a little home sick just now caused by some of the boys getting substitutes and

going home. William Paschal and Tom Pearsons substitutes have been received and are now performing duty. Paschal leaves for home this morning.
Pearson will stay a few days. Dr. Phillips [Philips] from Putnam is also here
with a substitute for Terry Dismukes, but he has not been accepted as yet.[40]
Col Willis is not exactly satisfied with his recommendations and has telegraphed to Savannah to some one to find out more of him. I reckon he will
be accepted, has been already by all except Col. Willis. It makes me feel bad
to see our boys leaving and putting in their places men we know nothing
of. Then we cannot but compare their present situation with our own. They
are free to go where they please and do as they please. The rest of us are still
bound fast and have not the knowledge that we will ever be free again. But
I intend to live in hope if I die in despair. I have a couple of over shirts and
my over coat which I shall try to send home by Paschal or Pearson. I drew
$160.00 yesterday from the government. I have now on hand about three
hundred dollars and some little owing to me. I could send you some but
will hold on until I get some more. When Bud comes on, if you should not
have plenty of money, just give him enough to bring him here, and then I
can supply him with as much as he wants or needs. Father there is no news
with us, not even a rumor today. I think now that we will remain here a
short time. I do dread the marching and fighting this summer but it will do
no good to be dreading for there is no other way but to go right ahead. Buds
coming troubles me. I am troubled much more on his account that on my
own for I would willingly serve for him and myself too if it could be so. If
it was not on his account and holding the position that I do, I would make
an effort to get a substitute or some position where I could be stationary.
But in condition it would not be an easy matter to do either. An officer can
hardly get his resignation accepted except upon a surgeons certificate. I am
anxious about Bud, to know when he will get here and all about everything
concerning him. I have given vent to my feelings pretty freely this morning. Several things set me to thinking. 1st these boys getting substitutes and
going home and from what Tom Pearson told me, while the young people of
Eatonton were dancing on Saturday night we were at that very time under
severe cannonading. Just make a comparison between the two parties. They
are quite a sympathetic set. You can say to them that our ball was larger,
more magnificent and ended more gloriously than theirs. I must close for
Paschal is nearly ready to leave for the depot. Dont think I am sick much or
low spirited. I will be certain to let you know when such is the case. Give my
warmest and best love to Mother, Bud, Emma, Mollie and all the rest of the
children. Kiss the little ones for twice. Tell Alfred I am getting on quite well
at present. Show him as much indulgence as you can consistent with your
own interest always in view that is firm. Do yourself justice and then allow
him as good a chance as possible for I think a great deal of him. My love to

all inquiring relations and friends Accept now my best wishes for your own and the whole familys wellfare. Also my love until death.

I Goodwin Scott

P.S. Write me soon about everything in general and especially about Bud. Yours &c I. G. Scott

12th Ga Regt. Near Fredericksburg Virginia
May 19, 1863

Dear Father,

Thomas Pearson leaves here tomorrow for home. Whenever an opportunity of this kind presents itself, I never feel right unless I write, if it is only a few lines, for I know you always expect a letter. When any one comes from home here I always feel disappointed if I do not get one from you. I am particularly anxious to hear from home at this time. I received one letter from you since we came back to our old camps. I want to hear when Bud is coming. I want him to stay at home as long as he can but somehow I cannot but feel great anxiety on his account. There are now two substitutes in our company, Paschall and Pearson's. Dr. Phillips [Philips] is here now with one for Terry Dismukes but Col. Willis not being exactly satisfied with his character has telegraphed to Savanah for recommendations. I supose [suppose] we will know by tomorrow whether he will be received or not. It seems that Terry has bad luck for this is the third substitute he has tried. He wants to get off so bad. I hope that he will be meet with success this time. There has been a recent order issued by Gen. Lee requiring the substitute to be equal phisically [physically] and morrally [morally] to the man he substitutes for. None are taken unless they are well recommended. There is not much news afloat with us. Capt. Reid got back from Richmond this morning. He says that D. H. Hills Division is coming up here. Some came up on the train to day. Longstreet Corps is already here. There was a rumor in camps several days since that all the most distinguished Generals were in Richmond in consultation with the President. I dont know whether this is true or not, but if true and with all these reinforcements coming up here, something important is on foot.[41] I should not be surprised if we cross the river or flank these Yankies some way and send them howling back to Washington but this is all mere speculation on my part. I dont care about crossing the river much for I know there will be hot times. The Yanks will fight better over there than they will on this side for when they come over here they expect nothing short of a good thrashing and havent failed of getting that very thing whenever they have come so far. On yesterday there was a Division review. It was a grand sight. To stand and look upon eight or ten thousand men in an open level field, all maneuvering at the same time, bands playing and drums beating. I mentioned in the letter I wrote and sent you by William Paschall of receiving my box, Abners also. It was a great treat and we who have nothing to eat but meat and bread know how to appreciate such things. The Butter was a little rancid but not enough to hurt it much. The lard had melted and a little wasted. I have taken it out of the box and put some in a tin can. The rest in a jug. I broke off the mouth of the jug so as to make kind of a jar. I have not been able to do the good things from home justice. I have been on the sick list nearly ever since the fight. My stomach and bowels being disordered. I have been compelled to live as light as possible. At first I did not have any appetite to eat and what little I did eat generally made me sick. I am still on the sick list but if I feel as well tomorrow as I have today I shall report for duty. I am not exactly well yet and am weak. I have never taken my bed but have kept stirring around camps all the while. In a few days more should I continue to improve, I shall be all right. I hope we will not have to move until we can eat up our supply of provisions on hand. You will please accept my best thanks for yourself and mother for your trouble in fixing up and sending to me the box of nicities and goodies from home. We have stop drawing from the commissary except flour which will reduce our bills somewhat this month which is generally between fifteen and twenty dollars per month. The health of the company is pretty good. Some few complaining but none sick much. There has been several citizens here from Georgia since the fight. Among the number Mr. Malone and Furlow from Sumter who both have sons in the 4th Ga Regiment.[42] Mr. Yancy from Putnam, Dr. Phillips and Dr. Horne is in Richmond.[43] He came on after James Bullard but the Government was sending troops over the road so he could not come on. James Bullard had one of his legs amputated but is doing well. I understand they are transferring our wounded to hospitals in Georgia. If I were wounded and could not get a furlough I would prefer being in a hospital in Georgia for there would be some chance to get from there home, if not—relations and friends could visit me without much trouble. I must quit writing for tonight and finish in the morning. I am afraid this will be a very uninteresting letter for I have nothing of interest to write about but I always like to fill out the whole of a sheet for this paper I am writing on cost only four dollars a guiro. We have now a suttler in our regiment. Suttlers can make any quantity of money while an army is in camps for they can get almost any price for anything to have they sell.

May 20th, 1863. I feel very well this morning and have reported for duty. There is nothing new today that I have heard of. Tom Pearson has concluded to remain over until tomorrow and wait for Dr. Phillips. I heard from James Bullard on yesterday evening. He is doing well but the surgeon does not think it advisable for him to be moved yet. If he were moved and the large arteries should happen to break loose, he would most likely bleed to death. I am sorry he lost his leg for he was a good soldier and a brave boy. We hear here

that Flournoy Adams is about to get the appointment of Adjutant in some Ga. Regt.[44] The weather is fine though pretty warm in the day. The nights are cool and we can sleep under three blankets comfortably. The woods are perfectly green and the fields are full of grass. Our horses are beginning to improve in looks. Some of them have been very poor all winter. I should like so much if it could be so that I could be at home this summer to enjoy eating some of the nice fruit and vegetables you will have. While I was sick and could not eat any scarcely, I often thought of the tempting strawberries you mentioned in your letter but its no use thinking of things that are almost an impossibility. I want to see you all as bad as I have since I have been in service. I often see you all in my imagination. Write me soon and often. I am rather expecting a letter from you today for it is about time one was coming to hand. My love to all inquiring friends and relations. Remember me to the negroes. Accept my best love for all of you. Yours affect. I Goodwin Scott.
PS: Longstreets Corps I hear since writing is up beyond Gordonsville near the Rapidan river. Kiss little Stonewall Scott for me. What have you named him or are you never going to give him or wait and let him name himself. I supose [suppose] he will always be called Stonewall anyway. Tell Tuck, Fannie and Bobbie not to feel slighted for you may kiss them too.

May 21st 1863

Dear Father. I wrote Tuesday, Wednesday and am writing again this morning. Nothing new at all to day. Colquitt's Brigade of our division composed of the 6th, 19th, 27th, 28th, 23rd Georgia Regiments are transferred from here to North Carolina.[45] There has been a brigade already sent here to take their place. There will some of them leave today. I understand D. H. Hill has sent up for three Ga. Brigades. Who can tell but what ours may be one. I do not care about going much though I have never felt that we will go yet. I feel very well today though still a little puny. I shall send my overcoat by Tom Pearson with directions to leave it at Harwells Store in Eatonton and you can get it from there. If I were to keep it here it would certain to be lost. Dismuke has not heard from his dispatch to Savannah yet. There was no mail on yesterday it going on to Hamiltons Crossing.[46] Dr. Phillips [Philips] will leave today with Pearson. Nothing more at present. I will close hoping this letter may find you all in health. Now as always accept my love for yourself and all the family. I remain yours affectionately until death.
I. Goodwin Scott

Write me soon and give me all the news &c about everything that is going on at home and around there, how your crops look, garden, what Major and Bobie are doing. Yours as ever.
I. G. Scott

12th Ga Regt. Near Fredericksburg, Virginia
May 23, 1863

Dear Father,

I am here in camp almost alone for the Brigade is off on piket at the river, and has been since yesterday morning. They will remain five days. I was left here on duty to take charge of the camp. I have a guard and besides there are a good many sick here. But it seems very lonely and the weather is so warm. There is not much shade the growth being mostly pine which does not make much shade. There is a Hickory tree near my tent under which I am now sitting. My health is not good at present nor has it been since the fight although I am still doing duty. My stomach is out of order and does not digest food properly. I cannot eat much for fear of its making me sick. This is the reason of my being left here in camps. I should have prefered to have gone with the regiment for it is much pleasanter there than here but it is a long and warm walk which I did not care about taking. The duties here are very light. It is a hard matter when a man gets sick in camps for him to get well. It takes some time. I am very anxious to hear from home. I have received but one letter from you since the fight dated I believe 3rd May. I have come to the conclusion that Bud must be on the way and you have waited to write by him. I have nothing new to write. There was about a dozen cannon fired today somewhere below here on the river. I have not learned the cause. I saw a news paper which a Yankee swam across the river with on yesterday and gave to one of our boys. It was Frank Laslic [Leslie's] New York Journal.[47] It contained several pictures among the rest, the fight at Chancellorsville where it says Hooker repulsed the rebels. The Yanks and our men go into the river bathing together, exchange papers, swap tobacco for coffee &c. I sent my over coat and a finger ring home by Tom Pearson and instructed him to leave them in Eatonton at Harwells Store. You can get them from there and take them home. I tried to buy a nice Pistol to send home but could not get the man to let me have it. It was captured from the enemy. If I had known that the fight would have ended so soon I would have picked many little tricks and some that were nice to have sent home. But I never dreamed of coming back to our old camps again. Dr. Horne left here yesterday to visit Bullard at the hospital near Chancellorsville some seventy miles distant. He does not think of taking him home yet for he is doing well. We sent him some ham, tobacco, &c. Colquitt's Brigade has gone to N. Carolina but I dont hear anything about our going. I dont want to go either. Write to me soon. If you knew how anxious I am to hear, you certainly would. You must excuse the brevity of this epistle for I have nothing to write about and dont feel like writing if I had. If I should continue long in my present condition I shall make an effort to get off to some private house where I can get well. Such things as furloughs are played out up this way but I hope soon to be well. If I should happen to get sick much I will let you know immediately. Remember me to all friends and the negroes. I hope these lines may find you all well. Accept now my best wishes for your welfare and the welfare of the whole family. Your truly affectionate son until death.

I. Goodwin Scott

Camp 12th Ga Regt. Near Fredericksburg, Va.
May 30th 1863

Dear Father,

I feel like writing this morning though nothing special or of interest to communicate. To day is Saturday and I will not have an opportunity to mail my letter before Monday but I will write any how and have it ready. There will be an inspection this morning at 8 Oclock. Yesterday Rodes Division was reviewed by Gen. Lee which occupied the most of the day. There was quite a number of distinguished Generals present. Among the number Gens Lee, Longstreet, A. P. Hill, Early, Ed. Johnson, Rodes and others of less note. Every thing passed off nicely though very fatiguing to the men having to remain in the hot sun so long and do a good deal of marching. Gen. Johnson came around to see us. Told us all howdy and expressed great pleasure in meeting us again. Said he had always heard good accounts of us from every battle field. He said that we still looked rugged and had two or three good campaigns in us yet, that he was proud to once have commanded us and had hoped to have commanded us again, that he had not seen much said of us in the papers but found we were well known in the army and by all the Generals, and then finished by saying he thought a rain would help us—it being dry and dusty. He now commands Jacksons old Division. It is said that Gen. Ewell will be our Lt. General. I received your letters of the 20th and 22nd of this month which I assure was a great relief and also a great pleasure to hear that all were well but was truly sorry to hear of Mr. Mortons low state of health. From what you write I am afraid ere this that he is dead but I hope he may be spared for the sake of his family. His loss would be keenly felt by the community in which he resides. I am very anxious to hear from him. Charles and Thomas seem to be much distressed. They have not got any letters from home recently but heard some way that he was dead before I received your letter which I read to them. Will the family brake up if he dies? Write me all about things. I suppose you would like to know something of my health. When I wrote you last I was sick. I am now well with the exception of being a little weak and am somewhat reduced in flesh. You spoke in your letter of wishing that you had sent me a bottle of wine or Brandy. I would have given a good deal for some of either at that time but it is an article not to be had in this region. About tomorrow or next day I reckon Bud will leave home. I shall keep a lookout for him. I have arranged for him in a mess with William Winchel, Andrew Gorley and Zack Johnson, all good, easy, clever boys.[48] I will give you an idea of how I will arrange things. I will let the boys pay an equal portion of Franklins time and then I will take that and pay for the negroes which wait on me. This is the best arrangement that can be made under the circumstances as it is impossible for Bud to get in our mess at present but I will keep my eyes open. We have already two negroes in my mess which is plenty. Franklin can still do any little thing I may want. I am glad Flournoy Adams is coming on with him for I was a little uneasy as to how he would get along never having traveled any. As to mustering him in for the unexpired term of this Regt. I guess there will be no difficulty. We are all in for the war any way unless we are shot out of it and if you are not shot bad, you then stand a poor chance for instead of discharing, they send a great many to the hospitals as nurses. The news from Vicksburg for the past few days is a little encouraging but I am still uneasy and do not think we are out of the woods there yet.[49] There is nothing new upon the Rappahannock. The report that Lee intends crossing the river has about died out. I cant tell but should not be surprised if he made a move in some direction before long. I heard yesterday that Ewell would take us up the valley. This is merely one of the many rumors about camp. I supose [suppose] Tom Pearson has reached home by this time. I wrote you about him. Sending also my overcoat and ring by him. I wrote again the other day by Dr. Horne and have sent several by mail. So I dont think you can complain of my not writing. The boys are always after me about writing so much. I wrote to Aunt Catherine and Emily a few days since.

May 31st. I did not finish my letter on yesterday as I could not sent it off before tomorrow morning. We received orders last night to hold ourselves in readiness and if we heard three signal guns to march immediately to Grace Church, the head quarters of Gen. Rodes.[50] It is said that the enemy are moving but in what direction I do not know. It is thought by some they are falling back to Washington in order to send reinforcements out west. I do not believe this. Others think they will move round to the Paninsula [Peninsula]. There are various opinions about their movements. I dont think we can lay here much longer as we are. Everything is very quiet this morning and this like other orders may turn out unnecessary. I hope so at least. Today is Sunday and we shall have preaching. I see the candidates for Governor of Georgia are beginning to work the mines. Yesterday we received some documents from Governor Brown. I believe he had them sent to every company in the Regiment. There is in it an extract from the Confederate Union showing how much he has done, what a good friend he is to the Soldier, also his message to the legislature recommending the passage of resolutions asking congress to increase the Soldiers pay. I had just as soon for him to come right out and asked me for my vote. I dont know that we will be allowed to vote at all. The Virginia troops all voted. Write me who are the candidates and who is the most prominent. Also your views upon the subject. I think Brown has had it long enough and ought not to be so greedy. The boys are all well and doing finely. I want to see you all very much but have no idea when I shall have that pleasure. I can only hope that it may not be long. My love to all relations and inquiring friends. How does Stonewall come on? I should like to see him about now. Remember me to all the negroes and accept my best wishes and love for yourself and the whole family. I remain your devoted son until death. Affectionately,

I. Goodwin Scott

P.S. Have you ever had my old boots fixed up? If not have it done. Also keep a lookout for leather for me a new pair. If you can get my measure I prefer Nigle of Eatonton to make them.[51]

Chapter 9

Second Northern Campaign

*" . . . have escaped thus far unhurt through the protection
of a divine providence."*

*Learning on June 2, 1863, that Federal forces stationed on the Peninsula
had moved northward, General Robert E. Lee began to move his army
from the Fredericksburg front in a westward direction. He did not wish to
fight in the ravaged counties of northern Virginia or close to Washington,
where the enemy could retreat into the defenses of the city. If he marched
north, Lee reasoned, he could provision his army from north of the Potomac River. Drawing the Federal army after him, he would clear Virginia
of Federal troops, possibly force Federal troops to be withdrawn from
other fronts, and fight the next battle on ground of his choosing.*

*Rodes's division received orders to advance on June 3, placing his
division in motion on the morning of June 4 toward Culpepper Court
House. During a rest stop on June 7, Irby Scott penned his first letter to his
father since being camped near Fredericksburg. Scott had suffered from
sore feet during the march, possibly because he brought from home a new
pair of shoes when he returned to the army after his wounded furlough.
In his letters of July 8 and July 16, Scott continues to address the worn-out
condition of his shoes from the recent northern campaign.*

*Nicholas Ewing "Bud" Scott, younger brother of Irby, enlisted on
June 1, 1863, in Company G, Twelfth Georgia. It does not appear he departed Putnam County on his enlistment date to join the army located at
Fredericksburg. Irby knew his brother would enlist in early June, and he
expressed much concern in his letters through May. Irby was also afraid
that, if the army left Fredericksburg, Bud would have to march after the
army. Bud and the slave Franklin reached the army without incident.
Franklin may have remained on the south bank of the Potomac River
while Irby and Bud crossed into Maryland.*

*About 1 p.m. on Wednesday, July 1, after what is reported as an "an
extremely fatiguing and rapid march . . . ," Colonel Edward Willis of the*

Twelfth Georgia formed his regiment in line of battle in a wheat field on the right side of the Middletown Road, one and one-fourth miles north of Gettysburg, Pennsylvania. The Twelfth Georgia was on the extreme left of Doles's brigade, which sat on the left flank of Rodes's division. Doles's brigade was in a position to attack the Federal right flank and rear. Rodes "trusted to his gallant brigade," Doles's brigade, to hold the Federal right until General Early's division arrived. When relieved by Early's division, Doles, without orders, attacked the Federal force in his front. The Twelfth Georgia followed the retreating Federals through the town of Gettysburg, halting on the southern edge.

On July 2, the Twelfth Georgia remained on Middle Street in the town of Gettysburg, skirmishers thrown out to their front. Nothing transpired except occasional skirmishing and annoyance from sharpshooters. Irby Scott missed the fight on July 1, joining the command sometime on July 2. Except for July 1, the Twelfth Georgia saw limited service during the Battle of Gettysburg. While lying in line of battle on July 3, General Doles requested assistance from batteries on the road leading from Gettysburg to Fairfield, to dislodge Federal sharpshooters in houses on his front. Scott details the effects of friendly cannon fire on his company when some of the shells burst in their lines.

Scott penned his July 8 letter to his father while camped in Hagerstown, Maryland, stating that he and Bud escaped unhurt. Irby briefly chronicles the activities of the regiment during and after the Battle of Gettysburg. Bud earned the respect of his older brother and undoubtedly the rest of the company by his conduct during the campaign.

Once on the south bank of the Potomac River, Scott wrote from Darkesville, Virginia. In this letter, he gives additional details of the army's retreat to the south bank of the Potomac. While crossing the river, many lost their shoes in the mud of the canal, the river, and the south bank of the river. Irby and Bud did not lose their shoes in the mud, but both were dirty and in need of clean clothes. Irby Scott and the men were able to rest and regain their strength at Darkesville. On July 22, the men resumed the march up the valley, and with the skirmish on July 23 ended the second northern campaign.

Richmond June 5th, 1863

Dear Father,

I arrived here this evening about 6 o'clock. I should have written to you before now but did not have the chance. I did not miss connection between here and home. This is the first time I have had today ever since I left home. I will leave tomorrow morning about 6 o'clock for Gordonsville. The army has moved from where it was when I left home. It is rumored here that

Gen Lee is crossing the Rappahannock. I saw a gentleman who came down from Gordonsville today. He told me that Rhodes [Rodes] Division was marching towards Gordonsville. I am in hopes that I will over take them at Gordonsville. I have got my passport and transportation tickets ready for tomorrow. I got here safe and am well. I must close as it is late. Your most affectionate son until death. N. E. Scott

PS: Franklin says give his love to all the negros and his wife. Franklin seems to be very well satisfied. N.E.S.

I am staying tonight at the Spotswood Hotel. Capt. Fitchpatrick and Charly Harris will go up to Gordonsville to find their Regiment so we will be together that far.[1] I must close. Give to all the family and inquiring friends. Your son until death.

Richmond June 6th, 1863

Dear Father.

I arrived here safe yesterday evening. I wrote you a letter last night stating that I would leave for Gordonsville this morning but I could not leave. The train that I expected to leave on was press to carry soldiers up to Fredricksburg [Fredericksburg]. I will try again in the morning but I am afraid that the train will be pressed again. They would let no one go on the train but the regiment they were carrying on. There is a regiment of soldiers just came into the city from towards Petersburg. It is rumored here that the fight is going on at Fredricksburg. My regiment has moved from where it was. I went to the intelligence office. They told me they were near Gordonsville. Charley Harris division is at Fredricksburg. He and Capt Fitchpatrick will go on up to Gordonville [Gordonsville] together in the morning. There is a great many troops going on up to Fredricks [Fredericksburg]. I had no difficulty in getting this far. I met connection on every road. I dont think I was off the cars more than five hours from home here. Having to lay over to day I will get rested though I wasent [wasn't] tired much when I got here. Franklin seems to be enjoying himself very much. I gave him a pass today and think he went nearly all over the city. Must close as it is late. I remain your most affectionate son until death. N. E. Scott

Ten miles Culpeper Court House
June 7th, 1863

Dear Father

I wrote you last from our old camps near Fredericksburg, we are now some distance from there. We commenced the march last Thursday morning going almost direct to Orange Court House. Crossing the Rapidan at the same place we did last summer when we went to Manassas & Maryland we have marched three days, resting yesterday, last night rumors reached that a portion of the enemy crossed the river near Fredericksburg and were driven back across the river again it is said that was the reason of our stopping yesterday.[2] We are now on the direct road to Culpeper and I heard this morning that we would go there tonight. I have no idea where we are going to. I think it is a flank movement it may be the enemy are changing their base of operations higher up the river. Time will soon reveal all. I have suffered a good deal with sore feet and the heat has been intense. My health is very good. I am a little uneasy about Bud, for fear he may come up to Fredericksburg and have to march all around after us he could go back and around on the railroad to Culpeper if he stays at home a while longer he will strike it right to miss this trip and fight. We have just stopped to rest a while we rest ten minutes in an hour. It rained last night and to day it is cooler and we have no dust. My love to all the family and all friends, if I have time I will write more your affectionate son

I. G. Scott

P.S. the boys are all well and getting on pretty well. I have just learned that Longstreets Corps is ahead of us and have crossed the Rappahannock.[3] When you have me a pair of boots or shoes made I want them full nines the shoes I have are too short to march in. I will write again as soon as possible. Love to all.

Yours as ever untill death

    IGS

Camp Near Martins Post—Maryland
United States   June 17th 1863
Dear Father,

    I reckon you will be a little surprised when you receive this letter and find I am in Maryland. Getting there you may say almost without a fight of any consequence. I wrote you last from Culpeper Court House. I supose [suppose] you have seen an account of the Cavalry fight there.[4] Rhodes [Rodes] Division was ordered to suport [support] Stewart [Stuart] and we reached the field in time to see the fight close. My Regt were down in sight of the river when they crossed but none of the infantry were engaged. We remained there a day or two when we again took up the line of march via Front Royal, from there to ——— little town Milwood. Run the enemy from Berryville, then from Bunker hill and again from Martinsburg crossing the river here about dark on the 13th inst. We did not capture many of the enemy but captured all their artillery at Martinsburg. Not a man in our Regt hurt up to this time. While we were doing this Ewell with Johnsons and Early's Division was hammering away on Millroy [Milroy] at Winchester.[5] I have not learned the particulars of their fight but hear they took every thing and that Millroy [Milroy] escaped with fifteen hundred men. We have just come in from picket and learn we will march from here in the morning, that all our baggage wagons will be sent back to Winchester which indicates we will penetrate farther into the United States but have no idea in what direction we will move, but should not be surprised if something should turn up in a few days. My own health and Buds is very good. Bud has stood the march very well yet sometimes he would get a little ———— about their marching so hard.[6] We have had to wade all the rivers on our march. My feet have been very sore but have got better. Franklin is well and stands it finely. Him and Bud are in a mess with Gorley Winchel and Johnson. He has been with my mess until today. While we were at Culpepper we thought that we would have a brush with the enemy. Bud wanted a gun and has been in ranks ever since. I think we will get along well. I have been treated well since I have been across the river. Quite a difference between the looks of things here and in Virginia. These people do not feel the effects of war much. I must close my hurriedly written letter. When I have the time I will write more of everything. Accept for yourself and all the family my own & Buds best love through life. Your affec. Son.

    I. Goodwin Scott

Franklin dispatch to his wife.

    Dear Fanny. I am in Maryland. I am not out of heart of seeing you again. My love for you is strong. Take care of my children, and kiss them both for me. I have been marching nine days and have got on finely and my health is better than it was when I left home. Remember to give my love to Alfred and all the rest of my fellow servants and all the family. I should like to see them all. I have not made much money only about seventeen dollars. When there is more time I will write again.[7] Accept my love for yourself and my children.

    Your affectionate husband. Franklin Scott.

P.S. We are at Williamsport instead of Martins Port Maryland. Kiss the little Buds & sisters for me.

Hagerstown Maryland July 8th 1863
Dear Father

    It is with pleasure I hail another opportunity of communicating to you of my own and [B]ud's safety both of us have escaped thus far unhurt through the protection of a divine providence. You see from the heading of my letter that we have fallen back reaching this place on yesterday evening. I wrote you a letter from Carlisle Penn. from which place we turned back rather in the direction of Baltimore and met the enemy at a small place called Gettysburg where we had a desperate fight of three days duration.[8] I was not in the first days fight which was opened by our division and resulted in a complete victory taking possession of the town and driving the enemy a considerable distance. I was behind sick in an ambulance. Bud went through and came out safe. I joined them the second day when just at dark we were ordered to charge some batteries and approached to within one hundred yards of the enemys line of battle when the order was countermanded. They were situated upon two high hills and both well fortified, we then fell back and threw up earth works about half way between ours and the enemys Guns, we nearly encircled the yanks and charges were made from two sides our men took their Guns, but were compelled to abandon them and fall back.[9] On the third day another attempt was made we opened one hundred pieces cannon on them, to which they replied with a considerable number. It was as if the whole element was bursting up, as I said just now we were about middle way between our guns & the enemys every shell passing over our line there were several which was shot from our guns which burst in our own lines one struck and bursted in my company tearing off William Winchells arm, which has since been amputated at the shoulder joint also burning and bruising Henry Marshall and Wm Waller there was an incessant picket fire all the time a great many of the enemys balls coming over us in our ditches, wound some few.[10] The third night we fell back a short distance to a range of hills trying to draw the enemy out, but they would not come.[11] That night we commenced our retreat, and have since found out that the enemy were retreating at the same time.[12] We crossed the mountain and arrived here yesterday evening there were a few yankee cavalry who followed us to this side of the mountain. The enemy admit a loss of twenty thousand, ours was considerable, all of ten or fifteen thousand. I saw nearly five thousand prisoners we had taken in one squad in the first days fight our division is said to have taken about eight or nine thousand. You must be satisfied with this description of our campaign so far. We had only two men wounded the first day James A. Beall shot through the pelvis died two days afterwards Andrew Gorley, severely shot through the hip with a grape shot was getting on well where we left, Gorley and Winchell were both left. Waller and Marshall I suppose have probable gone back with the rest of the wounded. Bud has kept well so far and stands it like a man. My own health has been bad up to this time, but I have managed to get on pretty well so far. Thomas and Charles Morton are both wounded. Charlie has a flesh wound through the thigh Tom I think in the arm. Whit Tompkins came out safe. I do not know what our future movements will be. I understand the Potomac river is pretty high from the recent rains. I have not heard where the enemy are. I have it rumored that Beauregard is here with an army, but I do not believe it. I hardly think Gen Lee intends crossing the river yet. We captured any amount of horses, cattle,

wagons &c. I have not heard from Franklin since he left us I supose it was well he did not go for there would have been a chance for him to have been captured. Some few are missing.[13] I must close as the mail will go off soon. I received your letters of the 21st June last night and was glad to hear you were all well and had such fine crops. The crops here are the finest I ever saw. I never saw such wheat which they are now harvesting, this is a fine section of country. I hope you all are well and shall look for another letter soon. Continue to direct your letters to Richmond and direct them to be forwarded on. Tell Alfred I am still safe and hope to return home one of these days.[14] I think often of you all from your letter I am affraid you are rather desponding let this not be the case, but hope for the best. Accept now my best wishes and love for your welfare and that of the whole family. My love to all friends and relations, remember me to all the negroes. From your affectionate son.
I. Goodwin Scott
I commenced to write with ink but the paper was to wet. Have me a pair of boots made as soon as you can. I have nearly worn out my shoes. Get Neagle of Eatonton to make them No 9s full size, and high in the instep. You had best have Bud some made he will need them after a while boots or shoes either will do him. Send mine by the first opportunity.

Camped Near Darkesville Va. July 16th 1863
Dear Father
    I know you are all uneasy about myself & Bud so I will try to allay your fears as far as I can by letting you know that we are both safe on this the South side of the Potomac. We are now in camps about 15 miles from Winchester and two or three from Bunker hill.[15] I wrote you about the fight at Gettysburg from which place we fell back slowly to Hagerstown where we threw up some fortifications and lay in line of battle for three days waiting for the enemy to attack us.[16] But it seemed he was affraid and we had only some skirmishing on the night of the 13th. We commenced our retreat again towards the river which owing to the heavy rain was impossible. We managed to get across a pontoon bridge over which we crossed our artillery and wagons and a portion of our troops. As for my corps we had to wade the river.[17] I never have seen just such a time. We commenced marching just at night and marched all night in the rain. When we reached the river we had to wade up the old canal nearly waist deep in mud, which smell awful then into the river we plunged the river four or five hundred yards wide and waist deep to me.[18] We crossed safely to this side where into the mud we went again up to our knees and trudged on till day when we halted and rested awhile. Since yesterday we have come only ten miles and I am in hopes we will rest awhile. Bud has stood up finely during the whole march and is now well. I have not been well but have got on pretty well, and am better now

than I have been, and am in hopes to soon be entirely well. I received a letter from aunt Emily Wright to day they were all well. I want to hear from home very bad and hope when I do hear that you are all in the enjoyment of good health and getting on well in every other respect. I was glad to hear you had such fine crops. If you have had as much rain lately as we have had you have had enough for it has rained almost every day for the last two weeks. The enemy have not attempted to cross the river. I think the next move will probably be towards Manassas though I cant tell any thing about it as yet. I hope soon to have a clean suit of cloths for I am pretty dirty just about this time. I do not think we made any thing by our campaign into Maryland and Pennsylvania. Our army is badly in need of cloths and shoes. A great many are bare footed. Mine are nearly worn out. I shall draw a pair from the government if possible as soon as the wagons come up from Stantoun [Staunton]. I have not heard from Franklin he and the other negroes are with the wagons. I shall look for them in a few days. Ab. Zachry found me last night at Martinsburg, he has been quite sick but is now nearly well.[19] I have written about all of interest and will give Bud a chance to write some. This is all the paper I have with me. My love to all my friends and the negroes, accept now my most devoted love for all the family untill death. Yours most affectionately.
I. Goodwin Scott.

Dear Father,

As Goodwin has left room enough for me to write I will try and write you a few lines, as I know you begin to want to hear from me by this time. I reckon you have heard before this time that I and Goodwin went through the battle safe, though cannot see how we escaped without being hurt. I went through the whole battle, I dont reckon the yankees ever fought harder than they did at Gettysburg. The first evening we attack them in an open wheat field and fought them about one mile the first thing our brigade done was to charge a battery. The yankees would walk back about ten steps and load and fire at us. We got in about fifty yards of the yanks several times. The whole battlefield was covered with the killed and wounded. But enough of this. I should like to be at home to get some of the good fruit, I often think of the good peaches which I know is nice. I dont expect to see home soon unless I get wounded. I dont see any prospect of the war closing. It is reported here that Vicksburg has fallen if so this war will last several years longer.[20] I think it will encourage the yanks and make them try harder to subjugate us. Charly & Thomas Morton was both wounded in the battle. Charly was wounded in the thigh & Tom in the arm.[21] Tell mother I will write to her the first chance I get which I hope wont be long. We get your letters regular nearly one a month. I had rather see a letter from home than any thing else I must close as it is getting too dark I cant see how to write. Give my love to the whole family, and all friends. I remain your most affectionate until death.

N. E. Scott

I have the diarrhea. It has not made me sick yet. I havent seen the first man with measles yet. I am hoping I wont take them.

Nicholas Ewing Scott

Camped near Luray, Va.[22]

July 26th 1863

Dear Father,

It was with the greatest pleasure I had this opportunity to write you a short letter. You must excuse its brevity. I shall try and condense as much as possible for the mail leaves this morning at ten o'clock and I want to try and write several short letters. We are now near Luray a little town on the west side of the blue ridge mountains. I wrote you last from Darksville. We came from there to Winchester via Front Royal to this place. When we reached Front Royal, Rights [Wrights] Brigade had been left to guard a pass there in the mountain and the enemy attacked them. Rodes Division was ordered to their suport [support].[23] We reached there in time to see a little fight in which the 3rd Ga Regt were engaged and suffered a good deal by having a good many wounded. I saw Chiss Slade and Nathan Dejarnette [DeJarnette] wounded, neither one seriously.[24] The enemy were repulsed without our assistance. We remained till some time in the night and then came on several miles this side of Front Royal. Now we are here at the foot of the mountains. Reached here last night and will remain probably until tomorrow when I expect we will pass over to the east side of the blue ridge. The weather is extremely warm and oppressive though we have marched quite moderately thus far. Last night we had a nice shower which will do great good especially in keeping down the dust. Our army needs rest very bad for the men are worn down marching foot bare &c. A great many are barefooted though there has been a good many shoes distributed. I am almost barefooted myself and not much prospect of getting any soon. I can make out a few days longer and then I may get a chance to draw a pair from the government. I wish you to send my boots by the first good opportunity. King Etheridge I expect will leave before you can have them made.[25] Have Bud some made. He can draw some here when he needs them. He will write you. Franklin & the other negroes came to us the 24th and our baggage wagons arrived yesterday morning. My things are safe. Franklin was sick two or three weeks after we left him but has entirely recovered. He was not sick enough to be confined, he says he fared very well. Sends his love to his wife and children, Alfred & all the other negroes. My own health has improved a great deal and I believe I am about well again though this is the way of flesh. Bud is all right. You would have thought so if you could have seen him pitch into the Beef and Bread for breakfast. I believe the company are all well. We get any quantity of Black & Dew Berries, Green apples &c to eat which I think are a great luxury. Longstreet & A. P. Hill have crossed the mountain higher up and are somewhere down towards Culpepper Court house. Johnsons division is camped about one mile and a half from here. I dont know where Gen Early is. We are moving about the same way we did last fall when our army went around to Federicksburg [Fredericksburg]. I should not be surprised is there was a battle fought soon. I must close by sending my love to all friends, yourself and the whole family. Remember me to Alfred and all the negroes. Tell Major, Bobie and Fannie I have some little thing I brought from Pennsylvania for them if I dont loose them. I remain your most affectionately.

I. G. Scott

Chapter 10

Rapidan Front

"We may remain here some time. . . ."

The Battle of Gettysburg had not produced a military victory for the Army of Northern Virginia. Losses to the army in men, equipment, and officers had been appalling. On the plus side of the ledger were the vast stores and herds of horses, mules, cattle, sheep, and hogs taken in Maryland and Pennsylvania. Lee's army needed time to rest and recuperate.

As the month of July ended, Lee and his army were once again in Virginia. General Mead's Federal Army had done very little after the Battle of Gettysburg to impede the retreat of the Army of Northern Virginia. A notable exception in attempting to cut off Lee's advance up the valley occurred at Manassas Gap on July 23. Rodes's division provided about 250 sharpshooters to assist General Ambrose R. Wright's brigade repulse the Federal Third Corps at Manassas Gap. After clearing Manassas Gap, Rodes's division resumed its march up the valley, resting at Luray. The division arrived on July 29 at Madison Court House by way of Thornton's Gap and Sperryville.

Once at Madison Court House, Virginia, Bud Scott wrote his mother, telling her that two of his messmates were wounded at Gettysburg. This left only Bud, Franklin, and one other man in his mess.

About August 1 the Twelfth Georgia moved southwestward from Madison Court House to Orange Court House. The Scotts were now feasting on dew berries, blackberries, and apples. There had been an issue of sugar and the men were frying apples, making apple pies, and roasting apples. Rest and a change of diet, for Irby, was a welcome relief.

Shortly after the Gettysburg campaign, Confederate authorities announced a general amnesty for all deserters and took steps to return to the army all sick and wounded, and men at home. During August, soldiers in great numbers began to report back to the army. While in camp at Orange Court House, Irby and Bud drew three months' pay. Irby wished to send some of it home, but knew he would have to pay for Franklin's return home, his commissary bill, and for a pair of shoes. He also wanted to pay for the clothes and boots he obtained at home during his wounded furlough.

While camped at Orange Court House, Irby Scott tells his father he was on "the lookout for a pistol for you." Whether he acquired one is unknown. Captured Federal pistols were plentiful and many of the men, including Irby, had already sent pistols home or otherwise disposed of them. Irby carried a Remington Model 1861 army revolver, also known as the Remington Old Model army revolver. The term "army" does not imply the branch of service, but rather the caliber, which was .44. This model was produced by E. Remington Sons, Ilion, New York, from 1862 until 1863, with a total production estimated at around nine thousand. Most, if not all, were sold to the U.S. government. Irby Scott must have picked up the gun on a battlefield or acquired it from a soldier who had picked it up on the battlefield.

Irby Scott and the men remained in camp at Orange Court House during the month of August and part of September. While camped at Orange Court House, his letters portray life in camp with plenty to eat, weather at times hot and sultry, furloughs being issued, and a most enjoyable period of rest and relaxation. The men spent much of each day in company, battalion, and brigade drill.

After the defeat at Gettysburg, the army turned to God. Being so near death in the campaigns of 1862 and 1863, many men realized their own mortality and turned to religion to uplift their spiritual life. They looked to God to regain His favor in hopes of defeating the northern host. Through God's blessing and their righteousness, the Confederate nation would be victorious.

Once on the south bank of the Rappahannock River, after the Battle of Bristoe Station on October 14, 1863, the Twelfth Georgia established their camp near Kelly's Ford. Shortly after going into camp, Colonel Willis sent a detail of about one hundred men over the river to purchase blankets, overcoats, and other items from local citizens, who had picked up the items from the battlefields and Federal camps. Crossing at Kelly's Ford, the detail moved down the river eight miles to Ellis's Ford. Bud Scott, a member of the detail, returned on the evening of October 26 with a good blanket and some soap. A special assignment required Irby Scott and the men to depart Kelly's Ford on November 2.

Camped Near Madison Court House
July 30th 1863
Dear Mother,

As I have nothing to do this evening I will try to write you a few lines to let you know that I am well and in the enjoyment of good health. Goodwin received letter from Father to day dated the 17th July which I assure you we was glad to get. You dont know how glad I am to get a letter from home. It is the next thing to seeing you all. We are camped about four miles from Madison Court House I think we will rest here a few days as the men are worn out from marching so much. I think we will go on to Gordonsville when we leave here though I cant tell where we will go. I have stood the march very well better than I thought I could we marched one day about 30 miles since we crossed the Potomac we marched all day and all knight, we generally march from 10 to 15 miles a day. Franklin came to us at Frontroyal [Front Royal] he is well. About clothing you wanted to know what I would need. I want Father to have me a pair of shoes made for winter. I can draw a pair of shoes from the Government that will do for the summer, the shoes that I wore from home are nearly worn out.[1] I will need some pants next fall. My coat will last me all winter. My jeans coat at home will do when I need another. I will also need some socks, that is about all I will need. If I should need any thing else I will let you know. I should like to have some of the good fruit at home. I have seen a few ripe peaches. We get apples and dew berries as many as we can eat. This is the greatest country for dew berries I ever saw. The crops in this portion of the State looks very well. Corn silking & taseling. My mess got cut up pretty bad at Gettysburg. Andrew Gorley Billy Winchel Zack Johnson and myself was in a mess together.[2] Two out of four was wounded. There is no one but me and Zack Johnson and Franklin in my mess. That is as many as I care about being in a mess with until I get into winter quarters. I should like to see all the best in the world, how does Bob and little Stonewall look. I want you to write me what you have named little Stonewall. I am anxious to know. I must close give my love to Father and all the family and all inquiring friends your most affectionate son until death
N. E. Scott

P.S. I put a piece of my hair in this letter. I dont believe you have any of my hair.

Orange C. H. Virginia
August 5th 1863
Dear Mother

It is with no little pleasure I write you a few lines this morning to inform you that myself Bud & Franklin are all the enjoyment of fine health. We are all getting on as well as we could expect plenty to eat and lying around in camps. The weather is extremely hot. I dont know that I ever felt warmer weather in Georgia or any where else than we have had here for the last week. We are now camped within one mile of Orange Court house on the South side of town in sight of the railroad. The iron horse has passed several times this morning and while I write I can hear his shrill voice in the distance.[3] We camped for several days on the west of town and moved here yesterday evening. We may remain here some time or we may leave here at any time. We have a very nice cool place and are quite comfortably situated. Our fly or tent is stretched beneath shade of some oaks while all around are the small yankee tents of the company. Some of the boys are naping, others lazzing about and the rest are cooking. Some of them have been out and bought some vegetables they brought in the first roasting ears of corn I have seen. We have had very few of such things this season. The crop of dew & black berries have been tremendous. There has been a little sugar issued by the government and we have had a splendid time making pies and blackberry jam which I assure you is no little luxury to this soldier who has been feeding on bread & beef. The berry season is about over and the apples are taking their place which we make into pies fry them, bake, roast &c. often (as the saying is) does my mouth water for some of your nice vegetable dinners which no one could appreciate more than myself. I sometimes think of the various nice things you all have at home for instance Milk and peaches. I wont mention any more and will leave the subject for its making me hungry to think of them. There is no news of importance. The mail is about to leave I will close and write again in a day or two. My love to all. I expected to write a long letter when I first commenced writing. Accept now my best love for yourself and the whole family. I remain your affectionate son untill death.

I. G. Scott

P.S. Franklin talks of wanting to come home in September which I cannot approve for he has only been here about two months yet and if he thinks of going home every three months he will not be of much service here. I am willing for him to go home this fall or winter he has made about $80 dollars.

Yours &c. IGS

Orange Court House Virginia

August 9th 1863

Dear Father,

I am here in camp with nothing to do. I always get worn out and tired when that is the case. So I have concluded to employ my time this morning in writing you a long letter perhaps, if I can find enough to compose a long one for we are dry for news as it seems both armies are lying still recruiting for the fall campaign. I never saw the like of men returning to the army.

Every train of cars is full and have been ever since we have been here. If they continue to come in for a few days longer as they have up to this time, our army will be fully as strong as it was before we went into Maryland. It seems that all the hospitals will soon be clear of sick, besides there are a good many conscripts and men from home on furlough. We had an inspection this morning and tomorrow I expect we will have to begin to drill twice a day. We have a nice camp and are now getting plenty flour, meal, bacon & beef. I wish you could see our boys cook and eat. They have many ways of cooking the same thing so as not to tire of it. We have drawn a little sugar lately and there has been thousands of dew and blackberries and we made pies, jam, &c. There are plenty of suttlers here now but it takes all the money a man has to buy the least little thing. We are now paying the government for bacon $1.00 per pound, beef $.30 cents, flour 17 cts, sugar from the suttlers $2.50, small ginger cakes three for a dollar, soda $4.00, butter from $2.00 to 2.50, lard $2.00. Our commissary bills will be pretty high for the last two months. We have been busy for the last day or two making out the muster and pay rolls. We will draw money in a few days. Bud will draw his bounty August 10th. I did not finish writing my letter on yesterday and have nothing new to write you. This morning every thing very still and quiet. I received your letter of the 2nd on yesterday. King Etheridge got back yesterday evening and brought us a good deal of news from home about things.[4] Generally, he says there are stirring times about there when he left among the conscripts, &c. Bud & Franklin are both getting on finely. Bud has no one in his mess now but Zack Johnson since Winchel and Gorley were wounded. Franklin has lost all his clothes except a shirt. He put them on a wagon on the march and when he went to get them they were gone. He picked up a good light coat somewhere and put his new in his knapsack so that was lost too. I guess he will now learn from bad experience that it will not do to trust wagoners or any one else to much. He can get shirts and things here plenty until fall. He will send by Henry Marshalls boy, Jim, $20.00 dollars to his wife. He wishes you to take the $20.00 bill and let her have smaller ones. Henry Marshall has processed a furlough in Richmond and his boy will go there today and both will leave for home in the morning. I have heard nothing from Winchel or Gorley since we left them. Thomas Morton has come back to his Regiment. I have not seen him. The company are all well and are now pretty well all shod. I have been unable so far to procure shoes. My old ones do finely in camp. I understand there is some in camp to sell. I will look them up this morning. I expect we will draw money today. I am undetermined as yet whether to draw any this time or not. With what I have on hand and what is owing to me, I will have between 2 & 3 hundred dollars on hand but there are two months commissary bill to pay, a pr shoes to buy and so on. I see from your letter you are making Brandy. If I were in your place I

should make some to sell for it is commanding high prices. Bud wrote a letter which I will send with this by Henry Marshall. Franklin wrote one to his wife which he wishes you to read and send to her.[5] I have written about all the news and every thing else I can think of now. As to what clothing we will need this fall I hardly know. I have never worn my new suit yet. I don't think I shall wear my coat until I can have it altered in the collar. The collar is so long and wide. I cant tell what Dusenberry [Dusenbury] was thinking about.[6] He shall never cut another for me. I shall want some pants, probably a jean coat which I do not want grey. I prefer a very dark brown or some other deep color, a pr or so of drawers and some other little things. Bud will also need the same coat, pants, drawers, socks and probably one or two shirts. You can have these things made and when Franklin comes home I will let you know what to send. I have just inquired of Bud about his letter and find he has not finished it yet. He is a hard case. I cannot get him to write. If I get after him about it, he generally gets mad so I shall let him alone. He is always very anxious to see your letters but never wants to write himself but for me to do all of it. I want to see you very much. Tell Bobie I have a jews harp for him & major which I will send home to him when Franklin comes home. Also a little tea pot for Fannie. Tell them both to write to me again. My love to all friends. Remember me to the negros. I remain your affectionate son.
I. G. Scott

Camped near Orange Court House
August 9th, 1863
Dear Father,

It is with much pleasure that I attempt to write you a few lines. I have been thinking for several days that I would write but have neglected it until the present. We received a letter from you today dated 2nd August which King brought which we was more than glad to get. I am always anxious to see a letter from home as it is the next thing to seeing you all. We are camped about one mile from Orange Court House on the Railroad between Orange Court House and Gordonsville. We are faring well at this time. We got a plenty to eat. We get flour and meal, bacon and beef. We can buy cakes from the sutlers and many other little things but have to pay a good price for them. Every thing sells almost out of reason. I have never heard a word from none of our boys that was wounded at Getysburg [Gettysburg] except Henry Marshall and Billy Waller. Thomas Morton came to us last week. His wound was not entirely well but it was healing very fast. His wound was very slight. Capt Reid is fixing to pay us off today. I will draw one months wages and a bounty of 50 dollars.[7] I think we will be camped here a week or two. Everything is quiet here now. I dont think we will have a fight soon. Our army is recruiting very fast. There is a great many soldiers coming in from

hospitals and other places. I would write more but Jim, Henry Marshalls boy is ready to leave and wants (to) send this letter by him. We get mail once every day. I must close. Give my love to Mother and all the family and inquiring friends. Your most affectionate son until death death.
Nicholas E. Scott

Orange C. H. Va.
August 15th 1863
Dear Father

Mr. Gartrell from Cutts Artillery leaves for home in the morning and will go to Putnam.[8] So I will write you merely to inform you that myself, Bud & Franklin are all well and doing well. I cannot write much as it is late, and Abner Zackry is now ready to go over and see him at his camp. There is no news of interest with us every thing quiet. I have not heard a cannon since I have been here and I hope I may never hear another so I keep living. I think we will have a big rain this evening for it is thundering very heavy and the rain in sight. We have had a good deal of rain for the last few days and the weather is nothing like as warm as it has been. The soldiers continue to come in from home and the hospitals. I should not be surprised if the enemy does not make haste in their preparations we will be ready first and attack him. I expect our army is nearly as strong as it was when we went into Pennsylvania. We have nothing to do except to drill twice a day, the rest of the time we lay around camps doing nothing. Our sutlers brings in a good many little things to eat, but they ask exhorbitant prices. At the rates of prices now we who have to buy our rations and clothing will not have much spare money to lay up. I drew three months pay the other day and have now something over four hundred and fifty dollars on hand. Bud has about a hundred and forty. I do not know whether to send any home or not. If I should happen to get wounded or sick I will have need for it besides I have two months commissary bill to pay, a pair shoes & so on to buy. I think I shall wait until I send Franklin home this fall. I dont expect we will draw any more soon. Then I will have to pay Franklins expenses home and back. I did want to send home enough to pay for my suit of uniform and boots and may do it yet. I am on the lookout for a pistol for you which will cost $40 that is a good one and I wont buy any other sort. They are not very plenty here.[9] The most of the boys have sent them home or otherwise disposed of them. I think I can manage to get one to send by the time Franklin will come to see you all. Bud wants to send you about $40 or $50. I did not think to write about our shirts in my last letter. I have one good one, which I have never worn. Bud will need some, our vests are good. We will want coats, pants, socks, shirts, over shirts, drawers &c. almost a little of every thing. If we dont need them when Franklin comes home I can let you know. Franklin thinks of coming in September, but I hardly think I shall let him come until October. It will owing to circumstances. Remember me to all friends and the negroes. Bud joins me, also Franklin in love to you all. Yours affectionately.

I. Goodwin Scott

Orange Court House Virginia
August 20th 1863
Dear Mother

It has been but a few days ago since I wrote to father sending my letter by Mr Gartrell who was going home on sick furlough, and expected to go to Putnam. It seems when I have the chance of writing, and do it not, that I have done wrong. I know from my own feelings how anxious you look for letters. I cant help expecting letters when I know I will not get any. Ever since the mail train of cars pass I am sure to think about a letter from home. I am not complaining that you all do not write. If you do not have more to write about than I do at present. I consider it pretty hard work to fill one of these small sheets. As for news there is none. I do not know that I have ever experienced as quiet a time in the war as the present. Since we have been here I have only heard the sound of one or two cannons and very little firing of small arms about the camps. Gen Lee has commenced issuing furloughs at the rate of two for every hundred men. We had a drawing in our regiment between the companies as to which should send a man home first. We missed and will have to wait. I supose until these return. For several days past we have had details of men cleaning up, and arranging our camps. We are now well fixed up, and from appearance may remain here some time. There is always a calm after a storm. But this calm cannot last long ere the thunders begin to be heard again. I am now thinking of the fall campaigns though there are no appearances of its commencing very soon. The warm sultry weather has passed away and for several days it has been quite pleasant. The nights pretty cool enough so for a man to sleep under a couple of heavy blankets. We are doing very well in every respect. They feed us pretty well, on bacon, beef, corn meal, flour. Sometimes Irish potatoes & green corn. On yesterday I helped to eat two nice water melons, which cost six dollars each. There are a good many brought up on the cars for sale. There are cakes, cider, apples &c a plenty at the suttlers shopes. So there is no end to spending money until your pocket is exhausted. The company are all well. I have not been able to get a pair of shoes as yet, though I expect to send to Richmond in a few days by some one. While here in camps my old ones answer every purpose. There are two men in the company who are entirely barefooted. I dont see why the government does not furnish us shoes and clothing. We have received none since we have been at this camp. I succeeded in getting my coat collar fixed by a tailor in the 4th Ga regt. it only cost me one dollar when if I had it done in Richmond it would have cost five or ten. Bud and Franklin are both doing finely and are well. I received a letter from father a few days since. I reckon Henry Marshall is at home now. I wrote by him and Franklin sent twenty dollars by Jim (Marshalls boy) to his wife. I guess Flournoy Adams and several others now at home will have to report here shortly or they will have an enrolling officer after them. Let Stonewall name himself. I cant pick out one. Kiss him and all the little children for me. Remember me to all friends especially those who think enough of me to inquire after me. Franklin sends his love to all. Write me all the news Bud joins me in love to yourself and the whole family. Your affectionate son untill death.

I. Goodwin Scott

Orange Court House Va

Thursday Morning August 27th, 1863

Dear Father

I reckon it is about my time to write again although I have nothing of interest to communicate. Times with us are extremely dull. Nothing to enliven us except the dull monotonous routine of camp life. They keep us pretty busy drilling twice each day company or battalion drill in the morning and battalion or brigade in the evening. I dont reckon you hardly know the difference between battalion and brigade drill. Battalion drill is simply one regiment drilling at a time. Brigade is several regiments. On yesterday Gen. Ewell reviewed and inspected our brigade. All quite on the front lines. Not even any picket fighting that I can hear of. We are very anxious to hear the news from Charleston.[10] There was nothing there in the papers on yesterday. I am affraid Charleston will go up. The company is generally well. There are some five or six of the boys here from the 3rd Ga.[11] It is a right hard matter for us to get permission to leave camps. I supose it on account of being in a division with North Carolina troops with whom they are very strict.[12] We are all getting on firstrate, plenty to eat &c. and expecting a supply from Richmond to day or tomorrow. Capt Reid and Ab Zachry both have boxes from home there, and we have made arrangements to have them brought up. Myself, Bud & Franklin are all in good health at present. Bud wrote a letter a few days since to you or Mother. I believe he improves every day. He grows & has fillen up considerably. Camp life agrees with him finely, he has never complained but two or three days since he joined us. I see the people of Putnam are giving it to those who refuse confederate money. I saw the proceedings of a meeting held there on the 11th of this month, that night.[13] I want you all to back them all over. I consider them among our worst enemy and would not care if all of them with the croakers were banished from the country. The soldiers are in fine spirits and willing to fight to the bitter end, if need also to sacrifice all they have not only their property but their lives. I must close as they are around getting up the mail. Mother may cut my coat straight breasted, but to make the same allteration in the collar. My love to all friends and the negroes, Franklin sends his love to his wife and children Bud joins me in love to you and all the family.

Your affectionate son untill death.

I. Goodwin Scott

Kiss the little ones for me.

Camped Near Orange C. H. Va.

Sept 3rd 1863

Dear Father,

I received your and Mothers letter several days ago and was more than glad to get it, and to hear that you all were well and doing well. I am always glad to get a letter from home, as it is the next thing to seeing of you all. Goodwin got a letter from Jacob Filer yesterday he said he had just received a letter from you and you wrote all was well. Jake wrote he had been very sick, and was awful tired of staying at the hospital, he said he was going to try to be sutler of our Regiment.[14] I dont think there is much chance for him, we have a very good sutler, he generally keeps a good supply on hand, of most every thing. It was rumored here in camps that we was going to be sent to Tennessee, but I dont put any confidence in the rumor you can hear any kind of rumors in camps that you want to hear. Just such rumors as that is going the rounds in camps all the time.

We have [a] nice place to camp. It is all cleaned up nice. We have to clean up our camps every day, and have company drills every morning, and Regiment every evening, and Brigade drills once a week, that is about all the duty we have to do, except guard duty which comes off about once in two weeks. We are enjoying ourselves very well at this time. Abner has been sick for the last two or three days but has got about strait again, all the rest of our company is well. Mother wanted to know whether I would need another coat or not. I think my coat will last all the winter. There is a revival going on in camps now. There is about fifteen or twenty to be baptized in our Regiment. This evening at three oclock Jack Johnson and John Dannelly are to be baptized this evening. We have meeting twice a day.[15] I have drawn a bounty and one months wages. I have 1490 dollars [*believed to be 149 dollars*] on hand and will draw again in a few days for two months. Goodwin & Franklin is well I must close as they have come a round after the mail. I remain your most affectionate son until death.

N. E. Scott

Orange Court House Va
September 10th 1863
Dear Father

Knowing your constant anxiety to hear from me and Bud, I will write you a short letter this morning though I am cannot as usual inform that we are well. Myself and Bud both have severe colds on yesterday I suffered a great deal with the head ache. But to day with the exception of soreness I feel much better, and think by tomorrow I shall be about straight again. Bud was quite sick for a day and night had considerable fever. I was fearful he was going to have a spell of fever or pneumonia. But he has nearly recovered his usual health with the exception of a bad cold. Bad colds are prevailing to a great extent among the men. Other than that there is no sickness dont feel uneasy about me and Bud for there is no danger now of our being sick more than a common cold will make one. If either one of us should be sick at any time you shall know it immediately. I received your letter of the 30th inst a few days since and was very sorry to hear mother had been sick and also glad to hear she had got better. I hope by this she has entirely recovered. I have no news of any importance to write you. We are still at our same old camp getting plenty to eat, every few days we have vegetables of some kind. We have had several nice dishes of ham and snap Beans. To day we will have potatoes and Tomatoes. What we eat costs us something these times for instance Beef at 40 cts a pound. Bacon 60 cts corn meal 0.5 cts. Flour 12 3/4 cts. sugar 12 c. Peas 4 1/4 c. Green corn $4.00 per Bushel Rice 10 c. soap 75 c. Salt 0.3 cts., these are the government prices. Things not bought from the government cost us much higher Irish potatoes from $2.00 to $3.00 per bushel, snap beans $1.00 per gallon, water mellons (common size) from $4.00 to $6.00 & so on. The commissary bill for our mess for the month of August was $101.16 this includes only what we bought from the government. I do not know how much besides that we bought, but the amount was not small. There is not much chance to save money here every thing good to eat a soldier sees he wants and if he has the money he will buy. It was partly for this reason that I sent you the money by Capt Reid and then I wanted to pay for my boots &c. I heard that Capt Reid had reached home and I reckon you have received the money $200.00 and the little presents for the children also all the news. Leather is very high higher than I anticipated. If you could get a pair of old boot legs and have them footed it would save a good deal of leather and also expense. I left a pair of old ones at home which I reckon would do very well. I have a splendid pr of shoes and do not want any more at the present. I want a pr of boots for winter. So you need not send me any. I know boots will be very high but I have the money to pay for them and while I am in the war I am going for comfort if it takes all I make. You may

have my coat cut straight breasted, but tell mother to not have the collar so wide and long. My uniform pants are a little to long. Say half an inch, as to hats we can make out a while longer. I expect we can get them easier here than you can. I could get them now in Richmond, but they are very high. I supose for a good one $50.00. I will keep a lookout and get some when we need them or see a good chance. When you write give me a few notes about the politics in the county and State as I have very little chance of learning any other way. I have been opposed to Joe Brown for several reasons one, his opposition to Jeff Davis & the administration.[16] But if Joshua Hill is the candidate of the reconstructionist or union candidate I shall vote for Brown and regret that I am only allowed one vote for if I had ten thousand I would cast them all against Hill.[17] I hear that Jeff Adams will run for the legislature.[18] If I am rightly informed he is opposed to Davis and the administration. Col Nisbet was in our camp a few days since electioneering around.[19] I supose The Countryman will post us up as soon as the candidates come out. It pitches into Hill about right.[20] Capt Reid takes the Countryman and we get it regulary.[21] Franklin sends his love to his family and is quite well. I have set the first of next month for him to come home if nothing happens and will make the best arrangements for him I can. Tell Bobbie his little letter done me a great deal of good that I sent his harp by Capt Reid and that he must learn how to play on it. Tell him to write me again soon and give me all the news. Tell mother I will get all the buttons I can which are eagerly sought after by all the soldiers for the coats we get have wooden Buttons. If I cannot get any you need not trouble about them for I can have those on my old coat put on, as I will have no use for that when I get the new one. Remember me to all friends also to the negroes. Bud joins me in love to you Mother and all the family. Yours in love. I. Goodwin Scott
You had better sent Buds shoes the first chance.

Mortons Ford Rapidan River Va
Sept 30th 1863
Dear Father,

I guess it is time that I was writing you again or I will fail to write once a week. We are still here on the River facing the enemy whose camp is plainly visible on some high hill not a great way I supose from Culpeper Court House there pickets are along the other side of the river.[22] I have given out a fight here, unless we cross and attack them which is hardly probable there are various rumors in camp as to the emenys and also our movements, but none of them are scarcely ever reliable so I shall leave them out. We have moved our camp a short distance from where we first camped. Our Regt is now off to itself in a beautiful piece of woods with water convenient. Camp clean & nice with our tents all arranged in order &c. Just about as comfortably situated as we could be under the circumstances. There is not a man sick in the company with the exception of Henry Thomas who has Diarhea [diarrhea] and is up and about.[23] My own & Buds health is splendid. Bud has grown and fattened since he came to the army had his hair shingled &c you would hardly know him. Capt Reid brought us all the things you sent safe also letter. My hat fit me exactly so did Buds we are well satisfied with them. The Brandy and figs were very nice. I expect Franklin will be home shortly. Some of the officers and men from here will be going home in a few days one from our company I reckon if he can get his furlough approved. Capt Harris of Morgan I think has applied which will be a good chance as he will go straight to Madison.[24] I will send him shortly.[25] I cant say exactly when for there is no telling what may turn up, but if things go on as they are now he may leave in four or five days or it may be ten days so look for him when you see him. I will write by him for what we need. I may send a few things home by him. If you cannot get buttons for my coat I can take those off the coat I have now. I am a great mind to send my old coat home but I dislike to wear my new one every day. Such clothes cost to much. We have just come off picket this morning we are one day in every four pretty light but our post is not more than half a mile or so from camp. Remember me to all friends and the negroes. Bud joins me in sending our best love to you, Mother and all the children. I remain as ever your devoted and affectionate son.

    I Goodwin Scott

Near Kellys Ford Va October 26th 1863
Dear Father,

    It has been some time since I wrote you last (or it seems so to me). We were then at Warrenton in pursuit of the enemy who run like pretty fellows untill they reached their fortifications at Centerville and Alexandria. The day after I wrote we had a little skirmish capturing a few prisoners &c.[26] Some of Hills forces the same day were engaged at some point on the railroad near Manassas or Bristol Station. Stuart with his cavalry also fought them beyond Manassas capturing a good many prisoners this was about all the fighting done. Our corps only went as far as Bristol Station we than comenced destroying the rail road and bridges on our return by piling up the cross ties and burning them with the irons placed upon them so as to bend when they were heated.[27] I think the road was torn up from near Centerville to the Rappahannock river. We are now camped near Kellys ford which is about eleven miles east from Culpeper Court House. I intended writing as soon as we got back on this side of the river but it was several days before we got into any regular camp. We were then ordered on picket at the river where we remained untill yesterday evening so this morning is the first good opportunity I have had to write and then I never like to write untill we settle after such trips as our last. I am glad to inform you that myself and Bud are both well and enjoying splendid health at this time there is not a man sick in the company. I am not pleased with the country around here or with our present camp the country here somewhat resembles the glade land of Putnam being so far as I have seen a low flat springy land.[28] If it rains much our camp will be very muddy and then there is no good spring water near. In some of the regts. they are digging wells but with what success I do not know. Some of the Regiments I believe all but ours have built cabbins but our boys do not seem disposed to build yet as there are chances of our not remaining here this winter. We cannot yet tell what the enemys programe may be of course our movements will depend entirely upon his. He may take the old Fredericksburg route if so we will have to front him there and besides there is plenty of time to build before winter fully sets in. I have been very anxious for several days to write you in reference to Franklin. I see from the papers that a good [number] of our soldiers have been exchanged among them Henry Marshall. Cap Reid has ordered him back to the company. Franklins furlough I reckon will be out about the time Henry will come back.[29] If you would see him you no doubt could make arrangements to send him along with Henry and probably you might send me a small box of eatables. If you fail to make arrangements with Marshall do not send me any box by him or encumber him with too many things as I am affraid he could not get along with them.[30] I think we will probably remain somewhere in this section this winter. So you can send him along when you think best. Bud is not in camp today while we were on the river yesterday Col Willis sent a detail of about one hundred men (ten from our company) over the river to hunt up and buy blankets over coats &c from the citizens where they had them from the yankees. They have not returned yet, but will be back this evening I reckon. A few of the enemys cavalry followed us near to the river where we crossed above here but there has been none down this way. I am affraid some of us will be sent west this winter. I prefer staying in Va. I believe I wrote for all I wanted from home. If you get this letter in time which no doubt you will try and make the arrangements with Marshall. Send Bud a pair of drawers. I received a letter from Aunt Emily Wright. I hear the negroes in some places are getting a little unmanageable. Give my love to all inquiring friends. Also remember me to the negroes. Thomas Spiveys & Green Spiveys negro boys are missing supposed they have gone to the yanks.[31] I will close and if Bud gets back in time this evening before the mail leaves he can if he wishes add a postscript. My best to mother and all the children. Yours in love.

I Goodwin Scott

P.S. Bud has just returned bringing with a good blanket & some soap. Most all the boys got something Bud says he will write in a day or two as he is to tired now and also wishes to fix up his tent. I can hear cannon this evening some ten miles. I supose across the river. I guess it is ours and the enemys cavalry. It is said that Gen. Doles has received an order where there are three officers to a company one can go home on furlough if such be the case my time will come one of these days.[32] I have given way for Abner to go first this time as I remained at home longer than he did. Capt Reid has been detailed to act as Quarter Master for about twenty days but look for me home when you see me. I will come when ever I can. This evening we had a settlement of commissary bills &c. I drew two months pay the other day after paying all my debts I have two hundred & sixty five dollars on hand and the government owes me nearly one months pay. So you see how I stand cant save much these times after paying all expenses. Nothing more at present. I remain yours truly

    I.G.S.

Camp near Kelly Ford VA
October 30th, 1863
Dear Father.

    Mr. McMillan who was lately sent on to our company as a conscript has been discharged and leaves for home this evening.[33] I have concluded to write you a few lines to inform you that Bud & myself are both well and enjoying good health at this time. Bud wants to write but there is an inspection today and he has to clean up his gun and the camp before he can write. I wrote you only a few days since. It seems letters come from home very slow lately and I am anxious to hear from home. Write what day Franklin will leave home so I may know when to meet or send to the railroad after the things he will bring with him. Nothing new with us. All quiet along the Rhappahammock [Rappahannock]. I hear nothing of the Yanks. They are granting furloughs to officers where there are three to the company. Abb. Zachry has applied. Say nothing to Mrs. Boswell about it as he may wish to take them on surprise. My time comes next but when the time will come I cannot tell. This war business is very uncertain. Look for me when you see me. The weather has been quite cool but it has clouded up and turned warm. I think we shall have rain John Little came back to the company on yesterday. The company all well. Nothing more at present. Remember me to Alfred. Tell him I have not forgotten him. Also to all the negroes. My best respects to all friends & my best love to mother & all the children. I remain your most devotedly.

    I. Goodwin Scott

N.S.
Dear Mother,

    As Goodwin has left a sheet for me to write, I will add a few lines as it has been sometime since I have written. I should have written before now but did not have a good chance since we was put on picket about three days after we got here and stayed on picket three days. I have been busy all the time since I came off picket fixing up my bunk and cooking &c. The men are busy fixing up their houses for winter. I dont think I shall build a cabin yet as I dont think we will stay here. I should not be surprised if we did not move farther back for this country is to level and flat to camp in. The Yankees stay a good distance off ———. I dont think there will be any more fighting this winter. There is no news of any importance with us. I went down the River the other day on a detail to get Blankets and overcoats. I got a good blanket. I could of got as many overcoats as I could carry. They was blue and I did not want them. The Yankees have taken nearly everything the people have on their side of the River. From Manassas to the river on the road we came they have burned nearly every house. They destroy nearly everything as they go. We have had some right cold weather. There was ice day before yesterday. I will close as I have nothing worth writing. Give my love to Mother and all the children. Most affectionately

N. E. Scott

P.S. Tell baby and Major howdy for me. I want to know whether they learned to play upon their jews harps and whether little Fannie has made any tea or coffee in her pot. Kiss all the little ones for me.

IGS

Chapter 11

Detached Duty

"We get a plenty to eat. . . ."

Confederate policy changes and aggressive action by authorities had brought many men back to the army by August 1863. General Lee knew there were healthy men of conscription age, as well as stragglers, convalescents, and deserters who had fled to the Blue Ridge Mountains to avoid service. On November 2, 1863, Lee detached, to the Shenandoah Valley, the Twelfth Georgia and the First South Carolina Infantry Regiments, for provost duty. Charles Huston of the First South Carolina told his father, on November 7, "the mountains have become a resort for all deserters & delinquents. . . . Gen Lee has thought it expedient to lead a select party . . . to arrest these traitors."

On the evening of October 31, Colonel Edward Willis of the Twelfth Georgia, who led the select party, came to Jedediah Hotchkiss, "seeking maps of the Valley, ect." The men of both regiments were not informed of their mission to arrest deserters, absentees, stragglers, and conscripts along the Blue Ridge. Leaving Kelly's Ford on November 2 and marching through Front Royal, the combined command arrived at Chester's Gap on the night of November 3, where the force was divided. The First South Carolina remained on the east side of the Blue Ridge while the Twelfth Georgia moved into Powells Fort, a valley west of the Blue Ridge. Once in the valley the Georgians proceeded southward through Powells Fort, coming out next to Luray, then "traveled up the valley as far as Swift Run Gap."

Because of an unexpected Federal advance against Kelly's Ford and Rappahannock Station on the Rappahannock on November 7, both the Twelfth Georgia and the First South Carolina were recalled to Lee's army before completing their work in the valley. Irby Scott and the men began their journey back to the brigade by way of Luray through Swift Run Gap, then through Stanardsville and Gordonsville, rejoining the brigade at Morton's Ford on November 14.

From November 14 until the evening of November 26, the Twelfth Georgia remained at Morton's Ford. On the morning of November 27 they were relieved from picket duty by a cavalry detachment and rejoined the division, where they were held in reserve, near Locust Grove. During the afternoon and night of November 27 the Twelfth Georgia supported various brigades of Rodes's division in the engagement near Payne's Farm. On the morning of November 28 the Twelfth Georgia marched to Mine Run, where they were held in reserve until the morning of December 2, when they occupied the entrenchments and learned the Federals had retreated.

On December 8, Jedediah Hotchkiss once again prepared a map, at the request of Colonel Edward Willis, of part of the Shenandoah Valley. Three days later, on December 11, Irby Scott and the men marched from Morton's Ford back to the valley to resume the work they had begun in early November. Arriving at Stanardsville, Virginia, on December 13, the men cooked two days' rations and loaded wagons with another two days' worth. At Stanardsville the regiment was divided into a right and left wing, and from there the men conducted "a four days scout amongst the hollows in the eastern side of the Blue Ridge." Scott and Company G, belonging to the right wing, proceeded north in the rain. After four days, the right wing passed through Simmon's Gap into the valley at the south end of Massanutten Mountain.

Once in the valley, Robert Young, in a January 3, 1864, letter to his cousin, says "the regiment reformed at Conrads Store in Rockingham County on the west of the Blue Ridge and kept moving up the valley sending out scouts as we moved." Traveling up the valley on the Port Republic Road, they passed the 1862 battlefield of Port Republic. Irby Scott, and the other veterans of the battle, surely described for Bud the Battles of Port Republic and Cross Keys as they walked over the battlefield. On January 6, the men moved closer to the village of New Hope and put up winter quarters.

Unfortunately, only one letter survives from Irby Scott detailing the Twelfth Georgia's sojourn in the valley. Four missives written by Bud survive, along with one incomplete letter likely written by Irby. When the regiment began their first mission in November they may not have been able to post letters home because of the separation from the army. During their second mission into the valley they were near enough to Staunton and the Virginian Central Railroad for the men to post correspondence home and receive boxes.

It is apparent that life in the valley had an advantage, with plenty to eat, fresh milk, and furloughs being issued to men who had not been home. With little fear of being shot at, the men continued to scout the area. Their time in the valley appears to have been a holiday.

Mortons Ford Dec. 8th 1863

Dear Father.

As Mr. Marshall leaves for home today I will write you a few lines. We received yours and Mothers letters by Lt. Zachary which I assure you we was glad to get. I reckon you have heard before this that we were safe. None of our company got hurt in the last fight. We only had three men wounded in the Regiment. We had a bad time while we were in line of battle. We were in line of battle four days and nights and the weather was as cold as I ever saw it. Our Regiment was not engaged with small arms but was under shelling. Mead backed clear out of it this time and it is a good thing for him he did. If he had of fought us he would of got one of the best whipping ever a Gen did get.[1] We received the thing you sent by Lt. Zachary. I would write more but Mr. Marshall is ready to start. Me and Goodwin and Franklin are well.

Your most affectionate son until death.

N. E. Scott

P.S. I want you to send us a box. I think by the time it gets here we will be in winter quarters. I should not be supprised if our regiment did not take winter quarters in the valley this winter. Colonel Willis thought it very probable we would go.[2]

N. E. Scott

Camped Near Piedmont

Jan 6th 1863 [*should be 1864*]

Dear Father

As it has been some time since I have written you a letter I will try and write you a few lines to let you know that I am well. I should have written before now but did not have a chance to send my letters. We have had quite a rough time since we left the Brigade. The weather is very cold and the ground is covered with snow. We will move to day and put up winter quarter. We will then be in about eight or ten miles of Stannton [Staunton]. We have caught a good many deserters, and men absent without leave. I went over the battlefield at Port Republic. The bones of the dead men are strewn all over the field, it is an awful sight to look at the battlefield now. Abner Zackry has been quite sick for the last six or eight days, he has the irocipn-lons [erysiplas] in his face and head, but is a great deal better now.[3] I think he will be up again in a few days, he is at a Private house about one mile from camps. Goodwin and Franklin are well. I will close as I have nothing else to write at present. I remain your most affectionate son until death.

Nicholas E. Scott

Camped Near New Hope, Va[4]
January 10th, 1864
Dear Father,

Tomorrow I will have an opportunity of sending a letter to Eatonton by Dr. Etheridge who is going home on furlough. I expect you think I do not intent to write again but I have plenty of excuses such as irregularity of mails, Building houses for winter quarters &c besides I am the only officer with the company and have all the business to attend to, which of late has been no small item itself. I have made out muster & pay rolls and almost hundreds of smaller reports and returns. Hope I have already named enough to satisfy you that my chances has not been very good for writing. So I will write something more interesting. We are now building our winter quarters between Staunton and Port Republic about ten miles from the former place. We can hear the cars whistling very plain.[5] There is two little villages about one mile and a half each from our camp. One is called Piedmont, the other New Hope. We have a nice camp with plenty of wood and water convenient. We are now engaged in putting up houses. Some of the boys have near enough completed to move in and be very comfortable. They will all be through in a few days. I have known some of them to work until midnight revving out boards &c. I have built a body of logs and stretched my tent over them which is a much better roof than boards to keep out snow. I have a good chimney and fireplace. I have now to fix up a bunk and stop a few cracks with mud and then I have a good house. There has been some of the coldest weather for the past ten days that I have seen since we left the Alleghany mountains. The ground is now covered with snow and no prospect of its thawing soon. Today is not quite so cold but cold it seems to me for any use. That is one reason we have progressed so slow in building. Just leave the fire and it felt like freezing in a very short time.

I supose [suppose] you have all heard by this time that Abner Zachry has been quite sick with Erysipilas [Erysipelas] in his face and head.[6] He is staying at a house near camp and has been there about ten days. He is much better now. Dr. Etheridge says he will be well enough to come to camp in a few days. I was going to send to Staunton and telegraph to Mr. Boswell to let him know of it that he might come on and take care of him but Dr. Etheridge told me not to do it, that he would get better and that it would frighten them all at home. I have not seen him in several days but hear every day. I have been so busy fixing up that I have not had time to go. Bud wrote home a few days since. We are both well. So is Franklin. Franklin sends his love to all. James Dannelly [Danielly] came to the company on the 8th of this month. Two more of the company will be home in a few days, Harry Etheridge & Oliver.[7] The election for county officers was held Wednesday. Suther got nine votes and Spivey 7 for Sheriff. Henry Reid one. I got a letter

from Wm. Hearns [Hearn] saying that Clinton Tucker was a candidate also besides about twelve others has [8]
[*Letter stops here.*]

Camped Near Piedmont Va.
January 31st 1864
Dear Father
It is with much pleasure that I avail myself of this opportunity of writing you a few lines. I intended to have written before now but have neglected it until the present. We received yours and Mothers letters yesterday of 21st and 22nd of January. Which I assure you we was glad to receive. I was sorry to hear that little Bobby was sick, but I hope he is well before this. I have been sick with the janndice [jaundice] about a week and a half, but I am entirely well now. I was not sick much. We are fixed up very well for living. I and Goodwin and Abner have a cabin put up with a large tent stretched over it and it do good. We have got a good bunk fixed up out of plank. Charles and Franklin has a little cabin put up with stick and dirt chimney.[9] They are just as warm as a plastered house. So you see we are fixed up very well. We get a plenty to eat we get Flour, pork, beef cabbage milk and many other little things. Franklin goes out twice a week and brings in a turn of cabbage and milk, Abner has just got a box from home.[10] Goodwin wrote to Richmond about one box. Sanlsbury wrote he would send it on to Staunton just as soon as it got there.[11] I should like to come home this winter but I dont think there is much chance. They are giving furloughs to all the men that has never been home. I hope my time will come next summer if they continue to give them. I will close as I know of nothing else to write about just now. Give my love to Mother cousin Mary Thomason and all the children and all inquiring friends. I remain your most affectionate son until death.
Nicholas Ewing Scott
Goodwin and Franklin are well.[12]

Camp Taylor February 21st 1864
Dear Father,
As I will have a good chance to send a letter off tomorrow by Henry Thomas who leaves for home on furlow [furlough] I will write you a few lines to let you know that I am well and in the enjoyment of good health. I received your letter a few days ago which gave me no little pleasure to hear from home. I received my box on the eighteenth of this month and the cap of syrup. Every thing came through safe. I am living Scrumptiously on the good things at this time. I am in hope[s] I may get home before long to enjoy some of the good things there. Our Regiment has sent up a petition to go to Savannah Georgia. There is a Regiment there that wants to exchange

places with us. I am in hopes that we may succeed in getting there. Colonel Hardeman is going to write out the petition in the morning and send it up to President Davis.[13] Every man in the Regiment signed the petition except two or three officers. The colonel of the other Regiment is very anxious to exchange with us. If I get to Savannah I will fell [feel] almost like I was at home. I intent to have me a pair of shoes made tomorrow if the shoemaker will take confederate money. They have closed up all the stores in Harrisonburg and Newhope and wont sell a thing for confederate money. I thank you and Mother for the nice things you sent us in the box. I will close as know of nothing else to write about. Give my love to all the family and except [accept] a large share for yourself. I remain your most affectionate until death.

Nicholas E. Scott

Camp Taylor, Va
March 25th, 1864
Dear Mother,

It is a pleasant task this morning for me to sit in my little hut by a good fire to write you a short letter. Myself, Bud & Tom are all enjoying splendid health at this time and I hope when this letter reaches you that it may find you and all the family enjoying the same Blessing.[14] Yours and fathers welcomed letters by John Dannelly [Danielly] was received last night and their content eagerly pursued for I was extremely anxious to hear from home not having heard from you since I left. I was sorry to hear of fathers defeat and have great hopes of his being successful in getting a detail. He wrote me not to let it trouble me. But it does trouble me when I think of you all left there by yourselves with no one but negroes to depend upon. I cant help from feeling bad. Still I know you will do your best and with Alfred to help you, you will get along as well as anyone could under the same circumstances.[15] I wrote home soon after my arrival in camp which I hope you have received ere this.[16] Abner Zachry had his knee badly hurt two nights ago. He has not been able to walk since. He and one of the boys got into a little frolic or tussle in the tent. His foot got hung somehow under a ——— box and falling strained his knee joint. It is badly swollen and I am afraid it will be some time before he will get over it entirely. I was glad to hear that Cousin Mollies school was getting more interesting. You wrote that Mr. M ——— had his house &c burnt up lately. His house was burnt when I was at home. I supose [suppose] that was the time you had ———. You stated that you heard we had we had orders to march. There has been no such orders since I came back. The ground has been buried in snow for several days. It was the largest snow of this winter. It is snowing now while I write. I should not be surprised if it did not snow a good deal before it quits. I was sorry to hear

that there was danger of loosing the fruit crop. I have had no change to getting those little things for ——— I tried in Wilmington but did not succeed. I will keep a look out for them and procure them the first opportunity. Gen Lee has quit giving furloughs for a time or it may be for good until the coming campaign is over. Tom gets along firstrate and does finely. Congress has passed an act giving officers one ration and allowing them to buy clothing from Quartermasters. It took effect on the 5th of this month. I wrote cousin Mollie a few days since. Give my respects to all friends &c. Remember me to all the negroes. Write me soon and often. My love to yourself, Cousin Mollie and all the family. I remain your son truly untill death.
I Goodwin Scott

Chapter 12

1864 Overland Campaign

"I have not been touched as yet am well though broken down phisically."

Irby Scott and the company had expected to leave Camp Taylor and the valley on April 12, but did not begin the march to the main army until April 14. When Scott arrived in camp near Orange Court House, he and the company found shelter in the vacated cabins of General Johnson's brigade. Unfortunately, the letter Scott wrote home when he reached the brigade is missing, and we are denied details of the march from the valley and comments on his elevation to the rank of first lieutenant.

Upon taking command of all Federal forces, General Ulysses S. Grant determined to bring all of the North's manpower and material superiority to bear on the Confederacy. Grant waged a war of attrition, depriving the Army of Northern Virginia of the strategic initiative, fixing it in place, disrupting communications, and denying it supplies.

On May 2, 1864, General Lee met his corps and division commanders at the signal station on Clark Mountain, Virginia. At this meeting, Lee gave his opinion that the Federal army would cross the Rapidan River on the right flank of the Confederate army at Germanna and Ely's Fords. On the following day, Lee's prediction was realized when the Army of the Potomac began to cross the Rapidan. About noon on May 4, Irby Scott and the men left their camp near Orange Court House, marching on the Orange Turnpike toward Locust Grove.

Grant had hoped to pass through the wilderness swiftly. Had his wagon train not slowed his movement, he would not have stopped in the Wilderness in the early afternoon of May 4. On the morning of May 5, Scott and the company formed in line of battle, in a dense pine thicket along the Orange Turnpike near Saunder's Field. Shortly after midday the Confederates advanced upon Federal General Charles Griffin's division of General Gouverneur K. Warren's Fifth Corps. As the southerners marched forward, the Federal line charged Doles' brigade, enfilading the Forty-fourth Georgia. Colonel Willis, of the Twelfth Georgia, seeing the predicament of the Forty-fourth Georgia on his left, ordered the Twelfth Georgia to charge. "Though hard pressed," Doles had held his ground. Battle's brigade moved forward to the main line, relieving Doles' brigade. Doles then formed on the left of Battle.

At the end of the second day, May 6, Grant knew he would not be able to gain a "decided advantage from the fighting in this forest" and hoped to steal a march on Lee by sending Warren's Fifth Corps to the southeast to seize a critical road junction at Spotsylvania Court House. Grant knew that advancing to Spotsylvania Court House would keep the Army of the Potomac between Lee and Richmond, and that the country around Spotsylvania Court House afforded the opportunity to operate on open ground.

By the afternoon of May 7, intelligence received at Confederate headquarters convinced Lee that preparations were underway for a movement by the Army of the Potomac. By late afternoon, Lee sent the First Corps, now commanded by Major General Richard H. Anderson, in the direction of Spotsylvania Court House.

Anderson's Confederates outmarched Grant and at once began constructing field earthworks to bolster their defensive position. Expecting an attack by the entire Federal army at any moment, Confederates continued to strengthen their position. By the afternoon of May 9 their earthworks resembled an inverted V, which the soldiers named the Mule Shoe. Ewell's Second Corps occupied a large portion of the Mule Shoe. Irby Scott and the Twelfth Georgia held trenches on the western flank of the Mule Shoe in what would become known as Doles' salient.

On May 10, Union Colonel Emory Upton received permission to lead a brigade-sized attack against the western face of the Mule Shoe. Upton believed the only way to breach the Confederate earthworks was to reach them quickly. There would be no firing or reloading during the charge and no yelling at its commencement. Once the attacking force breached the earthworks, their initial goal would be to widen the gap to allow supporting troops to pour in. Forming in the edge of a pine thicket, Upton's skirmishers cleared Doles' skirmishers from their front. About 6:35 in the evening, the Federal attack began with a yell, contrary to orders.

Irby Scott, in his June 8 letter, tells his father about the attack on May 10 and that the Federal attack broke through the Georgians' earthworks. Scott remained in the earthworks until he saw Federal soldiers capturing men. He and a number of the men ran from the entrenchments, risking being shot. While running, Scott lost contact with his brother. It was not until the next morning, on May 11, that Irby saw his Bud "a corpse." Though Irby Scott could not attend to the burial of his brother at the McCoull house, other men of the company buried Bud. On a plank at

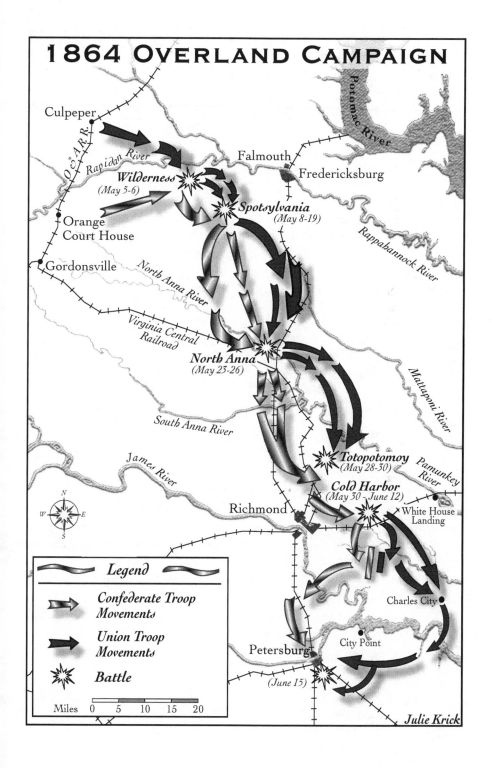

the head of his grave, one of the men carved Bud's initials, company, and regiment. Bud had been mortally wounded during an attack to retake the captured works.

Irby Scott's June 8 letter reveals that he had reached the bottom of his endurance, causing him to reflect on his own mortality and the horrors of the preceding month. He hoped that God would spare him and allow him to return home. Scott committed himself to his country and even more so to the men of the company.

Early on the morning of June 13, General Lee learned no Federal troops remained in his front at Cold Harbor. Lee issued orders for his army to move southward to block the roads to Richmond. Federal operations in the Shenandoah Valley gave Lee much concern, and he dispatched the Second Corps, under Lieutenant General Jubal A. Early, on an independent operation to remove the Federal threat from the valley.

Camped Near Mortons Ford
April 28th 1863 [*should be 1864*]
Dear Father,

I reckon you are begining to look anxiously for a letter from me before now. Goodwin wrote a letter to you as soon as we got to the Brigade. I thought I would wait a few days before I wrote as I did not think it was necessary for us both to write at the same time. We are now on picket about two miles from Mortons ford. I expect we will stand picket about a week, this is the first picket duty I have had to do since the first of December our picket duty comes on about once every other week, now. The most of our army is camped near Orange Court House about twelve miles from here. I expect they will move down near the breast works in a few days. A good many of Gen. Longstreets army is camped at Gordonsville. I am looking for a big fight to come off every day both sides are making preparations for a fight. A great many of Lincolns troops times expires next month I think we will have the fight before their time expires, this is my views about it though I cant tell. I am well Goodwin and Tom are well. I would write more but they have come around after the mail. I will close by remaining your most affectionate son until death.
N. E. Scott
P.S. To day I am nineteen years old.[1]

In line of Battle May 6th 1864
Dear Father,

As I have an opportunity to write a few lines and send them off to be mailed. I wish to inform you that we have been fighting since Thursday morning. The regt has been engaged and lost about sixty five killed and wounded.

The casualties in our company were Elisha Perryman Killed, David Denham wounded in leg (flesh) Thomas Avery severely in head, James Oliver severely in throat, the rest all safe & well.[2] I came out untouched. Bud was shot through the leg of his pants. We are between Mine Run & Chancellorsville our line extends I expect to Fredericksburg. We have whiped them every where we have fought. We are not well fortified, all in good spirits. I expect there will be more hard fighting yet. Nothing more at present. I forgot in my haste to state that Terry Dismukes was taken prisoner.[3] Solomon Batchelor missing. Longstreet is on our right. Hill in the center & Ewell on the right. Col Willis was slightly wounded in thigh. Capt Briggs and Lt Perry killed.[4] We had a pretty tight time one or two brigades fighting a whole corps of yanks. We were soon reinforced when we charged & made them give leg bail pretty fast. They have charged our works on the line several times but have been repulsed and driven back some distance. Cheering news from all parts of the line. We will whip certain. My love to all inquiring friends & the negroes. Bud joins me in love to all. I remain yours affectionately.
I. G. Scott

In line of Battle near Spotsylvania C. H. Va
May 16th 1864
Dear Father
All is quite in front this morning except the occasional firing of the skirmishers or pickets. I have written you two letters since the fight began, but fearing that those letters might not reach you and having a chance to send off another letter I have concluded to write you only a few lines. In my second letter I wrote you of Buds death he died fighting gallantly for his Country and his rights. I had him buried in a garden at the house of Mr. McCool [McCoull] about two miles north of Spotsylvania Court House.[5] His name was marked upon a board at the head of his grave. Our Reg & Brigade is now very small the 12th Ga numbers about one hundred men. The enemy has fallen back a little from our front. There is various reports some say he is crossing back over the river. There has been no fighting since Friday evening. Both armys have suffered terribly. I hope the fighting is over though I fear not. The men are all broke down. The weather has been bad very rainy. We are well fortified and await the enemys movements. I sent you a list of the killed, wounded & missing from the company. I made out a list since and sent it to Capt Sid Reid to dispatch home. There also has been sent a list of the casualties of the Regt & Brigade to one of the Macon papers. James W Davis was reported as missing, but I am now satisfied that he was killed from a description of a man found and buried by some of the men of the Regt. I have not been touched as yet am well though broken down phisically [physically]. My love to all the whole family. Yours truly untill death.

I. Goodwin Scott

Hanover Junction May 25th, 1864

Loved ones at Home

I embrace this opportunity of writing you a few lines to let you know that through the mercies of a kind providence I am well and safe thus far. Not having received the least injury I have written three letters home since the fight commenced but am afraid owing to the confused state of the mails & raids upon the railroads that they have never reached their destination. You have no doubt, if not from my letters, learned the heart rending intelligence of Buds death. He was killed May 10th in the evening about dark the ball entering his head above the left eye, passing out at the back of the head. I did not know he was dead until the next morning. I made inquiries that night and was told that he was safe. I did not try to hunt for him that night thinking he was lost from the company and would find us that night or next morning. It would have been useless to have searched for him as it was dark, the pines thick & no one knew where to look. He was found next morning by Bob Jenkins within a few feet of the trenches. I cannot describe my feelings when I learned his fate. I try to console myself that he died in a good cause, fighting gallantly for his country. He was a brave boy and a more gallant soldier never lived. I was told by one of the regt who was near him that he was in the front leading the charge, that when the ball struck him he threw up his hands & fell dead. He looked very natural. Some one had robbed his pockets and taken every thing of any value, even his memorandum book. We had orders to move immediately and I sent four men to bury him in a garden near by. He had no coffin but I had him wraped in a new tent and a blanket. I have since been to his grave. He is buried at the house of a Mr. Neil McCool [McCoull] two miles north of Spotsylvania Court House. At his head upon a board is N.E.S., Co G, 12th GA Regt. So it is, he is no more. God has seen fit to take him from us, from those who loved him dearly. He was liked by all who knew him. I could hardly write you the sad news of his death knowing how much it would grieve you. I think of him every hour in the day and feel lonely for I always had an eye to his comfort. More than for myself. I would rather if it had been the will of God for him to have been spared. At least to have visited home. He was much ——— in looks and disposition. But the worst of all he was not prepared for death. I must stop writing upon the subject and try to dismiss it from my mind. It makes me feel so sad. Do not give way to your grief more than you can help. I know this will be hard to do for I loved him as much as you. We are now at Hanover Junction in line of battle. But I dont think there will be much fighting here. I am of the opinion that the enemy will move around to the Paninsula [Peninsula]. He seems to evade a fight.

You get more news from the papers than I could give as to army movements. Our line of battle is about two hundred yard from the depot at the Junction. I saw Cousin Duke & Irby Goodwin Marshall on the 8th inst.[6] Duke came to see me yesterday morning. I have not seen Woodlief or Ben Shivers.[7] They are in the same Regt. I tried to telegraph you the list of casualties in the company but could not send a dispatch through. I sent you a list in a former letter. Since then J. W. Dannelly [Danielly] & J.W. Williams are missing. Supose [suppose] to be prisoners.[8] There is now only 17 men with the company able for duty. Before the fight we had 42 guns. Tom is somewhere in the rear and is getting along well. I am anxious to hear from home. Got the letter sent by Abner. I hope this letter may reach you and find the family all well. My love to all the family and accept a share for yourself. Your truly. I. G. Scott.

In line of Battle 10 miles
from Richmond
June 4th 1864
Dear Father,

I embrace this opportunity to let you know that I am safe thus far yet I have been in a fight almost everyday. I am almost worn out with fatigue loss of sleep &c. I have never seen such a time in my life. We have (I believe) whiped or repulsed every assault of the enemy and we it seems not more than begun the fight from the way the enemy hold on. We have lost many of our best officers and men among them Gen Doles & Col. Willis James Mansfield was wounded several days since.[9] No others in my company since I wrote you last. This fight I am convinced will seal the fate of the Confederacy for good or bad. Tom is well, Abner and all the boys except John Parker are also well.[10] I dont know whether Parker is sick much or not. The mail is about to leave for Richmond, I must close hoping one of these days to meet you and tell you all verbally. My love to all the family and all friends. Your affectionate son as ever.
I. Goodwin Scott

Camped 10 miles from Richmond
on Mechanicsville Road
June 8th, 1864
Loved ones at Home,

How thankful do I feel this morning to an all wise providence, that I am still spared and allowed the privilege of communicating through the medium of pen & ink. My thoughts &c to those who are near & dear to me almost a thousand miles away. I say to those who are near and dear to me.

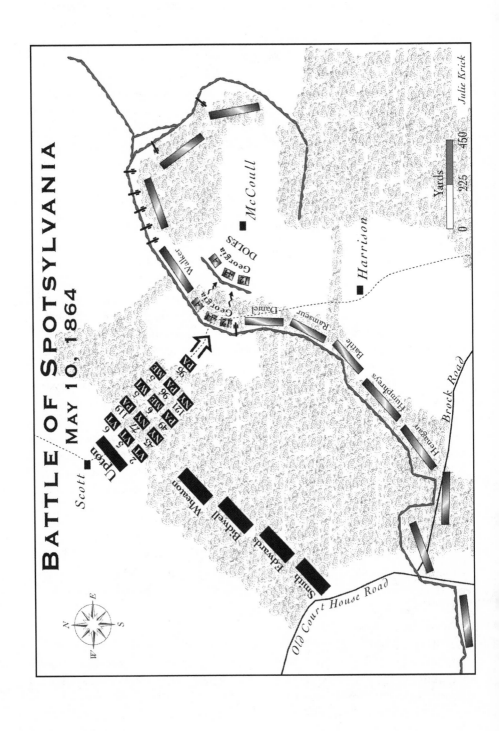

BATTLE OF SPOTSYLVANIA
MAY 10, 1864

Julie Krick

Yards
0   225   450

Yes, rendered doubly dear, because of the trials, difficulties and sufferings through which I have lately passed and expected to have to still endure. Should I through Gods mercy be spared, I hope and pray that I may be permitted to live and return home once more as a freeman to enjoy the blessings of peace & liberty for which I have toiled so hard. I long to see you all, but God only knows when, if ever I shall have that pleasure. Yet there is a hope. Yet there is a hope to which I shall cling to the last. I am as well as I could expect to be. I have been a little unwell and am troubled a little at this time with diarhea [diarrhea] which is almost a general thing owing I supose to the water & so much exposure. We are now for the first time with the exception of one day out of line of battle. We had orders to move this morning at daylight but have not moved as yet. I dont know where we will go. I never was so near worn out in my life. I scarcely have any energy left. There has been very little fighting for two or three days more than skirmishing between the pickets. I received your most welcome letter of the 30th on yesterday. Nothing is so reviving to the soldier as letters from home. You wished to know all the particulars of Buds death. On the evening of the 10th of May the enemy charged our works breaking the line of the 44th Ga Regt. We were on the right of the brigade the 4th Ga to our left & the 44th on their left in rear of the works was a dense pine thicket and the line making a curve. We could with difficulty see what was going on except in our front & right. As soon as the enemy made a breach in the line they poured through and turning to the right & left commenced pouring a fire right down the line and also passing in our rear. We remained in the ditch untill I saw the enemy shooting & capturing men within forty yards of us. Some of us ran taking the risks of being shot while others remained and were taken prisoners the company got separated in the run and I did not see Bud any more untill the next morning a corpse. Reinforcements were sent to us and we drove the enemy back and retook our works about dusk. I made inquires after Bud and was told that he was safe. Owing to the confusion and darkness I thought he had lost the regiment we took our positions in the works where we remained untill morning. Bob Jenkins found him about a hundred yards from us near the works. There was one of the regt close by him when he was shot who says he was fighting gallantly. He was struck just above the left eye. The ball coming out at the back of the head, he fell backwards. I do not think he ever spoke or moved and did not suffer any. Some one had robbed his pockets of everything. I had him buried at the house of Neil McCool [McCoull]. He had no coffin but was buried in a blanket & a pr of new tents the best that could be done. On a board at his head is marked N. E. S. Co "G" 12th Ga Regt. I could not see to it myself for we were ordered to move. I went to his grave afterwards. Henry Marshall & William Dannelly [Danielly] know where it is.[11] Deeply am I grieved at his death, one so young, and full of promise. I have felt sad ever since his death. I have not shed a tear. I cannot cry. I wish I could it would to some extent relieve my feelings it seems that all the finer sensibilities of my nature are gone. It may be that he was taken from us for some good and we must try and resign ourselves to Gods will. You wish me to get a position somewhere out of danger. I have thought of this, but there are always so many looking out for these places. Unless a man has some influential friends high in office to help him he does not stand much chance. I will keep a lookout for some place.

[On the bottom of page 2 of the original letter, the following is written.]
(dont let any one besides the family read this letter say nothing about my wishing to get another position) I am now detailed to command the 2nd Corps of sharp shooters from our brigade this is only temporary.[12] I do not like the position at all. The duty is very heavy and the responsibility great. I will get out of it as soon as possible. I do not know of any position that is vacant at present. I should like to leave the Regiment & brigade for we have no officers left in my opinion capable of commanding. In the death of Col Willis the Regt lost its best friend. I shall get some place if I can. I have nothing now to bind me to the Regt or Co. more than to be with those I am acquainted. I shall try and do my duty to my Country & myself and for your sake as well as my own will not expose myself any more than I can help. There has been no casualties in the company since I wrote last. Gen. Breckenridge has gone to the valley with troops to meet Hunter who is at Staunton.[13] You wanted to know if I wanted money &c. I have but little money at present and cannot use it for there is nothing to buy. If I should get wounded and get to Richmond I can get money there or let you know so that you can send me some. I am needing a pr of pants, but expect to get some from the government in a day or two. Tom stays the most of his time out at Capt Reids wagons he does not venture up often. He does not do exactly to suit me sometimes. He stays to far in the rear. I shall give him a little talk he is unthoughted. He is as fat as you ever saw him.[14] I have written all I can think of that would interest you. I hate to stop writing. Write to me often at least once a week if not oftener. My best love to Mother, Cousin Mollie and all the children. Remember me to all inquiring friends & the negroes. Cheer up all of you & dont give way to your grief, struggle against your feelings. I remain your ever devoted son as long as life shall last.
I. Goodwin Scott

In early May 1866, the ladies of Spotsylvania Court House, Virginia, met "for the purpose of making arrangements to pay respect to the memory of the Confederate soldiers . . . whose remains lie within its limits (county)." The ladies hoped "if found practical, to gather into one common cemetery all of the remains." In June 1866, the women incorporated into the Ladies' Memorial Association of Spotsylvania. This Ladies' Memorial Association survives today, with the purpose of perpetually caring for the Spotsylvania Confederate Cemetery.

Sometime in late 1866 or early 1867, Irby H. Scott, father of Nicholas E. Scott, made an effort to locate and bring the remains of his son home to Putnam County, Georgia. Two of the men who were responsible for interning Nicholas knew the location of the grave and helped mark it. In February 1867 Mr. James W. Stewart of Spotsylvania Court House, Virginia, wrote Mr. Scott that he had found the grave site of Nicholas. Apparently Irby H. Scott decided not to bring his son home, because Nicholas is buried in the Confederate Cemetery, Spotsylvania, Virginia, Georgia section, row L, grave 5.

Feb 15th 1867

Mr Scott

Dear sir I received your letter ——— to your son some time ago & I would have replied to it sooner, but we had such bad weather that it was impossible for me to look for him at that time. Since the weather has gotten good I have been searching for him & found a man lying about 20 feet south of & old log stable & about 15 feet above Clecks grave. I examed the grave & found he had been shot about the right eye the ball coming out back of the head & from appearances his hair seem to be a dark brown he had on a check shirt & I think a blue blouse coat he had on brown pants nor shoes that I could discover his grave was North & South. The head South & I think from all appearances a small man or common size. I put some planks around him & covered up the grave well & put a pen around it so that nothing can get to the grave. You can let me know if I have found the right grave or not. If not I will search again. I forgot to state he was buried about 2 feet deep. Very respectably your friend.

James W. Stewart

Spotsylvania Court House, Va

Chapter 13

Final Word Home

"Although cut off from home I think of you often."

It is a shame no letters survive that Irby Scott may have written home during the 1864 Valley campaign. Once Federal General Philip H. Sheridan began offensive operations in mid-September, there were fewer opportunities to write as the men marched, skirmished, and fought three decisive battles until mid-October. There is also a possibility some of his letters may have been destroyed during Sherman's march through Putnam County, Georgia, in late 1864.

On June 13, 1864, Scott and the Second Corps marched from Richmond to Charlottesville, where they boarded trains to Lynchburg, Virginia. Recent Federal damage to the rail line from Charlottesville to Lynchburg made travel slow. General Jubal A. Early could only move half of his command to Lynchburg by June 17. Rodes's division followed on June 18. By the afternoon of June 18 the Battle of Lynchburg was coming to an end, and Scott and the men arrived after the battle had concluded. Federal General David Hunter, far from his base of supplies, and facing a shortage of ammunition and believing General Early outnumbered him, withdrew during the night of June 18. General Early, and the 12th Georgia, pursued General Hunter to Salem, then on June 21 turned down the valley toward Lexington.

After the Battle of Lynchburg, Irby Scott and the men would begin one of the most important military campaigns in the Shenandoah Valley. During the first phase, Early's army cleared the valley of Federal control, crossed the Potomac River, and threatened the defenses of the Federal capital. On the march down the valley, Scott passed through Lexington, where he and the men marched past the grave of General Stonewall Jackson "with arms reversed" in "perfect silence." A member of Scott's company wrote that the grave of Jackson was "covered with flowers and Confederate Flag hung over" the grave site.

Before crossing the Potomac River, Irby Scott and the men skirmished with Federal troops on Boliver Heights, and on the next day, July 5, entered Harper's Ferry. Crossing the Potomac River into Maryland near Sharpsburg on July 6, after a day of rest, the men crossed South Mountain by Crampton's Gap, moving toward Frederick, Maryland. At Frederick, on July 9, Federal defenders fell back toward Monocacy Junction, resisting Confederate passage of the river for most of the day. Following the Battle of Monocacy, the road toward Washington provided a clear avenue for the advancing Confederate army. On July 11 Scott and the men advanced near the fortifications of Washington.

In the late afternoon of July 12 Scott and the men, in line of battle before Fort Stevens, received orders to support the skirmish line. During the ensuing skirmish, Captain Abner R. Zachry received a wound to the side of his chest. On the evening of July 12 all of the badly wounded, including Captain Zachry, were left in the hands of the Federals when General Early withdrew his army. Scott, as first lieutenant, now found himself in command of his company, a position he held until the surrender at Appomattox Court House, Virginia, on April 9, 1865. Scott could not receive a promotion to captain, because no provisions in the Confederate army regulations allowed the promotion of an officer to the position of an officer held as a prisoner of war.

After testing the defenses of the city of Washington, the 12th Georgia withdrew to Virginia, where the Second Corps continued to operate along the Potomac River during July and August. On August 7 the second phase of the campaign began when General Sheridan took command of all Federal forces in the theater. Sheridan would be admonished "that nothing should be left to invite the enemy to return" and to "Bear in mind, the object, is to drive the enemy South." Five weeks passed as Sheridan assembled his force. In mid-September he began active operations against Confederates in the valley.

General Sheridan learned on September 18 that General Early had sent Gordon's and Rodes's divisions to Martinsburg, West Virginia. Sheridan also learned that Confederate General Richard Anderson, with General Joseph Kershaw's division and Major Wilfred Cushaw's artillery battalion, had been recalled to General Lee. Now with General Early's army reduced and dispersed, Sheridan attacked Winchester, Virginia, on September 19, from the east. To hold General Rodes's and General Gordon's Confederates north of Winchester, two Federal cavalry divisions provided a supporting attack.

Between nine and ten o'clock on September 19, Rodes's division arrived on the left of Ramseur's hard-pressed division. Irby Scott and the men of Cook's brigade anchored the left of Rodes's division. Sheridan's force had stalled in the Berryville Canyon, and to take advantage of the gap in the Federal line, Rodes attacked the Federal line. Federal General Emory Upton, who had attacked the Twelfth Georgia at Spotsylvania on May 10, waited until Confederates closed within two hundred yards before giving the order to fire, followed by the order "Forward Charge." Irby Scott and the men of General Philip Cook's Confederate brigade suffered the brunt of the Federal volley and charge. Rodes's left crumbled and the men retired to their original position. During the counterattack General Rodes was mortally wounded. With no Confederate reserves, the weight of the Federal attack from the east and the north forced the Confederates to retire west and south toward Winchester. About 5 p.m., General Early realized he might be overwhelmed, and his line of retreat cut issued orders for the army to retire up the Valley Turnpike toward Newtown.

On the morning of September 20, Irby Scott and the men marched at daylight to Fisher's Hill, south of Strasburg. Upon reaching Fisher's Hill, the men, on the left of the line, commenced construcing earthworks. Dismounted cavalry protected the extreme left of the line. Major General Stephen D. Ramseur now commanded General Rodes's division.

General Sheridan planned a flanking movement on the Confederate left while his force demonstrated in front of the Confederate works. During the night of September 21, General George H. Crook's corps moved toward the right of the Federal army. Advancing in darkness, using the cover of the woods of Little North Mountain, he positioned his force on the left flank of the Confederate defenders on Fisher's Hill. On the morning of September 22, dismounted Federal cavalry attacked the Confederate left front while Crook moved into position on the Confederate left. At about the same time, a similar feint on the Confederate right occurred, shortly followed by a general engagement along the entire Confederate line.

General Crook's corps assaulted the extreme left of the Confederate line, brushing aside Confederate dismounted cavalry slamming into Ramseur's division. As the Union tide rolled over and behind the Confederate left, Federal troops assaulted in front, overwhelming Ramseur's brigades. Irby Scott and the men more than likely stayed in position until General Battle's brigade, which had been moved to confront the advancing Federals, had been routed on their rear and left flank. It is likely the 12th Georgia retired at this time. General Early withdrew his shattered force to Woodstock, about twenty-fives miles to the south, where he took up a defensive position on Mount Jackson. On September 25 the 12th Georgia retired to Brown's Gap.

General Lee once again sent General Joseph Kershaw's infantry division and also General Thomas Rosser's cavalry division to reinforce Early. With these additional troops, Early decided to close on the Federal position at Cedar Creek. By October 13 Early's army again occupied Fisher's Hill. There Early began to plan an attack on the Federal army located on the north bank of Cedar Creek. Confederate General Gordon and other officers ascended to the top of Massanutten Mountain on October 17. From the top of the mountain a full view of the Federal camp and all aspects of the camp could be viewed. Once back at Fisher's Hill, a decision was made to attack the Federal left flank on the morning of October 19. On October 18, about 8 p.m., Gordon and his division departed Fisher's Hill on their flanking movement. After a fatiguing march, at times in single file, Irby Scott and the men formed in line of battle to wait for the fighting to commence. Once the attack began, about 5:30 a.m., the Twelfth Georgia surged toward the lines of the Union Eighth corps, catching many of the Federal defenders half-dressed or asleep in their tents.

Upon reaching the Valley Turnpike, Scott and the men came under fire from Federal artillery on Red Hill. However, the smoke of battle and the early morning fog obscured the massed Confederates from Federal artillery fire. Halting on the turnpike for about an hour, skirmishers moved to the front until a Confederate battery came into position on the right of the turnpike. About 8 a.m., Confederate artillery commenced firing on Red Hill. Shortly afterward the Twelfth Georgia advanced against the position the Federal Sixth Corps had held on Red Hill, where they re-formed and replenished cartridge-boxes.

About 3:30 p.m. Confederate skirmishers retired into the main line before an advancing Federal line of battle. On the Confederate left, the battle line began retreating in confusion. The Twelfth Georgia fell back two hundred years to a stone fence. They held the center of the line and for an hour and a half held against the Federal Sixth Corps. Once Federal cavalry and infantry gained the rear of the Confederate right flank, the entire Confederate line broke and retreated in confusion toward Fisher's Hill. On October 20, General Early withdrew toward New Market, where the Confederate army remained throughout the rest of October and most of November. While at New Market, Brigadier General Bryan Grimes took command of the late General Ramseur's division.

On December 8, the Second Corps, now under General John B. Gordon, left the valley to report to General Lee around Petersburg. The Twelfth Georgia departed the valley on December 14, arriving in Staunton the following day, where they boarded cars for Richmond. During the balance of December, January, and much of February, Scott and the men rested in reserve at Camp Rodes in Petersburg. In late January 1865 Irby Scott's company consisted of nine enlisted men, plus two officers, and one corporal.

On February 5–7, 1865, an engagement near Hatcher's Run required Scott and his fellow soldiers to march from Camp Rodes toward the sound of battle. Upon their arrival, the 12th Georgia learned they were not needed, and returned to camp. On February 23, the 12th Georgia departed Camp Rodes for the extreme right of the army to protect the South Side Railroad and the Boydton Plank Road. On February 28, Special Order No. 55 officially assigned Major General Bryan Grimes to command of Rodes's old division. One of the men of Irby Scott's company stated that they did "not like him because he is tyrannical like all North Carolina officers."

On February 25, 1865, Irby Scott wrote his last surviving letter home while camped near Sutherland's Station, Virginia. Before the move to the extreme right of the Confederate line, all their baggage had been sent to Richmond, indicating preparations for active service. From the time Scott arrived in this new camp until early March, the weather was cool and rainy, leaving the roads and the surrounding area a muddy mess.

Southside Railroad Va
Camped near Southerners Station
Feby 25th 1865
Dear Father,

As a man is going to leave here for Georgia this evening I avail myself of the opportunity to sending a letter by him. This is our only chance now to get our letters through. I am well and getting on very well. We have abandon our winter quarters near Petersburg and are now camped near the right of our lines on the Southside road we moved only about twelve miles. Sent to Richmond all our extra blankets, baggage &c. to Richmond. There are many speculations in regard to whether we will take a position on the right of the army or go to N. Carolina. We have no shelter except our little small tents.[1] The weather at present is not cold but cloudy and raining. I received my boxes all right & was well pleased with them. I am anxious to hear from home and shall look for a letter by Bob Jenkins. There is nothing new with us. Write me every opportunity that presents itself. Tom is well and sends howdy to all.[2] I will close for fear I will not get my letter ready before the man leaves. My warmest love and affection for yourself mother and all the children. My respects to all friends. Remember me to all the negroes. Although cut off from home I think of you often. No chance to come home at present or untill Sherman is whiped from the railroad.[3]
Your affectionate son as ever.
I. Goodwin Scott

In March 1865 Robert E. Lee turned to General John Gordon to study the Federal lines and suggest a course of action. General Gordon's plan called for a predawn assault against Fort Stedman, Battery X to the north and Batteries XI and XII to the south. After capturing the initial objectives, the Confederate infantry would expand their breach by turning left and right. In the early morning hours of March 25, Irby Scott and the men of his division comprised the last of the three columns for the assault's first phase.

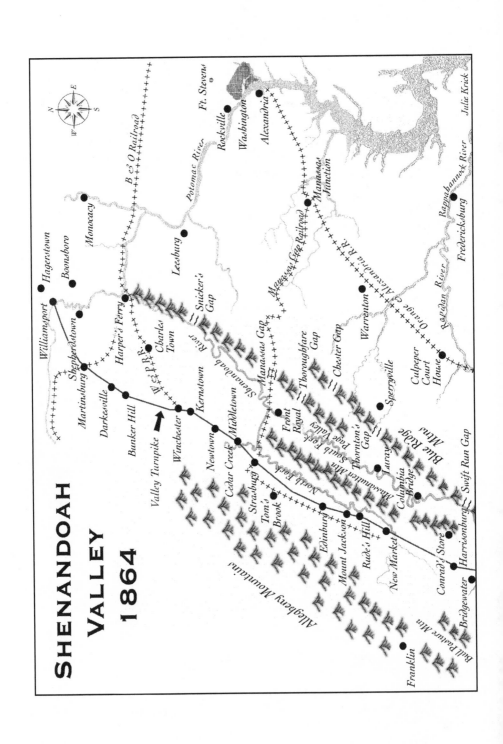

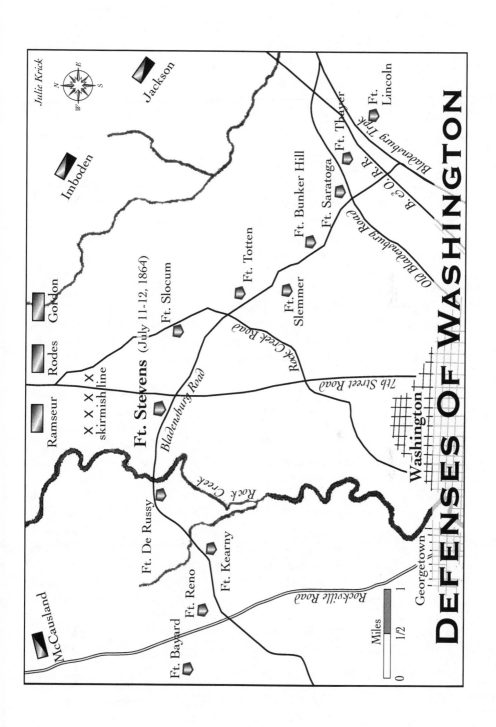

DEFENSES OF WASHINGTON

Fort Stedman Batteries X and XI fell to the advancing Confederates, but the rapid movement, darkness, and the maze of trenches caused confusion. Many attacking Confederate soldiers lost their way. Federal gunners began to fire into the mass of southerners. Expected reinforcements never arrived, and the Confederate attackers retired back to their entrenchments.

On April 2, Grant ordered a general assault along the Confederate lines. About 4 o'clock in the morning, two divisions of the Federal Ninth Corps attacked the portion of the line Irby Scott and the men defended. Breaching the Confederate line near where they were posted, the soldiers of Cook's brigade were pushed back. Counterattacking, the men regained control of the line. After dark, on April 2, the Twelfth Georgia evacuated the line, marching north through Petersburg. In just seven days, the Army of Northern Virginia would surrender at Appomattox Court House, Virginia, on April 9, 1865.

Only eight men of Company G, Twelfth Georgia, surrendered at Appomattox. Another six men of the company serving on detached duty also surrendered. First Lieutenant Irby G. Scott, in command of the company, surrendered and received his parole.

A number of the men of the Twelfth Georgia walked to Danville, Virginia, where they took the train to Greensboro, North Carolina. From Greensboro they reached the Savannah River by train and were walking when they crossed into Georgia. Once reaching Georgia, the trip home would be mostly on foot.

After the surrender, Irby Scott aided his father in the management of the family plantation. In 1861 the value of the Irby H. Scott property amounted to $29,563. In 1866 the value fell to $7,016, in part from decreased land values but primarily from the emancipation of the family's slaves.

On August 9, 1865, sixteen former slaves signed a contract with Irby H. Scott. This contract required Scott "to furnish said freed men and women and their children now members of his family with food, and clothing and to treat them in every way humanely also to give them one sixth part of the whole crop raised on his plantation this year 1865." The freed men and women agreed to "bind ourselves to continue to perform the work on his plantation, and elsewhere as directed . . . and not to leave said plantation without permission from said Irby H. Scott." Franklin, who had joined Irby in the army, signed the contract, and one can only guess his wife did also. One other former slave, Alfred, also signed the contract. Both Franklin and Alfred are said to be buried in the Irby H. Scott family burial ground.

In February 1875, veterans of the "Putnam Light Infantry" met and chose Irby G. Scott to serve on a committee to prepare a record of the company. Throughout the remainder of his life, Scott committed his energy and financial resources to the men who had served in the Confederate army. He was a member of the R. T. Davis Camp of the United Confederate Veterans, and solicited contributions for the construction of the Putnam County Confederate Monument and the Atlanta Soldiers' Home. At the annual meeting of the Davis Camp, held on Veterans' Memorial Day, 1924, Irby Scott became commander, a position he held until his death on May 25, 1925.

Irby Scott married Florence E. Williams of Jones County, Georgia, on May 26, 1880. Reverend Asa Marshall, former chaplain of the Twelfth Georgia and member of Company G, united the couple in marriage. Scott family lore claims that the Williams family was of a higher social standing than the Irby Scott family, and that Irby courted Florence by mail. He is said to have written irresistible letters to woo her. To their union three children survived to adulthood.

The Irby Goodwin Scott letters provide a vivid portrait of an everyday soldier and the men of his company. Defending the family fireside may have been the motivation for Scott's entrance into the life of a soldier. As the war progressed, his attachment to family grew stronger. At one point Scott expressed his desire to repay his father and mother for their support while in the army, though he felt he could never fully repay them. It is also clear from the Irby G. Scott letters that the bond of brotherhood among the men of his company helped sustain him throughout the horrors of war. Scott's letters are about endurance, sacrifice, duty, and the sense of community with the men of the company. Country, liberty, and peace to live a freed man took on greater importance. Once Irby Scott returned home, after the army surrendered, he became the everyday citizen as he had been the everyday soldier. His commitment to family, community, and to the men who served the Confederacy continued throughout the remainder of his life.

Irby G. Scott wearing a military jacket. Date unknown. Courtesy of T. G. Scott.

Mary Ellen Tompkins Scott, mother of Irby G. and Nicholas Scott. From the editor's collection.

Irby H. Scott, father of Irby G. and Nicholas Scott. From the editor's collection.

Camp Bartow earthworks face northwest toward East Fork, Greenbrier River. From the editor's collection.

Home of George Gibbons, Bridgewater, Virginia. General "Stonewall" Jackson, Col. Z. T. Conner, Rev. Dr. Dabney, Jedediah Hotchkiss, and others dined with Mr. Gibbons on May 18, 1862. From the editor's collection.

Travelers Repose was a stagecoach stop and post office on the Staunton–Parkersburg Turnpike on the east bank of the Greenbrier River. Before and during the battle of October 3, 1861, the stage stop served as a hospital. This modern home is said to have been built on the prior foundation of the stagecoach stop. From the editor's collection.

Tompkins Inn, owned by his maternal grandfather, is where Irby G. Scott as a young man would have met and talked to travelers going and coming from Milledgeville, Georgia. From the editor's collection.

McCoull House. This photograph was taken in 1864, shortly after the battle of Spotsylvania. Courtesy of the Fredericksburg and Spotsylvania National Military Park.

George Pierce Doles (1830–1864), first commander of what has become known as the Doles-Cook brigade. Scott and the soldiers of the Twelfth Georgia were transferred to this brigade on January 9, 1863. Courtesy of National Archives.

Edward S. "Ned" Willis (1840–1864), colonel of the Twelfth Georgia, January 22, 1863. Colonel Willis was mortally wounded at Bethesda Church, Virginia, and died May 31, 1864. On June 8, 1864, Scott wrote his father, stating, "In the death of Col Willis the Regt lost its best friend." Courtesy Christopher L. Ferguson.

Reverend Asa M. Marshall, ca. 1895, chaplain of the Twelfth Georgia. Reverend Marshall married Irby G. Scott to Florence E. Williams, May 26, 1880, in Blountsville, Jones County, Georgia. Courtesy of Georgia Archives, Vanishing Georgia Collection, Put193.

Dr. Nathaniel E. Walker, ca. 1860–1864, surgeon of the Forty-fourth Georgia. Dr. Walker, a physician of Putnam County, Georgia, joined the Forty-fourth Georgia at the outbreak of the Civil War. Dr. Walker treated Robert E. Lee for his injured wrists at the beginning of the 1862 Maryland campaign. Courtesy of Georgia Archives, Vanishing Georgia Collection, Put220.

R. T. Davis Camp No. 759, U.C.V., April 26, 1911. The men are standing around the Confederate memorial, with the Eatonton Hotel in the background. Irby G. Scott helped raise funds for the memorial and is likely in this photograph. Courtesy of Georgia Archives, Vanishing Georgia Collection, Put111.

General Phillip Cook (1817–1894), ca. 1880.
Enlisted April 29, 1861, Company I, "Macon
County Volunteers," Fourth Georgia, promoted
to colonel, Fourth Georgia, November 1, 1862.
After the death of General George Pierce Doles,
promoted to brigadier general, August 5, 1864,
and assigned to command Doles's Brigade.
Courtesy of Library of Congress.

Irby G. Scott later in life, date unknown. Courtesy of T. G. Scott.

Irby G. Scott carried a Remington Model 1861 army revolver, also known as a Remington Old Model army revolver. The term "army" does not imply the branch of service but rather the caliber (.44 caliber). From the editor's collection.

Mary Ellen Tompkins Scott (1821–1909), seated on the right of her sisters. Ca. 1885–1890. Courtesy of Georgia Archives, Vanishing Georgia Collection, Put083.

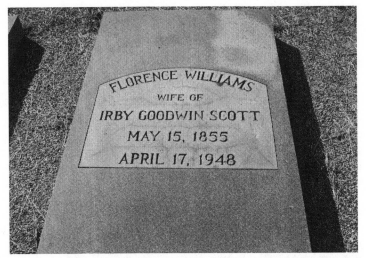

Florence Williams Scott's memorial marker at Harmony Baptist Church Cemetery, Putnam County, Georgia. From the editor's collection.

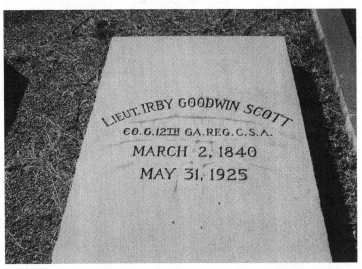

Irby Goodwin Scott's memorial marker at Harmony Baptist Church Cemetery, Putnam County, Georgia. From the editor's collection.

Flag of Company G, Putnam Light Infantry. The flag is silk of the first national design, with a blue field containing seven stars representing the seven seceding states as of June 1861. On Friday, June 14, 1861, Miss Fannie J. Reid presented the company with this flag. Private collection.

Detail of the obverse side of Company G, Putnam Light Infantry flag. The Latin phrase *Venimus ut Vincamus* translates to "we came that we might conquer." Private collection.

Aerial view of the prehistoric Rock Eagle located on the Irby H. Scott plantation, now the Rock Eagle 4-H Center property. The photograph's date is unknown, but it was taken before an observation tower and fence enclosure were installed at the site in the 1930s. Courtesy of the National Park Service, Southeast Archeological Center.

Appendix

ROSTER OF COMPANY G, PUTNAM LIGHT INFANTRY, TWELFTH GEORGIA INFANTRY REGIMENT

The National Archives' "Compiled Service Records of Confederate Soldiers in Organizations from the State of Georgia" provides the primary source material for this roster. Another primary source is the "Pension Applications of Confederate Soldiers and Widows who applied from Georgia." While reading the letters of Irby Goodwin Scott, it becomes apparent that Irby tried to inform his family about the condition of the company's men. Of the 113 in the company, Scott writes of seventy-five of these individuals in his letters. Of course, the men with whom he had the closest association are mentioned more than once. There are at least four sources for the roster, but none of them agree in every case. By using these four sources, Irby Scott's letters, and the National Archives records, a comprehensive roster has been developed.

Demographic information is taken from U.S. census returns, tax digests, and court records in Baldwin, Morgan, and Putnam Counties, Georgia. Additionally, other primary-source letters and diaries have been used to enhance the information on many of the soldiers. The Eatonton Putnam County Historical Society and the former archivist of Morgan County, Georgia, both contributed much additional information for the men in the roster.

ADAMS, BENJAMIN FRANKLIN. Born Putnam County, Georgia, September 11, 1843. In 1860 resident of Putnam County, Georgia. Listed as eighteen-year-old farmer in the household of his father, Jonathan Adams, a wheelwright. Owned no property. Enlisted as private at Camp Bartow, Virginia, October 10, 1861. Wounded in left hip joint in a skirmish near a bridge two miles northeast of Front Royal, Virginia, May 30, 1862. Detailed as ambulance driver, and as a teamster for brigade medical wagon. Captured at Cedar Creek, Virginia, October 19, 1864. Exchanged. Surrendered, Appomattox, Virginia, April 9, 1865. Living in Pennington, Georgia, after the war. Died July 30, 1911. Buried Antioch Baptist Church Cemetery, Godfrey, Morgan County, Georgia. The Madisonian (Madison, Georgia): "Death of Mr. B. F. Adams. When Mr. Ben F. Adams died at his home in Pennington last Saturday Morgan County lost a mighty good citizen. He was an old Confederate soldier, an honest man, true friend and kind neighbor."

ADAMS, IRBY HUDSON. Born Putnam County, Georgia, March 31, 1843. In 1860 resident Putnam County, Georgia. Listed as seventeen years old in the household of his father, David Rosser Adams Sr., and mother, Eliza Hudson. Owned no property. Enlisted as private, April 4, 1862. Discharged on account of disability, July 21, 1862. He was commissioned by Governor Joseph Brown in October 1862 a captain to organize and drill those subject to military duty in the 368th (Eatonton) militia district. Enlisted near Augusta, Georgia, January 2, 1864, in the Twenty-seventh Georgia Battalion and elected first lieutenant, Company B. In December 1864 he was captured near Savannah, but escaped. Promoted to captain following the battle at Bentonville, North Carolina, March 21, 1865. Surrendered Greensboro, North Carolina, April 26, 1865. Married first Florence Reid, December 20, 1871, Putnam County, Georgia. Married second Julia C. (Hudson) Jordan, February 1, 1883, Putnam County, Georgia. Married third Eppie Elder, 1886/1887, Barnsville, Georgia. After the war he was engaged in banking and insurance. Died in Eatonton, Georgia, March 22, 1900. Buried Pine Grove Cemetery with his three wives, Section 1, Division A, Lot 120, Eatonton, Georgia. *Eatonton Messenger* (Eatonton, Georgia) issue of March 24, 1900: "DEATH OF CAPTAIN ADAMS: . . . here was a man who was universally liked. We doubt if anybody remembers ever having heard an unkind word uttered about him. He numbered his friends by the number of his acquaintances, and for them he had a cheerful word. He was well and widely known in business and military circles. He was long a member of the Methodist church and died in the hope and belief of eternal life. He has answered the final roll call."

ADAMS, JAMES QUINTON "PUT." Born Philadelphia, Pennsylvania, 1835. In 1860 resident Putnam County, Georgia, having arrived only a short time before the strife began. His father, was a physician in Philadelphia, killed when thrown from his buggy. Enlisted as private June 15, 1861. Detailed in Commissary Department August 31, 1861. Appointed commissary sergeant April 30, 1862. Appointed regimental commissary sergeant and clerk May 1, 1863; brigade commissary sergeant 1864. Surrendered, Appomattox, Virginia, April 9, 1865. Married Nannie C. Rogan, June 23, 1869, a member of a well-known east Tennessee family. James Adams died Eatonton, Georgia, July 31, 1896. Buried Pine Grove Cemetery, Section 1, Division A, Lot 87, Eatonton, Putnam County, Georgia. *Eatonton Messenger* (Eatonton, Georgia) issue of August 8, 1896: "A SUDDEN DEATH. WHILE ON THE WAY HOME, MR. J. Q. ADAMS SEIZED WITH APOPLEXY. . . . Mr. Adams was a gentleman of much more than average intelligence, and in his career he had filled with satisfaction to all concerned several important local offices. He was an enthusiastic Mason, and several others of the secret orders of Eatonton found in him a valuable member. Pleasant, sociable and gentlemanly, he will be missed by his many friends and the public generally."

ADAMS, JOHN COLLINGSWORTH. In 1860 resident Putnam County, Georgia. Listed as nineteen years old, born Putnam County, Georgia, in the household of his father, David Rosser Adams Sr. Owned no property. Enlisted as private, June 15, 1861. Appointed musician. Wounded severely in side at McDowell, Virginia, May 8, 1862. Patient in a private home in Staunton upon being removed from the battlefield at McDowell. Admitted to general hospital, Charlottesville, Virginia, June 16, 1864, owing to dysentery and transferred to convalescent camp June 18, 1864. Wounded in the forehead just below the hairline, "where a minié ball seemed to have entered lengthwise," at about sundown, Summit Point, Virginia, August 21, 1864. Of this wound, though appearing to be bad, Robert Young stated, "I saw him he was walking about and looked pretty well." He was wounded again and received at United States Army Depot Field Hospital, as a prisoner of war, Winchester, Virginia, September 19, 1864, with a flesh wound of the head. Transferred to another hospital October 20, 1864. Supposed to have died soon after at Mt. Jackson. John C. Adams is not listed on the memorial marker at the Mt. Jackson Cemetery nor is he listed in *Confederate P.O.W.'s: Soldiers & Sailors Who Died In Federal Prisons, & Military Hospitals In The North.* This work was compiled in the Office of the Commissioner for Marking Graves of Confederate Dead, War Department, 1912.

ADAMS, JOSIAH FLOURNOY "COY." Born Putnam County, Georgia, April 9, 1844. In 1860 resident of Putnam County, Georgia. Listed as sixteen years old in the household of his father, Benjamin Franklin Adams. Enlisted as private, June 15, 1861. Absent sick August 1862, on sick furlough from September 17, 1862, until discharged by order in 1863. Appointed sergeant while on sick furlough. Elected second lieutenant of Company A. A. H. Reid's company, Sixty-sixth Georgia Infantry Regiment, August 8, 1863, while home on sick furlough. This company subsequently became Company F, Sixty-sixth Georgia Infantry Regiment. Wounded Peachtree Creek, Georgia, July 20, 1864. Absent wounded August 31, 1864. His company and regiment surrendered Greensboro, North Carolina, April 26, 1865. At the time of the surrender he was at Charlotte, North Carolina, on detached service. Married Fannie Elizabeth Moore of Greene County, Georgia, on August 10, 1865, in Putnam County, Georgia. Died January 17, 1910, Putnam County, Georgia. Buried Pine Grove Cemetery, Section 1, Division B, Lot 235, Eatonton, Georgia. *Eatonton Messenger* (Eatonton, Georgia) issue of January 20, 1910: "DEATH CALLS MR. FLOURNOY ADAMS: Died at his home in this city Sunday night after a few weeks' illness. . . . Although a young man, Mr. Adams with the spirit of the south at the close of the civil war went to the front as a Georgia volunteer and has ever remained true and loyal to the lost cause and to his Confederate comrades. He was always a great lover of music, possessed a fine bass voice, and characteristic of the Adams family, he was never happier than when he was singing with the Sunday School children while he made his home in the county, as well as after joining the Methodist choir in Eatonton."

ALFORD, GREEN B. Born August 21, 1823. In 1860 resident Putnam County, Georgia. Listed as thirty-six-year-old carpenter in the household of his sixty-six-year-old father, William Alford. Value of whole property $325. Married Martha Ann Arnett August 14, 1851, in Columbia County, Georgia. Enlisted as private, June 15, 1861. At Harrisonburg, Virginia, sick since September 29, 1861. Discharged on account of disability at Allegheny Mountain, Virginia, December 25, 1861. At age forty-three mustered at Eatonton, Georgia, as a private, Company A, Augusta Arsenal Battalion, Georgia Local Defense, September 11, 1863. Subsequently this company became, Company A, Twenty-seventh Battalion, Georgia Volunteer Infantry, Arsenal Guard. From the compiled service record it appears he was absent sick a great deal of the time. Discharged from the army on surgeon's certificate of disability. In 1907 he was living in Morgan County, Georgia, at the age of eighty-one. His pension was transferred to Putnam County, Georgia, in 1907 owing to his residence in Putnam County, Georgia.

ALFORD, HENRY WILLIAM. In 1860 resident Putnam County, Georgia. Listed as twenty-two years old, born Georgia, in the household of William Alford, his father. Half brother to Green B. Alford. Married Georgey E. Coats January 30, 1859, Putnam County, Georgia. Owned no property. Enlisted as private, June 15, 1861. Slightly wounded Malvern Hill, Virginia, July 1, 1862. Slightly wounded at Cold Harbor, Virginia, June 27, 1862. Killed at Winchester, Virginia, September 19, 1864.

ALFORD, WILLIAM H. In 1860 resident Putnam County, Georgia. Born 1839, Georgia. Listed as twenty years old in the household of his father, John Allen Alford, and mother, Jerusba Paschal. Owned no property. Enlisted as private June 15, 1861. Slightly wounded at Cedar Run, Virginia, August 9, 1862. Killed at Chantilly, Virginia, September 2, 1862, by a ball to the bowels.

ALFORD, WILLIAM. Born Morgan County, Georgia, April 1825. In 1860 resident Putnam County, Georgia. Owned 574 acres in Putnam County, Georgia, twelve slaves, value of whole property $11,480. Married Susan Bryant January 25, 1849, Morgan County,

Georgia. Enlisted as private June 15, 1961. Sick in Lynchburg, Virginia, hospital June 30–August 31, 1864. Admitted March 16, 1865, Farmville, Virginia, hospital owing to rheumatism. Admitted Petersburg, Virginia, March 25, 1865. Paroled at Lynchburg, Virginia, April 1865. Lived in Jasper, Morgan, and Wilkes Counties, Georgia, after the war. Died February 5, 1909, Emanuel County, Georgia.

Arnold, William Thomas. In 1860 resident Putnam County, Georgia. Listed as seventeen years old in the household of his father, Wiley Arnold. Owned no property. Enlisted as private June 15, 1861. Slightly wounded in the thigh at Allegheny Mountain, Virginia. December 13, 1861. Absent sick Staunton, Virginia, returned to the company March 22, 1862. With ordnance train in late 1862. Wounded Gettysburg, Pennsylvania, July 1, 1863. Captured at Spotsylvania, Virginia, May 10, 1864, transferred to Elmira, New York, August 10, 1864. Transferred to Point Lookout, Maryland, February 20, 1865, and paroled for exchange. Living in Marshall, Texas, after the war. Died Marshall, Harrison County, Texas, March 12, 1915. *Eatonton Messenger* (Eatonton, Georgia) issue of April 2, 1915: WILLIAM T. ARNOLD: . . . He was only eighteen when he volunteered and served gallantly and faithfully three years with Jackson and Lee in Virginia, and then a year in Prison. . . . Married and lived the life of a good Christian citizen, loved and respected by all who knew him. It is said that the attendance on his funeral was the largest ever seen in Marshall there being over five hundred present, including the W. P. Lane Camp, UCV and sons of Veterans.

Athon, Absalom William. Born in Surry County, North Carolina, August 1, 1833. In 1860 resident Schley County, Georgia. Listed as a twenty-three-year-old overseer in the household of George Dikes. In the 1861 Putnam County, Georgia, tax digest he is listed as only paying a poll. Enlisted as private June 15, 1861. Absent sick Stribbling Springs, Virginia, December 12, 1861. Slightly wounded at Snicker's Ferry, Virginia, August 1, 1864. His wound caused a stiff leg, and his left arm and hand were so shrunken and emaciated he could do no work with them. Married Artemesia Ophelia (Pearson) Davis, widow of John A. Davis, November 22, 1866. Died Milledgeville, Georgia, January 26, 1918. Buried Avolona Church Cemetery, Putnam County, Georgia. *Union Recorder* (Milledgeville, Georgia) issue of January 30, 1918: " . . . Mr. Athon was a devoted and upright man and his long life has been a blessing and benediction to all who have come under his influence. He was a member of the Methodist Church and was a regular attendant upon its services, always manifesting great interest in public worship of Him, who he served faithfully."

Avery, Thomas G. Born Social Circle, Walton County, Georgia, about 1838. In 1860 resident Morgan County, Georgia. Listed as twenty-one years old in the household of his father, Henry F. Avery, and his stepmother, Mary Brown Avery. Owned no property. Enlisted as private, June 15, 1861. During the summer of 1863 on provost guard. Severely wounded at Wilderness, Virginia, May 5, 1864, by a minié ball to the eye, returned to duty from Farmville, Virginia, hospital July 13, 1864. Slightly wounded at Winchester, Virginia, September 19, 1864. Paroled at Staunton, Virginia, May 1, 1865. Said to have died in 1870 owing to wounds he received in the war. Thomas is likely buried in an unmarked grave in the Arthur Avera(y) Family Cemetery, Putnam County, Georgia.

Badger, Charles Robert. Born Putnam County, Georgia, 1832. In 1860 resident Putnam County, Georgia. Owned no property. Released at Richmond, Virginia, June 24, 1861. He did not muster into Confederate service with Company G, Twelfth Georgia Infantry Regiment. Enlisted as private December 5, 1861, Company C, 2nd Battalion, 2nd

Brigade, Georgia State Troops, "Dennis Guards," Putnam County, Georgia. Mustered out May 1862. Enlisted at Fort Jackson as private May 11, 1862, Captain Anderson's company, "Republic Blues," First Regiment Georgia Infantry. This company subsequently became Company C, First Regiment, Georgia (Olmstead's) Infantry. In July 1864, while in the vicinity of Atlanta, he was sent to the hospital owing to sickness. In November and December 1864 he was stationed at Camp Wright, a convalescence camp, located at Macon, Georgia. His duty at Camp Wright is not shown. Muster roll for December 31, 1864, shows him with Company B, 2nd Battalion Troops and Defenders, Macon, Georgia, on provost guard duty at Eatonton, Georgia, from January 4, 1865. Captured at Macon, Georgia, April 20 or 21, 1865, where he was paroled. Died September 12, 1893, Eatonton, Georgia. Prior to his death he was the coroner for Putnam County, Georgia. Buried in Pine Grove Cemetery, Eatonton, Georgia. *Eatonton Messenger* (Eatonton, Georgia) issue of September 16, 1893: "LOCAL . . . He was a gentleman of integrity and high character, a consistent Christian and one whom nobody had occasion to speak ill."

BARNARD, LEEMAN J. In 1860 resident Putnam County, Georgia. Listed as thirty-three-year-old farmer in the household of Wilkins Linch. Real estate $325, personal estate $2,000. Enlisted as private June 15, 1861. Discharged on account of rheumatism January 3, 1862. Reenlisted Company G, 12th Georgia Infantry Regiment, October 1, 1863, at Macon, Georgia. Discharged disabled owing to chronic rheumatism at Bunker Hill, Virginia, August 31, 1864. At the time of his discharge he was thirty-seven years of age, 6 feet 2-1/2 inches tall, fair complexion, gray eyes, dark hair, and by occupation a farmer. Never married. Died November 21, 1899, Putnam County, Georgia. Buried Avolona Church Cemetery, Putnam County, Georgia. *Eatonton Messenger* (Eatonton, Georgia) issue of November 25, 1899: "DEATH OF L. J. BARNARD: . . . He was a good neighbor and was honest and straightforward in his dealing. He was in the war and was loyal to the cause for which the South fought. He was never married and lived at the time of his death with his nephew, J. J. Melton."

BATCHELOR, CORDY. Born Putnam County, Georgia, October 10, 1842. In 1860 resident Putnam County, Georgia. Listed as seventeen years old in the household of his father, Cordy Batchelor, and mother, Mary Corine. Owned no property. Enlisted as private June 15, 1861. Captured at Front Royal, Virginia, May 30, 1862. Exchanged from Fort Delaware at Aiken's Landing, Virginia, August 5, 1862. Slightly wounded at Chancellorsville, Virginia, May 2, 1863. At general hospital, Camp Winder, Richmond, Virginia, December 3, 1863, owing to fever. Furloughed December 18, 1863. In hospital Macon, Georgia, January 1864 and from there furloughed for thirty days. Severely wounded in the left hip, the ball passing through the back, at Spotsylvania, Virginia, May 10, 1864. Surrendered Appomattox, Virginia, April 9, 1865. Living in Morgan County, Georgia, at the time of his death on August 7, 1905.

BATCHELOR, DAVID. In 1860 resident Putnam County, Georgia. Listed as twenty-seven-year-old farmer, born Georgia, married, no children. He was the son of Cordy Batchelor and Mary Corine. Value of personal estate $100. Enlisted as private May 14, 1862, at Augusta, Georgia. On June 12, 1862, he was sent sick to the hospital at Staunton, Virginia. During much of his service his record shows him absent sick. Admitted to Ocmulgee Hospital at Macon, Georgia, March 17, 1864. Returned to duty April 12, 1864. Mortally wounded in the back and left arm at Spotsylvania, Virginia, May 10, 1864.

BATCHELOR, EARLY. In 1860 resident Putnam County, Georgia. Listed as twenty-four-year-old farmer in the household of his father, Cordy Batchelor, and mother, Mary Corine.

Owned no property. Enlisted as private April 4, 1862. Captured at Front Royal, Virginia, May 30, 1862. Exchanged from Fort Delaware at Aiken's Landing, Virginia, August 5, 1862. Captured at Spotsylvania, Virginia, May 10, 1864. First transferred to Point Lookout, Maryland, then transferred to Elmira, New York, July 15, 1864, arriving there July 28, 1864. Released July 11, 1865, upon taking oath of allegiance. Unable to travel until July 26, 1865. Married Matilda B. Haddock, Putnam County, Georgia, July 12, 1861. Died 1891.

BATCHELOR, JESSE T. Born Putnam County, Georgia, July 20, 1835. In 1860 resident Putnam County, Georgia. List as twenty-three-year-old clerk in the household of G. G. Green. Owned no property. Fourth sergeant June 15, 1861. Appointed first sergeant October 7, 1861. On recruiting duty in Georgia, March 20 to April 24, 1862. Severely wounded at McDowell, Virginia, May 8, 1862, in left arm below the elbow, leaving his wrist stiff. Discharged, disabled December 26, 1862. On the Putnam County, Georgia, militia roll in 1864 he is shown as a thirty-year-old overseer, detailed. Married Camilla Margaret Beall, daughter of Caraline and Allen A. Beall, September 20, 1863, Putnam County, Georgia. Mrs. Batchelor survived her husband by sixteen years, dying July 6, 1925. Jesse Batchelor died Eatonton, Georgia, December 27, 1909. Buried Beall Family Cemetery, Putnam County, Georgia. *Eatonton Messenger* (Eatonton, Georgia) issue of December 30, 1909: "MR. J. T. BATCHELOR DIES SUDDENLY: One of Putnam's oldest and best citizens passed away last Sunday night. He was a consecrated Christian gentleman, quiet and unostentatious in his daily life and a citizen who will be missed. . . . Although they had no children of their own he and his wife reared to manhood and womanhood several adopted children. He has long been called a father, to the fatherless and his home a happy haven of the orphans that came under his love and care. Married Camilla Margaret Beall, daughter of Caraline and Allen A. Beall September 20, 1863, Putnam County, Georgia. Mrs. Batchelor survived her husband by 16 years dying July 6, 1925."

BATCHELOR, LEVERETT. Born Putnam County, Georgia, July 30, 1830. In 1860 resident Putnam County, Georgia. Listed as twenty-nine-year-old farmer. Married Sarah Lancaster, January 21, 1851, Putnam County, Georgia. Four children in the household. Value of personal estate $250. Enlisted as private October 10, 1861. Wounded severely at McDowell, Virginia, May 8, 1862, in right arm between the elbow and shoulder, the ball then entering the body, striking the right lung and breaking several ribs. Admitted to General Hospital Number 9, Richmond, Virginia, May 31, 1864, owing to an old wound of the right arm. Returned to duty September 5, 1864. Surrendered, Appomattox, Virginia, April 9, 1865. Married Sarah Lancaster January 21, 1851. Residing in Putnam County, Georgia, after the war. Died at his daughter's home in Morgan County, Georgia, July 19, 1911. Buried Buckhead Cemetery, Morgan County, Georgia. *Eatonton Messenger* (Eatonton, Georgia) issue of July 29, 1911: "DEATH OF MR. L. BATCHELOR . . . At the close [of the war], Leverett and his four brothers returned home and as good citizens entered heartily into the work of restoring the southland. In this Leverette was engaged almost to the end of his life having worked more than forty years after surrender . . . I am all the more pleased to write this memoir because my comrade was so quiet and unassuming in life."

BATCHELOR, RICHARD. Born June 1840, Putnam County, Georgia. In 1860 resident Putnam County, Georgia. Listed as twenty-year-old farmer in the household of his father, Cordy Batchelor, and mother, Mary Corine. Owned no property. Enlisted as private April 4, 1862. Captured at Front Royal, Virginia, May 30, 1862. Exchanged Aiken's

Landing, Virginia, August 5, 1862. Wounded at Fredericksburg, Virginia, December 13, 1862. Captured at Spotsylvania, Virginia, May 10, 1864. First transferred to Point Lookout, Maryland, then transferred to Elmira, New York, July 15, 1864, arriving there July 28, 1864. Released June 19, 1865, upon taking oath of Allegiance. Married Ella Seay, September 14, 1869, Green County, Georgia. Died Putnam County, Georgia, November 29, 1910. Buried Crooked Creek Cemetery, Putnam County, Georgia.

BATCHELOR, SOLOMON. In 1860 resident Putnam County, Georgia. Listed as twenty-two years old, born Georgia, in the household of his father, Cordy Batchelor, and mother, Mary Corine. Owned no property. Enlisted as private June 15, 1861. Discharged, disabled, October 15, 1861. Reenlisted Company G, 12th Georgia Infantry Regiment, May 14, 1862. Muster roll for August 31, 1862, shows him absent sick. On June 12, 1862, he was sent sick to the hospital in Staunton, Virginia. Muster roll for December 31, 1862, shows him absent sick at Staunton, Virginia. Slightly wounded in the hand, a finger shot off, at Chancellorsville, Virginia, May 5, 1863. On wounded furlough July to October 1863. It appears he may have been listed as missing on May 5, 1864 in the Wilderness, and later appears as captured at Spotsylvania, Virginia, May 10, 1864. Paroled at Elmira, New York, February 13, 1865. Received at Boulware & Cox's Wharves, James River, Virginia, for exchange late February 1865. Married Lucy Ann Smith, November 29, 1866, Putnam County, Georgia. Died Putnam County, Georgia, February 14, 1878. Buried Batchelor Cemetery, Putnam County, Georgia.

BEALL, JAMES ALEXANDER. Born November 13, 1841, Putnam County, Georgia. In 1860 resident Putnam County, Georgia. Listed as eighteen years old in the household of his father, Allen Alexander Beall. Owned no property. Enlisted as a private, June 15, 1861. Slightly wounded in the ankle at McDowell, Virginia, May 8, 1862, by a spent ball. Wounded in the bowels by grapeshot July 1, 1863, Gettysburg, Pennsylvania, where he died. Memorial marker at Beall-Webster-Wheeler Cemetery, Putnam County, Georgia.

BEALL, JOSEPH JAMES. Enlisted as private July 20, 1861. Severely wounded at McDowell, Virginia, May 8, 1862. Admitted general hospital June 8, 1862, Charlottesville, Virginia. Wounded in left leg and captured at Winchester, Virginia, September 19, 1864. Amputation of left leg on the field at Winchester, Virginia. Admitted from camp of prisoners of war to general hospital with amputation of lower third of left leg. Received Fort McHenry, Maryland, November 19, 1864, from West Buildings Hospital, Baltimore, Maryland. Transferred to Point Lookout, Maryland, January 2, 1865. Transferred to U.S. General Hospital, Point Lookout, Maryland, late January 1865. Released on taking the oath of allegiance June 4, 1865. Carried to his home June 6, 1865.

BEDELL, JOHN K. In 1860 resident Eatonton, Georgia. Listed in the household of doctor J. G. Gibson. Owned no property. First sergeant June 15, 1861. Left sick at Richmond July 7, 1861, discharged October 7, 1861, on account of sunstroke at Richmond, Virginia. Died at the residence of his brother-in-law, Samuel Pearson, October 31, 1872, Eatonton, Georgia. Buried Pine Grove Cemetery, Eatonton, Georgia, Section 1, Division A, Lot 8, on the lot of Sparks Lawrence and Annie Lou Dennis Lawrence.

BULLARD, JAMES N. Born March 5, 1843 Putnam County, Georgia. In 1860 resident Putnam County, Georgia. Listed as eighteen-year-old farmer in the household of his father, James M. Bullard. Enlisted as private June 15, 1861. Slightly wounded at Second Manassas, August 28, 1862. Wounded at Chancellorsville, Virginia, May 2, 1863, by grapeshot in left leg, necessitating amputation four inches above knee. At home, wounded, close of war. In 1864 James N. Bullard was one of the enrolling officers for the 306th and 309th Military Districts Putnam County, Georgia. Died September 5, 1891. Buried at Harmony Church Cemetery, Putnam County, Georgia. His memorial marker gives the year of death as 1892.

CARTER, ROBERT O. In 1860 resident Eatonton, Georgia. Listed as fourteen years old in the household of his father, William B. Carter. Owned no property. Enlisted as private February 15, 1862. Slightly wounded at Cedar Run, Virginia, August 9, 1862. In late 1862 detailed in the quartermaster department. Wounded in left leg Spotsylvania, Virginia, May 11, 1864. Wounded in head at Fort Steadman, Virginia, March 25, 1865. Admitted Jackson Hospital, Richmond, Virginia, March 28, 1865, transferred and admitted General Hospital, Danville, Virginia, April 5, 1865. Teacher in Florida after the war. Died in Florida November 1896. *Eatonton Messenger* (Eatonton, Georgia) issue of November 28, 1896: " . . . He was a man possessed of many rare virtues and the highest and most manly traits. There was nothing mean or low or little in his make up. He scorned dishonor and abhorred meanness. He had filled a wide sphere of usefulness as a teacher in public schools . . . and he will be sadly missed."

CARTER, THOMAS W. In 1860 resident of Eatonton, Georgia. Listed as a twenty-two-year-old overseer, born Georgia, in the household of K. Marchman. Owned no property. Enlisted as private, June 15, 1861. Cut off from the regiment at Front Royal, Virginia, on May 30, 1862. Detailed in Pioneer Corps June 1863. Served throughout the war mostly in the Pioneer Corps. Said to have died in Texas after the war.

COCHRAN, BANNISTER R. In 1860 resident Putnam County, Georgia. Listed as thirty-eight-year-old farmer, born Georgia, married, with seven children. Value of whole property $875, which consisted of two slaves, $500 money and solvent debt, and a small amount of other property. Married Serene Voss, January 4, 1846, Putnam County, Georgia. Enlisted as private June 15, 1861. At hospital, Winchester, Virginia, May 27, 1862. Captured after the Battle of Sharpsburg, September 28, 1862. Paroled at Fort McHenry, Maryland, October 9, 1862. Sent to Fort Monroe, Virginia, for exchange. Received at Aiken's Landing, Virginia, October 13, 1862. Exchanged November 10, 1862. Left sick at Frederick County, Virginia, November or December 1862. Transferred to general hospital, Danville, Virginia, on December 15, 1862, and on December 21, 1862, is listed deserted. There is no service record after December 1862. Probate records, Putnam County, Georgia, show he had died by January 1865.

COCHRAN, MARK A. COOPER. Born December 27, 1833, Morgan County, Georgia. In 1860 resident Shepherd district, Morgan County, Georgia. Listed as twenty-two years old in the household of his father, Bannister Cochran. Owned no property in 1861. In 1862 his estate is shown to be $280. Enlisted as private June 15, 1861. Injured left leg on forced march 1861. Absent sick Staunton, Virginia, October 14, 1861. Discharged, disability at Staunton, Virginia, November 29, 1861. Married first Susan Ann McDaniel in Morgan County, Georgia, April 19, 1863. Married second Mary McAllister in Morgan County, Georgia, March 15, 1888. Living in Morgan County, Georgia, after the war. Died at Soldiers' Home, Atlanta, Georgia, August 16, 1920.

CONNANT, OLIVER H. P. In 1860 resident Putnam County, Georgia. Listed as thirty-nine-year-old farmer, born South Carolina, married with two children. Value of whole property $4,525, which consisted of a town lot, five slaves, money and solvent debt, and $1,125 in other property. Enlisted as private June 15, 1861. Discharged at Stribling

Springs, Virginia, January 25, 1862. Enlisted May 10, 1863, as second sergeant, Company A, Captain A. H. Reid's company, Sixty-sixth Georgia Infantry Regiment. This company subsequently became Company F, Sixty-sixth Georgia Infantry Regiment. Killed near Calhoun, Georgia.

COUGHLEY, JOHN. Enlisted as private June 14, 1861. Substitute. Wounded by bayonet and captured at Spotsylvania, Virginia, May 12, 1864. Admitted Old Capitol Prison U.S.A. Hospital, Washington, D.C., May 14, 1864. Transferred to Lincoln U.S.A. General Hospital May 20, 1864. On roll of prisoners of war at Fort Delaware, Delaware, June 17, 1864. Exchanged September 30, 1864, from Fort Delaware. Admitted to Jackson Hospital, Richmond, Virginia, October 7, 1864, furloughed for thirty days October 11, 1864. Said to have been killed after the surrender.

DANIELLY, JAMES W. Appears to be the son of William and Martha Danielly in the 1850 Putnam County, Georgia, census. Enlisted as private July 25, 1862. Admitted May 4, 1863, Chimborazo Hospital Number 4, Richmond, Virginia, transferred May 9, 1863 to Chimborazo Hospital Number 2, Richmond, Virginia. Transferred to Camp Jackson August 6, 1863. Wounded at Spotsylvania, Virginia, where he was captured May 20, 1864. Died of wound at Elmira, New York, February 14, 1865. Buried Woodlawn National Cemetery.

DANIELLY, JOHN E. Born Putnam County, Georgia, June 20, 1842. In 1860 resident Putnam County, Georgia. Listed as eighteen years old in the household of his father, William Danielly. Owned no property. Enlisted as private June 15, 1861. Wounded Cold Harbor, Virginia, June 27, 1862. Admitted Farmville, Virginia, general hospital July 22, 1862, returned to duty August 11, 1862. Detailed as butcher July 16, 1864. Surrendered, Appomattox, Virginia, April 9, 1865. Living in Randolph County, Georgia, after the war, where he died March 9, 1922. *Cuthbert Leader* (Cuthberth, Georgia) issue of March 16, 1922: " . . . Mr. Dannelly spent the greater part of his life in and near Shellman where he had a great many friends."

DANIELLY, WILLIAM H. In 1860 resident Putnam County, Georgia. Listed as twenty years old in the household of his father and mother, William and Martha Danielly. Owned no property. Enlisted as private June 15, 1861. Muster roll for August 30, 1862, shows him as a nurse at hospital. Captured at West View, Virginia, September 1, 1862. Exchanged. Wounded, through and through, by musket ball to right ankle, fracturing the tibia and fibula, and captured at Winchester, Virginia, September 19, 1864. Admitted from the field to U.S.A. Depot Field Hospital, September 24, 1864. Admitted to U.S. General Hospital Baltimore, Maryland, December 18, 1864. Admitted to Point Lookout, Maryland, January 31, 1865. Released at Point Lookout, Maryland, on June 5, 1865. Married Clementine D. Sudduth February 13, 1869, Putnam County, Georgia. His first wife may have died, for in the 1870 census his wife is listed as Adeline, nineteen years old. William Danielly died February 8, 1886.

DAVIS, EDWARD S. "EDD." In 1860 resident Putnam County, Georgia. Listed as seventeen years old in the household of his father and mother, William C. Davis and Elizabeth Mason Davis. Born Putnam County, Georgia. Owned no property. Enlisted as private June 15, 1861. Appointed fourth sergeant October 7, 1861. Slightly wounded in an arm at Allegheny Mountain, Virginia, December 13, 1861. Appointed third sergeant December 25, 1861. Killed McDowell, Virginia, May 8, 1862. His body was returned to Putnam County, Georgia, and he is buried Pine Grove Cemetery, Eatonton, Georgia, Section 1,

Division A, Lot 24. *The Countryman* (Turnwold-Putnam County, Georgia) issue of Tuesday, May 20, 1862: "OUR SOLDIER BOYS: . . . In order to testify the respect of our community for the fallen braves, the Confederate flag floated at half-mast over the town, the bell tolled, and all the houses of business were closed. Every mark of respect was shown the memory of the lamented young men, not only on account of their dying for their country, but on account of the great number of friends which their amiable dispositions had won for them, while yet in life."

DAVIS, JAMES W. Enlisted as private June 15, 1861. Cut off from the regiment at Front Royal Virginia on May 30, 1862. Slightly wounded Cedar Run, Virginia, August 9, 1862; slightly wounded in a hand, Second Manassas, Virginia, August 28, 1862. Wounded in the arm, breaking the small bone at Chancellorsville, Virginia, May 2, 1863. Muster roll for December 31, 1863, shows him under arrest. Killed at Spotsylvania, Virginia, May 10, 1864.

DAVIS, RICHARD TARPLY. Born Elbert County, Georgia, August 17, 1825. Educated at Emory College, where he graduated with high honors. In 1854 a mason in Rising Star Lodge 4, Eatonton, Georgia. In 1860 resident Eatonton, Georgia. Listed as thirty-five-year-old attorney, married with two children. Married to Margaret Ann Park January 8, 1849. Value of whole property $11,050, which consisted of sixty-five acres in Putnam County, a town lot in Eatonton, seven slaves, money and solvent debt, kitchen and household items, and $400 in other property. He was elected a member of the Georgia Secession Convention, and his abilities were immediately recognized by his being appointed a member of the committee on foreign relations. Captain, Company G, 12th Georgia Infantry Regiment June 15, 1861. Severely wounded in the thigh at McDowell, Virginia, May 8, 1862. Died from his wound May 22, 1862, at Staunton, Virginia. Patient in a private home in Staunton at the time of his death. His remains were returned to Eatonton. Burial in the family cemetery of his father-in-law, Dr. Andrew Park. Removed to Pine Grove Cemetery, Eatonton, Georgia, Section 1, Division A, Lot 114 when Park home was later sold. *The Countryman* (Turnwold-Putnam County, Georgia) issue of Tuesday, May 27, 1862: "Capt. Davis was possessed of those moral and religious qualities which give a man high position wherever he goes. Added to these were intellectual endowments of no mean order. . . . he possessed refined and cultivated belles-letters tastes, and acquirements. These made him a good speaker, and a ready writer, both in prose and verse. He wrote poetry occasionally as a pastime, and his poems evince sentiment of a high order, chaste diction, and easy versification. With the laurels which he had gathered at the forum, in the senate, on the fields of letters, and the more dazzling field of battle, the deceased had a bright future before him."

DAVIS, WILLIAM H. In 1860 resident Milledgeville, Georgia. Listed as twenty years old, born North Carolina, in the household of his parents, Anderson and Sarah Davis, in Milledgeville, Baldwin County, Georgia. Occupation listed as operative in manufactory. Enlisted as private June 15, 1861. Killed at Allegheny Mountain, Virginia, December 13, 1861. Anderson Davis of Baldwin County, Georgia, father of William H. Davis, applied for his unpaid army wages.

DENHAM, DAVID. Born in Georgia, March 20, 1845. In 1860 resident Putnam County, Georgia. Listed as fourteen years old in the household of his father, John Denham. Owned no property. Enlisted as private April 4, 1864. Wounded at Wilderness, Virginia, May 5, 1864, just below the right knee, leaving the leg stiff. Admitted General Hospital Number 9, Richmond, Virginia. February 14, 1865, transferred to Jackson Hospital. Wounded by gunshot in upper left thigh and captured at Fort Steadman, Virginia (Hatchers Run),

March 25, 1865. In Lincoln General Hospital, District of Columbia, April 10, 1865. Took oath of allegiance June 6, 1865. Married F. L Weems October 4, 1870, Putnam County, Georgia. He and his wife were living in Lincoln County, Georgia, with one of their children, where he died February 12, 1933. *Lincoln Journal* (Lincolnton, Georgia) issue of February 16, 1933: "MR. DENHAM IS LAID TO REST DOUBLE BRANCHES. . . . He was highly respected and held the admiration of all those who came under his influence during his life. Until ill health prevented he was one of the most active and public spirited citizens of his community."

DENHAM, JOHN T. Resident Putnam County, Georgia. Listed as sixteen-year-old farmer in the household of his father, John Denham. Owned no property. Enlisted as private June 15, 1861. Left sick in Richmond July 7, 1861, with pneumonia. Slightly wounded in ankle at McDowell, Virginia, May 8, 1862. Admitted to hospital June 8, 1862, Charlottesville, Virginia. Transferred to Lynchburg, Virginia, hospital June 16, 1862. Wounded by stray shot at Lynchburg, Virginia, May 20, 1864. Died of wounds July 12, 1864, at Ladies' Relief Hospital, Lynchburg, Virginia. Buried in Confederate Cemetery at Lynchburg, Virginia, No. 8, 2nd Line, Lot 194, Ladies' Hospital.

DISMUKES, GARLAND TERRELL "TERRY." Born Putnam County, Georgia, October 14, 1841. In 1860 resident Putnam County, Georgia. Owned no property. Enlisted as private June 15, 1861. Appointed corporal. Severely wounded in shoulder at McDowell, Virginia, May 8, 1862. Appointed third corporal August 7, 1862. Captured at Wilderness, Virginia, May 5, 1864, and exchanged October 30, 1864. Captured at Fort Steadman, Virginia, March 23, 1865. Released at Point Lookout, Maryland, June 26, 1865. Married Laura C. Lawrence October 5, 1865, Putnam County, Georgia. Died Dovedale community, Baldwin County, Georgia, April 17, 1903. Buried Dismukes Family Cemetery, Baldwin County, Georgia, Route 212, just inside Baldwin County line. Cemetery was in the garden of the old Dismukes place. *Union Recorder* (Milledgeville, Georgia) issue of April 21, 1903, front page: "MR. G. T. DISMUKES DEAD. . . . He was a gallant and brave Confederate soldier, during the civil war. He was a kind hearted man, and a good neighbor."

EAKIN, JAMES L. Born Putnam County, Georgia, October 4, 1823. In 1860 resident Putnam County, Georgia. Listed as thirty-seven-year-old farmer. Value of whole property $1250, which consisted of three slaves and a small amount of other property. Enlisted as private June 15, 1861. Died of tuberculosis September 15, 1861, at Camp Bartow, Virginia. *The Countryman* (Turnwold-Putnam County, Georgia), Tuesday, May 20, 1862: "The deceased was an honest man, and a brave soldier. No one could say naught against him. Modest and unassuming in his disposition, he was a kind friend, and an obliging neighbor."

ETHERIDGE, HENRY C. "HARRY." Resident Putnam County, Georgia. Listed as fifteen years old in the household of his guardian, James A. Etheridge. Value of whole property $9,347, which consisted of nine slaves and $3,847 in money and solvent debt. Enlisted as a private June 15, 1861. Appointed fourth corporal April 16, 1863. Musician, November 1863. Surrendered Appomattox, Virginia, April 9, 1865. Living in Chattooga County, Georgia, after the war.

ETHERIDGE, JAMES ALLEN. Born Jones County, Georgia, January 16, 1828. In 1860 resident Putnam County, Georgia. Listed as thirty-two-year-old physician. Dr. Etheridge attended first the Medical College of Georgia at Augusta, from which he graduated in 1848, and finished his course in Philadelphia in March 1849. Widowed with two children, his wife of Jones County, Georgia, Henrietta Curtis Drewry, dying on Sunday, October 7, 1860. Value of whole property $8,455, which consisted of a town lot in Eatonton, seven slaves, $1,575 money and solvent debt, and $280 in other property. Enlisted as first lieutenant June 15, 1861. Wounded severely in bowels at McDowell, Virginia, May 8, 1862. Patient in a private home in Staunton, Virginia, upon being removed from the battlefield at McDowell. Promoted assistant surgeon. Appointed surgeon of the Twelfth Georgia Volunteer Infantry Regiment, April 26, 1862, to take rank March 22, 1862. Afterward major and brigade surgeon of the Doles-Cook brigade. After the war he was a physician in Eatonton, Georgia. Married Corinne Drewry of Jones County, Georgia, sister of his first wife, on January 26, 1864. She died January 1, 1895. In 1876 Dr. Etheridge and family moved to Dallas, Texas, for a period of time. Died Eatonton, Georgia, September 30, 1893. Buried Pine Grove Cemetery, Section 1, Division A, Lot 19, Eatonton, Georgia. Both wives are buried with him. *Eatonton Messenger* (Eatonton, Georgia) issue of October 7, 1893: "A Good Man Gone. Dr. Etheridge Gone To His Reward. . . . He was through life a man of the strictest morality, truth, honesty and integrity. . . . As a citizen, a legislature, a physician, a Mason, a friend, husband and father, he did his duty and won respect and admiration of the public."

FEILER, JACOB. Born Prussia in Europe November 1839. Enlisted as a private, June 15, 1861. Slightly wounded Richmond, Virginia, June 26, 1862, and slightly wounded Malvern Hill, Virginia, July 1, 1862. In a September 3, 1863, letter written by Nicholas E. Scott to his father, he relates that Jacob had written Scott's brother Irby that he had been very ill and was tired of being in the hospital. From the compiled service records it appears Jacob remained away from the company in an absent wounded status until the close of the war. Said to have been captured near Natchez, Mississippi. Living in Columbus, Georgia, in 1906, having moved there between 1870 and 1880.

GHOLSON, JOHN E. In 1860 resident Putnam County, Georgia. Listed as thirty-year-old farmer in the household of R. J. Wynn. Owned no property. Enlisted as private June 15, 1861. Wounded in the leg, Second Manassas, Virginia, August 28, 1862. Captured at Spotsylvania, Virginia, May 10, 1864. Transferred to Elmira, New York, July 15, 1864. Released at Elmira, New York, June 16, 1865. Buried Memory Hill Cemetery, Milledgeville, Baldwin County, Georgia, west side, Section E, Lot 5.

GORLEY, THOMAS E. In 1860 resident Putnam County, Georgia. Listed seventeen years old in the household of his father, William Ayres Gorley. Owned no property. Enlisted as private December 5, 1861, Company C, 2nd Battalion, 2nd Brigade, Georgia State Troops, "Dennis Guards," Putnam County. Mustered out May 1862. Enlisted as a private, Company G, "Putnam Light Infantry," Twelfth Georgia Volunteer Infantry Regiment, May 14, 1862. Cut off at Front Royal, Virginia, May 30, 1862, but was able to rejoin his unit. Died of typhoid fever near Winchester, Virginia, June 5, 1862. It is said that a sergeant from the "Muckalee Guards," Company A, Twelfth Georgia, dug his grave. Memorial marker at Gorley Family Cemetery, Putnam County, Georgia.

GORLEY, WILLIAM ANDREW. In 1860 resident Putnam County, Georgia. Listed as nineteen years old in the household of his father, William Ayres Gorley. Owned no property. Enlisted as private June 15, 1861. Slightly wounded at McDowell, Virginia, May 8, 1862. Wounded at Sharpsburg, Maryland, September 17, 1862. Wounded in the thigh, July 1, 1863, but did not break the bone and captured at Gettysburg, Pennsylvania. Died of wounds July 15, 1863, at Gettysburg, Pennsylvania. Memorial marker at Gorley Family Cemetery, Putnam County, Georgia.

GRIGGS, CINCINNATUS W. In 1860 resident Putnam County, Georgia. Value of whole property $5,862, which consisted of 486 acres, four slaves, $545 money and solvent debt, and $201 other property. Enlisted as private June 15, 1861. Left sick at Richmond July 7, 1861. After July 7, 1861, the record is not clear as to his status with the army. From the compiled service record, General Lee detailed him to general hospital, Camp Winder, Richmond, Virginia, September 12, 1863. Captured Jackson Hospital, Richmond, Virginia, April 3, 1865, and paroled there April 25, 1865.

HASKINS, JAMES WOODSON. Born in North Carolina, September 12, 1846. In 1860 resident of Putnam County, Georgia. Listed as fifteen years old in the household of Martha A. Johnson. Owned no property. His father and mother died when he was about three years of age. His uncle, Woodson Johnson, brought him to Georgia, adopted him, and raised him as one of his children. Enlisted as private, June 15, 1861. Severely wounded at Camp Allegheny, Virginia, December 13, 1861, above left hip, the ball crossing through the back muscles, fracturing the crest of both hips and lower spine; the bullet came out on right hip. Sent to Staunton, Virginia, hospital March 2, 1862, and later to Lynchburg, Virginia, hospital. Discharged on account of wounds September 5, 1862, and sent home on a stretcher. In the winter of 1864 he joined a cavalry troop with Major Burns and served with him in South Carolina until the surrender. Married Tommie Webster. He died July 29, 1916, Eatonton, Georgia. Buried Philadelphia Church Cemetery, Putnam County, Georgia. *Eatonton Messenger* (Eatonton, Georgia) issue of August 4, 1916: "DEATH OF A CONFEDERATE SOLDIER: James Woodson Haskins . . . leaving Eatonton June 18 for Virginia, before he was 17 years old. . . . Like so many other young men of the South . . . he came home to a devastated country but with the high hopes of youth, he joined with others in efforts to rebuild the homes and save the social structure of the South. . . . He married Miss Tommie Webster who has shared with him the ups and downs of life, and while they did not accumulate much property they have raised and trained six fine young men and three gentle, lovely women who are following in habits of industry, probity and good citizenship and hold the respect and high esteem of all who know them."

HETLAND, ANTHONY A. In 1861 resident Putnam County, Georgia. Owned no property. Enlisted as private June 15, 1861. Killed at Sharpsburg, Maryland, September 17, 1862.

HITCHCOCK, WILLIAM L. In 1860 resident Eatonton, Putnam County, Georgia. Listed as thirty-eight-year-old physician, with a wife and child in his household, and $700 personal estate. Enlisted as second corporal June 15, 1861. Died of fever at Camp Bartow, Virginia, September 29, 1861. Buried Camp Bartow in the evening of September 29, 1861.

HOLLIS, JOHN. In 1860 resident Putnam County, Georgia. Listed as fifty-six-year-old farmer, married with two children. Owned $270 in personal property. Enlisted as private, June 15, 1861. Died of fever at Allegheny Mountain, Virginia, October 8, 1861. In other sources, August 1861 is listed as the date of death, which is not correct.

HUBERT, MATHEW A. Enlisted as private December 5, 1861, Company C, 2nd Battalion, 2nd Brigade, Georgia State Troops, "Dennis Guards," Putnam County, Georgia. Mustered out May 1862. Enlisted as a private, Company G, "Putnam Light Infantry," Twelfth Georgia Volunteer Infantry Regiment, March 28, 1863. Gunshot wound to the right side of head at Spotsylvania, Virginia, May 10, 1864, by one of his own men, who was shooting from behind him. Admitted General Hospital Number 9, Richmond,

Virginia, May 18, 1864. Admitted Jackson Hospital, Richmond, Virginia, May 22, 1964. Furloughed for sixty days, May 27, 1864. Killed at Petersburg, Virginia, March 29, 1865.

HUDSON, IRBY GIBSON "CHAP." Born May 8, 1831, Eatonton, Georgia. Son of Irby Hudson Jr. and Jane Frances Flournay. In 1854 a mason in Rising Star Lodge 4, Eatonton, Georgia. In 1860 resident Putnam County, Georgia. Listed as twenty-nine years old with whole property of $1,300, which consisted of money and solvent debt. Enlisted as private, June 15, 1861. On May 30, 1862, he was cut off from Company G at Front Royal, Virginia, afterward living among the farmers of the neighborhood. It is reported by a former comrade that Hudson was knocked off the upper bridge at Front Royal, that "a yankee ran his horse against I. G. H. and knocked him off. . . ." He rejoined the 12th Georgia in time to participate in the Seven Days battle near Richmond. Slightly wounded Cold Harbor, Virginia, June 26, 1862. Slightly wounded Sharpsburg, Maryland, September 17, 1862. Appointed commissary sergeant, Twelfth Georgia Infantry Regiment, August 1863. Surrendered, Appomattox, Virginia, April 9, 1865. Died Elberton, Georgia, December 21, 1895. Buried Pine Grove Cemetery, Eatonton, Georgia, Section 1, Division B, Lot 86. *Eatonton Messenger* (Eatonton, Georgia) issue of December 28, 1895: "PROF. IRBY G. HUDSON: . . . He was educated at Emory College by the late David Rosser Adams, and soon after his graduation there he chose school teaching as his life work. His career as an educator was interrupted by his four years service in the war, but was resumed when the war was over. As an educator he became well known in Georgia and filled some of the best positions in several colleges. . . . Prof. Hudson was a devout church member. He was very fond of the Methodist church and his piety was unquestioned. He was of a social disposition and the ties of his younger days were very strong."

JENKINS, ROBERT HUDSON. Born Putnam County, Georgia, January 11, 1843. In 1860 resident Eatonton, Putnam County, Georgia. Listed as sixteen years old in the household of his father, Robert Cater Jenkins. Owned no property. Third sergeant June 15, 1861. Appointed second sergeant December 25, 1861. Wounded slightly in head at McDowell, Virginia, May 8, 1862. Appointed first sergeant December 26, 1862. Unable to march to Pennsylvania in 1863 because of a sore leg. After crossing the Potomac River back into Virginia, during the 1864 Valley campaign, Jenkins is said to have been sick about July 15, 1864, and riding in a wagon with the commissary train. There is an indication that Jenkins received a furlough in late January 1865 and returned home. Living in Haddock, Jones County, Georgia, after the war. Died May 24, 1907, Eatonton, Georgia. Buried Pine Grove Cemetery, Section 1, Division A, Lot 80, Eatonton, Georgia. *Eatonton Messenger* (Eatonton, Georgia) issue of May 31, 1907: "DEATH OF MR. ROBERT C. JENKINS: . . . Mr. Jenkins was a loyal and brave soldier in the civil war and his love for the lost cause and his fellow comrades never wanted . . ."

JENKINS, WILLIAM FRANKLIN "FRANK." Born Sumter County, Georgia, March 26, 1845. In 1860 resident Eatonton, Putnam County, Georgia. Listed as fourteen years old in the household of his father, Robert Carter Jenkins. Owned no property. Frank was the youngest member of the company, being only sixteen when he enlisted. Enlisted as private June 15, 1861. Appointed first corporal August 7, 1862. Slightly wounded twice at Cedar Run, Virginia, August 9, 1862. At dusk, severely wounded twice, at Second Manassas, Virginia, August 28, 1862, once in the side, and while lying wounded on the battlefield, his leg was shot with a shell. After the battle in private home, wounded, at Middleburg, Virginia, where he was captured and paroled. Appointed ordinance sergeant, Cook's brigade, May 2, 1864. Surrendered, Appomattox, Virginia, April 9, 1865. After the war he attended the University of Virginia and graduated from the Law Department. He returned to Eatonton, Georgia, to practice law. He represented Putnam County, Georgia, in the General Assembly. Was chairman of the board of county commissioners of Putnam County and later the first mayor of Eatonton after the city was incorporated. Served as judge of the Ocmulgee Circuit and was a trustee of the Georgia Soldiers' Home. Elected assistant adjutant general of the Confederate Veterans of Georgia, his commission arriving the day of his death. Died Eatonton, Georgia, December 17, 1909. Married Leila U. Head of Webster County, Georgia, in 1870. Buried Pine Grove Cemetery, Section 1, Division B, Lot 227, Eatonton, Georgia. *Eatonton Messenger* (Eatonton, Georgia) issue of December 30, 1909: "JUDGE W. F. JENKINS, SR. SLEEPS 'NEATH THE SOD OF PUTNAM: . . . countless friends throughout Georgia have paid tribute to him as a brave and gallant defender of the lost cause, a fearless and impartial judge, a generous and loyal friend and above all a noble Christian gentleman. He was a man who never let his right hand know what his left hand did in the way of charity, and yet the writer has both before and since his death had abundant testimony from his friends both white and black, of occasions when financial as well as legal aid has been given unstentedly. . . . With the 'Boys in Gray' he was ever a hero among their heroes of the wearers of the gray. They knew him best and loved him most. They came to him with their sorrows and shared with him their joys, knowing his generous and sympathetic heart beat for his Confederate comrades, to whom his heart and purse were ever open."

JOHNSON, BENJAMIN F. Born Putnam County, Georgia, March 5, 1841. In 1860 resident Putnam County, Georgia. Listed as nineteen-year-old clerk in the household of B. F. Adams. Personal estate $3,500. Third corporal June 15, 1861. Discharged at Greenbrier River, Virginia, August 30, 1861, on account of disability. Enlisted in the Twenty-seventh Georgia Battalion, Augusta, Georgia, September 11, 1863, as first lieutenant, Company A, Augusta Arsenal Guard. Promoted to captain April 25, 1864. Ordered to report to light batteries at Savannah, Georgia, September 4, 1864, station Fort McAllister. Absent without official leave October 13, 1864. Sick in hospital December 25, 1864. Surrendered April 26, 1865, and paroled May 1, 1865, at Greensboro, North Carolina. Residing in Atlanta, Georgia, after the war, assistant to Secretary of State Phil Cook. Died December 30, 1916. Buried Pine Grove Cemetery, Section 1, Division C, Lot 261, Eatonton, Georgia. *Atlanta Constitution*, issue of December 31, 1916, front page, continued on page three: "CAPTAIN JOHNSON DIED LAST NIGHT For Thirty Years He Had Served as Chief Clerk in the Office of Secretary of State. . . . Captain Johnson was a valiant soldier of the confederacy, and was noted for his bravery. A story oft told among veterans is how Captain Johnson's unflinching fortitude was responsible for getting a trainload of ammunition across the bridge over the Savannah river to Charleston while the bridge was under artillery fire. Captain Johnson always remained true to the ideals of the old south and those for which the old south fought."

JOHNSON, JOHN DAVID. Enlisted as private June 15, 1861. At Harrisonburg, Virginia, sick September 20, 1861, returned to camp March 17, 1862. Killed at Second Manassas, Virginia, August 30, 1862.

JOHNSON, ZACCHEUS B. "JACK," sometimes seen as Zack. Born Putnam County, Georgia, February 28, 1843. In 1860 resident Putnam County, Georgia. Listed as nineteen years old. His guardian, T. F. Cowles, controlled whole property of $3,300, which consisted of five slaves and $500 in money and solvent debt. Third sergeant October 31, 1861, Company B, 2nd Battalion, 2nd Brigade, Georgia State Troops, "Calhoun Greys," Putnam County,

Georgia. Mustered out May 4, 1862. Enlisted as a private, Company G, "Putnam Light Infantry," Twelfth Georgia Volunteer Infantry Regiment, May 14, 1862. Wounded Front Royal, Virginia, May 30, 1862. Wounded Cold Harbor, Virginia, by the shock of a bomb June 17, 1862. Wounded Chancellorsville, Virginia, May 2, 1863. Sprained his ankle just before the Battle of Gettysburg and was not with the regiment. Detailed courier to General Doles October 13, 1863. Transferred to Confederate States Navy, James River Squadron, October 1864. When Richmond was evacuated in 1865, ordered by Captain Tucker, C. S. N., to report to President Davis's chief of staff and was then placed as one of the guards of the ambulance train, and served as such to Washington, Georgia, where he was discharged. Washington, Georgia, was the site of the last Confederate cabinet meeting. Married Sarah Evelyn Harrison November 28, 1877, Putnam County, Georgia. Residing in Milledgeville, Georgia, after the war, where he was usher of the Georgia State Sanatorium. Died Milledgeville, Georgia, November 4, 1922. Buried Memory Hill Cemetery, west side, Section G, Lot 44, Milledgeville, Georgia.

KILPATRICK, WILLIAM T. In 1860 resident Putnam County, Georgia. Son of Thomas W. Kilpatrick and Mary Henry Terrell Crafton. His father died in 1856. Listed as sixteen years old, born Georgia, in the household of his eighty-year-old great grandmother, Kitie Garland Terrell, his administrator. His administrator controlled an estate for three children with a whole value of $21,955, which consisted of land, slaves, and money. Enlisted as private June 15, 1861. Died of measles, Camp Allegheny, Virginia, August 14, 1861. First death in the company. *Savannah Republican,* issue of September 7, 1861: " . . . Wm. T. Kilpatrick, a young man, amiable and exemplary in all his conduct, and beloved by all his associates, has been taken from our midst. With simple ceremony and sad hearts, we buried him far away from home and friends, where perhaps none that knew him will ever look upon his grave again. Ah! How sad the experiences of life often are! Written by Captain Richard T. Davis"

LITTLE, ALGERNON FORRESTER. Born Putnam County, Georgia, May 6, 1842. In 1860 resident Putnam County, Georgia. Listed as eighteen-year-old farmer in the household of his father, Kinchen Little. Owned no property. Second sergeant June 15, 1861. Mortally wounded in a thigh at Allegheny Mountain, Virginia, December 13, 1861. Died of wounds at Camp Allegheny December 25, 1861. His body was returned home. Buried in Stinson-Little Cemetery, Putnam County Georgia. *The Countryman,* (Turnwold-Putnam County, Georgia) issue of Tuesday, May 6, 1862: "OBITUARY. . . . Falling far away from home, kind friends brought him, and laid him in the family burial ground, where he now sleeps upon the soil which his brave heart leaped to defend. The ground of old Putnam is consecrated by holding the ashes of those who have fallen in freedom's holy cause; and young Algie's bosom is one of the barriers that have kept the foot of the invader away from our country homes. Let us ever feel grateful to those who die to defend all that is dear to us."

LITTLE, FRANCIS MILTON. Born Putnam County, Georgia, October 22, 1837. In 1860 resident Putnam County, Georgia. Listed as twenty-three-year-old farmer in the household of his father, Kinchen Little. Value of whole property $5,979, which consisted of one slave, $5,049 money and solvent debt, and a small amount of other property. Enlisted as private June 15, 1861. Appointed fourth sergeant December 25, 1861. Severely wounded by Federal cannon fire in the right shoulder, fracturing the scapula and the head of the humerus at Cross Keys, Virginia, June 8, 1862. The flesh was nearly all torn from his shoulder. Sent to the hospital in Waynesboro, Virginia. Discharged, disabled, at Charlottesville, Virginia, July 14, 1862. Married November 15, 1863, to Anna Reid. Resident of Hancock County, Georgia, after the war. Died November 22, 1921. Buried in Little-Hudson Family Cemetery, Hancock County, Georgia. *Eatonton Messenger* (Eatonton, Georgia), issue of Friday, December 2, 1921: "DEATH OF MR. MILTON LITTLE. . . . He farmed all his life and was successful. During illness of 15 years his eyes failed and he became totally blind, but he retained a splendid memory and took active interest in everything around him."

LITTLE, JOHN WESLEY. Born Eatonton, Georgia, May 4, 1844. In 1860 resident Eatonton, Georgia. Listed as sixteen years old in the household of Elizabeth Little. Owned no property. He received his education in the common schools of Eatonton and was assisting Mr. Sidney Clark Prudden in the post office when the strife between the North and South began. Enlisted as private June 15, 1861. Slightly wounded in head at McDowell, Virginia, May 8, 1862. Appointed second sergeant December 26, 1862. Captured Wilderness, Virginia, May 6, 1864, having gone too far into the enemy's lines with Captain Harris and others of the command. Transferred from Point Lookout, Maryland, to Elmira, New York, August 10, 1864. His compiled service record shows him released Elmira, New York, June 21, 1865. On his pension application he indicated he was paroled in February 1865 and in Eatonton, Georgia, waiting for exchange at the close of the war. After the war he engaged in farming, but soon went into business in Madison, Georgia, and later in Atlanta as a commercial traveler and merchant. Married Martha N. Wilson of Morgan County, Georgia, May 1, 1867. Died Indian Springs, Georgia, May 25, 1903. Buried Atlanta, Georgia. *Eatonton Messenger* (Eatonton, Georgia) issue of June 13, 1903: "IN MEMORIAM: . . . In all this service John was known as a good soldier, always ready, always willing to go when and as far as anybody else could go, a favorite of Col. Willis, who loved a good soldier and despised a poor one. . . . He, like our comrade Dismukes, seemed to think that every old soldier was a part of himself, and always evidenced a great interest in his old company and its welfare."

LITTLE, LITTLETON LUDLOW. Born February 3, 1820, Putnam County, Georgia. In 1860 resident Putnam County, Georgia. Listed as a married forty-year-old farmer with seven children. Married Caroline E. Gregory, October 27, 1842, Putnam County, Georgia. Value of whole property $9,138, which consisted of 550 acres in Putnam County, ten slaves, and $588 in other property. Enlisted as private October 8, 1863. Discharged disabled at Morton's Ford, Virginia, December 11, 1863. He appears on the 1864 Putnam County, Georgia, militia list as forty-three years, eleven months as discharged soldier.

LITTLE, ROBERT JOHNSON. Resident Putnam County, Georgia. Listed as twenty-one-year-old farmer in the household of his father, Lewis Little. Owned no significant property. Fourth corporal June 15, 1861. Wounded in a finger at Sharpsburg, Maryland, September 17, 1862. Elected second lieutenant April 16, 1863. Left sick at Chambersburg, Pennsylvania, about June 23, 1863, and captured at Chambersburg, Pennsylvania, while sick. Admitted to West Walnut Street Hospital, Harrisburg, Pennsylvania, August 2, 1863. Paroled at Johnson's Island, Ohio, and sent to Fortress Monroe, Virginia, for exchange September 16, 1864. Received at Aiken's Landing, Virginia, September 22, 1864. Surrendered, Appomattox, Virginia, April 9, 1865. After the war he was engaged in farming. Died Putnam County, Georgia, March 22, 1883. Buried Bynum-Little Cemetery, Putnam County, Georgia.

LYNCH, HARVEY J. In 1860 resident of Putnam County, Georgia. Listed as seventeen years old in the household of his father, James N. Lynch. Owned no property. Enlisted as private June 15, 1861. Severely wounded, shot through the leg with a musket ball, bone not touched, Cedar Run, Virginia, August 9, 1862. Detailed as a farmer in Putnam

County, Georgia, for an unknown period. Surrendered, Appomattox, Virginia, April 9, 1865. Killed in Jasper County, Georgia, November 9, 1868. Buried Salem Cemetery, Putnam County, Georgia.

LYNCH, JAMES N. In 1860 resident Putnam County, Georgia. Listed as thirty-nine-year-old married farmer with seven children in the household. Married Amanda Lynch October 19, 1840, Putnam County, Georgia. His wife in 1860 is listed as blind. Value of whole property $34,950, which consisted of seven hundred acres, thirty-three slaves, $500 in kitchen and household furniture, and $4,050 in other property. Enlisted as private, Macon, Georgia, date of enlistment not shown. It appears he was on detached service in Putnam County, Georgia, as an overseer through the war. There is little information contained in his compiled service record.

MADDOX, FRANCIS ALEXANDER. Born Putnam County, Georgia, October 13, 1845. In 1860 resident Putnam County, Georgia. Listed fifteen years old in the household of his guardian, Allen A. Beall. A student at the school of Beman at Mount Zion, Hancock County, Georgia. He appears to have left school without consent of his uncle, who was his guardian, and enlisted. Value of whole property, administered by his guardian, $4,066, which consisted of six slaves and $366 in money and solvent debt. Enlisted as private June 15, 1861. Sent sick to Harrisonburg, Virginia, September 30, 1861. Cut off from the regiment at Front Royal, Virginia, May 30, 1862. Appointed third corporal August 7, 1862. Captured at Middleburg, Virginia, September 30, 1862, exchanged. Severely wounded in the foot at Chancellorsville, Virginia, May 2, 1863. Appointed fourth corporal November 1863. Captured at Spotsylvania, Virginia, May 10, 1864. Arrived Belle Plains, Virginia, May 19, 1864. Transferred to Elmira, New York, July 27, 1864. Released at Elmira, New York, June 16, 1865. At the time of his release his complexion was fair, with brown hair, gray eyes and five feet ten inches tall. Married first Margaret "Mina" S. Spivey October 17, 1865, Putnam County, Georgia. Married second Louella (Armor) Spivey, widow of Green Spivey. Died Putnam County, Georgia, December 8, 1920. Buried Philadelphia Church Cemetery, Putnam County, Georgia. *Eatonton Messenger* (Eatonton, Georgia) issue of December 10, 1920: "IN MEMORIAM OF BRO. F. A. MADDOX: . . . brother Maddox became a leading planter of Putnam County, overcoming the greatest obstacles and was financially as well as morally a successful man and mason. His modesty was such that many of his closest friends never heard from him any count of his experiences in the great American conflict in which he had borne so heroic a part. He was a consistent member of the Methodist Church as well as one who lived up to the moral requirements of order. All of which were pleasures to one of his nature, thus to live and act. No one ever knew him to do unto another, that which he would not desire done unto himself."

MADDOX, NOTLEY. Born Putnam County, Georgia, September 9, 1843. In 1860 resident Putnam County, Georgia. Listed as seventeen years old in the household of his guardian, Allen A. Beall, his uncle. Value of whole property, administered by his guardian, $2,901, which consisted of four slaves and $201 in money and solvent debt. Enlisted as private June 15, 1861. Wounded Bristow, Virginia, August 26, 1862. Severely wounded by a Union cannon shell at Second Manassas, Virginia, August 27, 1862, in the left thigh, breaking the bone just below the hip and leaving the leg three inches shorter. He did not reach home until about four months after being wounded. Detailed as sub-enrolling officer with the rank of first lieutenant in Pike County, Georgia, April 10, 1864. Captured at Zebulon, Georgia, April 19, 1865, and transferred to military prison at Macon, Georgia, April 23, 1865. Died Putnam County, Georgia, February 10, 1919. Buried Central Methodist Church Cemetery, Putnam County, Georgia. *Eatonton Messenger* (Eatonton, Georgia) issue of February 14, 1919: "DEATH OF VETERAN: . . . I take pleasure in testifying to memory of my friend and comrade, having known him 63 years and served side by side with him. As he was a good soldier, so he was a good citizen, honored and respected by all who knew him. Robert Young."

MAHONE, GIBSON G. In 1860 resident Putnam County, Georgia. Listed as sixteen years old in the household of his guardian, William Garrard. Value of whole property held by the guardian was $5,542, which consisted of four slaves and $3,242 in money and solvent debt. Enlisted as private June 15, 1861. Mortally wounded by Federal cannon fire at Cross Keys, Virginia, June 8, 1862. Both legs were broken and mangled just about his knees, dying within four hours of being wounded. Captain A. C. Philips, Company B, "Calhoun Greys," 2nd Battalion, Georgia State Troops, came to the company, camped near Charlottesville, to retrieve the remains of Gibson Mahone to return them to Putnam County.

MANSFIELD, JAMES L. In 1860 resident Putnam County, Georgia. Listed as thirty-year-old overseer, married with four children. Owned no property. Enlisted as private July 28, 1861. Admitted November 4, 1862, Episcopal Church Hospital, Williamsburg, Virginia, with pneumonia, transferred Petersburg, Virginia, and then to General Hospital, Farmville, Virginia. Returned to duty April 28, 1863. Wounded through both legs and permanently disabled at Bethesda Church near Cold Harbor, Virginia, May 30, 1864. Admitted May 31, 1864, to General Hospital Number 3, Richmond, Virginia, and transferred to Jackson Hospital, Richmond, Virginia. Furloughed for thirty days July 21, 1864.

MAPPIN, JAMES WILLIS. Born Georgia. In 1860 resident of Eatonton, Putnam County, Georgia. Listed as twenty-year-old railroad hand in the household of Jesse Simmons. Owned no property. Enlisted as private December 17, 1863. Wounded and captured at Spotsylvania, Virginia, May 10, 1864. Died at Point Lookout, Maryland, August 2, 1864.

MARSHALL, ASA MONROE. Born December 25, 1832, Jones County, Georgia. In 1860 resident Putnam County, Georgia. Enlisted as private June 15, 1861. Slightly wounded in an arm at Allegheny Mountain, Virginia, December 13, 1861. Appointed chaplain, Twelfth Georgia Volunteer Infantry Regiment, August 1, 1862, but refused to leave the ranks, serving as private until it was convenient to get a horse. Then, not having a saddle to suit him, he followed the command. At the opening of the battle of Cedar Run, August 9, 1862, one of the enemy's horses was wounded, and as it passed on he took the saddle and retired to his posting near regimental headquarters. He was often with the company in camp and on the march. Resigned March 10, 1864. In the letter approving his resignation, dated February 18, 1864, Colonel Edward Willis indicated "Reverend Marshall had received a call from a Church in Putnam County. He was anxious to accept not only for the good of the community, but as a young preacher for his own improvement." Reverend Marshall was a Missionary Baptist minister who graduated, in 1860, from Mercer Institute, formally located at Penfield in Greene County, Georgia. Upon graduation he was ordained a minister, in December 1860, and he accepted the school in Putnam County at Harmony, and began teaching. He was serving Harmony and Eatonton churches when the war began. For many years after the war, he was a trustee of Mercer College. He was a Baptist minister in Putnam County, Georgia, after the war and preached primarily at Harmony and Ramoth Baptist Churches. For a short period was at Eatonton Baptist Church while church was searching for a new minister.

Married Rebecca Frances Paschal November 8, 1866, Putnam County, Georgia. Reverend Marshall died October 7, 1914, Eatonton, Georgia. Buried Harmony Baptist Church Cemetery, Section C, Putnam County, Georgia. A tribute by a comrade (Robert Young) at a memorial service November 18, 1914, Harmony Church, Putnam County, Georgia: " . . . Our hero was a true pupil of General Lee, who said, 'Duty is the sublimest word in the English language.' Whatever he believed to be his duty as a soldier, he did to the best of his ability. He obeyed orders always without complaint. As chaplain of the Regiment, he preached as often as circumstances allowed, ministered to the sick and wounded, and was often seen walking when he had insisted on a tired or sick soldier riding his horse."

MARSHALL, HENRY HARRIS. Born Georgia. In the household of his father, Stephen B. Marshall Sr. In 1860 resident Eatonton, Georgia. Listed as sixteen years old. Enlisted as private June 15, 1861. Slightly wounded in thigh at McDowell, Virginia, May 8, 1962. Because of this wound he was hospitalized for a time at Richmond, Virginia. Appointed corporal in 1862, fourth sergeant August 7, 1862, third sergeant December 26, 1862. Wounded by friendly cannon fire at Gettysburg, Pennsylvania, July 3, 1863. Left on the field, where he was captured, Gettysburg, Pennsylvania, July 4, 1863. Sent to Fort Delaware, Delaware, where he was exchanged July 31, 1863. Wounded in the fleshy part of the arm above the elbow, the ball coming out below, at Summit Point, Virginia, August 21, 1864. Sent to the hospital at Charlottesville. On wounded furlough August 31, 1864. After the war was a member of the Atlanta police force. Died of cancer of the mouth and throat in Atlanta, Georgia, June 27, 1894. *Eatonton Messenger* (Eatonton, Georgia) issue of June 30, 1894: "DEATH OF H. H. MARSHALL . . . He was a brave Confederate soldier, a steadfast friend, and a true man in every relation . . ."

MARSHALL, STEPHEN B., JR. Born Eatonton, Georgia, August 22, 1836. In 1860 resident Eatonton, Georgia. Listed as twenty-four-year-old bookkeeper for the Eatonton Factory Company, in the household of his father, Stephen B. Marshall Sr. Value of whole property $3,100, which consisted of five slaves, money and solvent debt, and $300 in other property. Junior second lieutenant June 15, 1861. In October 1861 on duty in Georgia. Elected first lieutenant March 1, 1862. Received a through and through wound of the right foot at McDowell, Virginia, May 8, 1862. Owing to this wound, he was hospitalized for a time at Richmond, Virginia. Wounded in left leg, and then while lying wounded he was shot in the foot at Fredericksburg, Virginia, December 13, 1862. Resigned April 16, 1863. Graduated Emory College, later taking a bookkeeping course at Nashville, Tennessee. Returning home, he married Hattie H. Slade, the daughter of the late Judge Daniel Slade, November 20 1860, in Putnam County, Georgia. Died in Eatonton, Georgia, September 20, 1898. He and his wife are buried Pine Grove Cemetery, Section 1, Division A, Lot 91, Eatonton, Georgia. *Eatonton Messenger* (Eatonton, Georgia) issue of October 15, 1898: "STEPHEN B. MARSHALL . . . As a soldier he was all that a soldier should be—in authority over his men as his rank required him to be, solicitous of their welfare, subordinate to his superior officers, self-sacrificing in devotion to the Confederacy, brave in battle and active and cheerful in camp. He was willing to give his heart's blood for the south and he returned home after the war ended, and like a true soldier took up again the responsibilities of civic life, met its hardships, smiled upon his old friends, formed new friendships in his career as a hotel proprietor, remained steadfast in his love for the cause of the Confederacy, and at length passed peacefully away. . . . His life was not one of ease but he met its vicissitudes, faced its disappointments and struggled against its hardships with the courage and determination of a manly man, and amid life's battles he had a cheerful word for his friends and a tender solicitude and ready comradeship for his wife.

McDade, William Timothy. Born February 22, 1822, near Athens, Alabama. In 1860 resident Putnam County, Georgia. Listed as thirty-eight-year-old liveryman. Married Henrietta Walker of Monroe County, Georgia, September 27, 1846, later had six children. Value of whole property $9,574, which consisted of a town lot in Eatonton, six slaves, money and solvent debt, and $1,500 in other property. A mason in the Masonic Lodge of Eatonton, Georgia, since 1854. Besides hiring out horses and buggies, he ran the old swinging stages to all towns around, carrying mail and passengers. Enlisted as private September 12, 1863. November and December 1863 provost guard at Corps Headquarters. Mr. McDade was not in good health, not fit for the ranks, therefore, Captain Alexander Reid secured for him a position in the Pioneer Corps, building bridges, laying crossways, and the like. In January 1864 elected judge of Inferior Court, Putnam County, Georgia, and furloughed 1864. Died Putnam County, Georgia, June 12, 1890. Buried Pine Grove Cemetery, Section 1, Division A, Lot 105, Eatonton, Georgia. *Eatonton Messenger* (Eatonton, Georgia) issue of June 14, 1890: "W. T. McDade. . . . He was one of Putnam's prominent and useful citizens, and an efficient member of the Methodist church."

McDonough, John. Enlisted as private June 15, 1861. Deserted near Front Royal, Virginia, about July 25, 1863.

McGettrick, Barsby M. In 1860 resident Eatonton, Georgia. Listed as thirty-year-old clerk, born Ireland, in the household of Stephen B. Marshall Sr. Value of whole property $1,259, which consisted of money and solvent debt. Enlisted as private June 15, 1861. Appointed hospital steward by surgeon Henry K. Green, August 9, 1861. His compiled service record states he was discharged at Allegheny Mountain, Virginia, January 1862. However, in a letter written by Robert Young, dated July 12, 1862, he is shown still with the army. Also in a letter written by Irby Scott, dated July 20, 1862, he was still with the company. No additional details can be found.

McLeroy, David D. Born Georgia, March 20, 1839. Enlisted as private June 15, 1861. Sent sick to Harrisonburg, Virginia, September 30, 1861. Slightly wounded in a leg at Allegheny Mountain, Virginia, December 13, 1861, and sent to Staunton, Virginia. Wounded in the small of his back by grapeshot Chancellorsville, Virginia, May 3, 1863. On muster roll dated October 30, 1863, he is shown absent sick since October 1, 1863. Muster roll dated December 31, 1863, shows him at home with leave. Captured at Spotsylvania, Virginia, May 10, 1864. Sent to Belle Plains, Virginia, May 19, 1864. Transferred to Elmira, New York, July 27, 1864. Released at Elmira, New York, June 16, 1865. At the time of his release his complexion was florid, with dark hair, blue eyes, five feet six inches tall. Living in Oconee County, Georgia, after the war.

Middleton, Alexander "Alec." In 1860 resident Putnam County Georgia. Listed as twenty-five-year-old farmer in the household of his widowed mother, Nancy Middleton. Value of whole property $100. Enlisted as private June 15, 1861. Severely wounded in the groin Allegheny Mountain, Virginia, December 13, 1861. Died of wounds at Staunton, Virginia, January 15, 1862. Buried in a trench, Confederate section, Thornrose Cemetery, Staunton, Virginia, January 25, 1862. There is no marker at Thornrose Cemetery. His mother applied for his pay after his death. A memorial marker is said to be located at Salem Cemetery, Putnam County, Georgia. However, during a survey of Salem Cemetery in April 2007, no marker could be located.

Moore, John M. In 1860 resident Putnam County, Georgia. Listed as seventeen years old in the household of his father, Richard Moore. Owned no property. Enlisted as private June 15, 1861. Killed Sharpsburg, Maryland, September 17, 1862.

MORTON, HENRY W. "WAT." In 1860 resident Putnam County, Georgia. Listed as nineteen years old in the household of his father, Henry Morton. Owned no property. Enlisted as private June 15, 1861. Died of typhoid fever at Camp Bartow, Virginia, at 2:15 a.m. September 19, 1861. Buried at Camp Bartow on the evening of September 20, 1861. At the time of his death, Irby G. Scott and Thomas Spivey of Company G were by his side. Wat was shrouded in his uniform and buried in a coffin made by Frank Suther of the company. Irby Scott cut his name on a plank and placed it at the foot of his grave. At the head of his grave Irby placed a rock onto which Wat's initials were engraved.

OLIVER, JAMES M. In 1860 resident Putnam County, Georgia. Listed as thirty-year-old overseer in the household of Alfred Westbrooks, who was the superintendent of the Eatonton factory. Value of whole property $60. Enlisted as private July 20, 1861. Wounded at Malvern Hill, Virginia, July 1, 1862. Severely wounded in left jaw at Wilderness, Virginia, May 5, 1864. Admitted to Jackson Hospital, May 20, 1864, and given a sixty-day furlough. He last reported July 24, 1864, and there are no records after this date.

ONEIL, R. A. Refused to enter service and discharged at Richmond, Virginia, June 26, 1861.

PARKER, JAMES R. In 1860 resident Putnam County, Georgia. Listed as eighteen-year-old farmer, in the household of Austin Parker. Enlisted as private June 15, 1861. Severely wounded in the face, the ball passing through his cheeks, and a second ball struck him in the breast and came out his back at McDowell, Virginia, May 8, 1862. Absent wounded from the company from May 8, 1862, until May 10, 1864, when he is shown absent without leave. Appears on register of the Invalid Corps, Provisional Army Confederate States, with a date of retirement October 19, 1864. Living in Lincolnton, Georgia, after the war.

PARKER, JOHN S. In 1860 resident Putnam County, Georgia. Listed as twenty-seven-year-old married farmer with three children. Married F. E. Denham December 25, 1853, Putnam County, Georgia. Personal estate of $100. Enlisted as private May 14, 1862. Muster roll for December 31, 1863, shows him detailed as a shoemaker for the regiment. Absent sick and admitted June 1, 1864, to Jackson Hospital, Richmond, Virginia. Transferred to Huguenot Springs, Virginia, hospital July 8, 1864. Gunshot wound with compound fracture of lower third left femur at Cedar Creek, Virginia, October 19, 1864. Amputation of middle third, left femur, on the field. Captured and admitted to U.S.A. Depot Field Hospital at Winchester, Virginia, October 20, 1864, and died there, as result of leg amputation, November 8, 1864.

PASCHAL, HOMER VIRGIL. Born Morgan County, Georgia, May 15, 1837. Listed in the 1861 Morgan County, Georgia, tax digest with $300 in money and solvent debt. Enlisted as private, June 15, 1861. Listed on muster roll dated August 31, 1862, as absent without leave. Listed as deserter on muster roll dated December 31, 1862. Appears on morning report, Jackson Hospital, Richmond, Virginia, dated December 31, 1863, as deranged. Discharged on account of mental disability at Jackson Hospital, Richmond, Virginia, February 17, 1864. It appears Homer joined Talbot Scouts, a Cavalry Company attached to the 1st (Galt's) Infantry Regiment, Georgia State Line, in October 1864. Surrendered Milledgeville, Georgia, at the close of the war. Residing in Putnam County, Georgia, after the war. Married Harriet Glenn Floyd October 18, 1865, Putnam County, Georgia. During his lifetime he changed his name from Virgil Homer to Homer Virgil. Died Milledgeville, Georgia, June 11, 1911. Buried Alexander-Chambers Cemetery, at Turnwold

Plantation, Putnam County, Georgia. *Eatonton Messenger* (Eatonton, Georgia) issue of July 1, 1911: "OBITUARY: Fifty years ago this month he volunteered in defense of his home and loved ones, going to the seat of war in Virginia, in the Putnam Light Infantry, Co. G., 12th Ga. Regt., Capt. R. T. Davis commanding. After a year's hard service in the Virginia, mountains, he returned to Georgia broken down in health."

PASCHAL, WILLIAM C. Born Putnam County, Georgia, August 31, 1839. In 1860 resident Eatonton, Georgia. Listed as twenty-year-old doctor in the household of his father, William R. Paschal, and mother, Mary Ann Ingram. Owned no property. Enlisted as private June 15, 1861. On muster roll dated August 31, 1862, shown as absent as nurse. Captured at Middleburg, Virginia, September 30, 1862. Exchanged. On furlough December 31, 1862. Furnished a substitute. He appears on the 1864 Putnam County, Georgia, militia list as a twenty-four year, five-month-old farmer, and his exemption is substitute. Married Mary Kimbrough of Greene County, Georgia. Living in Dawson, Georgia, after the war. Died Dawson, Georgia, October 26, 1912. Buried Cedar Hill cemetery, Dawson, Georgia. *The Dawson News* (Dawson, Georgia) issue of October 29, 1912: " . . . Twice served Mercer University as Trustee, and for 5 or 6 years was Vice President of the Board. He was a man of great liberality in other ways, and numbers of boys and girls have been helped in school and many poor people have enjoyed his benefactions. As a friend he was loyal, as a christian he believed in God and his church and as a business man he was honest and successful."

PEARMAN, WILLIAM W. Orphan of W. W. Pearman, and his guardian was James Pearman. Enlisted as private June 15, 1861. Cut off from the regiment at Front Royal, Virginia, May 30, 1862. Wounded in a leg Second Manassas, Virginia, August 28, 1862. In the official report of Major Isaac Hardeman, dated May 9, 1863, early on the evening of May 4, 1863, Captain J. N. Beale, of Company B, was ordered to take command of a detachment of forty men to act as skirmishers in front of the brigade. At eight o'clock the following morning, May 5, the skirmish line was ordered forward. Advancing under heavy Federal cannon and musket fire, Captain Beale determined that the enemy was in great numbers. In this skirmish, Major Hardeman declared, William W. Pearman was killed. However, the official Compiled Service Record shows W. W. Pearman was killed at Chancellorsville, Virginia, May 4, 1863. He was killed instantly when shot through the head.

PEARSON, WILLIAM THOMAS. In 1860 resident Putnam County, Georgia. Listed as eighteen years old in the household of his father, Samuel Pearson, a wealthy planter. Owned no property. Enlisted as private June 15, 1861. Severely wounded in arm at McDowell, Virginia, May 8, 1862. His wound was so severe that Dr. Etheridge wanted to amputate his arm, but William would not allow Dr. Etheridge to remove arm. Tom was a patient in a private home in Staunton, Virginia, upon being removed from the battlefield at McDowell. In General Hospital Number 16, at Richmond, Virginia, from wounds, September 1, 1862. Paid commutation of rations while on wounded furlough October 9, 1862 to May 14, 1863. Furnished a substitute. Enrolling officer Putnam County, Georgia. Married December 11, 1866, Putnam County, Georgia, to Elizabeth Caroline "Carrie" Harwell, daughter of T. B. and Elizabeth Harwell. Died Putnam County, Georgia, April 2, 1888. He, his wife, and a daughter are buried Pine Grove Cemetery, Eatonton, Georgia, Section 1, Division A, Lot 37, in unmarked graves. His grave is only marked with a small stone, with C. S. A. and the number 25, placed by the Dixie Chapter, Daughters of Confederate Veterans, in 1923.

PERRYMAN, ELISHA B. Enlisted as private June 15, 1861. At home on leave of indulgence (furlough) December 1863, he returned to the company camped near New Hope, Virginia, on January 14, 1864. Killed at Wilderness, Virginia, May 5, 1864.

PORTER, JOSIAH F. "JOE." Born Putnam County, Georgia, July 20, 1840. Enlisted as private June 15, 1861. Shown as absent without leave in September 1862. Shown on muster roll for December 31, 1862, as arrested. Captured at Spotsylvania, Virginia, May 10, 1864. Received at Elmira, New York, July 30, 1864, from Point Lookout, Maryland. Released at Point Lookout, Maryland, May 14 1865, his occupation was listed as student. Died Soldiers' Home, Atlanta, Georgia, August 4, 1925. Buried in the Confederate Cemetery at Marietta, Georgia, August 5, 1925. *Eatonton Messenger* (Eatonton, Georgia) issue of January 7, 1926: "VETERAN PORTER OF COMPANY 'G' DEAD: . . . Porter returned to Eatonton but drifted to Macon after his mother moved to Milledgeville leaving no relatives here. He found work in Macon and advanced to be a trusted engineer of the old E.T.V. & G.R.R., now the Southern Railway. He lived at the Soldiers Home part of last year and died there August 4, 1925 at the age of 85."

PRITCHARD, DONALDSON. Born in North Carolina. In 1854 a mason in Rising Star Lodge 4, Eatonton, Georgia. In 1860 resident Putnam County, Georgia in the household of N. Hudson. Listed as fifty-five-year-old overseer. Owned no property. Enlisted as private, June 15, 1861. Muster roll dated December 31, 1861, shows him sick at Harrisonburg, Virginia. Returned to camp March 28, 1862, and sent sick to Atlanta, Georgia, April 20, 1862, where he was discharged July 21, 1862. He must have come back to the company for a short while, as he was said to be going home in the July 20, 1862, letter written by Irby Scott. Died December 29, 1870, Putnam County, Georgia. Buried Concord United Methodist Church Cemetery, Putnam County, Georgia.

REID, ALEXANDER HUDSON "AB." Born Putnam County, Georgia, April 7, 1840. In 1860 resident Eatonton, Georgia. Listed as twenty-year-old dentist in the household of his father, David Henry Reid, and mother, Susan Elizabeth Adams. Owned $300 in personal estate. Enlisted as private June 15, 1861. Severely wounded at McDowell, Virginia, May 8, 1862, under the left lower rib by minié ball, which passed through and came out near the spinal column. Ball cut the larger stomach, causing all discharge from the bowels to pass through the hole left by the ball, causing permanent disability. Patient in a private home in Staunton, Virginia, upon being removed from the battlefield at McDowell. Discharged disabled prior to October 1863. Organized Company F, Sixty-sixth Georgia Infantry, and commissioned captain August 8, 1863. He remained with the company until January 19, 1864, when he returned home because of the effects of his earlier wound. Resigned April 12, 1864, on surgeon's certificate of disability. Married Mary Ann Rogan December 7, 1865, Putnam County, Georgia. Died Eastman, Georgia, June 14, 1899. Buried with his wife, Pine Grove Cemetery, Section 1, Division A, Lot 25, in an unmarked grave, Eatonton, Georgia. *Eatonton Messenger* (Eatonton, Georgia) issue of June 17, 1899: "BRIEF LOCAL ITEMS: . . . He was desperately wounded in the bloody battle of McDowell May 8, 1862, and probably never recovered fully from the wound. He was made a captain in 1864, and was a gallant soldier."

REID, ALEXANDER SIDNEY. Born Putnam County, Georgia, November 8, 1839. In 1860 resident Eatonton, Georgia. Listed as twenty years old in the household of his father, Andrew Reid, and mother, Mary Ann (Clopton) Reid, a wealthy planter family. Owned no property. Second lieutenant June 15, 1861. On recruiting service in Georgia March 11 to April 26, 1862. Elected captain May 22, 1862. Acting quartermaster for the regiment in late 1863. Colonel Edward Willis recommended "Sid" Reid for the position of assistant quartermaster. Appointed captain and assistant quartermaster January 27, 1864, to take rank November 16, 1863. Assistant quartermaster of Doles's brigade, Grimes's division, Second Corps, Army of Northern Virginia, October 1, 1864. On March 22, 1865, relieved as captain and assistant quartermaster of Cook's brigade and assigned to the charge of the supply train of Grimes's division. Surrendered, Appomattox, Virginia, April 9, 1865, as captain and assistant quartermaster of Grimes's division. "No officer in the regiment was more popular, for he was always in a good humor with himself and the rest of mankind, and he made friends wherever he went." (In Thomas, *Doles-Cook Brigade,* 236.) Married Mary Elizabeth "Lizzie" Grimes (August 23, 1846–March 21, 1916) of Sparta, Georgia, November 8, 1866, Putnam County, Georgia. Resided in Eatonton, Georgia, after the war. Died December 2, 1909. Both Alexander and his wife are buried at Pine Grove Cemetery, Section 1, Division B, Lot 187, Eatonton, Georgia. Ab Lee, body servant to Captain Reid, served through all four years of the war. At the Doles-Cook Brigade Association reunion in 1900, Lee was made an honorary member of the association by unanimous vote. *Eatonton Messenger* (Eatonton, Georgia) issue of December 4, 1909: "CAPT. A. S. REID PASSES AWAY: Had been in perfect health until a few weeks ago. Was taken sick in Atlanta. . . . A man of charming social qualities, a gentleman of the old school, generous to a fault in friend or foe alike he made friends wherever he went and held them. That in his public career he should not have been misunderstood and made enemies, would have been unnatural and direct opposition to the laws of human nature. A loyal true hearted citizen, a devoted husband and father, and loyal friend he will be sadly missed in Eatonton and Putnam." *Eatonton Messenger* (Eatonton, Georgia) issue of December 11, 1909: "AN UNUSUAL TRIBUTE AT FUNERAL OF CAPT. A. S. REID. An unusual touching feature of the funeral service, was the presentation of a handsome silver loving cup to the widow of Capt. Reid. . . . The loving cup had been purchased for presentation to Capt. Reid by his countless admirers and constituents in Eatonton and Putnam, but unfortunately had not been presented before the illness and death of Putnam's representative."

REID, DAVID HENRY. Born Eatonton, Georgia, June 16, 1842. In 1860 resident Eatonton, Georgia. Listed as seventeen years old in the household of his father, Andrew Reid, and his mother, Mary Ann (Clopton) Reid, a wealthy planter family. Owned no property. Enlisted as a private April 4, 1862. Wounded in the arm at Front Royal, Virginia, May 30, 1862. He was discharged after furnishing a substitute in December 1862. He appears on the 1864 Putnam County, Georgia, militia list as twenty-one years old and his exemption is substitute. Served in Prudden's Battery in 1864. In November 1864 was commissioned captain on staff of General Samuel Read Anderson; paroled under such commission, and in such position at Milledgeville, Georgia, May 1865. Never married, residing in Eatonton, Georgia, after the war. Died at the Confederate Soldiers' Home in Atlanta February 3, 1915. Buried Pine Grove Cemetery, Section 1, Division A, Lot 110, Eatonton, Georgia. *Eatonton Messenger* (Eatonton, Georgia), issue of February 12, 1915: "He was a first honor graduate of South Carolina's leading college prior to the civil war, and a member of one of Georgia's best known families." Editor's note: his correct date of birth is June 16, 1842, per family Bible: his tombstone reads "born January 16, 1843" and his obituary gives a date of birth as June 30, 1842.

REID, EDWARD BUTLER "EDD." Born Putnam County, Georgia, September 17, 1841. In 1860 resident Eatonton, Georgia. Listed as eighteen years old in the household of his father and mother, Edmund Reid and Elizabeth (Terrel) Reid. In 1861, his guardian and uncle, Judge David Henry Reid returned for taxes one slave, with a value of $700. Enlisted as private June 15, 1861. Killed McDowell, Virginia, May 8, 1862. His body was returned to Putnam County, Georgia. Buried Pine Grove Cemetery, Section 1, Division A, Lot 109, Eatonton, Georgia. *The Countryman* (Turnwold-Putnam County, Georgia), Tuesday, July 12, 1862: "OBITUARY . . . 'His noble regard for truth,' says one very near to him, 'and his conscientious discharge of duty, rendered him lovely to his companions and friends; while his affectionate nature was only equaled by his self-sacrificing disposition, and his heroic devotion to justice and right.' He was a nature's soldier, with an intuitive sense of a soldier's honor and duty. He leaned with heroic reliance upon his own arm, not only to meet the battle of life, but also to meet the invader of his country's soil. When asked by a fond mother, at parting, to pray and put his trust in the Almighty, he said, 'Ma, don't give yourself any uneasiness about me: I am old enough to think for myself, now': thus intimating that prayer and trust in God had occupied his unsolicited attention."

REID, JAMES HENRY. Born Putnam County, Georgia, May 8, 1840. In 1860 resident Eatonton, Putnam County, Georgia. Listed as nineteen years old in the household of his father, James Lewis Reid. Enlisted as private June 15, 1861. Died of dysentery at Staunton, Virginia, December 20, 1861. Memorial marker at Pine Grove Cemetery, Section 1, Division A, Lot 118, Eatonton, Georgia.

REID, RICHMOND ALEXANDER. Born June 29, 1829, Putnam County, Georgia. In 1860 resident Eatonton, Georgia. Listed as thirty-year-old money lender in the household of his father and mother, Edmund Reid and Elizabeth (Terrel) Reid. Personal estate $25,000. Enlisted as private June 15, 1861. Appointed assistant commissary sergeant July 6, 1861. Appointed captain, commissary department, to report to Twelfth Georgia Infantry Regiment, July 9, 1861. Appointed assistant quartermaster, Twelfth Georgia Infantry Regiment, May 28, 1863. Resigned as assistant quartermaster as he was appointed provost marshal, Second Corps, Army of Northern Virginia, in 1863. Resigned as captain October 14, 1863. Married Leonora H. Rosser December 5, 1866, Putnam County, Georgia. Died Eatonton, Georgia, September 28, 1882. He and his wife are buried Pine Grove Cemetery, Section 1, Division A, Lot 109, Eatonton, Georgia.

RICKERSON, HENRY R. Born in Georgia, August 16, 1840. In 1860 resident Eatonton, Georgia. Listed as twenty-year-old mechanic. Owned no property. Enlisted as private August 2, 1861. Severely wounded in thigh at McDowell, Virginia, May 8, 1862. Wounded by shell fragment to the foot April 29, 1863. Robert Young, in his letter dated May 9, 1863, states Henry cut his big toe off with an ax a few days before the Chancellorsville fight. This statement by Robert Young seems to indicate the April 29 date. In General Hospital, Farmville, Virginia, August 3, 1863, owing to stricture of urethra, returned to duty August 18, 1863. Captured at Winchester, Virginia, September 19, 1864. Took oath of allegiance to U.S. government at Point Lookout, Maryland, released, on joining U.S. Army, October 8, 1864. He then served in the Fourth Volunteer Infantry, Regular U.S. Army. Married Mary E. Brown, a widow, December 20, 1885, Rutledge, Morgan County, Georgia. Until this marriage, he had not been previously married. Died September 14, 1910, Rutledge, Georgia. Buried Rutledge Cemetery in the town of Rutledge. His grave is located in the center of the cemetery.

SCOTT, IRBY GOODWIN. Born Putnam County, Georgia, March 2, 1840. In 1860 resident Putnam County, Georgia. Listed as twenty-year-old farmer in the household of his father, Irby H. Scott. Value of whole property $194, which consisted of a small amount of money and $194 in other property. Enlisted as private June 15, 1861. Elected junior second lieutenant August 7, 1862. In his August 13, 1862, letter Irby informs the family, "I was struck by a spent ball on the hip but it did not hurt me any." He would have been struck August 9, 1862, during the battle of Cedar Run. Wounded in shoulder and thigh at Second Manassas, Virginia, August 27, 1862, when an enemy shell exploded nearby and killed and wounded several men. First lieutenant April 21, 1864. In command of the company after July 12, 1864, when Captain Zachary was wounded and captured. From June 1864 in command of 2nd Corps of sharpshooters from the brigade for nearly a year. Surrendered, Appomattox, Virginia, April 9, 1865. Married May 26, 1880, to Florence E. Williams, Blountsville, Jones County, Georgia. Irby died Putnam County, Georgia, May 31, 1925. Buried Harmony Baptist Church Cemetery, Putnam County, Georgia. Irby applied for the Cross of Honor through the Dixie Chapter of U.D.C. on April 10, 1900. *Eatonton Messenger* (Eatonton, Georgia) issue of June 5, 1925: "Front page IRBY GOODWIN SCOTT: . . . Unassuming as a soldier, so was he in private life. Popular but never asking office. At request of Grand Jury he served several terms as County Commissioner, respected and loved by every one who came in contact with him. MR. GOODWIN SCOTT DIES ON MONDAY: . . . Mr. Scott was a quiet, unassuming man, but his splendid qualities were well known and appreciated by a large number of friends in the town and county. He has made Putnam a useful citizen."

SCOTT, NICHOLAS EWING "BUD." Born April 28, 1845, Putnam County, Georgia. Brother to Irby G. Scott. In 1860 resident Putnam County, Georgia. Listed as fifteen years old in the household of his father, Irby H. Scott. Owned no property. Enlisted as private June 1, 1863. Killed at Spotsylvania, Virginia, May 10, 1864, during the counterattack to recapture the works. He was "shot through the head and killed about night-fall near the works but a little to the left of the part occupied by Company G." (*Eatonton Messenger,* May 17, 1913.) His body was carried in his blanket, on May 11, about two hundred yards to the rear of the works, and buried in a fence corner near the McCoull house. After the war he was interned in the Confederate Cemetery, Spotsylvania, Virginia, Row L, Number 5. Nicholas had not married before his death. *Eatonton Messenger* (Eatonton, Georgia) issue of May 17, 1913: "A WAR INCIDENT: By Robert Young, Co. G. 12th Ga. 'So the remains of our dear comrades are in the care of the U.D.C. of Virginia. Noble women of Virginia—We Georgians who served in Virginia, through three and four years of that devastating war can never forget the kindness of the Virginia, ladies of those days. Their daughters continue their good works.'"

SPIVEY, THOMAS ROBERSON. Born July 22, 1839. In 1860 resident Putnam County, Georgia. Listed as twenty-year-old farmer, with three children, married to Mary T. Gallaway, December 22, 1853, Putnam County, Georgia. Value of whole property $2,839, which consisted of six slaves and $539 in other property. Enlisted as private June 15, 1861. Appointed fifth sergeant in 1863. Wounded in the neck, Spotsylvania, Virginia, May 10, 1864. Wounded in right elbow, leaving it stiff and permanently disabled at Cedar Creek, Virginia, October 19, 1864. Admitted general hospital, Charlottesville, Virginia, March 1, 1865, in Lynchburg, Virginia, hospital at close of war, and paroled there April 1865. Died Putnam County, Georgia, October 24, 1910. Buried in the Spivey Family Cemetery, near Philadelphia Church, Putnam County, Georgia. *Eatonton Messenger* (Eatonton, Georgia) issue of December 17, 1910: "IN MEMORIAM: In the death of Mr. Thomas R. Spivey, Putnam county loses one of her best citizens; and as his life and example are so worthy of emulation, so helpful and instructive, and so full of inspiration. . . . It is the universal testimony of the surviving comrades of Thomas R. Spivey, that there was no better soldier in this regiment than he. He was always ready for duty brave as a lion, quiet and uncomplaining and never lost either courage or hope from defeat and disaster. . . . His highest ambition was to live right and to treat his fellow man right and he never sought public office but once when he served the people of his county as sheriff."

STUBBS, THOMAS JEFFERSON. Born December 1, 1836. In 1860 resident Putnam County, Georgia. Listed as nineteen years old in the household of his widowed mother, Elizabeth J. (Davis) Stubbs. Owned no property. Enlisted as private June 15, 1861. Sick Harrisonburg, Virginia, September 29, 1861. Returned to camp March 28, 1862. Severely wounded in the bowels at McDowell, Virginia, May 8, 1862, the ball remaining in his body until his death many years later. Absent wounded since May 8, 1862, and appointed sub-enrolling officer June 10, 1863 at Eatonton, Georgia. He remained on the rolls of the company through the war, though he never returned to the army after being wounded. Married Mary Griggs, November 22, 1862, Putnam County, Georgia. Thomas Stubbs died June 8, 1891, Houston County, Georgia. Buried Andrew Chapel Cemetery, Dennard Community, Houston County, Georgia.

SUTHER, SAMUEL FRANK. In 1860 resident Putnam County, Georgia. Listed as 24-year-old carpenter, born in North Carolina, in the household of William S. Spivey. Personal property $50. Enlisted as private June 15, 1861. Muster roll dated December 31, 1861 shows him sick at Staunton, Virginia. Wounded in the back at McDowell, Virginia, May 8, 1862. Admitted to General Hospital Number 18 Richmond, Virginia, September 28, 1862. Wounded Chancellorsville, Virginia, May 3, 1863. Captured at Winchester, Virginia, September 19, 1864. Sent first to Harpers Ferry, Virginia, then transferred to Point Lookout, Maryland. Released at Point Lookout, Maryland, May 14, 1865. Married Julia Ann Marie Rogers December 30, 1866, Putnam County, Georgia. Living in Selma, Alabama after the war. Died July 23, 1896 Selma, Alabama.

SUTHER, WILLIAM W. In 1860 resident Putnam County, Georgia. Listed as 43 years old, born North Carolina, married with one child. Married to Martha Lynch, Putnam County, Georgia. Enlisted as private April 4, 1862. Severely wounded in side at McDowell, Virginia, May 8, 1862. Captured at Spotsylvania, Virginia, May 10, 1864. Arrived Point Lookout, Maryland, May 14, 1864. Transferred to Elmira, New York July 27, 1864. Released at Elmira, New York June 19, 1865. At the time of his release he had dark hair, blue eyes and was 5 feet 11 inches tall. Died at home of his only child Mrs. H. C. Barney in Macon, Georgia, October 20, 1894. Buried Pine Grove Cemetery, Eatonton, Georgia, Section 1, Division A, Lot 103. *Eatonton Messenger* (Eatonton, Georgia) issue of October 27, 1894: ". . . he was a good natured and well meaning man, and his honesty was never questioned. As a builder and worker he was careful. Reliable and ———, and when he undertook a job there was no doubt that it would be well done."

THOMAS, HENRY WALTER. Born Eatonton, Georgia, June 15, 1842. His mother was Mary C. (Turner) Thomas. Listed in the household of his father and stepmother, Gabriel R. and Juda A. (Fears) Thomas. Enlisted as a private May 14, 1862, at Augusta, Georgia. On the way to the army Henry was taken sick with diarrhea seven miles south of Front Royal and was left "with a very clever family" to recuperate. Captured near Front Royal, Virginia, June 9, 1862. Imprisoned at Washington, D.C., and Fort Delaware, Delaware. Exchanged at Aiken's Landing, Virginia, August 5, 1862. On sick furlough from August 14, 1862, to January 27, 1863. Appointed hospital steward Twelfth Georgia Infantry Regiment May 6, 1864. Surrendered, Appomattox, Virginia, April 9, 1865. Married Amanda Barnett in June 1870 at Milledgeville, Georgia; she died in 1871. Residing Atlanta, Georgia, after the war, where he was a clerk in the office of the secretary of state of Georgia. Died in Milledgeville, Georgia, 1909. Buried Memory Hill Cemetery, Milledgeville, Georgia, east side, Section I, Lot 63, grave 9; his wife is buried in grave 10. *Eatonton Messenger* (Eatonton, Georgia) issue of April 24, 1909: "DEATH OF CONFEDERATE VETERANS. Several weeks ago there died in Milledgeville a confederate Veteran who did not receive the honors that he deserved. . . . Henry W. Thomas, son-in-law of Hon. Samuel Barnett, [Nathan Crawford Barnett is the correct name of the Secretary of State] for many years Georgia's secretary of state, [Thomas] was historian of the Doles-Cook brigade and in that capacity did for his comrades a service whose value can hardly be over estimated."

THOMAS, LOVIC HULL "TUCK." In 1860 resident Eatonton, Georgia. Listed as fifteen years old in the household of his father and stepmother, Gabriel R. and Juda A. (Fears) Thomas. Owned no property. Enlisted as private June 15, 1861. Slightly wounded in arm and back of head at Allegheny Mountain, Virginia, December 13, 1861. Slightly wounded in arm at McDowell, Virginia, May 8, 1862. On wounded furlough from May 13, 1862, to February 26, 1863. Wounded Chancellorsville, Virginia, May 3, 1863. Admitted to hospital, Charlottesville, Virginia, June 16–18, 1864, owing to dysentery. Flesh wound of the right thigh, Kernstown, Virginia, July 12, 1864. Admitted to hospital, Winchester, Virginia, July 22, 1864, transferred to C. S. A. Hospital, Charlottesville, Virginia, July 30, 1864. Furloughed August 5, 1864 for sixty days. Detailed in quartermaster's department, Grimes's division, February 1865. Surrendered, Appomattox, Virginia, April 9, 1865. Died Milledgeville, Georgia, March 7, 1908. Buried Memory Hill Cemetery, Milledgeville, Georgia, west side, Section D, Lot 108, grave 1.

VINING, ELIJAH. Born 1838 Georgia. In 1860 resident Eatonton, Georgia. Listed as twenty-four-year-old grocer in the household of G. C. Green. Value of whole property $100, which was money and solvent debt. Enlisted as private June 15, 1861. Muster roll dated December 31, 1861, shows him in Harrisonburg, Virginia, sick since September 29, 1861. Returned to camp March 25, 1862. Captured at Spotsylvania, Virginia, May 10, 1864. Transferred from Point Lookout, Maryland, to Elmira, New York. Released Elmira, New York, June 19, 1865. At the time of his release complexion fair, auburn hair, hazel eyes, 5 feet 7 inches tall. Died Eatonton, Georgia, January 21, 1876. Buried Pine Grove Cemetery, Eatonton, Georgia, Section 1, Division A, Lot 98. *Eatonton Messenger* (Eatonton, Georgia) issue of Saturday, January 22, 1876: "Sudden Death—We are sorry to chronicle the death of Mr. E. Vining, Deputy Sheriff, Putnam County. . . . Mr. Vining was an honest man, and about 40 years of age. He leaves a wife and two little children to mourn his untimely end."

WALKER, THOMAS A. "PHONZ." In 1860 resident Putnam County, Georgia. Listed as twenty-nine-year-old farmer, married with three children. Married Putnam County, Georgia, to Sarah Elizabeth Faver, January 3, 1854. Shortly after the war, Sarah married second John A. Avera. Her second husband was also a Confederate veteran. Personal estate $1,500. Enlisted as a private July 20, 1861, at Monterey, Virginia. Wounded slightly in head at McDowell, Virginia, May 8, 1862. Admitted General Hospital Number 21, Richmond, Virginia, October 14, 1862. Transferred to Camp Winder, Richmond, Virginia, November 17, 1862. One of the men of the company has indicated that Thomas was AWOL (Absent Without Leave) for a period of time and then dropped from the rolls as a deserter. There is no evidence in the compiled service record showing Thomas was listed as AWOL or that he had been dropped from the rolls as a deserter. It can be surmised from the compiled service record he was still recovering from his wound. Mortally wounded Winchester, Virginia, September 19, 1864.

WALLER, CHARLES B. In 1860 resident Putnam County, Georgia. Listed as twenty years old in the household of his father, H. H. Waller. Owned no property. Enlisted as a private March 13, 1862, at Camp Allegheny, Virginia. Muster roll dated August 30, 1862, shows him absent wounded. Died of smallpox at Winchester, Virginia, October 25, 1862. When it was discovered he was infected with smallpox, the company was separated from the regiment.

WALLER, WILLIAM H. In 1860 resident Putnam County, Georgia. Listed as twenty-one-year-old carpenter in the household of his father, H. H. Waller. Owned no property. Enlisted as private June 15, 1861. Promoted to second corporal. Admitted C. S. A. Hospital, Winchester, Virginia, May 27, 1862. Wounded by friendly cannon fire at Gettysburg, Pennsylvania, July 2, 1863. Left on the field and captured at Gettysburg, Pennsylvania, July 3, 1863. Arrived at Fort Delaware, Delaware, October 22, 1863. Died April 1, 1864, Fort Delaware.

WELCH, REUBIN R. In 1860 resident Putnam County, Georgia. Value of whole property $540, which consisted of money and solvent debt. Enlisted as private June 15, 1861. On special duty at hospital December 27, 1861. Killed Cedar Run, Virginia, August 9, 1862, by a piece of shell or grapeshot from an enemy cannon. He was killed instantly, the ball passing entirely through his breast.

WELCH, THOMAS H. Enlisted as private April 4, 1862. Deserted prior to December 31, 1862.

WHALEY, NICHOLAS E. "NICK." In 1860 resident Putnam County, Georgia. Listed as nineteen-year-old farmer in the household of Jos. Whaley. Owned no property. Enlisted as private June 15, 1861. Said to have died of pneumonia at Camp Allegheny, Virginia, December 25, 1861. On November 6, 1861, Nick was in Staunton, Virginia, ill; if he ever returned to camp, it is uncertain. There is no later record. From the Irby G. Scott letter of January 9, 1862, Nick's body was returned home.

WILLIAMS, FRANCIS M. In 1860 resident Putnam County, Georgia. Owned no property. Enlisted as private June 15, 1861. At Harrisonburg, Virginia, sick September 30, 1861. Killed McDowell, Virginia, May 8, 1862.

WILLIAMS, JAMES WESLEY. In 1860 resident Morgan County, Georgia. Listed as twenty-three-year-old overseer in the household of James M. Zachry. Value of personal estate $200. Enlisted as private June 15, 1861. Sent sick to Harrisonburg, Virginia, September 30, 1861. Absent without leave September 15–20, 1862. Wounded at Spotsylvania, Virginia, May 8, 1864, and captured there May 18, 1864. Released Elmira, New York, June 14, 1865. At the time of his release he was 5 feet 6 inches tall, with blue eyes. Died at the home of his brother, K. C. Williams, in Atlanta, January 5, 1914. Buried Brownwood Baptist Church Cemetery, Morgan County, Georgia. *The Madisonian* (Madison, Georgia) issue of January 8, 1914: "MR. WES WILLIAMS DEAD. . . . He was a confederate veteran and one of the best men who ever lived in the county. He was once a merchant in Madison."

WILSON, JAMES LAWSON. Born in Putnam County, Georgia, February 22, 1841. In 1860 resident Putnam County, Georgia. Listed as twenty-year-old farmer in the household of Austin Parker. Owned no property. Enlisted as private June 15, 1861. Appointed fifth sergeant July 21, 1862, fourth sergeant 1864. Captured at Front Royal, Virginia, May 30, 1862. Exchanged at Aiken's Landing, Virginia, August 5, 1862. Wounded, right ankle, Sharpsburg, Maryland, September 17, 1862. Admitted, September 25, 1862, to General Hospital Number 7, Richmond, Virginia. Returned to duty October 14, 1862. On detached service February 18 to March 18, 1863. Wounded at Winchester, Virginia, September 19, 1864, gunshot wound of left lower arm, with deformity of wrist. In Lynchburg, Virginia, hospital wounded, at close of the war. On his application for the Cross of Honor in

1900, Wilson says he was paroled at Macon, Georgia. Married Nancy Elizabeth Parker, December 22, 1859. Elected superintendent of the Soldiers' Home, Atlanta, Georgia, 1901. Died Eatonton, Georgia, October 22, 1902. Buried Wilson Cemetery, Putnam County, Georgia. *Eatonton Messenger* (Eatonton, Georgia) issue of November 15, 1902: "A TRIBUTE TO THE MEMORY OF CAPT. JAS. L. WILSON. . . . He was a true, valiant soldier of the cross and it is not strange that he was a brave soldier in the war, for we are taught the righteous are as bold as a lion. . . . Soon after the war he was unanimously elected sheriff of Putnam county which office he filled with honor, firmness and gentleness, a number of years. . . . In the very beginning of the war between the states he volunteered for service. He was a brave and faithful soldier for four years."

WILSON, WILLIAM E. Born in Georgia. In 1860 resident Putnam County, Georgia. Listed as forty-six-year-old farmer. Married with six children in the household. Value of whole property $25,420, which consisted of 580 acres Putnam County, forty acres Lumpkin County, twenty-four slaves, $3,780 money and solvent debt, and $1,800 in other property. Enlisted as private June 15, 1861. Served as nurse at Harrisonburg, Virginia, from September 29, 1861, to at least the end of December 1861. Discharged over age, July 21, 1862. He appears on the 1864 Putnam County, Georgia, militia list as fifty-two-years, three-months-old farmer. Died June 1882.

WINCHEL, WILLIAM H. In 1860 resident Putnam County, Georgia. Listed as twenty-nine-year-old farmer in the household of A. Winchel. Value of whole property $1,515, which consisted of one slave, money, solvent debt and other property. Enlisted as private June 15, 1861. Cut off from the regiment at Front Royal, Virginia, May 30, 1962. Wounded in the head by a spent ball, but the skin was just broken, Cedar Mountain or Slaughter Mountain, August 9, 1862. Wounded in arm by friendly cannon fire and left on the field Gettysburg, Pennsylvania, July 3, 1863. His arm was amputated at the shoulder by Dr. Etheridge. Died as result of amputation in hospital at Gettysburg, Pennsylvania, July 8, 1863. *The Countryman* (Turnwold-Putnam County, Georgia) issue of February 16, 1864: "TRIBUTE OF RESPECT. . . . Although unusually strongly attached to the hearth-stone around which he was reared, yet he never, even for once, quit his post to return and gaze on the anxious faces of those whose morning, noon, and evening sacrifices were for his welfare and preservation. From boyhood, he had been a meek and consistent member of the Baptist Church at Harmony, and we console ourselves with the belief that, in his dying hours, he was cheered and sustained."

YOUNG, ROBERT. Born June 21, 1843, at Stralane, near Londonderry, County Tyrone, in the providence of Ulster, Northern Ireland. In 1860 resident Eatonton, Putnam County, Georgia. Listed as sixteen years old in the household of his cousin, William T. Young. Owned no property. Third sergeant December 5, 1861, Company C, 2nd Battalion, 2nd Brigade, Georgia State Troops, "Dennis Guards," Putnam County, Georgia. Discharged May 1862. Enlisted as a private, Company G, "Putnam Light Infantry," 12th Georgia Infantry Regiment, May 14, 1862. Wounded in side at Malvern Hill, Virginia, July 1, 1862 by a piece of shell. Admitted Chimborazo Hospital Number 1, Richmond, Virginia, July 3, 1862. Returned to duty July 5, 1862. Admitted Chimborazo Hospital Number 2, Richmond, Virginia, January 13, 1863, owing to hernia. Returned to duty January 17, 1863. Wounded in the right shoulder near the collarbone, Chancellorsville, Virginia, May 3, 1863. Wounded through the fleshy part of the left leg below the knee, Summit Point, Virginia, August 12, 1864. Moved by ambulance to Winchester, Virginia, August 23. Be-cause of this wound, Robert Young was away from the army for five months. On April 1, 1865, at Petersburg, Virginia, Robert was part of a detail of between twenty-five and thirty men on picket, eighty to one hundred yards in front of the main line. At daybreak on April 2, Federal troops broke through the picket line. Robert and the others retired to the main line, where he found his rifle fouled. While clearing the fouled rifle, he attempted to get away, but was overpowered by the pursuing Federal troops. Captured at Petersburg, Virginia, April 2, 1865. Arrived City Point, Virginia, April 4, 1864. Released Point Lookout, Maryland, June 22, 1865. On release his complexion was fair, with brown hair, blue eyes, 5 feet 8 inches tall. Married Susan Frances Adams, daughter of Jefferson Adams and Susan Meriwether Adams. Residing in Eatonton, Georgia, after the war, where he was the adjutant of R. T. Davis Camp #756, United Confederate Veterans. Young was active in Confederate veteran activities in Putnam County, Georgia. Robert Young, it is believed, may have accumulated much valuable material on the Twelfth Georgia and Confederate Veterans living in or near Putnam County, after the war. Unfortunately, disputation of this material is unknown. It is feared all of his material may have been destroyed by the family after his death. Died Putnam County, Georgia, January 13, 1927. Buried Pine Grove Cemetery, Eatonton, Georgia. *Eatonton Messenger* (Eatonton, Georgia) issue of January 21, 1927: "MR. ROBERT YOUNG PASSES TO BEYOND: . . . He was one of the distinguished citizens of Putnam, one of the county's truly great men, and during a long, useful and unselfish life, he held the confidence and esteem of every other Putnamite. . . . He was prominent in church affairs, being during his long membership in the Eatonton Presbyterian church Clerk of the session, Sunday school superintendent, treasurer, deacon, elder and ruling elder, and so long as his health permitted he was a regular attendant at all services, and took an active part. He was a prominent Mason, and served in various offices in Rising Star Lodge No. 4 and rose to the rank of Worshipful Master."

ZACHRY, ABNER ROWAN. Born Morgan County, Georgia, June 6 1841. In 1860 resident Putnam County, Georgia. His father died two years after the birth of Abner. Listed as nineteen years old in the household of his uncle and guardian, Josias Boswell.[1] His guardian controlled an estate for Abner and A. J. Zachary with a value of $22,900. Enlisted as first corporal June 15, 1861. Wounded at Allegheny Mountain, Virginia, December 13, 1861. Cut off from the regiment at Front Royal, Virginia, on May 30, 1862. Elected junior second lieutenant August 7, 1862, later second lieutenant. Promoted to first lieutenant April 16, 1863, and captain April 21, 1864. Gunshot wound in the side of his chest, and left on the field at the Confederate hospital, where he was captured, at Fort Stevens, near Washington, D.C., July 12, 1864. Admitted July 14, 1864 to Lincoln General Hospital, Washington, D.C., then to General Hospital Old Capital Prison, September 19, 1864. Sent to Fort Delaware, Delaware, October 21, 1864. Released at Fort Delaware, June 17, 1865. At his release he is shown to have blue eyes and was 6 feet 4 inches tall. After the war, he moved to Morgan County, Georgia, where he farmed. Married first Eugenia Alexander Lyle, in 1866 in Jackson County, Georgia. Eugenia died in January 1885, a few days after giving birth. Married second Martha "Mattie" Singleton, February 24, 1886, Putnam County, Georgia. Martha had been the schoolteacher for the Zachry children. While sitting with his family on the night of December 16, 1896, he was murdered. The assassin fired through a window, and Abner was instantly killed. Buried in the Baldwin-Wright Cemetery, north of Eatonton, Georgia, on U.S. Highway 441.

Notes

Introduction

1. In an April 1863 letter Scott asked if his brother Bud (Nicholas) walked to school, as it would be good for his brother to condition himself for entrance into the army. This letter suggests that the school was within walking distance of the Scott plantation and most likely the school under Mr. Shell at Union Chapel Methodist Church.
2. A bird-shaped mound representing the form of an eagle lying on its back with extended wings, the head turned toward the east. White quartz rock makes up the building materials of the rock effigy. The breast of the bird is seven to eight feet above ground level, tapering to two feet at the head, tail, and the tip of the wings. Measured from the top of the head to the tip of the tail, the eagle is 102 feet long. From the tips of the wings across the body is a distance of 120 feet.
3. A review of the 1859 to 1862 Putnam County, Georgia, Tax Digests verifies the number of slaves on the Scott plantation and those for which he was agent.
4. In the computation of the 1866 Putnam County Tax Digest, the value of the Scott plantation had been reduced to a total value of only $7,016, a loss of more than $22,000. Some of the loss was from decreased property values. The loss of the human property accounted for most of the reduced value.

Chapter 1

1. Camp Fairfield was located at the Fairfield Race Course two and one-half miles from the center of Richmond in Henrico County. The company remained here until June 26.
2. Irby Hudson Scott, father of Irby G. Scott and Nicholas E. Scott.
3. This is a rumor. Fearing Federal troops, after their success on June 13 at Romney, Virginia, would advance into the Shenandoah Valley and trap his small command, General Joseph E. Johnston evacuated Harper's Ferry on June 15, falling back to Bunker Hill.
4. Richard T. Davis (1825–1862), captain, June 15, 1861.
5. Nicholas E. "Nick" Whaley, private, June 15, 1861. Died of pneumonia December 25, 1861. H. W. "Wat" Morton, private, June 15, 1861. Died of fever September 1861.
6. Sarah Tompkins (1780–1862), grandmother to Irby G. Scott, residing in the household of her son-in-law Irby H. Scott.
7. Young boys would travel from the city to sell newspapers in the camps to earn spending money.
8. This was only a rumor, as there is no mention of an insurrection in the Augusta newspaper.
9. Zephaniah Turner Conner (1811–1866). Appointed lieutenant colonel of the Twelfth Georgia, July 2, 1861; promoted to colonel December 13, 1861, owing to the promotion

of Colonel Edward Johnson to brigadier general. Conner was charged under the fifty-second article of war for neglect of duty. Relieved of command and cashiered from the Confederate army, December 27, 1862. His release from the army was a result of his conduct at Front Royal, Virginia, on May 30, 1862.

10. Charles R. Badger, released at Richmond, Virginia, June 24, 1861. He did not muster into service. He later served in Company C, "Dennis Guards," Putnam County, Georgia, Second Battalion, Second Brigade, Georgia State Troops. After service with the "Dennis Guards" he served in Captain Anderson's company, "Republic Blues," First Regiment Georgia Infantry. This company subsequently became Company C, First Regiment Georgia (Olmstead's) Infantry. He served through the war, and at the time of his death, in 1893, was coroner for Putnam County, Georgia.

11. Scott and those men in the company who had not been inoculated were vaccinated against smallpox.

12. Nicholas Ewing "Bud" Scott, brother to Irby G. Scott. Entered service as a private on June 1, 1863.

13. Jacob "Jake" Feiler, private, June 15, 1861. Wounded Richmond, Virginia, June 26, 1862. A "mess" was typically a group of four or five men grouped together for the purpose of sharing cooking duties.

14. Jim Pike, body servant of Abner Rowan Zachry. Zachry enlisted as first corporal on June 15, 1861.

15. Camp Reservoir, located two miles from Richmond in Henrico County, Virginia, near the reservoir for the city of Richmond. The Twelfth Georgia was camped here until at least July 7, 1861.

16. Henry Morton, father of "Wat" Morton, was a planter in Putnam County, Georgia, with large landholdings. He was the first minister for Union Chapel Methodist Church, located on land Irby H. Scott had given the trustees of the church in 1855.

17. Alexander Sidney "Sid" Reid, second lieutenant, June 15, 1861. Later captain and quartermaster of Cook's Brigade.

18. Mumps, not as contagious as measles, a common childhood disease caused by a virus usually spread through saliva or mucus from the nose. Symptoms are fever (often high), headache, and swollen and painful glands under the jaw. As the glands swell it may become difficult to eat or drink. Measles is a serious infection that spreads very easily from person to person. Symptoms are fever (often high), fatigue, runny nose, cough, and watery red eyes. Complications include pneumonia, ear infections, and diarrhea. During the Civil War there was no vaccine for mumps or measles and many of the men had not been exposed to measles or mumps as children. Many in the company became ill with measles and mumps after the regiment arrived in the mountains of Virginia.

19. Robert A. O'Neal did not muster into service. He later served in Company B, "Calhoun Greys," Second Battalion, Georgia State Troops, a militia company from Putnam County.

20. Unable to accurately identify Major Perryman. Mathew Henry Talbot, enlisted as first lieutenant, Company I, Ninth Georgia Infantry Regiment, June 10, 1861. Elected captain June 16, 1862. Resigned June 4, 1863, for health reasons, accepted July 17, 1863. After his resignation he served as captain and volunteer aid-de-camp to General William Henry Talbot Walker.

21. Richmond A. "Rich" Reid, private, June 15, 1861. Appointed captain of commissary department, to report to the Twelfth Georgia, July 9, 1861.

22. Abner Rowan Zachry, first corporal, June 15, 1861. Promoted to first lieutenant April 16, 1863, and captain April 21, 1864. Stephen B. Marshall Jr., junior second lieutenant, June 15, 1861.

23. Asa A. Shell, teacher for the Irby H. Scott family. In 1860 listed as a married teacher with three children. Mr. Shell died in Putnam County, Georgia, in late 1865 or early 1866.

24. Confederate General Robert S. Garnett's small Confederate force occupied Laurel Hill and Rich Mountain in northwestern Virginia. In early July Federal forces advanced on Martinsburg, Virginia, causing Confederate outposts to fall back towards Winchester, Virginia.
25. John T. Denham, private June 15, 1861.

CHAPTER 2

1. John K. Bedell, first sergeant, June 15, 1861. Left sick at Richmond July 7, 1861, and discharged October 7, 1861.
2. Cincinnatus W. Griggs, private, June 15, 1861. Left sick at Richmond July 7, 1861. Detailed to general hospital, Camp Winder, Richmond, Virginia, September 12, 1863.
3. William Campbell Scott (1807–1865), at the outbreak of the war colonel, 102nd Virginia Militia, later brigadier general, Virginia Militia. Appointed colonel, Forty-fourth Virginia Infantry, June 14, 1861. Resigned his commission January 14, 1863.
4. Robert Selden Garnett (1819–1861); his command was located at Laurel Hill (Belington, Virginia) and Rich Mountain, Virginia. Mortally wounded July 13, 1861. Scott did not know of the death of General Garnett at the time of this letter.
5. From July 21, 1861, to August 13, 1861, the Twelfth Georgia camped on the summit of Allegheny Mountain. At times this camp is referred to as Camp Yeager, because the property was owned by John Yeager Jr. Later, the same location was known as Camp Allegheny. Camp Yeager/Camp Allegheny is also referred to as Camp Baldwin, named after the colonel of the Fifty-second Virginia, John B. Baldwin, when the Fifty-second Virginia was the only regiment camped on the summit.
6. Henry Roots Jackson (1820–1898) commanded the brigade sent to reinforce General Robert S. Garnett. Recognizing the importance of blocking the Staunton–Parkersburg Turnpike against a Federal advance, Jackson ordered the Twelfth Georgia to the summit of Allegheny Mountain. He commanded the brigade composed of the Third Arkansas, Thirty-first Virginia, and First and Twelfth Georgia Regiments.
7. Cheat Summit Fort, at an altitude of nearly four thousand feet, was initially occupied on July 13, 1861. Between July and August the Fourteenth Indiana Regiment, commanded by Colonel Nathan Kimball, fortified the summit with an earth and log fortification as a means of controlling the Staunton–Parkersburg Turnpike. Two Federal regiments were on the western base. A well-equipped Federal cavalry force numbering five hundred, and twenty-six pieces of artillery, were available and operating in the area.
8. Thomas A. "Phonz" Walker, private, July 20, 1861. Bill, an unidentified person not listed in company roster. He may not have been accepted for service. James M. Oliver, private, July 20, 1861. Scott refers to him as Mr. Oliver.
9. Scott is referring to Federal soldiers captured by scouting parties on the roads in the vicinity of Allegheny Mountain and toward Greenbrier River and Cheat Mountain. From captured Federal soldiers vital intelligence would be gathered and passed along to higher headquarters.
10. Colonel Johnson, noting the different uniform arrangements of the several companies of the regiment, preferred the men to acquire uniform pieces from the government in order that the men look alike.
11. Tom, a slave on the Irby H. Scott plantation. Tom did join Scott in 1864.
12. First (Ramsey's) Georgia Volunteer Infantry Regiment was formed in Macon, Georgia, in April 1861 and commanded by Colonel James N. Ramsey. Serving first at Pensacola, Florida, before moving to Virginia to serve under General Robert S. Garnett in northwestern Virginia. Routed during the Battle of Laurel Hill, the regiment rendezvoused at Staunton. Ramsey was rebuked, after the Battle of Laurel Hill, for granting furloughs,

rather than reorganizing and refitting the regiment. Furloughs were suspended and the regiment was made ready for additional service in the mountains of Virginia.

13. Asa Monroe Marshall, private, June 15, 1861. Appointed chaplain of the regiment, August 1, 1862.

14. Cullen S. Criddle, also seen as Credille, a fifty-two-year-old farmer, and his wife Jane were residents of Putnam County. In the 1864 Georgia Militia roster he is listed as fifty-six years old and a farmer.

15. Charles Duke "Charlie" Morton, private, May 13, 1862, Company F, "Putnam Volunteers," Forty-fourth Georgia regiment. Appointed fifth sergeant in 1862. Wounded at Gettysburg, Pennsylvania, July 1, 1863. Wounded at Winchester, Virginia, September 19, 1864. Surrendered, Appomattox, Virginia, April 9, 1865. Thomas A. Morton, private, May 13, 1862, Company F, "Putnam Volunteers," Forty-fourth Georgia regiment. Killed at Fisher's Hill, Virginia, September 22, 1864.

16. The Putnam Light Infantry camped on soft and spongy ground. To remedy this situation, all members of the company were ordered out on July 30 to scrape off and pave the streets and walks. Smooth, thin slate rock, from a nearby deposit, was used as paving material.

17. The First Battle of Manassas, July 18–21, 1861.

18. George Brinton McClellan (1826–1885) commanded Federal troops in northwestern Virginia in 1861. His victory at Laurel Hill (Belington, Virginia) and Rich Mountain, Virginia, propelled him into command of the Army of the Potomac and into the office of general in chief November 1, 1861. The Federal troops in northwestern Virginia controlled the mountains, rivers, and lines of communications, and protected the Baltimore and Ohio Railroad.

19. Pierre Gustave Toutant Beauregard (1818–1893) commanded Confederate forces in northern Virginia and commanded the battlefield during the First Battle of Manassas. Having possession of Alexandria and Arlington Heights is rumor.

20. Edward Johnson (1816–1873) commissioned colonel of the Twelfth Georgia June 26, 1861. On December 13, 1861 he was promoted to brigadier general and took command of the brigade to which the Twelfth Georgia was assigned. At the beginning of the Valley campaign of 1862 he was wounded at McDowell, Virginia, May 8, 1862 and did not rejoin the Twelfth Georgia. He is most often referred to as "Alleghany Johnson."

CHAPTER 3

1. Camp Bartow, named after Colonel Francis S. Bartow (1816–1861), was located on the east bank of the Greenbrier River, Pocahontas County, Virginia, today Bartow, West Virginia. Prior to being established on the east bank of the Greenbrier River, Camp Bartow was located one mile east, farther up the mountain on the Staunton–Parkersburg Turnpike. At times this camp is seen as Camp Travelers Rest or Travelers Repose. It is also referred to as Camp Garnett, but most often as Camp Bartow.

2. James H. Reid, private, June 15, 1861. Died of disease December 20, 1861. Solomon Batchelor, private, June 15, 1861. Discharged disabled October 15, 1861.

3. James L. Eakin, private, June 15, 1861. Died of tuberculosis at Camp Bartow.

4. Thomas W. Carter, private, June 15, 1861.

5. This is a rumor. On August 4 President Davis wrote General Beauregard that to have followed the Federal retreat after the Battle of Manassas "would have been extremely hazardous." Federal forces retreated into the strong defenses of Washington City after the battle.

6. Solomon Batchelor, private June 15, 1861. Discharged, disabled, October 15, 1861. Reenlisted Company G, 12th Georgia Infantry Regiment, May 14, 1862.

7. Green B. Alford, private, June 15, 1861. Discharged disabled December 25, 1861.

8. Josiah Boswell, uncle to Abner R. Zachry.
9. C. Nicholas "Nick" Featherston enlisted May 31, 1861, at Atlanta, Company G, Seventh Georgia Infantry Regiment, and was elected second lieutenant. Elected captain September 10, 1861. Relieved from duty as captain of the company May 12, 1862, because enlistment expired. In October 1863 appointed second lieutenant of artillery to rank from May 2, 1863, and was ordered to report for duty to chief of ordnance. On June 4, 1864, he was serving as lieutenant of artillery and ordnance officer of Neely's brigade.
10. No. 9 is the number assigned to the mess of which Scott was a member. Two forts on the North Carolina Outer Banks protected Hatteras Inlet. On August 26 Fort Clark was occupied and on August 28 Fort Hatteras was captured. Hatteras Inlet was now closed to blockade runners.
11. Turner is likely a slave on the plantation of Josiah Boswell, uncle to Abner R. Zachry.
12. Mr. Whaley is Joseph Whaley, father of Nicholas E. Whaley.
13. Emerline O. Boswell, wife of Josiah Boswell and aunt to Abner R. Zachry.
14. John Hollis, private, June 15, 1861. Died of fever October 8, 1861.
15. Homer Virgil Paschal, private, June 15, 1861. He survived his fever. Henry R. Rickerson, private, August 2, 1861. He survived his fever.
16. After reorganization and refitting in Staunton, the First (Ramsey's) Georgia was placed in the brigade commanded by General Daniel S. Donelson.
17. Mary Ellen (Tompkins) Scott (1821–1909), mother to Irby G. Scott and Nicholas E. Scott. It is believed she is buried next to her husband, Irby H. Scott, in the family burial ground on the former Scott property.
18. Typhoid fever is a life-threatening bacterial infection of the intestinal tract. Typhoid germs are passed in the feces and are spread by eating or drinking water or foods contaminated by feces from the infected individual. Symptoms are high fever, diarrhea, stomach pain, constipation, headache, and malaise. Complications are high fever, loss of appetite, diarrhea, pneumonia, delirium, and coma.
19. Thomas R. Spivey, private, June 15, 1861.
20. Samuel Frank Suther, private, June 15, 1861. Wounded at McDowell, Virginia, May 8, 1862.
21. Robert Carter Jenkins (1818–1888) and Caroline Francis "Hudson" Jenkins (1821–1884). Father and mother to Robert H. Jenkins and William F. Jenkins. Mr. Jenkins was a large landowner in Putnam County, Georgia. Robert H. Jenkins, third sergeant, June 15, 1861. Wounded at McDowell, Virginia, May 8, 1862.
22. Colonel Edward Johnson; this is a reference to G. L. VonBlucher, a Prussian field marshal from 1819. Colonel Johnson is most often referred to as "Allegheny Johnson" and is at times referred to as "Old Clubby." Johnson was known to carry a large thick club into battle because of his disdain of sword or pistol.
23. Samuel Dawson, first lieutenant, June 15, 1861, Company A, "Muckalee Guards," Twelfth Georgia, Sumter County, Georgia. Elected captain April 12, 1862. Killed McDowell, Virginia, May 8, 1862.
24. Albert Rust (1818–1870) recruited the Third Arkansas Infantry Regiment and served as colonel of the regiment. Appointed brigadier general March 4, 1862. See OR, Series 1, Volume 5, pages 191–92, for the report for the reasons why Colonel Rust did not attack Cheat Summit on September 12, 1861.

Chapter 4

1. Under the direction of Lieutenant Colonel Seth M. Barton of the Third Arkansas, from the middle of September through October, the men fit for duty began throwing up and improving gun emplacements, rifle pits, and obstructions on the left flank, on the road to Green Bank.

2. Grand Guard is usually a force of one hundred men posted in advance of camp. Part of this guard would have been posted near Shavers Fork of the Cheat River about nine miles in advance of Camp Bartow.

3. William L. Hitchcock enlisted as second corporal June 15, 1861. Died of typhoid fever at Camp Bartow, Virginia, September 29, 1861.

4. In September 1861 Dr. Henry K. Green informed General Henry Jackson he had received an offer from the people of Harrisonburg to take four hundred of the sick men.

5. On September 20, 1861, Federal Colonel James Mulligan surrendered his hilltop position at Lexington, Missouri, to General Sterling Price. Colonel Mulligan had expected General Fremont to send aid, but none came.

6. His reference to branch, which the men stood in during most of the battle, was a mill race.

7. Official casualties for the Twelfth Georgia are listed as six killed, thirty-three wounded, and thirteen missing or captured.

8. James N. Ramsey (1821–1869), colonel, First (Ramsey's) Georgia Infantry Regiment, from April 3, 1861, to March 18, 1862, when the regiment disbanded. Colonel Ramsey was with the advanced guard as officer of the day. Fearing capture, he and others of the advanced guard scrambled up Burner Mountain and out of the fight.

9. William Starke Rosecrans (1813–1898) entered the Federal army in 1861, serving as a brigade commander during General George B. McCellan's northwestern Virginia campaign. When General McClellan left northwestern Virginia to take command of the Union army, General Rosecrans took command to oppose General Robert E. Lee in northwestern Virginia. This dispatch, if actually received, was not correct. General Robert E. Lee determined to provoke General Rosecrans to attack his fortified position on Sewell Mountain. General Rosecrans withdrew on October 5 without attacking.

10. On leaving their home state, the Seventh Indiana was presented a fine silk banner. The banner was missing when the regiment reached Cheat Summit Fort. The color-bearer, when the regiment halted to permit the artillery to fire on the defenses of Camp Bartow, placed the banner in a fence corner for protection, then he fell asleep. He simply forgot to retrieve the banner when aroused.

11. On October 10, four additional cannon arrived in camp: two twelve-pound howitzers and two six-pound rifled guns, for a total of twelve cannon. All of this construction was in anticipation of another Federal attack.

12. There is no evidence Thomas S. Robins mustered into service with the company. In the letter dated October 21, 1861, Scott states that Robins and Lawrence would leave Camp Bartow in the evening. Robins later enlisted as a private in Company A, Ninth Regiment Georgia State Guards, on August 4, 1863, at Eatonton, Georgia. Leverett Batchelor, private, October 10, 1861. Wounded at McDowell, Virginia, May 8, 1862. There is no record of a Lawrence in the muster records of Company G, Twelfth Georgia. Benjamin F. "Ben" Adams, private, enlisted at Camp Bartow October 10, 1861.

13. Lieutenant Marshall had been on duty in Georgia since September 1861.

14. William D. Terrell, resident of Putnam County, Georgia. He is listed in the 1864 Putnam County Militia roster as a fifty-three-year-old farmer.

15. Brown Rifles, Company B, Third Georgia Infantry Regiment. The Brown Rifles was the first company raised in Putnam County.

16. On October 4–5, 1861, the Third Georgia and North Carolina troops attacked and defeated Federal forces on Chicamacomico Banks, North Carolina. This affair is known as the "Chicamacomico races." Chicamacomico is the name commonly given to Pea Island, North Carolina. The Third Georgia at this time was stationed on Roanoke Island, North Carolina.

17. Mark A. Cooper Cochran, private, June 15, 1861. Discharged disabled November 29, 1861.

18. Henry K. Green (1818–1867), appointed surgeon, Twelfth Georgia, July 4, 1861. He was slightly wounded in the hand by a spent ball December 13, 1861. Doctor Green was later dropped from the regimental roll by Special Order 104/7 dated May 6, 1862.

19. Joseph E. Brown, governor of Georgia from 1857 to 1865.

20. Susan Elizabeth Morton (1847–1939), daughter of Henry Morton and sister to Henry W. "Wat" Morton. Susan Morton is buried at Pine Grove Cemetery, Eatonton, Georgia. She married Ralph Jones, former overseer on the plantation of Thomas and Sarah Head.

21. Lou Jones cannot be identified.

22. John M. Zachry, third sergeant, June 10, 1861, Company D, Twelfth Georgia. Transferred to Company H, Twenty Seventh Georgia, September 18, 1863.

23. Caroline Francis "Hudson" Jenkins, mother of Robert Jenkins.

24. Emma Catharine Scott, sister of Irby G. Scott. "Mollie" is Mary Elizabeth Scott, sister of Irby G. Scott.

25. John E. Danielly, private, June 15, 1861.

26. This is a rumor.

27. Benjamin Harvey Wright, husband to Emily E. (Tompkins) Wright. She is granddaughter of Sarah Tompkins.

28. The Federals were more than likely driven across Shavers Fork of the Cheat River about nine miles in advance of Camp Bartow.

29. John Brown Baldwin (1820–1873), appointed colonel Fifty-second Virginia Infantry Regiment August 19, 1861. His health was broken at Allegheny Mountain, Virginia, and he was not reelected on May 1, 1862.

30. William F. Brown, captain, Company F, "Davis Guards," Twelfth Georgia Infantry Regiment. Mustered into service at forty-seven years of age. Killed at Ox Hill, Virginia, September 1, 1862, while commanding Trimble's brigade. He was in command of the Twelfth Georgia Infantry Regiment at Cedar Run/Slaughter Mountain, Virginia, and Second Manassas until General Trimble was wounded, when he was placed in command of the brigade, and served in that capacity throughout the Battle of Second Manassas.

31. James Woodson Haskins, private, June 15, 1861. Wounded Camp Allegheny, December 13, 1861.

32. On October 31, the men of the regiment were paid in treasury notes. For part of his pay Scott received a Confederate bond. In Company A only thirty-nine men were present for pay. The remainder were likely absent sick in Harrisonburg or Staunton.

33. "Major" is Giles Eli Scott (1855–1923), brother of Irby G. Scott.

34. Mary Jane Moore cannot be identified.

35. Many of the men made rings from slices of root from the laurel shrubs that covered the mountains.

36. A green tomato relish.

37. Most likely Shavers Fork of the Cheat River, about nine miles from Camp Bartow.

38. James Deshler, captain on the staff of General Henry R. Jackson, acting as brigade adjutant. When General Jackson left the brigade he served on the staff of Colonel Edward Johnson. During the battle of Alleghany Mountain he was shot through both thighs.

39. On May 28, 1861, the ladies of Eatonton and Putnam County came together and formed the Soldier's Relief Society of Putnam County. This society provided the first two companies leaving the county with jackets, pants, flannel and cotton shirts, haversacks, havelocks, and other necessary clothing items. The Society in Putnam County continued to supply the men with uniform parts, socks, gloves, and undergarments during the war. The Inferior Court of Putnam County enacted a tax to purchase supplies for the Soldier's Relief Society.

40. This is a rumor.

41. Hannah is a slave on the Scott plantation. It was not unusual for slave children to be named by members of the plantation household.

42. Irby Gibson "Chap" Hudson, private, June 15, 1861. On May 30, 1862, he was cut off from Company G at Front Royal, Virginia, afterward living among the farmers of the neighborhood.

CHAPTER 5

1. Camp Allegheny, located eleven miles southeast of Camp Bartow, near the summit of Valley Mountain on the Staunton–Parkersburg Turnpike, Pocahontas County, Virginia. John Yeager Jr. owned the property on which Camp Allegheny was located. In some sources Camp Allegheny is referred to as Camp Yeager and Camp Baldwin. Prior to establishing Camp Bartow, the Twelfth Georgia was first encamped at Camp Allegheny.
2. William Wing Loring (1818–1886) commanded the Army of the Northwest. His order is found at OR 51, pt. 2, p. 388. During the winter campaign of 1861–62 he was to cooperate with General Thomas J. Jackson. He and Jackson clashed over the conduct of the campaign. Removed from command under Jackson, Loring saw service in the western theater.
3. Josiah F. "Joe" Porter, private, June 15, 1861.
4. Irby G. "Chap" Hudson, private, June 15, 1861. Wounded during the Seven Days Battles. Green Spivey, in 1860 a resident of Putnam County, Georgia. Brother to Thomas R. Spivey, of Company G.
5. Mark H. Blanford, captain Company K, "Marion Guards," Twelfth Georgia, Marion County, Georgia. Wounded in the arm at McDowell, Virginia, May 8, 1862, necessitating amputation. Elected lieutenant colonel of the regiment January 24, 1863. Resigned June 9, 1863.
6. Green Brier road is the Staunton-Parkersburg Turnpike.
7. Colonel William L. Jackson commanded the 31st Virginia. However, during the battle of December 13, Lt. Col. Francis M. Boykin most likely commanded the regiment.
8. William H. Davis, enlisted as private, June 15, 1861.
9. Algernon F. Little, second sergeant, June 15, 1861. Mortally wounded Camp Allegheny December 13, 1861. Alexander Middleton, private, June 15, 1861. Wounded Camp Allegheny December 13, 1861. William Thomas Arnold, private, June 15, 1861. Slightly wounded at Allegheny Mountain, Virginia, December 13, 1861. Absent sick Staunton, Virginia; returned to the company March 22, 1862. Lovic Hull "Tuck" Thomas, private, June 15, 1861. Edward S. Davis, private, June 15, 1861. Appointed fourth sergeant October 7, 1861. David D. McLeroy, private, June 15, 1861. Slightly wounded at Allegheny Mountain, Virginia, December 13, 1861, and sent to Staunton, Virginia.
10. Edward S. Davis, private, June 15, 1861. Appointed fourth sergeant October 7, 1861. James Henry Reid, private, June 15, 1861. Died of dysentery at Staunton, Virginia, December 20, 1861.
11. Joseph and Julia Whaley, parents of Nicholas Whaley.
12. Francis Milton Little, private, June 15, 1861. Appointed fourth sergeant December 25, 1861.
13. William Fredrick Little (1817–1880), son of Kinchen Little. In the 1864 Putnam County Militia roster he is shown as a forty-six-year-old farmer.
14. James Woodson Haskins, private, June 15, 1861. Severely wounded at Camp Allegheny, December 13, 1861.
15. William Thomas Pearson, private, June 15, 1861. Severely wounded, McDowell, Virginia, May 8, 1862. Robert J. Little, fourth corporal, June 15, 1861. Wounded at Sharpsburg, Maryland, September 17, 1862. Henry Harris Marshall, private, June 15, 1861. Wounded McDowell, Virginia, May 8, 1862. Henry C. Etheridge, private, June 15, 1861.
16. Colonel Edward Johnson, promoted to brigadier general, December 13, 1861.

17. This pistol could have been one Irby brought from home. In August 1863 he is on the lookout for a pistol for his father.

18. Mr. Suther is believed to be Sandy Suther. In 1860 a resident of Eatonton, Putnam County, Georgia. Listed as a thirty-three-year-old carpenter, with one child. Married to Ann E. Barnes. He was a house carpenter and skilled cabinetmaker.

19. Huntersville is about twenty-four miles southwest of Camp Bartow at the intersection of the Green Bank road and the Huntersville-Huttonsville Pike.

20. Green Bank, Virginia, now Greenbank, West Virginia, is located at the base of Allegheny Mountain and is accessible by road from Camp Allegheny.

21. There was no victory in Kentucky. Instead, the Kentucky line became useless. On February 8 a superior Federal force quickly overpowered Confederate defenders on Roanoke Island, North Carolina. It is unknown which Lee the newspapers claimed to be dead.

22. Lizzie Reid is Elizabeth Brewer Reid, daughter of Judge David Henry Reid and Sara Elizabeth (Adams) Reid.

23. Salley Collie; spelling of the last name is more likely *Colley.* Unable to identify this individual. This person may be through an Adams family connection.

24. Jesse T. Batchelor, fourth sergeant, June 15, 1861. Appointed first sergeant October 7, 1861.

25. Towards the Greenbrier River on the Staunton-Parkersburg Turnpike and the road from Camp Alleghany to Green Bank.

26. On March 11, 1862, the Federal Army occupied Manassas, Virginia, and on March 12 Federal troops marched into Winchester, Virginia, as General Stonewall Jackson marched southward, up the Shenandoah Valley.

27. Scott is likely referring to the Battle of Pea Ridge, also known as Elkhorn Tavern, Arkansas.

28. Cousin Sarah Reid is Sarah Elizabeth Adams Reid (1819–1889) married to Judge David Henry Reid. Judge and Mrs. Reid were ardent supporters of "The Cause." This Sarah Reid and Irby would have been first cousins once removed.

29. There was an undertone that the town boys may have felt they performed better under fire than the country boys. These differences, if any, did not continue once campaigning began in earnest.

30. Isham, commonly call "Smut," was the body servant of Lt. Stephen B. Marshall. It is said "he was the liveliest and rarest darkey in the regiment." Whether Isham knew someone at home was trying to injure Scott is not likely.

31. Thomas Jonathan "Stonewall" Jackson (1824–1863).

32. John David Johnson, private, June 15, 1861. At Harrisonburg, Virginia, sick since late September 1861. Notley Maddox, private, June 15, 1861. Elijah Vining, private, June 15, 1861. At Harrisonburg, Virginia, sick since late September 1861. William Franklin "Frank" Jenkins, private, June 15, 1861, was the youngest member of the company.

33. James Allen Etheridge, first lieutenant, June 15, 1861. Dr. Etheridge would later be promoted to surgeon of the regiment.

34. Abner Smead, major, Twelfth Georgia, June 15, 1861, and afterward lieutenant colonel, December 13, 1861. Lieutenant colonel and assistant adjutant general to General Edward Johnson. Colonel and assistant inspector general to General Thomas J. Jackson and General Robert S. Ewell. Willis Alston Hawkins, captain, Company A, "Muckalee Guards," Twelfth Georgia, Sumter County, Georgia. Promoted to major, December 13, 1861; lieutenant colonel, January 22, 1863. Resigned January 24, 1863. Hawkins was disgraced along with Colonel Z. T. Conner at Front Royal, Virginia, May 30, 1862. John McMillan, captain, Company C, "Davis Rifles," Twelfth Georgia, Macon County, Georgia. Killed at McDowell, Virginia, May 8, 1862.

35. The Society in Putnam County supplied the men with uniform parts, socks, gloves, and undergarments during the war. The Inferior Court of Putnam County enacted a tax to

purchase supplies for the Soldier's Relief Society. It is not know if the ten dollars Scott is referring to is in addition to the tax.

CHAPTER 6

1. Camp Johnson was located on Shenandoah Mountain astride the Staunton–Parkersburg Turnpike, in Augusta County, Virginia. General Order No. 10, Head Quarters Army of the North West, Camp on Shenandoah Mountain, dated April 6, 1862, "The present encampment of the troops will be known as Camp Shenandoah." Sometimes it is seen as Camp Johnson.
2. Reynolds Hotel was located at Rodgers toll gate on the Staunton-Parkersburg Turnpike.
3. Jim Pike was the body servant of Abner R. Zachry. Zachry had been wounded on December 13, 1861, and it may be that Jim Pike was returning to Georgia when Zachry was to return to the army. The next reference to Jim Pike indicates that upon his return he brought letters from Putnam County.
4. Madison, Morgan County, Georgia.
5. Spalding's Prepared Glue, liquid glue, was useful for mending furniture, toys, crockery, and glassware. Manufactured by Henry C. Spalding & Co., No. 49 Cedar Street, New York City.
6. Tolbert appears to be a well-thought-of slave on the Scott plantation. He is mentioned in several letters.
7. All of these officers were promoted on December 13, 1861.
8. Dr. James A. Etheridge, appointed surgeon of the Twelfth Georgia, April 26, 1862, to take rank March 22, 1862.
9. Henry K. Green (1818–1867), appointed surgeon, Twelfth Georgia, July 4, 1861. Slightly wounded in the hand by a spent ball, December 13, 1861. He was later dropped from the Regiment Roll by Special Order 104/7 dated May 6, 1862, and assigned to Atlanta. Special Order 139/11 dated June 17 1862, assigned him in charge of General Hospital, Montgomery, Alabama. He was relieved from duty at Montgomery by Special Order 35/25 dated February 11, 1864. It is clear from other sources that Dr. Green was not considered by the captains of the Twelfth Georgia a competent medical doctor and did not provide the necessary medical services to the men of the regiment. If formal charges were ever made the record is not clear.
10. *The Countryman,* a newspaper published in Putnam County, Georgia, on the plantation of Joseph A. Turner.
11. Three ordinary field hands sold for a total of $4,740.00.
12. Probably a slave on the Irby H. Scott plantation.
13. On April 16, 1862, the Confederate Congress enacted the Conscription Act requiring three years' service for all white males between age eighteen and thirty-five who were not legally exempt.
14. Fort Pulaski, a masonry fort, guarded the river entrance to Savannah, Georgia. After a thirty-hour bombardment, the fort surrendered on April 11, 1862. With the surrender of Fort Pulaski the main channel to Savannah was closed.
15. Irby Scott would not be elected a company officer until August 1862.
16. Fannie Jane Scott, sister of Irby G. Scott.
17. West View is about seven miles west of Staunton, on present-day Route 254, and four miles from Buffalo Gap.
18. Buffalo Gap is about twelve miles west of Staunton on the Staunton–Parkersburg Turnpike.
19. Lieutenant Alexander Sidney Reid and Ordnance Sergeant Jesse T. Batchelor had been in Putnam County in early April on recruiting duty. They returned to the army with

Irby Hudson Adams, William W. Suther, David H. Reid, Early Batchelor, and Richard Batchelor as new recruits.

20. William W. Pearman, private, June 15, 1861. Wounded August 28, 1862.

21. General "Stonewall" Jackson was reinforced by Major General Richard S. Ewell's division from General Joseph E. Johnston's army.

22. General Edward Johnson's Army of the Northwest received the Army of Northern Virginia–style, twelve-star flags in May 1862. Scott's letter is of the correct time frame. This style flag would have replaced any regimental flag used before this time. It is probable that Lieutenant Alexander Sidney Reid carried the company flag of the Putnam Light Infantry home while he was on recruiting duty in Georgia.

23. Virginia Central Railroad.

24. Edward Butler "Edd" Reid, private, June 15, 1861. Killed McDowell, Virginia, May 8, 1862. Francis M. Williams, private, June 15, 1861. Killed McDowell, Virginia, May 8, 1862.

25. Josiah N. Beall, second sergeant, Company B, "Jones Volunteers," Twelfth Georgia, Jones County, Georgia. Promoted to first sergeant August 10, 1861. Elected first lieutenant November 8, 1861. Wounded Manassas, Virginia, August 30, 1862. Wounded Sharpsburg, Maryland, September 17, 1862. Elected captain January 22, 1863. Commanding the regiment at the surrender, Appomattox, Virginia, April 9, 1865.

26. Nathaniel Prentiss Banks (1816–1894) commanded the Federal Fifth Corps of McClellan's army and had been ordered to cross the Potomac River to eject General Jackson from the valley. Banks, however was, expelled from the Shenandoah Valley during the 1862 Valley campaign with a loss of 30 percent of his command.

27. William C. "Billy" Paschal, private, June 15, 1861. Captured at Middleburg, Virginia, September 30, 1862, while on service as a nurse.

28. William R. Paschal, a fifty-six-year-old farmer from Putnam County, Georgia, and father to William C. Paschal.

29. Scott wrote on the top sheet of this letter "This is yankee paper." On the first sheet is a drawing of a soldier standing guard with "Arm For The Union" banner.

30. Scott is referring to the road General Johnson knew came from Harrisonburg in the rear of Shenandoah Mountain.

31. Battle of Front Royal May 23, 1862.

32. After his victory at Front Royal on May 23, General Jackson attempted to cut off General Banks's retreat route, on May 24, to Winchester on the Valley Pike. However, he was not able to trap the enemy.

33. Battle of First Winchester, May 25, 1862.

34. Richard Stoddert Ewell (1817–1872), major general, commanded a division in "Stonewall" Jackson's Valley Army.

35. This could be David Henry Reid, who had not reached the army by May 26, or Judge David Henry Reid, writing from Eatonton. Judge Reid was the father of Alexander Hudson Reid.

36. Sarah Tompkins died at the residence of her son-in-law, Irby H. Scott, on the morning of May 5, 1862, at the age of eighty-one. For a long time before her death she was completely helpless, having lost the use of her hands and feet.

37. This June 3 date is not correct. Scott is referring to the rout of the regiment at Front Royal on May 30, 1862.

38. General Jackson pursued Banks almost to Harper's Ferry before he was forced to withdraw up the valley.

39. David Henry Reid, private, April 4, 1862. Wounded in the arm at Front Royal, Virginia, May 30, 1862.

40. Lieutenant Taylor, unable to identify this person.

41. James Shields (1810–1879), Federal division commander at the time, defeated at Port Republic, Virginia, by Jackson's Valley Army. John Charles Fremont (1813–1890),

commanding an army in western Virginia, was to push to the east, working in consort with General Shields, to trap Jackson. Fremont failed in his attempt at Port Republic. When his army was merged with the army under the command of John Pope, he resigned rather than serve under Pope.

42. Gibson G. Mahone, private, June 15, 1861. Mortally wounded by Federal cannon fire at Cross Keys, Virginia, June 8, 1862.

CHAPTER 7

1. Reinforcements were being transferred to Richmond on the Virginia Central Railroad.

2. Captain A. C. Philips, Company B, "Calhoun Greys," Second Battalion, Georgia State Troops. This unit of state troops disbanded in May 1862. Philips appears in 1864 as a private in Pruden's Battery, Georgia Artillery, State Troops.

3. Henry Walter Thomas, private, May 14, 1862, at Augusta, Georgia. Captured near Front Royal, Virginia, June 9, 1862. Thomas compiled *History of the Doles-Cook Brigade* with the help of the brigade's survivors.

4. Robert Young in a letter to his cousin on November 8, 1912, states Chap Hudson was knocked off a bridge by a Yankee cavalryman, which saved Chap from being captured at Front Royal.

5. This is Reverend Asa M. Marshall, chaplain of the Twelfth Georgia.

6. Robert Young enlisted as third sergeant December 5, 1861, Company C, Second Battalion, Second Brigade, Georgia State Troops, "Dennis Guards" Putnam County, Georgia. Discharged May 1862. He enlisted as a private, Company G, Twelfth Georgia, May 14, 1862. Wounded in side at Malvern Hill, Virginia, July 1, 1862, by a piece of shell. Henry William Alford, private, June 15, 1861. Wounded at Cold Harbor, June 27, 1862.

7. Alfred, a slave belonging to Sarah Tompkins, grandmother of Irby G. Scott. At the death of his grandmother, Alfred was bequeathed to Irby G. Scott.

8. These statements give a glance of the paternalistic relationship between master and slave. Allowing Alfred to choose his own master is an interesting statement and implies trust.

9. Chickahominy River. McClellan and his army had retreated to Harrison's Landing on the James River.

10. William H. Winchel, private, June 15, 1861. Francis Alexander Maddox, private, June 15, 1861. William W. Pearman, private, June 15, 1861. James W. Davis, private, June 15, 1861. All of these men had been cut off from the regiment at Front Royal, Virginia, on May 30, 1862.

11. John H. Pearson, fifth sergeant, March 17, 1862. Wounded at Ellison's Mill, Virginia, June 26, 1862. Died of his wounds at Howard's Grove, Richmond, Virginia, July 8, 1862. William H. Montieth, first sergeant. Wounded at Ellison's Mill, Virginia June 26, 1862. Died of his wounds at Richmond, Virginia, July 7, 1862. Both men served in Company F, Forty-fourth Georgia, Putnam Volunteers, Putnam County, Georgia.

12. William A. Hudson, private, June 11, 1861, Company D, Ninth Georgia, Fort Gaines Guards, Clay County, Georgia.

13. Bartow is the child of Hannah, a slave on the Scott plantation. He was given his name by Scott and the men of his mess.

14. Bobbie is Robert Jefferson Scott, brother of Irby G. Scott.

15. On July 17, 1862, Federal soldiers captured Gordonsville, Virginia, a Confederate supply base.

16. Absalom William Athon, private, June 15, 1861.

17. James Alexander Beall, private, June 15, 1861. Severely wounded at McDowell, Virginia, May 8, 1862.

18. Henry William Alford, private, June 15, 1861.

19. A. F. Bird, a member of the Bird family of Swords Community, Morgan County, Georgia. Giles Tompkins, Scott's grandfather, bought Tompkins Inn from George L. Bird in 1812. The Birds then relocated to Morgan County. James Zachry, believed to be a son of Abner Zachary. Abner Zachary was married to Harriet Boswell. They had two children, Abner Rowan Zachary and Asa J. Zachery. It is believed that the "J" stands for James. There is no evidence in the Compiled Service Record of Abner Rowan Zachry that a substitute took his place in the ranks. Abner R. Zachry served through the war in Company G, Twelfth Georgia. Abner R. Zachry and Irby G. Scott were close friends and mess mates during the war. Wm. Gatewood is William Ellis Adams Gatewood (1828–1908), never married, son of Ainsworth Dudley Gatewood and Rebecca Ann Adams.
20. Cordy Batchelor was the father of five sons in Company G.
21. Freeman Perryman is Freeman W. Perryman, in 1860 listed as a thirty-nine-year-old farmer with seven children. He was a neighbor of Irby G. Scott.
22. Irby Hudson Adams, private, April 4, 1862. Discharged on account of disability, July 21, 1862. Barsby M. McGettrick, private, June 15, 1861. Appointed hospital steward by surgeon Henry K. Green, August 9, 1861.
23. William E. Wilson, private, June 15, 1861. Served as nurse at Harrisonburg, Virginia. Donaldson Prichard, private, June 15, 1861. Discharged July 21, 1862, because of health.
24. It appears Scott received a pass while camped near Richmond so that he could tend to personal matters in Richmond.
25. Believed to be Mrs. Emma L. (Wright) Leverett.
26. Virginia Central Railroad.
27. Many, if not all, of the men visited Montpelier, the home of former President James Madison.
28. Thomas E. Gorley, private, December 5, 1861, Company C, 2nd Battalion, 2nd Brigade, Georgia State Troops, "Dennis Guards," Putnam County. Mustered out May 1862. Enlisted as a private, Company G, "Putnam Light Infantry," Twelfth Georgia Volunteer Infantry Regiment, May 14, 1862. Died of typhoid fever near Winchester, Virginia, June 5, 1862.
29. William Andrew Gorley, private, June 15, 1861. Slightly wounded at McDowell, Virginia, May 8, 1862.
30. Jacob Feiler was born in Prussia in November 1839.
31. Mary Elizabeth Scott, "Mollie," sister to Irby Scott.
32. During late July and early August the Federal Army of Virginia was advancing towards Orange Court House.
33. Reubin R. Welch, private, June 15, 1861. Killed at Cedar Run, Virginia, August 9, 1862.
34. Harvey J. Lynch, private, June 15, 1861. Severely wounded at Cedar Run, Virginia, August 9, 1862.
35. William H. Winchel, private, June 15, 1861. Wounded by a spent ball at Cedar Run, Virginia, August 9, 1862.
36. Jubal Anderson Early (1816–1894).
37. Irby was struck during the Battle of Cedar Run or Slaughter Mountain, Virginia, August 9, 1862.
38. This could be acid reflux or some type of gastric distress, which was not unusual in the army, owing in part to diet and sanitation in cooking.
39. Charles, body servant of Abner Rowan Zachry. Charles was probably owned by Abner's uncle, Josiah Boswell. Uncle Joe is Josiah Boswell, uncle of Abner R. Zachy. Boswell served in Company "H," Fifth Georgia Militia, in the trenches of Atlanta during 1864.
40. General Robert E. Lee arrived at Gordonsville on August 15 to make plans for the offensive to clear northern Virginia of Federal troops. His plan to move the army across the Potomac River culminated in the Battle of Sharpsburg.

CHAPTER 8

1. The Bollingbrook Hotel was located at the northeast corner of Bollingbrook and Second Streets in Petersburg, Virginia. John Niblo and investors constructed the three-story hotel in 1828. It was demolished about 1933.
2. The Globe Hotel was located at 252 Broad Street, at the southeast corner of Broad and Jackson, in the heart of then-downtown Augusta. Weldon, North Carolina.
3. Madison, county seat of Morgan County, Georgia.
4. Concert Hall was located on Ellis Street approximately one block from the Globe Hotel. Scott was entertained by either the Thespian Family or Queen Sisters with the Palmetto Band. He does not state if he had a seat on the parquet (main floor) for $1 or in the gallery for 50 cents. Doors opened at 7:15 and the performances commenced at 8:00.
5. Unable to identify Whit Tompkins.
6. Organized in Augusta, Georgia, in 1861, the association's stated mission was to aid the government in caring for the sick and wounded men from Georgia. To this end the association and affiliated associations throughout Georgia collected all manner of supplies for the comfort of the sick and wounded soldiers from the state. As the war progressed, the association acted as a conduit for the distribution of boxes sent to the men in the army.
7. Rodes's division spent the winter in Caroline County, Virginia, near Grace Church, in present-day Corbin, Virginia.
8. General Edward Johnson did not take command of the division.
9. Robert Emmett Rodes (1829–1864) Promoted to brigadier general October 21, 1861, serving under Thomas J. "Stonewall" Jackson. He was assigned to command Daniel H. Hill's division in January 1863. General Doles's brigade, to which the Twelfth Georgia was assigned, served in Rodes's division.
10. Edward Shackelford "Ned" Willis (1840–1864) was attending the United States Military Academy at the outbreak of the war. After Georgia's secession, he tendered his resignation of his academy appointment on January 22, 1861. Ordered by the Confederate government to report to Colonel Edward Johnson as adjutant Twelfth Georgia, July 5, 1861. After the battle of Fredericksburg he took command of the Twelfth Georgia Regiment when the regimental commander was killed.
11. Emily E. (Tompkins) Wright, wife of Benjamin Harvey Wright. Granddaughter of Sarah Tompkins.
12. Cousin Mary Thomason is the daughter of Beverley and Sarah Thomason. Mrs. Mary Thomason was granddaughter of Sarah Tompkins, the grandmother of Irby G. Scott.
13. Thaddeus S. C. Lowe, who had been ballooning for several years before the war, became interested in using balloons for gathering military intelligence. In June 1861 he demonstrated the military potential of balloons. Shortly after his successful demonstration, his balloons and his services were contracted by the Union War Department.
14. Franklin, a slave on the Scott plantation, belonged to Sarah Tompkins, grandmother of Irby Scott. Upon the death of his grandmother, Franklin became the property of Irby's mother, Mary E. Scott.
15. Charlie appears to be a horse belonging to Scott.
16. On the afternoon of April 7, nine Federal ironclads attacked Fort Sumter in Charleston harbor. Battered by Fort Sumter and Fort Moultrie, the Federal fleet withdrew.
17. Mr. Terrell is likely William D. Terrell, who had visited the company in northwestern Virginia. Buck Head, Georgia is in the southwestern section of Morgan County, close to the Scott plantation.
18. Ab (or Abb) is the body servant of Alexander Sidney Reid. Scott initially felt comfortable sending money home by Ab but for some reason changed his mind.
19. On January 19, 1863, the Twenty-first Georgia became part of the new brigade, which included the Twelfth Georgia.

20. A Union flotilla that attacked Fort Sumter was repulsed.
21. Charlie is a horse that Scott had written about earlier.
22. Henry Reid "Stonewall" Scott, brother of Irby G. Scott.
23. Bob is Robert Jefferson Scott. Major is Giles Eli Scott. Both are brothers of Irby G. Scott.
24. The Fourth Georgia was brigaded in the same brigade as the Twelfth Georgia.
25. Alfred is the slave Scott inherited through his grandmother upon her death.
26. Charles M. "Charlie" Wiley entered service April 20, 1861, as sergeant, Company D, "Macon Volunteers," Second Independent Georgia Battalion. Discharged March 18, 1862, as the term of service of the unit expired. Appointed adjutant, April 11, 1862, of the Forty-fourth Georgia and served in this capacity until his resignation July 24, 1863.
27. Franklin, a slave belonging to Sarah Tompkins. Through the will of Sarah Tompkins, Franklin was given to her daughter, Mary E. Scott, mother of Irby G. Scott. Franklin did bring shaving equipment with him.
28. Franklin was trusted enough to be given money to pay his train fare if separated from Nicholas.
29. Battle of Chancellorsville.
30. Part of Federal General Hooker's army crossed the Rappahannock River at Kelly's and U.S. Fords, clear of the Confederate left flank. This movement is the beginning of the Battle of Chancellorsville.
31. Stonewall Jackson was wounded on the evening of May 2. General A. P. Hill assumed command of Jackson's corps, and he was wounded.
32. General J. E. B. Stuart was placed in command of Jackson's corps upon the wounding of General Hill.
33. Guiney's Station, about eighteen miles south of Fredericksburg on the rail line leading to Richmond. After Stonewall Jackson was wounded he was taken to Guiney's Station.
34. Unable to accurately identify Captain Green.
35. Unable to accurately identify this person. He is not a member of Company G.
36. Charles M. Wiley, adjutant of the Forty-fourth Georgia.
37. James N. Bullard, private, June 15, 1861. Wounded by grapeshot in left leg at Chancellorsville, Virginia, May 2, 1863. Robert Young, private, May 14, 1862. Wounded in the right shoulder near the collarbone, Chancellorsville, May 3, 1863. Francis Alexander Maddox, private, June 15, 1861. James W. Davis, private, June 15, 1861. Wounded in the arm, breaking the small bone, at Chancellorsville, May 2, 1863.
38. Longstreet's corps had been on duty south of the James River conducting a siege at Suffolk, Virginia.
39. Alexander "Ab" Hudson, private, June 15, 1861. Severely wounded at McDowell, Virginia, May 8, 1862.
40. Garland Terrell "Terry" Dismukes, private, June 15, 1861.
41. All of this activity is in preparation for the Second Northern Campaign.
42. Mr. Malone is the father of Private Charles E. Malone, Company K, Fourth Georgia, who had been wounded during the Battle of Chancellorsville on May 2, 1863. Mr. Furlow is the father of Private Charles T. Furlow, Company K, Fourth Georgia, who had been wounded during the Battle of Chancellorsville on May 2.
43. Mr. Yancy is most likely Erastus H. Yancey, private, April 26, 1861, Company B, Third Georgia. In 1860 he is listed in the household of Dr. W. L. Hitchcock as a "student of medicine." Dr. Phillips [Philips] is Dr. Abram Charles Philips (1825–1905), a doctor and farmer in Putnam County, Georgia. Dr. Horne is Dr. Charles Norsworthy Horne (1796–1872), buried at Antioch Church, Morgan County, Georgia.
44. Josiah Flournoy "Coy." Adams, private, June 15, 1861, discharged in 1863. Elected second lieutenant of Company A, A. H. Reid's company, Sixty-sixth Georgia Infantry Regiment, August 8, 1863, while home on sick furlough.

45. Colquitt's Brigade served on the coast of South Carolina and Georgia and in middle and east Florida from June 1863 to December 1863, returning to the Army of Northern Virginia for the 1864 Overland Campaign.
46. Hamilton's Crossing, four miles south of Fredericksburg, a critical supply base on the Richmond, Fredericksburg, and Potomac Railroad.
47. Frank Leslie's New York Journal (1855), with illustrations made by Leslie and his artist on the battlefield during the Civil War, are regarded for their historical value.
48. Zaccheus B. "Jack" Johnson, sometimes seen as Zack. First served with state troops on the coast of Georgia. Enlisted as a private, Company G, Twelfth Georgia, May 14, 1862. Detailed courier to General Doles, October 13, 1863.
49. On May 18 the siege of Vicksburg began, and on May 21 the siege of Port Hudson below Vicksburg began. On May 22 a second assault on Vicksburg began, and on May 27 Federals made their first assault on Port Hudson.
50. Grace Episcopal Church, Corbin, Caroline County, Virginia, served as a Civil War hospital. General Rodes's Division camped in the surrounding area.
51. James Neagle, a thirty-five-year-old shoemaker. Resident of Eatonton, Putnam County, Georgia.

CHAPTER 9

1. Nicholas E. "Bud" Scott spent at least one night and likely two at the Spotswood Hotel, at the southeast corner of Eighth and Main Streets, Richmond, Virginia. Unable to identify Capt. Fitchpatrick (likely Fitzpatrick) and Charly Harris.
2. A small force of Federal infantry had crossed the Rappahannock River, on a pontoon bridge, below Fredericksburg at Deep Run. Their crossing was only a feint.
3. James Longstreet (1821–1904) commanded the First Corps, Army of Northern Virginia.
4. Battle of Brandy Station June 9, 1863, considered the greatest cavalry battle of the Civil War.
5. Battle of Second Winchester, June 14–15, 1863.
6. From Scott's June 17 letter it appears Bud and Franklin reached the army camped at Culpeper, Virginia.
7. There is no evidence in any of the surviving letters that Franklin wrote home again.
8. It is unfortunate that this letter is missing and the details of it are not available. From this missing letter we would know where Franklin remained after the army crossed into Maryland. Rodes's division reached Carlisle, Pennsylvania, on June 27. Doles's brigade bivouacked on the campus of Dickinson College, with a portion of the brigade serving as guard for the town.
9. Scott and the Twelfth Georgia were to attack Cemetery Hill. General Early's division was to attack Culp's Hill.
10. William H. Waller, private, June 15, 1861. Both men were wounded by friendly cannon fire and left on the field at Gettysburg, Pennsylvania.
11. On the evening of July 4, Rodes's division retired to Seminary Ridge, behind the Lutheran Seminary.
12. The Second Corps, in the rear of the army, retreated on the Fairfield Road toward Fairfield.
13. On June 17 Franklin is shown in Maryland. If he crossed back into Virginia it is not known. Scott may be referring to missing body servants that may have crossed the Potomac River and stayed north of the river during the campaign.
14. Alfred is the slave Scott inherited from his grandmother, Sara Tompkins.
15. Darkesville, Virginia, now West Virginia, is on the Valley Turnpike, and is sometimes known as the Winchester Pike. Ewell's corps camped on the waters of Middle Creek.

16. Ewell's corps was fortified from the Williamsport–Hagerstown Turnpike on the north to just across the National Road west of Hagerstown.
17. A pontoon bridge and ferries were located at Williamsport. During the night of July 14, Ewell's corps crossed the Potomac River at Williamsport.
18. The old canal is the Baltimore and Ohio Canal, located on the north bank of the Potomac River.
19. Once across the Potomac River, Rodes's division initially camped at Big Spring three miles from Martinsburg, Virginia.
20. On July 3 Vicksburg, Mississippi, surrendered to Federal General Ulysses S. Grant. The formal surrender took place on July 4.
21. Charles Duke Morton and Thomas A. Morton, Company F, Forty-fourth Georgia Infantry. The Morton family and the Scott family were close friends.
22. Luray, Virginia, is south of Front Royal in Page County, between the Blue Ridge Mountains and Massanutten Mountain.
23. On July 22, 1863, Confederates skirmished with Federals at Manassas and Chester Gaps. The Federal Third Corps were to move forward on July 23 to attack the Confederates in Manassas Gap. This attack failed.
24. Lyman Chester Slade, private, April 26, 1861; first sergeant, April 30, 1862. Elected junior second lieutenant August 30, 1862. Wounded at Chancellorsville, May 3, 1863, and Gettysburg, July 1, 1863. Elected second lieutenant July 1, 1864. Surrendered at Appomattox, 1865. Nathan H. DeJarnette, private, June 1, 1861. Appointed sergeant major May 1, 1862. Wounded at Malvern Hill, Virginia, July 1, 1862, and Manassas Gap, Virginia, July 23, 1863. On furlough December 31, 1864, to February 28, 1865. Both men served in Company B, Third Georgia "Brown Rifles," Putnam County, Georgia.
25. King Etheridge was a slave, perhaps on the Scott plantation.

Chapter 10

1. Four months of marching have worn out the shoes Bud Scott brought from home.
2. Johnson, Zaccheus B. "Jack," sometimes seen as Zack, private, Company G, "Putnam Light Infantry," Twelfth Georgia Volunteer Infantry Regiment, May 14, 1862. Detailed courier to General Doles October 13, 1863.
3. Scott could hear the Orange and Alexandria Railroad.
4. King Etheridge is a body servant of one of the men in the company.
5. Franklin, a slave on the Scott plantation, likely could not write. Rather, Irby or Bud wrote the letters for him.
6. Samuel Solomon Dusenbury (1823–1871). Married to Pamelia Jane Avery November 1, 1855, Putnam County, Georgia. He is shown as a tailor in both the 1850 and 1860 Putnam County Federal Censuses.
7. Nicholas received a bounty because he enlisted and was not conscripted.
8. Joseph B. Gartrell enlisted September 10, 1862, at Washington, Georgia, as a private, Company C, "Sumter Artillery," also known as Cutt's Artillery, Eleventh Battalion, Georgia Artillery. Gartrell was absent sick most of 1863, being afflicted with rheumatism and discharged for disability July 29, 1863.
9. If Irby ever purchased a pistol and sent it home to his father it is not known. At the end of the war Irby returned home with a Remington Model 1861 Army revolver, also known as the Remington Old Model Army revolver.
10. On July 18, a Federal force attacked Fort Wagner, one of the forts protecting Charleston harbor. Failing to take it by frontal assault, the Federals besieged the fort, and it fell two months later.

11. Company B, Third Georgia consisted of men from Putnam County, and the five or six men in camp more than likely were Putnam County men.

12. Three of the five brigades in the division contained all North Carolina regiments. Some North Carolina units experienced problems with Absent With Out Leave (AWOL), and this may be what Scott is referring.

13. On August 25, *The Countryman* printed the report of the August 11 meeting. The meeting was called to discuss measures to sustain the currency of the Confederate states. A number of the county's citizens refused to accept Confederate notes for the payment of debt or merchandise.

14. Jacob Feiler had been absent from the army on wounded furlough since the Seven Days Battles. From this letter it appears Feiler had other health problems. In the Irby H. Scott Papers is found a letter from Feiler, addressed to Irby and Bud Scott's father, in which Feiler describes shopping for flatware in Augusta, Georgia, for the Scott family.

15. After the Battle of Gettysburg a spiritual revival swept through the camps.

16. Joseph Emerson Brown (1821–1894), Civil War governor of Georgia. Throughout the war Brown stressed strict adherence to states' rights and state sovereignty, lambasting the Davis administration.

17. Joshua Hill (1812–1891) was staunchly antisecession before and during the Civil War. He was an attorney, politician, and unsuccessful candidate for governor of Georgia.

18. Jefferson Adams (1823–1864) was a planter and attorney in Putnam County, Georgia. His wife was Susan Meriwether (1827–1923), daughter of Judge James Meriwether.

19. Reuben Battle Nisbet, captain, Company B, "Brown Rifles," Third Georgia, Putnam County, Georgia. Elected lieutenant colonel December 20, 1862, to rank from July 1, 1862. Wounded Malvern Hill, Virginia, July 1, 1862; wounded and captured Sharpsburg, Maryland, September 17, 1862. Exchanged. Detailed at Augusta, Georgia, because of wounds May 4, 1864. Retired disabled, May 16, 1864. Before and after the war, Colonel Nisbet was a physician in Eatonton, Georgia, where he died on April 10, 1901.

20. The local Putnam County newspaper printed a number of articles critical of Hill.

21. *The Countryman* newspaper printed in Putnam County, Georgia.

22. From at least September 15, 1863, to October 7, 1863, the Twelfth Georgia was camped at Camp Morton's Ford while they were on picket duty. Camp Morton's Ford was about fifteen miles northeast of Orange Court House, Virginia.

23. Henry Walter Thomas, private May 14, 1862, at Augusta, Georgia.

24. John H. Harris, second lieutenant, Company I, "Morgan and Henry Volunteers," Forty-fourth Georgia. Promoted to captain July 12, 1862. Killed at Winchester, Virginia, September 19, 1864.

25. Scott is referring to Franklin.

26. At Warrenton Springs on the Rappahannock River, a brigade of Federal cavalry blocked the advance of the division. Driving the cavalry before them, the Twelfth Georgia was the first to cross the bridge over the river. About three hundred Federals were captured.

27. Scott and the company played a limited part in the Battle of Bristoe Station. On their return to the Rappahannock River they destroyed much of the Orange & Alexandria Railroad.

28. The glade land in Putnam County is an area of flat low land, close to the Irby H. Scott plantation.

29. Though Franklin was a slave, he would have been issued a furlough, for a specific time frame, allowing him to travel and pass through the lines.

30. It is unknown if Franklin returned to the army with Henry Marshall. Franklin had returned to the army by January 1864.

31. Green J. Spivey, private, March 17, 1862, Company F, "Putnam Volunteers," Forty-fourth Georgia. Detailed as ambulance driver June 1864.

32. George Pierce Doles (1830–1864), captain, Company H, "Baldwin Blues," Baldwin County, Georgia, Fourth Georgia Infantry Regiment. Promoted to colonel, Fourth Georgia, May 8, 1861. Wounded at Malvern Hill, Virginia, 1862. Promoted to brigadier general November 1, 1862, commanding the brigade to which the Twelfth Georgia was assigned. Killed at Cold Harbor, Virginia, June 2, 1864.
33. Identity of Mr. McMillan is not known.

Chapter 11

1. General George Gordon Mead's Mine Run Campaign had failed.
2. Colonel Willis knew the regiment would return to the valley because he had asked Jedediah Hotchkiss to prepare a map of part of the Shenandoah Valley.
3. It is unknown what Nicholas was trying to spell. Robert Young in his January 3, 1864, letter to his cousin says, "Lieut Zachry has Paralysis in his face which is swelled up very bad he is at a house not far from camp."
4. New Hope, Virginia, is in the Shenandoah Valley about ten miles northeast of Staunton.
5. Irby could hear trains on the Virginia Central Railroad.
6. Zachry suffered from erysipelas, an acute disease of the skin.
7. James M. Oliver, private, July 20, 1861.
8. Wm Hearns is believed to be William Hearn, a thirty-one-year-old living in Putnam County, Georgia. Clinton Tucker is probably Clinton C. Tucker of Kingston Community, Morgan County, Georgia. Tucker married Martha T. Whaley on December 20, 1854, in Putnam County.
9. Charles is the body servant of Abner Zachry. Franklin and Charles shared their own cabin. Jim Pike, Zachry's other body servant, must have gone home.
10. One would guess Charles and Franklin went out together.
11. Sanlsbury is unknown; unable to identify anyone with a similar spelling.
12. This is the last reference to Franklin. He must have returned to the Scott plantation sometime after this letter and March 25, 1864.
13. Lieutenant Colonel Isaac Hardeman entered service as first sergeant of Company B, Twelfth Georgia, working his way through the ranks of the company. Promoted major January 22, 1863, and lieutenant colonel June 9, 1863.
14. Tom, a slave on the Scott plantation, must have accompanied Irby Scott to the army when he returned from furlough in March 1864.
15. Alfred, a slave on the Scott plantation, considered to be loyal and dependable. Alfred's is the first mark on the August 9, 1865, contract between the former Scott slaves and Irby H. Scott binding themselves to continue to work on his plantation.
16. Irby must have received a furlough, and Tom, a slave on the Scott plantation, must have accompanied Scott on his return to the army. On their return to the army they stopped in Wilmington, North Carolina.

Chapter 12

1. In less than two weeks Nicholas would be mortally wounded.
2. Elisha B. Perryman, private, June 15, 1861. At home on leave of indulgence, December 1863. David Denham, private, April 4, 1864. Wounded at the Wilderness, Virginia, May 5, 1864. Thomas G. Avery, private, June 15, 1861. Severely wounded at Wilderness, Virginia, May 5, 1864.
3. Garland Terrell "Terry" Dismukes, private, June 15, 1861. Captured at Wilderness, Virginia, May 5, 1864.

4. James Monroe Briggs, second lieutenant, Company I, "Lowndes Volunteers," Twelfth Georgia Infantry Regiment. Elected first lieutenant December 13, 1861; captain, May 8, 1862. Wounded severely in thigh at McDowell, Virginia, May 8, 1862; wounded Manassas, Virginia, August 30, 1862, and Chancellorsville, Virginia, May 3, 1862. Killed at Wilderness, Virginia, May 5, 1864. John I. Perry, private, June 10, 1861, Morgan County, Georgia, Company D, "Calhoun Rifles," Twelfth Georgia Infantry Regiment. Elected second lieutenant September 30, 1862. Killed at Wilderness, Virginia, May 5, 1864.
5. The McCoull House, a one-half story dwelling build of wood. Around the house were a number of outbuildings and the McCoull family burying ground. In 1860 Neil McCoull, age fifty, head of the household, is listed as a farmer. He owned six slaves. In the household were Eliza F. McCoull, age sixty-five, Mary A. McCoull, age sixty, and Milly M. McCoull, age forty-five. Neil McCoull had six hundred acres of land under his control; one hundred acres were described as "improved" and five hundred acres described as "unimproved." The rear of the McCoull house faced the Muleshoe East Angle and the front of the house faced the Harrison House, six hundred yards from the McCoull House. To the right of the front of the house was located Doles's Salient. The house sustained extensive damage during the Battle of Spotsylvania Court House, but was repaired and reoccupied after the war. It was destroyed by fire in 1921.
6. Irby Goodwin Marshall, private, December 11, 1862. Company K, Seventeenth Georgia, "Webster Confederate Guards," Stewart and Webster Counties, Georgia. Surrendered at Appomattox, Virginia, April 9, 1865. Not able to identify Duke Marshall in Company K, Seventeenth Georgia.
7. Woodlief S. Marshall, private, August 15, 1861, Company K, Seventeenth Georgia. Appointed hospital steward November 2, 1864. Surrendered at Appomattox, Virginia, April 9, 1865. B. F. Shivers, color sergeant, August 15, 1861, Company K, Seventeenth Georgia. Appointed regimental ensign December 1864. Surrendered at Appomattox, Virginia, April 9, 1865.
8. James W. Danielly, private, July 25, 1862. Wounded at Spotsylvania, Virginia, where he was captured May 20, 1864. James Wesley Williams, private, June 15, 1861.
9. General George Pierce Doles (1830–1864), killed at Cold Harbor, Virginia, June 2, 1864, by a minié ball fired by a Federal sharpshooter. At the time of his death near Bethesda Church, he was supervising the entrenchment of his line. Colonel Philip Cook of the Fourth Georgia took command of the brigade. Cook was promoted to general in August 1864. Colonel Willis, while in command of Pegram's brigade, was wounded on May 30, 1864, at Bethesda Church, by grapeshot. He died on May 31, 1864.
10. John S. Parker, private, May 14, 1862. Absent sick and admitted June 1, 1864, to Jackson Hospital, Richmond, Virginia.
11. William H. Danielly, private, June 15, 1861. Wounded at Winchester, Virginia, September 19, 1864.
12. Scott may have meant battalion of sharpshooters. In May 1863 two battalions of sharpshooters were created in the brigade, one of men from the Twelfth and Fourth Georgia, the other of men from the Twenty-first and Forty-fourth Georgia. Each battalion would relieve the other. Sharpshooters would advance in front of the line of battle.
13. John Cabell Breckinridge (1821–1875) served during the war primarily in the western theater before taking command of the Department of Southwest Virginia in 1864. Breckinridge served under General Jubal A. Early in the summer of 1864. Federal General David Hunter (1802–1886), after the Battle of Piedmont, Virginia, on June 5, 1864, yielded the Shenandoah Valley to General Early. Early promptly marched on Washington, D.C.
14. Tom must have spent most of his time with the wagon train, and from this letter it is clear that he was not as helpful to Scott as Franklin.

CHAPTER 13

1. Captured Federal shelter tents.
2. Whether Tom accompanied Scott home after the surrender is unknown.
3. General William Tecumseh Sherman (1820–1891). Sherman is most noted for his successful campaign to capture Atlanta, Georgia, and for his March to the Sea. On his March to the Sea, all of his army passed through Putnam County and one wing passed through Eatonton, Georgia, on the Madison Road, passing by the Tompkins Inn very close to the Irby H. Scott home site.

APPENDIX

1. Josian Boswell (1811–1882); in some sources the first name is shown as Josias and in others Jonas.

Bibliography

Unpublished Primary Sources

Alexander, Harrison, letter. CSA Collection, North Carolina Infantry, 21st. Eleanor Brockenbrough Library, Museum of the Confederacy, Richmond, VA.

Atkins, James W., diary. Georgia Department of Archives and History, Morrow, GA.

Carson, John J., personal papers. Civil War Miscellany, Georgia Department of Archives and History, Morrow, GA.

Casualty Reports of the Confederate States of America M836, Roll 5. Microfilm. National Archives, Washington, DC.

Company Muster Rolls, Company G, 12th Regiment Georgia Volunteer Infantry, June 15, 1861, August 31, 1861, August 31, 1862, October 31, 1863. Microfilm. National Archives, Washington, DC.

Compiled Service Records, Confederate General and Staff Officers and Non-Regimental Enlisted Men M331. Microfilm. National Archives, Washington, DC.

Compiled Service Records of Confederates in Organizations from the State of Georgia. Microfilm, Georgia Department of Archives and History, Morrow, GA.

Compiled Service Records Showing Service of Military Units in Confederate Organizations Georgia M861, Roll 10. Microfilm. National Archives, Washington, DC.

Confederate Service Record, Roster of Putnam Light Infantry, Company G, 12th Georgia Regiment, Doles-Cook Brigade, Army of Northern Virginia, Putnam County Roster. Microfilm. Georgia Department of Archives and History, Morrow, GA.

Ellis, John W., letters. Civil War Miscellany files. Georgia Department of Archives and History, Morrow, GA.

Eighth Census of the United States, 1860. Nonpopulation Schedules: Agriculture Putnam County, Georgia. Microfilm. Record Group 29. National Archives, Washington, DC.

Governor's Incoming Correspondence (Joseph E. Brown). Georgia Department of Archives and History, Morrow, GA.

Hutson, Charles J. C., Papers. Gilder Lehrman Collection. Gilder Lehrman Institute of American History, New York.

Kimball Papers. Lilly Library, Indiana University, Bloomington.

Letters Received by the Confederate Adjutant and Inspector General 1861–65 M474. National Archives, Washington, DC.

Letters Received by the Confederate Secretary of War 1861—1865 M437. National Archives, Washington, DC.

Pension Applications of Confederate Soldiers and Widows Who Applied from Georgia. Georgia Department of Archives and History, Morrow, GA.

Pfeiffer, Sarah Shields, Papers, letters of Henry T. Davenport. Atlanta History Center, Atlanta.

Putnam County, Georgia, Inferior Court, Tax Digests (1860–62). Putnam County, Eatonton, GA.

Records of Cross of Honor, Dixie Chapter U.D.C. Public Library, Eatonton, GA.

Rylander, John Emory, diary. In private hands.

Scott, Irby G. Letter. Irby G. Scott to father, September 30, 1861. Tom Atkins, Lavonia, GA.

———. Letters. Irby G. Scott to father, 1861–64. Patsy Scott Prickett, Asheville, NC.

Scott, Irby H. Papers. Rare Book, Manuscript, and Special Collections Library, Duke University, Durham, NC.

Scott, Nicholas E. Letters. Nicholas E. Scott to father, 1863–64. Patsy Scott Prickett, Asheville, NC.

Smithsonian Annual Report, 1877. "Aboriginal Structures in Georgia." 278–82.

Unfilled Papers and Slips Belonging to the Compiled Service Record, Addendum to the Compiled Service Records M347. National Archives, Washington, DC.

U.S. Census Office. Seventh Census (1850). Population schedules. National Archives, Washington, DC.

U.S. Census Office. Eighth Census (1860). Population schedules. National Archives, Washington, DC.

U.S. Census Office. Eighth Census (1860). Population schedules—slaves. National Archives, Washington, DC.

Waterman-Bacon-Sanders Family Papers. Sam Houston Regional Library and Research Center, Liberty, TX.

Young, Robert, letter to his cousin Miss Nannette Hudson. Museum of the Confederacy, Richmond, Virginia.

Young, Robert, Papers. Special Collections Library, Emory University, Atlanta.

Published Primary Sources

Adams, Charles R., Jr., ed. *A Post of Honor, the Pryor Letters, 1861–63. Letters from Capt. S. G. Pryor, Twelfth Georgia Regiment and his wife, Penelope Tyson Pryor.* Fort Valley, GA, 1989.

Batts, William. *A Foot Soldier's Account: Letters of, 1861–1865.* Georgia Historical Quarterly 50 (1960) 87-100.

Baxter, Nancy Niblack, ed. *Hoosier Farm Boy in Lincoln's Army. The Civil War Letters of Pvt. John R. McClure.* NP, 1971.

Beck, Brandon H., and Roger U. Delauter. *Early's Valley Campaign: The Third Battle of Winchester.* Lynchburg, VA , 1997.

Brett, Martin. *Experiences of a Georgia Boy in the Army of Northern Virginia 1861–1865.* Bullock County, Georgia, Historical Society, 1988.

Caldwell, J. F. J. *The History of a Brigade of South Carolinians First Known as "Gregg's" and Subsequently as "McGowan's" Brigade.* Philadelphia, 1866.

Clark, Walter A. *Under the Stars and Bars or, Memories of Four Years Service with the Oglethorpes, of Augusta, Georgia.* Augusta, GA, 1900.

Cook, Anna Maria (Green). *The Journal of a Milledgeville Girl 1861–1867.* Athens, GA, 1964.

Dayton, Ruth Woods, ed. *The Diary of a Confederate Soldier: James E. Hall.* NP, 1961.

Denison, Frederic. *Sabres and Spurs, the First Regiment Rhode Island Cavalry in the Civil War 1861–1865.* First Regiment Rhode Island Cavalry Veteran Association, 1876.

Dowdey, Clifford, ed. *The Wartime Papers of R. E. Lee.* Boston, 1961.

Garrett, Franklin. *Necology index.* Atlanta History Center, Atlanta, 1954.

Hermann, J. *Memoirs of a Confederate Veteran 1861–1865.* Lakemont, GA, 1974.

McDonald, Archie, ed. *Make me a Map of the Valley. The Civil War Journal of Stonewall Jackson's Topographer.* Dallas, 1973.

Official Atlas of the Civil War. New York, 1958.

Pool, J. T. *Under Canvass.* Terre-Haute, IN, 1862.

Southern Historical Society Papers, Richmond, Virginia, 1876–1959.

The Staunton–Parkersburg Turnpike Byway and Backways, Visitors Guidebook. Draft Copy, NP, ND.

Supplement to the Official Records of the Union and Confederate Armies. 100 vols. Wilmington, NC, 1994.

Taylor, Walter H. *Four Years with General Lee.* New York, 1878.

Thomas, Henry W. *History of the Doles-Cooke Brigade, Army of Northern Virginia C. S. A.* Atlanta, 1903.

Trout, Robert J. *With Pen & Saber: The Letters and Diaries of J. E. B. Stuart's Staff Officers.* Mechanicsburg, PA, 1995.

U.S. War Department. *The War of the Rebellion: A Compilation of the Official Records of the Union and Confederate Armies.* 128 vols. Washington, DC, 1880–1901.

Young, Robert. "Lost in Early's Valley Campaign, 1864." *Confederate Veteran* 29 (1921): 427.

SECONDARY SOURCES

Armstrong, Richard L. *25th Virginia Infantry and 9th Battalion Virginia Infantry.* Lynchburg, VA, 1990.

Ashcraft, John M. *31st Virginia Infantry.* Lynchburg, VA, 1988.

Baxter, Nancy Niblack. *Gallant Fourteenth: The Story of an Indiana Civil War Regiment.* Indianapolis, 1980.

Black, Robert C., III. *The Railroads of the Confederacy.* Chapel Hill, 1952.

Boney, F. N. *Rebel Georgia.* Macon, GA, 1997.

Bonner, James C. *A History of Georgia Agriculture.* Athens: University of Georgia Press, 1964.

Brown, Kent Masterson. *Retreat from Gettysburg: Lee, Logistics and the Pennsylvania Campaign.* Chapel Hill, 2005.

Bryan, T. Conn. *Confederate Georgia.* Athens, 1953.

Clemmer, Gregg S. *Old Alleghany: The Life and Wars of General Ed Johnson.* Staunton, VA, 2004.

Collier, Calvin L. *They'll Do To Tie To! The Story of the Third Regiment, Arkansas Infantry C.S.A.* Little Rock, 1959.

Driver, Robert J., Jr. *52nd Virginia Infantry.* Lynchburg, VA, 1986.

———. *58th Virginia Infantry.* Lynchburg, VA, 1990.

Freeman, Douglas Southall. *Lee's Lieutenants: A Study in Command.* 3 vols. New York, 1942–44.

———. *R. E. Lee. A Biography.* 4 vols. New York, 1934–35.

Griffin, Richard N., ed. *Three Years a Soldier: The Diary and Newspaper Correspondence of Private George Perkins, Sixth New York Independent Battery, 1861–1864.* Knoxville: University of Tennessee Press, 2007.

Folsom, James Madison. *Heroes and Martyrs of Georgia.* Macon, GA, 1864.

Hays, Louise Frederick. *History of Macon County.* Atlanta, 1933.

Henderson, Lillian. *Roster of Confederate Soldiers of Georgia, 1861–1865.* 6 vols. Hapeville, GA, 1955–64.

Krick, Robert K. *Lee's Colonels: A Biographical Register of the Field Officers of the Army of Northern Virginia.* Dayton, OH, 1991.

Lee, Fitzhugh. *General Lee: A Biography of Robert E. Lee.* New York, 1894.

Lesser, W. Hunter. *Rebels at the Gate: Lee and McClellan on the Front Line of a Nation Divided.* Naperville, IL, 2004.

Mahr, Theodore C. *Early's Valley Campaign: The Battle of Cedar Creek Showdown in the Shenandoah, October 1–30, 1864.* Lynchburg, VA, 1992.

Martin, David G. *Gettysburg, July 1.* Conshohocken, PA, 1995.

McPherson, James M. *What They Fought For, 1861–1865.* Baton Rouge, 1994.

Moore, Robert H., III. *The Charlottesville, Lee Lynchburg and Johnson's Bedford Artillery.* Lynchburg, VA, 1990.

Pfanz, Harry W. *Gettysburg—Culp's Hill and Cemetery Hill.* Chapel Hill, 1993.

Rhea, Gordon C. *The Battle of the Wilderness, May 5–6, 1864.* Baton Rouge, 1994.

———. *The Battles for Spotsylvania Court House and the Road to Yellow Tavern, May 7–12, 1864.* Baton Rouge, 1997.

Ruffner, Kevin C. *44th Virginia Infantry.* Lynchburg, VA, 1987.

Smedlund, William S. *Campfires of Georgia Troops, 1861–1865.* Marietta, GA, 1994.

Stutler, Boyd B. *West Virginia in the Civil War.* Charleston, WV: Educational Foundation, 1963.

Warner, Ezra J. *Generals in Blue.* Baton Rouge, 1964.

———. *Generals in Gray.* Baton Rouge, 1959.

Wert, Jeffry D. *From Winchester to Cedar Creek: The Shenandoah Campaign of 1864.* Carlisle, PA, 1987.

Zinn, Jack. *The Battle of Rich Mountain.* Parsons, WV, 1971.

———. *R. E. Lee's Cheat Mountain Campaign.* Parsons, WV, 1974.

Newspapers/Publications

The Countryman, Putnam County, GA, 1862–66.

Daily Constitutionalist, Augusta, GA.

Eatonton (GA) Messenger, 1870–1927.

Georgia Weekly Telegraph, Macon.

Harper's Weekly, March 24, 1860.

The Madisonian, Madison, GA.

Richmond (VA) Examiner.

Savannah (GA) Republican.

Index

Georgia Units (cont.)

and Burner Mountain, 31; and captured flag, 35, 228n10; and grand guard, 30; and mill race, 31; and sick men, 31; Guiney's Station, 111; Hagerstown, Maryland, 127; and fortifications, 129; and retreat from, 129–30; health, of, 4, 20, 22; and measles and mumps in camp, 8, 13, 14; and half of regiment sick, 2; indignation among men, 49; inspection, brigade, 74, 90; Jackson, "Stonewall" consolidation with, 75; mail from Staunton, 36; McDowell, battle of, 76; and causalities, 76; and scout to, 69, 70; Mine Run, battle of, 151; Monterey clothes sent back, 37; officer election, 94; Orange Court House, 87, 91, 93, 97, 125; and pickets close to, 85; and picket, Gordonsville, 87; Port Republic, battle of, 78–79; provost duty, 149; regiment, finest, 34; roads, blockading, 60, 61; rumor, moving, 39; Richmond clothes left, 86; and departing from, 10; and ordered to, 48; Savannah, petition, 153; scout, worst, 55–56; snowballing, 59, 60; Staunton arriving, 10; and going to, 48–49; and quartermaster arrangements, 7; strength, of, 78, 82, 87, increase in, 91; Spotsylvania Court House, 161; sugar issued, 134, 136; tents, burned, 47, and making pins, 63; transfer, 100; transportation forbidden, 71, 75; uniforms, 12, 225n10; Valley Campaign 1862, causalities, 78, 82; and marching, 79; and Valley Mills, 72; and West View, 72; Valley Campaign 1864, 169–72; wagon transportation, 49; West View, 72; Wilderness, casualties, 160; and strength, 161; Winchester, first battle of, 77; 19th Infantry, 52; 118; 21st Infantry, 100, 106; 23rd infantry, 118; 27th Infantry, 118; 28th Infantry, 118; 44th Infantry, 100, 108, 158; "Jones Volunteers", 76; "Putnam Light Infantry". *See* Putnam Light Infantry

Germanna Ford, Va., 157

Gettysburg, 124, 133; army worn out, 131; bare footed men, 130, 131; battle, description of, 127–29; clothes army need of, 130; earthworks, 128; friendly fire, 128;

march to, 126, 127; Middle Street, 124; Middletown Road, 124; retreat, 128, 129–30, 131; war effects of, 127

Gholson, John E., 202

Glade Land, Putnam County, Ga., 146

Globe Hotel, 100

Gordon, John B., 170, 171, 172, 173

Gordonsville, Va., 81, 91, 93, 125, 135, 149, 160; camp ground, 90; brigade inspection, 90; picket duty, 87; weather, 87, 96

Gorley, Thomas E., 202; burial, 91

Gorley, William Andrew, 91, 121, 137, 202; messmate, 127, 135; wounded, 128

Grace Episcopal Church, 121

Grant, Ulysses S., 158; Petersburg attack, 176; waging war, 157

Green, Henry K., 36; charges, 71; Harrisonburg, sick arrangements for, 228n4

Greenbank, W.Va., 60

Green Bank Road, 48; blockading 60, 61

Green Brier Road, 51

Greenbrier Creek, 11, 12

Greenbrier River, 10; leaving, 49; scout to 55–56

Greensboro, N.C., 176

Griffin, Charles, 157

Griggs, Cincinnatus W., 203

Grimes, Bryan, 172; tyrannical, 173

guard, 40, 45, 74, 142; grand, 31, 33, Camp Valley Mills, 75. *See also* picket duty

Guiney's Station, Va., 111

Gun Boats, Union, 84

Hagerstown, Md., 124, 127; area, description of, 129; fortifications, 129; retreat, 129–30; skirmish, 129

Hamilton's Crossing, Va., 109, 118

Hannah (slave), 46, child, 46; death child, 86. *See* Bartow (child)

Hannover Junction, Va., 162

Hardeman, Isaac, petition to Davis, 154

hardship, 43

harp, Jews, 138, 144, 148

Harper's Ferry, W.Va., 2, 78

Harris, John H., 145

Harrison's Landing, Va., 81

Harrisonburg, Va., 65, 73, 77; Confederate currency refused, 154; occupied, 65; sick arrangements for, 228n4; and sent to, 33, 36, 40

Harwells Store, Eatonton, Ga., 119, 118

Haskins, James Woodson, 42, 203; messmate, 55; skeleton, 88; wounded, 52, 55

Hatcher's Run, Va., 172

Hawkins, Willis A., 63, 71; Front Royal surrender proposed, 68

health, army, 106; 12th Georgia, 4, 20, 22; Putnam Light Infantry, 8, 22, 40; and Allegneny Mountain, 13; and in 1861, 49; and in 1862, 58, 59, 61; and in 1863, 101, 103, 137

Hearn, William, 153

herring, 108

Hetland, Anthony A., 203

Highland County, Va., 10, 11

Hill, Ambrose P., 81, 93, 120, 132; Overland Campaign, 161; wounded, 110

Hill, Daniel H., 116, 118

Hill, Joshua, opposition to, 144

Hitchcock, William L., 33, 203

Hollis, John, 203; death, 36; pants for Colonel Johnson, 46; sick, 22, 33

Hooker, Joseph, 100

Horne, Charles N., 117, 119, 121

Hospital Association, Georgia Relief, 102

Hotchkiss, Jedediah, Valley maps, 149, 150

Hubert, Mathew A., 203–4

Hudson. See Adams, Irby H.

Hudson, Irby Gibson, 19, 60, 88, 94, 96, 204; candidate for office, 94; Front Royal escaped, 84; flag received, xx; furlough, 86; sick, 46, 49

Hudson, William A., 88

Hunter, David, 166, 169

Huntersville, W. Va., 58, 69

Huston, Charles, 149

Indiana Units: 7th Infantry, flag captured, 35; 14th Infantry, 30; and Kimball, Nathan, 30

intelligence, 17

Isham "Smut" (slave), 62, 91

inspection, 106, 120, 137; brigade, 74, 90, 141

Jackson, Henry Roots, 11, 29, 58; force reduced, 29; Cheat Summit Fort attack, 26; Conner, communication from, 8

Jackson, Thomas J. "Stonewall," 65, 71, 73, 81, 90; Conner arrest of, 68; death, 113; "Foot Cavalry," 7; Front Royal, 12th Georgia detachment to, 66; grave, 169; movements depend on, 74; wounding, 110

Jackson, William L., 51–52, 230n7

Jake. See Feiler, Jacob

James River, 81, 85

jaundice. See diseases and illnesses

Jenkins, Caroline F., (Mrs. Robert C. (Hudson) Jenkins), 24, 38, 53; Camp Bartow, 33, 36

Jenkins, Robert C., 24, 38; Camp Bartow, 33, 36

Jenkins, Robert Hudson, 62, 79, 84, 204; fever, 24; found Nicholas Scott's body, 162, 165; officer, candidate for, 94, 95,107–8; sick, 33; sick furlough, 36

Jenkins, William F., 63, 86, 204–5

Jim, (slave), 139; furlough, 137; letter sent by, 139; money sent by, 137, 141

Johnson, Benjamin F., 205

Johnson, Edward, 45, 50, 51, 66, 71, 77, 85, 103, 120, 157; Camp Alleghany, 47, 48; Camp Bartow attack on, 30; camp, rode through, 75; colonel appointed, 1; brigade, pride in, 61; and inspection of, 74; Cheat Summit Fort attack, 25; discipline, xxv; dispatch from Colonel Scott, 7; division, 126, 132; furloughs, 56; Greenbrier River, battle of, 30, 34–35; and expedition to, 14; and reconnaissance of, 8; horse shot, 34; McDowell, 66; military experience, 1; Monterey withdrawal to, 8; "Old Blucher", 25, 227n22; pants, wants a pair, 46; picket orders, 45; regiment pride of, 61, 120; Shenandoah Mountain, 65, 66; transportation forbids, 71, 75; uniforms, 45, 225 n10; whiskey, ration, 45

Johnson, John David, 63, 205; hat size, 93; candidate for office, 94

Johnston, Joseph E., 29

Johnson, Zaccheus B., 121, 205–6, baptized, 142, messmate, 127, 135, 137

Jones, Lou, 37

Jones Volunteers, 76

pay, 62, 63, 90, 103, 115, 137, 138, 139, 142,
147; bounty, 105, 137, 138; Camp Bartow,
41, 44; Confederate bond, 20, 44; Kellys
Ford, 147; not paid, 12; treasury notes,
229n32
Payne's Farm, Va., 150
Pearman, William W., 73, 86, 111, 112, 213
Pearson, John H., 86
Pearson, William Thomas, 116, 117, 118,
119, 121, 213; overcoat sent by, 118, 119;
substitute, 115
Pendelton County, Va., 76, 77
Peninsula, 121, 123, 162; campaign effects
on men, 84
Pennsylvania, 130
Petersburg, Va., 26, 100, 101, 109, 125;
entrenchments, 176; Lee reporting to,
172; winter quarters 173
Perry, John I., 161
Perryman, Elisha B., 214; death, 161
Perryman, Freeman W., 88
Philips, A. C., 82
Philips, Abram C., Dr., 115, 116, 117, 118
Phonz. *See* Walker, Thomas A.
picket duty: Allegheny Mountain, 49; and
camp, 48; and attack on, 39, 40–41,
44; Camp Bartow, 40, 45; brigade, 119;
enemy close to, 84, 85; exposure, 45, 53;
Federal, 106, 144; and fraternizing with,
119; Gordonsville, 87; guard, 40, 45, 74,
142; and grand guard, 31, 33; and houses
built for, 53; Kellys Ford, 145; McDowell,
69; Morton's Ford, 160; no fires, 36, 43;
reinforcing, 45; tobacco for coffee, 102;
Valley Mills, 75; West View, 75. *See also*
guard
Piedmont, Va., 151, 153; winter quarters,
151
Pike, Jim (slave), 3; captured, 78; carpetbag,
6; duties, 12; fiddle, 21; furlough, 61;
home going to, 70; mail from home, 73;
mumps, 40; sick tending to, 24–25; wife
letters to, 21
plunder. *See* foraging and plunder
pneumonia. *See* diseases and illnesses
Pocahontas County, W.Va., 18, 19, 23, 35, 37,
39, 40, 42, 45, 48, 51, 53, 57
politics, 144
Pope, John, 81

Potomac River, 123, 124, 128
Port Republic, Va., 81, 82, 150; battle of, 78–
79; detached duty, battlefield tour 151;
Road, 150
Porter, Josiah F., 49, 214
Powells Fort, Va., 149
Price, Sterling, 33; Arkansas victory, 61
prisoners, Federal, 66, 77; Laurel Hill, 12;
Staunton sent to, 11
Pritchard, Donaldson, 89, 214
provisions. *See* rations and food
provost duty, 150
Putnam County, Ga., Confederate currency
sustaining, 141; Confederate monument,
177; county officials elections, 152–53;
Military Aid Association Soldier's Relief
Society, xx, xxii, 45, 46, 229n39; and expects payment, 63, 231n35; petition to
War Department, 53
Putnam Light Infantry, Allegheny Mountain, battle of, casualties, 52; and health
of, 13; and paving streets, 226n16; and
routine, 15; baggage storage, 5, barefooted men, 140; Buffalo Gap scout to,
74; Camp Johnson, 68; Chancellorsville, battle of, 109–12; and killed and
wounded, 112; Cheat Summit Fort attack
preparations, 22, 23; company meeting,
colonel, 2; complimented, 74; cooking
utensils, 2; county officials election, 152–
53; Cross Keys, battle of, 78–79; diarrhea,
3; drill, 72, 142; elections, officers, 107–
8; factions in, 62; fish, 108; flag, xx;
Front Royal escapees, 86; and officers
and NCO's, 78; and strength of, 78;
Gettysburg friendly fire, 128; hams cask
of, 57; health of, 8, 22, 40; and in 1861,
49; and in 1862, 58, 59, 61; and in 1863,
101, 103, 137; hometowns, xx; knapsacks
carried, 12; marquee, 38; McDowell,
battle of, casualities, 78; mustered, 3;
occupations, xx; organization, xix; Port
Republic, battle of, 78–79; sermon farewell, xx; shoes, 137; social status of men,
xx; Staunton hiring wagon, 10; strength
of, 1862 June, 78, 82; and July, 84, 85,
87; and 1864, May, 163; surrendered
number, 176; tents, 68; and making pins
for, 63; and Yankee, 136; uniforms, new,

sabbath, marching on, 13

Salem, Va., 169

Saunder's Field, Va., 157

Savannah, Ga., 72; petition to go to, 153–54; Sherman departs, xxvii; Colonel Willis, telegraph to, 115; river, 176

Scott, Giles Eli "Major", 44, 46, 107, bequest, 9; Irby wants to see, 86; jews harp, 138, 148; ring, 55, 60

Scott, Emma Catharine, 20, 75; ring sent to, 38; write, asked to, 42, 93, 107, 114

Scott, Fannie Jane, ring sent to, 72; tea pot, 138, 148

Scott, Irby Goodwin, 216; ambrotype, 96; bedclothes, 44; blankets, 92; and government draw from, 42; and grandmother sent, 19; body servant, xxiv; and needing one, 97; and relationship with, xxiv; Bollingbrook Hotel, 100; bowie knife, 57; broken down, 161, 163, 165; brother, advice to, 3, 6, 13; and anxious for, 112, and army travel to, 108–9; and arrangements for, 121; and from a veteran, 64; and clothes, wear brothers, 50; and company joining brothers, 104; and concern for, 107, 114, 126; and on enlistment, 105, 108; and Gettysburg march, 129; and praises, 141, 162; and stay home, 60; brother, burial 159–60; and on death, 161, 162, 165; and grief for, 162, 165–66; brotherhood, xxvi, xxix–xxx, 177; Brown, Governor, views on, 122, 144; box send, 102; cabins at Camp Shenandoah, 70; and detached duty, 152; and Kelley's Ford, 146; camp, cleaning, 140; Camp Alleghany, battle of, spared, 52; and dread of leaving, 63; Chancellorsville, battle of, 109–12; and rumor of a move, 113; and spared, 112; clothes, 12, 15, 62, 70; 71 63; and brother send with, 114; and carry on back, 36, 71; and clean, 130; and coat collar fixed, 140–41; and for fall, 92, 138, 139; and frock coat, 92; and Georgia buttons, 144, 145; and Government supplying, 75; and need of, 70, 139; and new, 99; and made, 104–5; and officers uniform, 105, 107, 109, 144; and overcoat sent home, 118, 119; and pants need, 94; and paying for 63, 134, 139; and plenty of, 55, 92; and

received from home, 43; and sent off, 37, 63; and send by, 92; and Staunton stored, 71; and storage at Richmond, 5; and uniform coat, 142, 143; and vest, 59; and wearing out, 57; colic, camp, 95; comfort, 4; and going for, 143; company, command of, 170; Confederate currency, sustaining, 141; Confederate monument, solicited funds, 177; cooking, 3, 41, 87; and tent, 55 and washing, 5; cotton, sell, 44, 50; detached duty responsibilities, 151; and weather,151; and winter quarters, 151, 152; Davis, Captain, dissatisfied with, 51, 54; dream, 63, 79, 96; duty, xxix, 177; and reason for service, 39, 142, 165; Eatonton celebration thoughts on, 113–14, 115; economical, 3; education, xxii; endurance, xxv, 58; enlistment, xix; family attachment to, 177; father aiding, 176; and anxious for, 21; and emotions, father leaving, 19; and expecting a visit, 15; and pistol for, 139; feet, sore, 79, 126, 127; and bare footed, 131; fighting, hard, 84; food box, 43, 44, 59, 82, 102, 114; and received, 117, 173; and not received, 79; food, cost of, 57, 96, 117, 137, and food at home, 136; and plenty of, 140, 141, 143; Fredericksburg, battlefield tour, 104; and winter quarters, 102; friendship, 92; furlough, 54, 56, 147, 154; and disappointed, 63; and drawing for, 140; and officers, 147; Gettysburg, battle of, 127–29; and friendly fire, 128; and Gettysburg retreat from, 128, 129, 131; and Hagerstown retreat from, 129; and march to Gettysburg, 126, 127; and safe, 128, 129; girls, nice looking, 75; grandmother death, 77; Greenbank trip, 60; Guiney's Station, 111; guard, officer of, 101, 103, 119; hair, lock of, 53; and from family 55; hardened, xxv, 79, 89; hat, 55, 59; and cost, 144; and need 57; and received, 92, 145; health, 62, 93, and during fall 1863, 143; and on the march 1862, 61; home cut off from, 173; homesickness, 13, 21, 38, 50, 72, 85, 96, 118; and army returning to, 101; and banish feelings, 13; and ceased to be, 75; and discontented, harm, 50; and home ties to, 88–89; and letters releave, 42; and substitutes cause, 114–15; horse, Charlie/

Suther, Sandy, 57
Suther, William W., 218
Sutherlands's Station, 173
suttler, 117, 137, 138; good supply, 142; prices high, 139
Swift Run Gap, 65, 149

Talbot, Mathew H., 5, 86
tax, clothing supplies, 229n39; dog law, 52; money for, 44
Taylor, George W., 99
Tebbs, William H., 47
Tennessee, rumor, 142
tents, baggage wagons with, 87; burned, 47; Camp Johnson, 68; cooking, 55; Gordonsville, 75; Lt. Reid, bringing, 71; pins, 63; planking, 22
Terrell, Willima D., 35, 105; Camp Bartow, 37
Third Corps, Federal, 133
Thomas, Henry Walter, 84, 91, 218–19; furlough, 153; sick, 145
Thomas, Lovic Hull, 52, 219
Thomason, Mary, 103, 114, 153
Thorton's Gap, Va., 133
Tolbert, (slave), 70, 92, 94, 97
Tom (slave), 12, 104, 155, 163, 166, 173
Tom, *See* Pearson, William T.
Tompkins, Giles, xxii–xxiii
Tompkins, Sarah, 2; febble health, 40, 46, 57; death, 77; ill, 6; sight lost, 73
Tompkins, Whit, 101, 103, 112, 128
Tompkins Inn, xxii–xxiii; Irby's interaction, xxiii
transporation, Johnson forbids, 71, 75
Travelers Repose, Va., 19. *See* Camp Bartow
Trimble, Isaac R., brigade, 99, 100
troops, time expires, 160
Tucker, Clinton C., candidate for office, 153
Turner (slave), 21
Twelfth Georgia Infantry. *See* Georgia Units: 12th Infantry
typhoid fever. *See* diseases and illnesses

United Confederate Veterans (UCV), 176
Union Chapel Methodist Church, xxii
Upton, Emory, 158, 170–71

vaccination, 1
Valley Army, 65, 81
Valley Mills, Va., 68, 72, 82; brigade inspection, 74; description of area, 73, 74; equipment hauled, 73; food, 74; guard, 75; rumors, 74; weather, 73
Valley Campaign, 1862, causalities, 78, 82, and marching, 79; and 1864, 169–72
Valley Turnpike, 171, 172
Vicksburg, Miss., 121, 130
Vining, Elijah, 63, 219
Virginia Central Railroad, 81, 91, 150
Virginia Units: 31st Infantry, 30; 44th Infantry, 7; and accidental shootings 10; and Cheat Summit Fort attack, 25; 52nd Infantry, 29; and scout worst, 55–56

Walker, Thomas A., 11, 22, 103, 219
Waller, Charles B., 219–20
Waller, William H., 87, 138, 220; wounded, 128
Warren, Gouverneur K., 157, 158
Warren County, Va., 77
Warrenton, Va., 145
Washington, D. C., 123; fortifications, 170
Wat. *See* Morton, Henry W.
Waynesboro, Va., 81
weather: Allegheny Mountain, July 1861, 14; Camp Alleghany, 47, 51, 52, 55, 57, 58; 60, 62; Camp Bartow, 19, 20, 31, 33, 38, 40, 43; Camp Shenandoah, 70, 71; Chancellorsville, 111; Cheat Summit Fort attack, 25; detached duty, 151, 152; Fredericksburg, 101, 113, 117, 119; Gettysburg retreat, 130; Gordonsville, 87, 96; Luray, 131; Kellys Ford, 147, 148; McDowell scout, 69; Mortons Ford, 151; New Hope, 152; Orange Court House, 134, 136, 139, 140; Petersburg, 173; Piedmont, 151; Spotsylvania Court House, 161; Valley Mills, 74; West View, 74
Welch, Reubin R., 220; death, 94
Welch, Thomas H., 220
Weldon, N. C., 100, 101
West View, Va., 65, 66, 72; brigade inspection, 74; description of area, 73, 74; equipment hauled, 73; food, 74; guard, 75; left, 77; rumors, 74; weather, 73

Whaley, Joseph, 53, 54, 61, gift to Irby Scott, 60; pay drawing son's, 96

Whaley, Julia, (Mrs. Joseph Whaley), 53

Whaley, Nicholas E., 220, clothes, 54; and boxed, 43–44; burial, 53, 56; death, 53; discharge offered, 43; Feiler attending, 56; health good, 3, 5, 15; and improving, 43; ill, 18, 20, 24; illness, last, 54, 56; lock of hair, 53; pay, 96; personnel effects, 56; removal home, 54; sick sent off, 35–36; shoes, 54; writing, not, 41

whiskey, ration, 45

whooping cough. *See* diseases and Illnesses

Wilderness, 157; battle of, 161

Wiley, Charles M., money sent by, 108, 112

Williams, Francis M., 177

Williams, Francis M., 76, 220

Williams, James Wesley, 163, 220

Williamsport, Md., 127

Willis Edward S., xxix; colonel promoted, 100; death, 163; detached duty, 149, 150; Gettysburg, 123–24; officers class, 103; Scott, Nicholas, muster, 107, 108, 113; special detail, 134, 146; substitute verifying, 115, 116; regiment loses best friend, 166; Wilderness, 158; wounded, 161

Wilmington, N. C., 109, 155

Wilson, James Lawson, 220–21

Wilson, William E., 89, 221

Winchel, William H., 86, 94, 101, 103, 121, 137, 221; messmate, 127, 135; wounded, 128

Winchester, Va., 60, 66, 68, 76, 82; baggage wagons sent to, 127; first battle of, 77; second battle of, 126–27; third battle of, 170; rumor, 61

wine, 70, 120; grandmother, from, 46

winter quarters, 41, 43; Camp Alleghany, 47, 48, 54; detached duty, 150, 151, 152; Fredericksburg, 102; Petersburg abandon, 173; Piedmont, 151; provisions low, 51

Woodstock, Va., 171

Wright, Ambrose R., brigade, 131; Manassas Gap, 133

Wright, Benjamin H., 40

Wright, Emily E. (Mrs. Benjamin H. Wright), 103, 121, 130, 146

Yancey, Erastus H., 117

Young, Robert, 150, 221–22; wounded, 84, 112

Zachry, Abner Rowan, 73, 74, 222; body servant, 95, 97; box from home, 43, 117, 141; camp arrival, 5; candidate for office, 94; captured, 78; and escaped 86; clothes needed, 94; erysipelas, 151, 152; fever, 83; friend, best, 92; furlough applied for, 147; hat size, 93; home still at, 3, 4; injured knee, 154; messmate, 55; officer elected, 95; sick, 130, 142; West View sick, 76; wounded, 170

Zachry, Asa J., substitute, fee paid, 88

Zachry, James, 88

Zachry, John M., 37–38

Zack. *See* Johnson, Zaccheus B.